STUDIES IN MEDIEVAL PHILOSOPHY

**STUDIES IN PHILOSOPHY
AND THE HISTORY OF PHILOSOPHY**

General Editor: Jude P. Dougherty

Studies in Philosophy
and the History of Philosophy   Volume 17

Studies in Medieval Philosophy

edited by John F. Wippel

THE CATHOLIC UNIVERSITY OF AMERICA PRESS
Washington, D.C.

Copyright © 1987
The Catholic University of America Press
All rights reserved

LIBRARY OF CONGRESS CATALOGING-IN-PUBLICATION DATA
Studies in medieval philosophy.
   (Studies in philosophy and the history of philosophy;
v. 17)
   Includes index.
   1. Philosophy, Medieval.   I. Wippel, John F.
II. Series.
B21.S78 vol. 17 [B721]   100 s [189]   86-23282
ISBN 978-0-8132-3082-5

Contents

Introduction   vii

1. ELEONORE STUMP, Boethius's *In Ciceronis Topica* and Stoic Logic   1
2. THÉRÈSE-ANNE DRUART, Al-Farabi and Emanationism   23
3. ARTHUR HYMAN, Maimonides on Creation and Emanation   45
4. GEORG WIELAND, Plato or Aristotle—a Real Alternative in Medieval Philosophy?   63
5. JAMES MCEVOY, The Divine as the Measure of Being in Platonic and Scholastic Thought   85
6. JOHN F. WIPPEL, Thomas Aquinas and Participation   117
7. BERNARD RYOSUKE INAGAKI, *Habitus* and *Natura* in Aquinas   159
8. JAMES F. ROSS, Aquinas on Annihilation   177
9. CALVIN G. NORMORE, The Tradition of Mediaeval Nominalism   201
10. MARILYN MCCORD ADAMS, William Ockham: Voluntarist or Naturalist?   219
11. STEPHEN F. BROWN, Ockham and Final Causality   249
12. EDWARD P. MAHONEY, Themes and Problems in the Psychology of John of Jandun   273

Index of Authors   289
Index of Subjects   294

Introduction

The following essays originated from papers presented in the fall of 1984 as part of the Catholic University of America lecture series in medieval philosophy. The medieval period in the history of philosophy ranges over many centuries, and some indication of that range is evident from the titles of these essays. In organizing them I have followed a roughly chronological plan. This was possible only up to a point; for while some of the lectures concentrate on one figure from the medieval period, others consider the development of a particular theme or concept in different thinkers. Thus in Chapter 4 Georg Wieland attempts to identify the intellectual conditions in the twelfth and thirteenth centuries (as distinguished from the mere availability of newly translated texts) which account for the favorable reception of Aristotle in the thirteenth century. In Chapter 5 James McEvoy traces the notion of measure (*mensura*), especially in its application to the divine, from Greek philosophy into the high Middle Ages. And in Chapter 9 Calvin Normore attempts to cast some light on the meaning of the term "nominalism" in its application to both twelfth- and fourteenth-century thinkers. This being so, I have used such essays as "bridge articles," as it were, in moving from chapters dealing with one particular thinker to those which take up another.

Medieval philosophical thought was by no means limited to the Latin West. Arabic and Jewish philosophy are represented in this volume by Thérèse-Anne Druart's treatment of emanation in Al-Farabi and by Arthur Hyman's examination of creation and emanation in Moses Maimonides. Since these two medieval thinkers both flourished before the Western "triumph" of Aristotelianism in the thirteenth century, it seemed appropriate to consider them in Chapters 2 and 3.

The volume begins, therefore, with Eleonore Stump's treatment of a work by Boethius (*In Ciceronis Topica*) and an examination of the light it may cast on a difficult point in the history of Stoic logic. As indicated, this is followed by chapters dealing with Al-Farabi and Moses Maimonides, and then by the transition pieces by Georg Wieland and James McEvoy. In Chapter 6 I concentrate on a rather non-

Aristotelian aspect of Aquinas's metaphysics—participation. In Chapter 7 Bernard Inagaki considers Aquinas's treatment of *habitus* in order to cast some light on his understanding of nature, especially human nature. James Ross directs Chapter 8 to Aquinas's views concerning annihilation, especially as these are presented in the *De potentia*. As already noted, in Chapter 9 Calvin Normore attempts to come to terms with the meaning of nominalism in the medieval period. Marilyn McCord Adams devotes Chapter 10 to an extensive investigation of the meaning of the term "voluntarist" in its application to the thought of William Ockham. Another facet of Ockham's thought is examined by Stephen F. Brown in Chapter 11, concerning the causation which he assigns to the final cause. This leads Brown to take up certain issues touching on the authenticity of some of Ockham's works. The volume concludes with Edward P. Mahoney's examination of the psychology of John of Jandun.

Because the contributors to this volume come from various countries and widely divergent backgrounds, I have not attempted to impose a rigidly uniform reference system on all of the contributions. What I have aimed for is consistency within each essay.

Funding for the 1984 lecture series and partial funding for this volume was provided by the Exxon Foundation. Since without that series the present volume would not have come into being, we are doubly indebted to the Exxon Foundation, that is, for the lecture series itself and for the resulting publication.

Finally, I would like to take this occasion to thank Jude P. Dougherty, Dean of the School of Philosophy at Catholic University, for his gracious and efficient organization and management of the original series of lectures, and for accepting this volume for Studies in Philosophy and the History of Philosophy. The various contributors share this sentiment, as many have already indicated to me. I would especially like to thank each of them both for their original lectures and for the challenging essays they have now submitted for publication.

J.F.W.

1 Boethius's *In Ciceronis Topica* and Stoic Logic

ELEONORE STUMP

INTRODUCTION

Boethius's *In Ciceronis Topica* is one of two treatises Boethius wrote on the subject of the Topics or *loci*. The other treatise is *De topicis differentiis*,[1] one of the last philosophical works he composed.[2] Together these two treatises present Boethius's theory of the art of discovering arguments, a theory which was enormously influential in the history of medieval logic.[3] *De topicis differentiis* is a fairly short treatise, but it is Boethius's advanced book on the subject; it is written in a concise, even crabbed, style, and it clearly presupposes acquaintance with the subject matter. In contrast, *In Ciceronis Topica* is Boethius's elementary treatise on the Topics. It was written shortly before *De topicis differentiis*[4] and is a commentary on Cicero's *Topica*, though it is a much larger and more comprehensive work than the *Topica*; and it is more than twice as long as the more tightly knit *De topicis differentiis*.

Cicero's treatise *Topica*, on Cicero's own account,[5] is his attempt to explain to his friend Trebatius what he himself takes to be Aristotle's system for discovering arguments. There is some mystery about this

---

1. An edition of this text can be found in J.-P. Migne, *Patrologia latina* (PL), vol. 64 (Turnholt: Brepols, n.d.), 1174–1216. For a translation and notes, see Eleonore Stump, *Boethius's De topicis differentiis* (Ithaca, N.Y.: Cornell University Press, 1978).
2. L. M. de Rijk, "On the Chronology of Boethius' Works on Logic II," *Vivarium* 2 (1964), pp. 159–60.
3. Cf. Stump 1978, and Stump, "Topics: Their Development and Absorption into Consequences," *The Cambridge History of Later Medieval Philosophy*, ed. Norman Kretzmann et al. (Cambridge: Cambridge University Press, 1982), 273–99. Cf. also Niels J. Green-Pedersen, *The Tradition of the Topics in the Middle Ages* (Munich: Philosophia Verlag, 1984).
4. De Rijk 1964, pp. 159–61. For an edition of this text, see *Ciceronis Opera*, ed. J. C. Orelli (Zürich: Fuesslini, 1833), vol. 5, pt. i; for the same text in the PL, see PL 64: 1039–1174.
5. Cicero, *Topica* I.1–5, and *The Letters to His Friends*, trans. W. G. Williams, Loeb Classical Library (Cambridge, Mass.: Harvard University Press, 1928), vol. II, VII, xix.

claim of Cicero's because, as has been recognized not only by modern scholars[6] but even by Boethius,[7] there is a vast difference between what Aristotle presents in his *Topics* as an art for the discovery of arguments and what we read in Cicero's *Topica*. Aristotle's system of discovery was transmitted and developed both by rhetoricians and by commentators on Aristotle, including, for example, Theophrastus, Eudemus, and Strato.[8] What we find in Cicero's *Topica* is an art of discovery which reflects the alterations and adaptations of Aristotle made by generations of such rhetoricians and commentators in the three intervening centuries.

Unlike Aristotle's treatment of the Topics, Cicero's is neither highly philosophical nor tied to the nature of the predicables (genus, property, definition, and accident); and the tools for aiding the discovery of arguments—the so-called Topics—are not a host of general principles, as they are in Aristotle, but rather a small set of classifications or differentiae for such general principles. In his *Topica* Cicero is attempting to teach Trebatius, in a brief and summary fashion, how to use these Topics, these differentiae of general principles, to generate a great variety of arguments which will be useful to him in arguing cases in courts of law. Because his *Topica* is an abbreviated treatment of the subject, Cicero does not spell out the way in which he expects the Topics to aid in the discovery of arguments; but Boethius in his leisurely and extensive commentary does. Consider, for example, the following passage.

Marriage by purchase was carried out by established ceremonies. The parties being married by purchase asked one another questions; the man asked whether the woman wanted to be a *materfamilias*, and she answered that she did. In the same way, the woman asked whether the man wanted to be a *paterfamilias*, and the man answered that he did. In this way, a woman came under the authority of her husband, and the marriage was called marriage by purchase. The woman was a *materfamilias* to her husband and had the status of a daughter of his. Ulpian describes this ceremony in his *Institutes*. Now a certain man in his last will bequeathed to his wife Fabia all his silver on the condition that Fabia would be not only his wife but in fact a definite species of wife, namely a *materfamilias*. The question is whether the silver was bequeathed to the wife Fabia. *The wife Fabia* is the subject; *bequeathed silver* is the predicate. So I ask myself what argument I can take from the things presented in the question, and I see that there are two kinds inhering in *wife:* one is only a wife and

---

6. For bibliography on this long-standing scholarly discussion, see H. M. Hubbell, trans., *Cicero's Topica*, Loeb Classical Library (Cambridge, Mass.: Harvard University Press, 1960), p. 380; and Stump 1978, pp. 20–21.

7. *De top. diff.* 1195c and 1200cff.; and *In Ciceronis Topica* (ICT), pp. 280–83 (PL 1051–54).

8. Stump 1978, pp. 208ff.

the other is a *materfamilias*, a status brought about by coming under the authority of the husband. If Fabia did not come under the authority of her husband, she was not a wife, that is, she was not that species of wife to whom all the silver was bequeathed. Consequently, since what is said of one species is not appropriately said of another, and since Fabia is not included in that species of wife which has come under the authority of the husband (that is, the species which is a *materfamilias*) but her husband bequeathed the silver to a *materfamilias*, it appears that the silver was not bequeathed to Fabia. So the question, as was said, is whether all the silver was bequeathed to the wife Fabia. The subject is *the wife Fabia;* the predicate is *bequeathed silver.* The argument is taken from something which is in the thing asked about, that is, from something which is in *wife*, which is being asked about; for a species of wife is in *wife*, which is being asked about, namely, that species which has not come under the authority of the husband. And this is related to *wife*, for every species (that is, every kind) is related to its genus. The argument is therefore made from something which is in the thing at issue, namely, from related things—from a kind belonging to a genus. The maximal proposition is 'what is said of a single species is not appropriate for another'.[9]

The argument in this case apparently has the following structure.

(1) The silver was bequeathed to a woman who was *materfamilias*.

(2) The wife Fabia is not *materfamilias*.

(3) *Materfamilias* is a species of wife.

(4) MP What is said of a single species is not appropriate for another.

(5) Therefore, the silver was not bequeathed to the wife Fabia.

9. ICT, p. 299 (PL 1071). All Latin quotations of this work are from the Orelli edition. My annotated translation of ICT is forthcoming. "Coemptio vero certis sollemnitatibus peragebatur, et sese in coemendo invicem interrogabant, vir ita: an sibi mulier materfamilias esse vellet? Illa respondebat, velle. Item mulier interrogabat: an vir sibi paterfamilias esse vellet? Ille respondebat, velle. Itaque mulier viri conveniebat in manum, et vocabantur hae nuptiae per coemptionem, et erat mulier materfamilias viro loco filiae. Quam sollemnitatem in suis institutis Ulpianus exponit. Quidam igitur extremo iudicio omne Fabiae uxori legavit argentum, si quidem Fabia ei non uxor tantum, verum etiam certa species uxoris, id est, materfamilias esset. Quaeritur, an uxori Fabiae legatum sit argentum. *Uxor Fabia* subiectum est, *legatum argentum* praedicatum. Quaero igitur, quodnam ex iis argumentum sumere possim, quae in quaestione sunt posita, ac video, uxori duas inesse formas, quarum una tantum uxor est, altera materfamilias, quae in manum conventione perficitur. Quod si Fabia in manum non convenit, nec materfamilias fuit, id est, non fuit ea species uxoris, cui argentum omne legatum est. Quocirca quoniam id, quod de alia specie dicitur, in aliam dici non convenit, quumque Fabia praeter eam speciem sit, quae in manum convenerit, id est, quae materfamilias sit, et vir matrifamilias legaverit argentum, non videtur Fabiae esse legatum. Quaestio igitur, ut dictum est, an uxori Fabiae omne argentum legatum sit; subiectum *uxor Fabia*, praedicatum vero *legatum argentum*. Argumentum ab eo, quod est in ipso, de quo quaeritur, id est, ab eo, quod est in uxore, de qua quaeritur. Est autem in uxore, de qua quaeritur, species uxoris, ea scilicet, quae in manum non convenit, quae ad eam affecta est. Omnis enim species ad suum genus refertur, id est, omnis forma. Factum est igitur argumentum ab eo, quod est in ipso, ab affectis, a forma generis. Maxima propositio est: Quod de una specie dicitur, idem in alteram non convenire."

The Topic for this argument is *kind*, or *species;* and it has a double role in the argument. First, it serves to suggest a class of middle terms which can unite or disjoin the subject and predicate terms of the question (*the wife Fabia* and *bequeathed silver*) and which thus provide the argument needed to prove the conclusion. In this case, the Topic gives rise to premiss (3) and the general strategy of the argument. And second, it is a differentia for a genus of general principles, picking out those generalizations or maximal propositions which concern species. In this way the Topic helps to discover the general principle, premiss (4), which in some sense warrants the argument. A great deal more could and should be said about Boethius's theory of discovery in general and about this argument in particular, but for my present purposes I want just to show briefly how Boethius intended his art of discovery to work and what sort of example he used to illustrate it.

Although the scholastics made extensive use of Boethius's works on the Topics, they relied on *De topicis differentiis* much more than on *In Ciceronis Topica*. That relative neglect is also characteristic of contemporary historians of medieval philosophy, who have in general concentrated on *De topicis differentiis* more than on *In Ciceronis Topica*. I do not mean to suggest that *In Ciceronis Topica* was not influential in the scholastic period or that its influence is not currently recognized. Abelard, for example, used *In Ciceronis Topica* in his *Dialectica;*[10] and, as far as we know, there are 30 manuscripts of it extant from the tenth to the fifteenth centuries.[11] But there are 170 manuscripts of *De topicis differentiis* from the same period,[12] and that greater number is indicative of the greater use made of it. Part of the reason that more attention has not been paid to *In Ciceronis Topica* by contemporary historians of philosophy (and perhaps this is even true of scholastic philosophers) is that by the standards of scholastic philosophical Latin, its Latin is difficult, certainly more difficult than that of Boethius's other philosophical treatises. But even more of an obstacle is the nature of the many examples which Boethius discusses in great detail. Because Cicero is writing for a lawyer, he deliberately tries to make the bulk of his examples legal issues; and because Boethius is writing a commentary on Cicero, he takes over the legal examples he finds in Cicero's text and labors to explicate them as well as the more theoretical portions of the *Topica*. It is unlikely that the technical terminology of these examples would have been very familiar to scholastic philosophers. The laws involved in Cicero's examples were designed to regu-

---

10. Cf., e.g., *Petrus Abaelardus. Dialectica*, ed. L. M. de Rijk (Assen: Van Gorcum, 1970), pp. 449.34–450.2, 459.26, 561.16–19, 582.8–10.
11. De Rijk 1964, p. 151, n. 2.   12. Ibid., p. 153, n. 1.

late institutions some of which had ceased to exist even by Boethius's time, as seems evident from the effort Boethius expends in explaining them; and in some instances Boethius himself had to have recourse to textbooks of Roman law in order to clarify Cicero's examples. For instance, in discussing Cicero's example about marriage quoted above, Boethius refers to a passage of Ulpian's manual, which is now no longer extant, to describe the rituals of a certain archaic form of marriage. In fact, Boethius's description of this ceremony, apparently taken from Ulpian's text, is still one of our main sources for this part of Roman law and culture.[13]

This fact indicates one of the characteristics of *In Ciceronis Topica* which should make it especially interesting to contemporary scholars; it is a marvelous source of information about Roman rhetoric and philosophy as well as about Boethius himself. There has been a tendency in recent years to portray Boethius as a hack, as someone who relied very heavily on just a few sources and whose writings are essentially just reproductions of someone else's thought. There has even been the suggestion that virtually all of Boethius's philosophical writings except the *Consolation* are nothing more than his verbatim translations of the marginalia he found in his particular copy of Aristotle's *Organon*.[14] What we see in *In Ciceronis Topica*, however, is a Boethius conversant with a wide variety of thinkers, doctrines, and works. Besides the various Roman jurists he cites, such as Ulpian,[15] Gaius,[16] and Julius Paulus,[17] and his general knowledge of Roman law demonstrated throughout *In Ciceronis Topica*, the text shows that Boethius is acquainted with a broad range of texts and thought. He cites four different works of Cicero, *Pro Caelio, Brutus, De inventione,* and *Tusculan Disputations*.[18] He gives extensive paraphrases of Marius Victorinus's book on definitions,[19] and he is thoroughly conversant with Victorinus's commentary on Cicero's *Topica*, which is now lost.[20] He quotes from Virgil's *Georgics*;[21] he twice cites the fifth-century Latin rhetorician Merobaudes;[22]

---

13. H. F. Jolowicz and Barry Nicholas, *Historical Introduction to the Study of Roman Law* (Cambridge: Cambridge University Press, 1972), pp. 115–16, n. 1.
14. James Shiel, "Boethius' Commentaries on Aristotle," *Mediaeval and Renaissance Studies* 4 (1958), pp. 217–44. For critical discussion of Shiel's thesis, cf. Eleonore Stump, "Boethius's Works on the Topics," *Vivarium* 12 (1974), pp. 77–93.
15. ICT, p. 229 (PL 1071). 16. ICT, p. 322 (PL 1095).
17. ICT, p. 303 (PL 1075–76).
18. ICT, pp. 341 (PL 1117); 292 (PL 1063); 355 (PL 1332); 372 (PL 1152).
19. ICT, pp. 324 ff. (PL 1098 ff.). For discussion of Victorinus's book on definitions, cf. Pierre Hadot, *Marius Victorinus* (Paris: Études Augustiniennes, 1971), pp. 163 ff.
20. Cf., e.g., ICT, pp. 270 ff. (PL 1041 ff.); 273 (PL 1044); 284 (PL 1055); 377 (PL 1156). For a discussion of Victorinus's commentary, see Hadot 1971, pp. 115–41.
21. ICT, p. 356 (PL 1134).
22. ICT, pp. 335 (PL 1109); 368 (PL 1147).

and he also seems familiar with Greek rhetorical terms and theory.²³ Finally, besides exhibiting familiarity with Aristotle's logic and the later commentators on it, he discusses Aristotle's *Physics* at some length;²⁴ and he devotes considerable attention to Stoicism, mostly Stoic logic but also Stoic physics.²⁵ In short, *In Ciceronis Topica* gives us strong evidence for supposing that Boethius did have a philosophical library, as he says in the *Consolation*,²⁶ that it had much more in it than a copy of Aristotle's *Organon* with marginalia, and that he made good use of what he had in that library.

Besides what *In Ciceronis Topica* shows us about Boethius, it is also a valuable source for us as a witness to the thought and culture of his period. For example, in its testimony to the contents of works no longer extant, such as Victorinus's commentary on the *Topica* or Ulpian's legal text, *In Ciceronis Topica* provides an important source for scholarship; and even when Boethius is not giving us evidence concerning books no longer extant but instead just presenting philosophical doctrines, *In Ciceronis Topica* sheds light on some important issues. For instance, in it Boethius explains his views on the nature of universals and on the relations between metaphysics and logic,²⁷ he gives a lengthy exposition of Aristotelian and Ciceronian theories of causation,²⁸ and, in an interesting digression, he discusses Stoic views of Fate in a way which helps to explain why the Stoics should have thought that the governance of all things by Fate is compatible with genuine freedom in human actions.²⁹

But perhaps the most interesting unexplored section in *In Ciceronis Topica* is Boethius's presentation of Stoic logic, and that is the part I want to concentrate on in this paper. Rather than dwell on the main theme of *In Ciceronis Topica*, the art of discovery and its instruments, the Topics, I want to focus instead on just that small part of Boethius's commentary in which he relates the Topics to Stoic dialectic or logic and reveals his understanding of that part of Stoicism. We are beginning to understand the ancient art of discovering arguments, and it has garnered increasing attention among contemporary scholars. But as far as I know, Michael Frede[30] is alone among recent historians of

23. Cf., e.g., ICT, pp. 297 (PL 1068); 325 ff. (PL 1099 ff.); 384 ff. (PL 1165 ff.).
24. ICT, pp. 367 ff. (PL 1145 ff.), esp. p. 373 (PL 1152).
25. Stoic logic is discussed throughout bk. V of ICT. For some discussion of Stoic physics, see ICT, pp. 367 ff. (PL 1146 ff.).
26. Cf. *The Consolation of Philosophy*, bk. I, prose 4 and 5.
27. Cf., e.g., ICT, pp. 312 ff. (PL 1084 ff.); 283 ff. (PL 1054 ff.); 293–97 (PL 1064–68).
28. ICT, pp. 367 ff. (PL 1145 ff.).
29. ICT, p. 367 (PL 1146).
30. Michael Frede, *Die stoische Logik* (Goettingen: Vandenhoeck and Ruprecht, 1974), pp. 148–53, 160–62.

philosophy in considering Boethius's contribution to our understanding of Stoic logic; and even he gives only a brief discussion of a small part of the relevant Boethian text. So in what follows I will concentrate on just the fifth book of *In Ciceronis Topica*, in which Boethius discusses the so-called undemonstrated modes or argument forms of the Stoics. I need to make plain here that my area of interest and expertise is Boethius and not the Stoics; but I think that in *In Ciceronis Topica* Boethius sheds some light on a vexing problem which has troubled students of Stoic logic for some time.

THE PROBLEM

As is well known, Stoic logic revolved around conditional propositions and arguments involving them, but what constitutes the definition of a conditional proposition was a matter of dispute among the Stoics. Scholars now are generally agreed that there were four distinct Stoic views concerning the truth of conditionals:

(1) a sound conditional is one which does not have a true antecedent and a false consequent;

(2) a sound conditional is one which neither could nor can have a true antecedent and a false consequent;

(3) a sound conditional is one in which the contradictory of the consequent is incompatible with the antecedent;

and

(4) a sound conditional is one whose consequent is in effect contained in its antecedent.[31]

The fourth definition is not associated with any particular Stoic and does not seem to have been popular with any major group of Stoics.[32] But Sextus Empiricus explicitly associates the first two with Philo and his teacher Diodorus Cronus;[33] and scholars tend to associate the third with Chrysippus.[34]

A small number of simple types of arguments incorporating a conditional proposition were singled out by the Stoics as 'undemon-

---

31. Cf. Benson Mates, *Stoic Logic* (Berkeley, Calif.: University of California Press, 1953), pp. 42 ff.
32. Cf. Mates 1953, p. 49.
33. Sextus, *Pyrrhoniae Hypotyposes* II.110–12.
34. Cf. William and Martha Kneale, *The Development of Logic* (Oxford: Clarendon Press, 1962), p. 129.

strated' (*anapodeiktos*). What exactly 'undemonstrated' means in this context is not clear; but whatever else it may mean, it seems intended to convey the idea that the validity of these types of argument is readily apparent and so does not need to be demonstrated. Chrysippus appears to have held that there are five undemonstrated types of argument. In Stoic logic the arbitrary constants are expressed not by letters of the alphabet as in Aristotelian logic but in general by number words; and they take as their values not the names of classes, as Aristotle's variables do, but instead entire propositions. As far as we can tell from the sources available to us,[35] Chrysippus's five argument forms are these:

(1)   (i) If the first, then the second.
       (ii) But the first.
       (iii) Therefore, the second.

(2)   (i) If the first, then the second.
       (ii) But not the second.
       (iii) Therefore, not the first.

(3)   (i) Not both the first and the second.
       (ii) But the first.
       (iii) Therefore, not the second.

(4)   (i) Either the first or the second.
       (ii) But the first.
       (iii) Therefore, not the second.

(5)   (i) Either the first or the second.
       (ii) But not the first.
       (iii) Therefore, the second.

By Cicero's time, however, it had apparently become customary to add two more argument forms to Chrysippus's list of five; in the description of Stoic logic in his *Topica*[36] Cicero gives seven rather than five argument forms. As Cicero presents them, the additional ones are these:

(C6)   (i) Not both this and that.
        (ii) But this.
        (iii) Therefore, not that.

(C7)   (i) Not both this and that.
        (ii) But not this.
        (iii) Therefore, that.

---

35. Cf. Kneale 1962, pp. 162–63.   36. *Topica* XIII.53–XIV.57.

This list of seven clearly presents us with a considerable problem, however, because it looks as if Cicero's sixth argument form is just a slightly reformulated version of the third, and the seventh looks blatantly invalid.

Different scholars have suggested different solutions to this problem. The Kneales suggest both that Cicero was confused and that the text of his *Topica* is defective.[37] They point out that in both Martianus Capella and an anonymous sixth-century author of a scholium on the syllogism the seventh argument form is assimilated to the fifth, and the third argument form is given in a way different from that in Cicero's *Topica*. Martianus in fact gives the third argument form in this way:

(MC3) (i) Not both the first and not the second.
       (ii) But the first.
       (iii) Therefore, the second also.[38]

On this basis the Kneales suggest that sometime before Cicero at least some Stoic logicians had revised Chrysippus's list of indemonstrable argument forms in such a way that Chrysippus's third argument form became the sixth and two new argument forms were added, the third the one we find preserved in Martianus Capella as third and the seventh very like the fifth:

(K7) (i) Not both not the first and not the second.
      (ii) But not the first.
      (iii) Therefore, the second.

(K7) differs from Cicero's seventh just in the addition of two negatives in the major premiss. The Kneales suggest that Cicero might have known the seventh argument in its (K7) form and that copyists' errors, producing the omission of two negatives, might have resulted in a defective text giving the last argument form as (C7), as our text now has it. Furthermore, they suggest, Cicero is just confused in his presentation of the third argument form, conflating the later Stoic list with Chrysippus's original list of five and so giving Chrysippus's third argument form twice, once in its original place, third in the list, and again in its revised location as the sixth argument form.

In his recent book on Stoic logic, Michael Frede disputes the Kneales' solution to the problem. As far as the seventh argument form is concerned, he marshals an impressive array of evidence to show that

---

37. Kneale 1962, pp. 179ff.
38. Cf. *De nuptiis Philologiae et Mercurii* IV.414–21.

Cicero's text is not corrupt.[39] Frede has found the same formulation of the seventh mode as Cicero's in Martianus Capella, Cassiodorus, Isidore, and Boethius (in *In Ciceronis Topica*). These authors, of course, are likely to have been influenced by Cicero; and it is possible to suppose that the text of Cicero's *Topica* might have been known to all these authors in the same corrupted form. But, as Frede points out,[40] it is surely implausible to suppose that all these authors would have tamely copied and transmitted a blatantly invalid form of argument. And Frede might have added that Boethius at any rate has no compunctions about criticizing Cicero and often stops in *In Ciceronis Topica* to indicate a point he thinks Cicero has got wrong.[41] Finally, Frede shows[42] that Philoponus appears to know of the sixth and seventh argument forms in Cicero's formulation, but that he argues against the seventh only on the grounds that it is a superfluous reformulation of the third argument form, *not* on the grounds that it is obviously invalid. In the face of this evidence, Frede concludes (quite correctly, I think) that Cicero's original formulation of the seventh argument form was just as our text now has it and that our current text is not the product of copyists' errors.

Frede also disputes the Kneales' suggestion that there is something wrong with the presentation of the third argument form as we now have it in Cicero's *Topica*. In fact, Frede seems able to build a stronger case for the Kneales' suggestion than they themselves do; he points out that not only Martianus Capella but also Boethius, Cassiodorus, and Isidore know the third argument form in the formulation the Kneales think the Stoics must have intended.[43] Furthermore, although the latest editions of Cicero's *Topica* follow manuscripts which give Cicero's description of the third form as

> (C) "cum autem aliqua coniuncta negaris et ex eis unum aut plura sumpseris, ut quod relinquitur tollendum sit, is tertius appellatur conclusionis modus"[44] ("but when you deny certain things which are conjoined and take one or more of them as the minor premiss, with the result that what is left must be taken away, this is called the third form of conclusion"),

the older editions (partly because of Boethius's reading) give this passage as

---

39. Frede 1974, pp. 157–67.　　40. Ibid., pp. 162–63.
41. Cf., e.g., ICT, pp. 361–62 (PL 1139–40) and 372 (PL 1151–52).
42. Frede 1974, pp. 163–64.　　43. Ibid., p. 160.
44. Cf., e.g., *Cicero's Topica*, trans. H. M. Hubbell, op. cit., XIII.54.

(C′) "cum autem aliqua coniuncta negaris, *et his alia negatio rursus adiungitur,* et ex his *primum* sumpseris, ut quod relinquitur tollendum sit . . ." ("but when you deny certain things which are conjoined, *and another negation is in turn added to these,* and you take *the first* of these as the minor premiss, with the result that what is left must be taken away . . .").[45]

As Frede points out, it would be easy enough to imagine that the italicized clause in (C′) had just been dropped in the course of the manuscript's transmission. At any rate, (C′) rather than (C) is on the face of it what Boethius seems to be reading in his copy of Cicero.

Against this evidence for the Kneales' suggestion that the third argument form cannot have been what we now have in Cicero's text, Frede raises two considerations. In the first place, he maintains, if (C′) was the original text, then it is hard to explain how the *aut plura* ("or more") of (C) might have crept into the manuscripts. And secondly, he claims, it is altogether possible that Boethius's text of Cicero had (C) rather than (C′) but that Boethius just interpreted the Ciceronian passage as (C′) anyway because the other things Cicero says about the third argument form are more compatible with (C′) than with (C). For example, Cicero claims that we can use the third argument form as well as the first to conclude 'the coin was bequeathed' from the assumption that the silver was bequeathed.[46] And the example Cicero gives in connection with the third argument form can be expressed in this way:

(CE) (i) Not both 'the silver was bequeathed' and not 'the coin was bequeathed'.
(ii) But the silver was bequeathed.
(iii) Therefore, the coin was bequeathed.

Frede thinks that although Boethius's copy of the *Topica* perhaps had (C), reading Cicero's example and description of what the third argument form was intended to prove might have convinced Boethius that Cicero really meant (C′). Therefore, Frede thinks there is no reason to suppose that Cicero's text was anything other than (C).

What Frede himself suggests is that in the sixth and seventh argument forms the major premiss is intended to be a special sort of disjunction. In general, the Stoics took a disjunction to be a proposition whose disjuncts are completely incompatible and cannot be true or false together; such a proposition is true when one and only one of its

---

45. Cf. Frede 1974, p. 160.   46. *Topica* XIII.53–54.

disjuncts is true.[47] But there is also some evidence that Stoics knew of a different sort of disjunction, subdisjunction. Different Stoics give somewhat different conditions for the truth of subdisjunctions; but Frede presents a generalized interpretation: subdisjunctions are true just in case the disjuncts cannot be true together although they can be false together and one of the disjuncts is true.[48] According to Frede, Chrysippus's list of five undemonstrated argument forms includes only conditionals, conjunctions, and disjunctions, but has no form based on subdisjunction.[49] As later Stoics became aware of and interested in subdisjunction, they may have felt the need to add to Chrysippus's list argument forms with a subdisjunction as the major premiss.

They are unlikely to have used the disjunction 'or' to frame such subdisjunctive premisses, since 'or' was already associated with disjunction; but they might easily have formulated subdisjunctive premisses as 'not-(p and q)'. If we interpret Cicero's sixth and seventh argument forms as subdisjunctions, Frede claims, we can make sense out of all the perplexing features of the Ciceronian argument forms. The sixth form is not a superfluous repetition of the third, because, in spite of the apparent similarity, the two forms depend on different propositions as their major premisses. The major premiss of the third is a negated conjunction, while the major premiss of the sixth is a subdisjunction; and thus different truth conditions apply to these different major premisses. Furthermore, on this interpretation, the seventh argument form turns out to be valid even in Cicero's formulation of it. If the major premiss of the seventh argument form, not-(p and q), is intended to be a subdisjunction, then p and q are such that although they can both be false, they cannot both be true and at least one of them is true. On those conditions, we can validly conclude q from the subdisjunctive major premiss and not-p as the minor premiss.

Finally, Frede's suggestion makes sense out of the ordering of Cicero's list. On the face of it, Cicero's list appears jumbled: two arguments with conditional major premisses, one with a conjunction as the major premiss, two with disjunctions as the major premisses, and two more with conjunctions as the major premisses. But if we take Frede's suggestion, the list turns out to be orderly, because the last two argument forms are not a return to the sort involving conjunctive major premisses but instead the start of a new sort involving subdisjunctive major premisses.

47. Frede 1974, pp. 93 ff.; Mates 1953, pp. 51 ff.; Kneale 1962, pp. 160 ff.
48. Frede 1974, pp. 98 ff. and esp. p. 165, n. 18. For different characterizations of subdisjunction, cf. Kneale 1962, pp. 160 ff., and Mates 1953, pp. 53 ff.
49. Frede 1974, pp. 164 ff.

The main evidence for Frede's view is that it makes sense of the text as we have it (though Frede presents some minor considerations which might be taken as indirectly confirmatory of his view).[50] On Frede's own account, the major evidence against his view is that none of our sources say anything directly associating the sixth and seventh argument forms with subdisjunction; and in view of the puzzling look of Cicero's list, someone might be expected to have mentioned that the last two argument forms depend on subdisjunction if that were in fact the case. Nonetheless, since he finds no good alternative to his interpretation of Cicero's list, Frede is prepared to stand by it as the best available explanation even in the absence of any direct textual evidence for it.

I think Frede's case for this view is perhaps somewhat weaker than he realizes. In the first place, in his argument to show that Boethius might have misread Cicero's text (C) as (C'), Frede in fact presents us with some reason for thinking that Cicero's text was in fact (C'), that the text as we now have it *is* corrupt. At any rate, if Cicero's text was what Boethius thinks it is, then Cicero's description of the conclusion of the third argument form and his example for it are consistent with the argument form he gives; but if the original text was what we now have in our current editions, there is an egregious mismatch which is difficult to explain between Cicero's third argument form and his example for it and explanation of it. Secondly and more interestingly, Frede is wrong in supposing both that the worst evidence against his view is the lack of textual support for it and that his view is the only reasonable explanation which fits all the data. There is an alternative explanation, philosophically sophisticated and historically interesting, in Boethius's *In Ciceronis Topica;* and in that explanation, which includes a detailed exposition of the seven undemonstrated argument forms, Boethius gives an analysis which is clearly incompatible with Frede's view. So there is at least one Roman witness against Frede's view and for a different interpretation; to that witness I want to turn next.

BOETHIUS'S INTERPRETATION

In his initial presentation of the first three argument forms, Boethius offers a description of the third form which is surprising, given our current text of the Ciceronian passage he is commenting on:

50. Ibid., pp. 165–66.

The first and second modes of hypothetical syllogisms arise from propositions which are connected. When a negation is added to a connected proposition composed of two affirmations and the whole proposition is negated, the third mode arises.[51]

This passage suggests that Boethius takes the major premiss of the third argument form to involve a conditional or connected proposition (as he calls it), not a conjunction, and that he furthermore takes it to be a negated conditional which itself contains a negated proposition. This suggestion is confirmed and developed a little later in the text:

The third mode occurs when a negation is inserted among the parts of a connected proposition composed of two affirmations and the negation itself is negated. . . . For example, if a negation is interposed among the parts of the proposition which we presented above—'If it is day, it is light'—it will become 'If it is day, it is not light'. If we negate it further, it will be this: 'It is not the case that if it is day, it is not light'; and the meaning of this proposition is that if it is day, it is not possible that it is not light. . . . In this case, if we assert in the minor premiss the former part of this supernegative proposition, namely, that it is day, it also follows that it is light, in the following way: 'It is not the case that if it is day, it is not light; but it is day; therefore, it is light'.[52]

This passage also shows us two further things about Boethius's view. In the first place, as this quotation illustrates and as is abundantly demonstrated throughout the text, Boethius adopts a Chrysippean account of conditionals according to which the opposite of the consequent cannot be true together with the antecedent of a true conditional. He does not, then, share our ordinary truth-functional analysis of conditionals but instead has a modal interpretation of them. Secondly, Boethius's description of the major premiss for the third argument form shows that he understands this mode as involving incompatibles. In explaining incompatibles earlier, Boethius says:

It is clear that incompatibles are produced from connected propositions; for if a mediating negation is inserted among affirmations when one affirmation

---

51. ICT, p. 355 (PL 1133). "Ex iis igitur propositionibus, quae connexae sunt, fit primus et secundus hypotheticorum syllogismorum modus. Addita vero negatione propositioni connexae ex duabus affirmationibus copulatae eaque insuper denegata tertius accedit."

52. ICT, p. 356 (PL 1133–34). "Tertius modus est, quum inter partes connexae atque ex duabus affirmationibus copulatae propositionis negatio interponitur eaque ipsa negatio denegatur, . . . ut in hac ipsa, quam superius proposuimus: *Si dies est, lux est.* Si inter has partes negatio interveniat, fiet hoc modo: *Si dies est, lux non est.* Ac si ulterius denegemus, erit ita: *Non, si dies est, lux non est.* Cuius propositionis ista sententia est: quia, si dies est, fieri non potest, ut lux non sit. . . . In hac igitur si priorem partem, id est, diem esse, in assumptione ponamus, consequitur etiam lucem esse, hoc modo: *Non, si dies est, lux non est; atque dies est: lux igitur est.*"

follows from another, it produces incompatibility in the following way. 'If it is day, it is light'—here an affirmation follows from an affirmation. But when I say, 'If it is day, it is not light', with the inserted negation the parts of the connected proposition are incompatible with one another.[53]

He recognizes a number of other ways of producing a proposition containing incompatibles, but this way may be taken as a kind of paradigm. In general, his criterion for such propositions seems to be this: if 'p entails q' is true then 'p entails not-q' is a proposition containing incompatibles.

Boethius himself goes on to stress the important relation between the third argument form and propositions containing incompatibles:

> this mode contains parts of a proposition which are incompatible with each other; that it is not light is in fact opposite to and incompatible with 'if it is day'. But the proposition is made true because the incompatibility of the consequent with the antecedent which is produced by the mediating negation is destroyed by the other negation, and the whole proposition regains the force of an affirmation. For because it is understood to follow and to be true that if it is day, it is light, it is incompatible and false that if it is day, it is not light. When this is itself in turn negated, it is true, in this way: 'It is not the case that if it is day, it is not light'. And it becomes similar to the affirmation 'If it is day, it is light', because a double negation produces an affirmation.[54]

This passage and Boethius's example for this argument form raise two concerns. First of all, he apparently takes

(1) It is not the case that if p, then not-q

to be equivalent to

(2) If p, then q.

This equivalence does not hold on truth-functional interpretations of conditionals. Nor does it hold on a Chrysippean analysis of conditionals, on which we apparently get the following version of (1):

(1′) It is not the case that necessarily if p, then not-q.

---

53. ICT, p. 354 (PL 1131). "Sed ex connexis repugnantes manifestum est nasci: namque ubi affirmatio sequitur affirmationem, his si media negatio interposita sit, repugnantiam facit hoc modo: *Si dies est, lux est.* Hic affirmatio sequitur affirmationem. At quum dico: *Si dies est, lux non est,* repugnant inter se partes propositionis connexae interposita negatione."

54. ICT, pp. 356–57 (PL 1134). "Hic autem propositionis modus partes inter se suas continet repugnantes: adversum quippe est ac repugnat, si dies est, non esse lucem. Sed idcirco rata propositio est, quia consequentium repugnantia facta per mediam negationem alia negatione destruitur et ad vim affirmationis omnino revocatur. Nam quia consequens esse intelligitur ac verum, si dies est, esse lucem, repugnat ac falsum est, si dies est, non esse lucem: quae denegata rursus vera est ita: *Non, si dies est, lux non est;* et fit consimilis affirmationi: *Si dies est, lux est;* quia facit affirmationem geminata negatio."

(1') is also clearly not equivalent to the corresponding version of (2):

(2') Necessarily, if p, then q.

Why, then, does Boethius equate (1) and (2)? One possible explanation is simply that he thinks the two negations in (1) cancel each other out, as is suggested by the last line in the passage above. Another more complicated and perhaps more satisfactory answer depends on considering the nature of the propositions which can be substituted for p and q. The third mode is the mode for incompatibles. So substitutions for p and not-q in a legitimate version of (1) must be incompatibles; and Boethius seems to understand (1) as expressing the negation of that incompatibility. If that is indeed how he reads (1), then on his reading (1) says that p and not-q cannot be true together, or that no p-world is a not-q-world. If we understand (2) on Boethius's reading to express a necessary connection between p and q, such that every p-world is also a q-world, (1) and (2) on these readings do seem equivalent.

Secondly, since on Boethius's views the major premiss of the third argument form in Boethius's formulation of it is equivalent to the major premiss of the first argument form, and since the minor premiss and conclusion of the first and third argument forms as Boethius presents them are the same, we may wonder why Boethius feels compelled to list the third argument form as a separate and distinguishable form of argument. This is a question Boethius himself anticipates, and he answers it in this way:

This [third] mode differs a great deal from the previous modes, because in the mode which arises from antecedents, the antecedent is asserted in order to support the consequent, and in the mode which arises from consequents, the consequent is destroyed in order to remove the antecedent; but in this mode neither of these things occurs. The antecedent is not asserted to corroborate the consequent, nor is the consequent destroyed in order to subvert the antecedent; rather the antecedent is asserted in order to destroy the consequent.[55]

In other words, Boethius tries to disarm this objection by pointing to the form of the inference. On this view of the third mode, it is a cross between the first two. The problem is that this interpretation of the

---

55. ICT, p. 356 (PL 1134). "Qui modus a superioribus plurimum distat, quod in eo modo, qui fit ab antecedentibus, ponitur antecedens, ut id, quod sequitur, adstruatur; in modo vero a consequentibus perimitur consequens, ut id, quod praecesserat, auferatur: in hoc vero neutrum est. Nam neque antecedens ponitur, ut, quod sequitur, confirmetur, nec interimitur subsequens, ut id, quod praecesserat, evertatur: sed ponitur antecedens, ut id, quod sequitur, interimatur."

third mode ignores the fact that it begins not with a conditional but with the negation of a conditional. If we consider just the conditional within the scope of the negation and ignore the negation, then Boethius's analysis of the third mode seems reasonable. But we need to remember that the conditional in the third mode is negated. On Boethius's own views the negated conditional is equivalent to the conditional of the first mode, and the minor premiss and conclusion of the third mode are identical in form to those of the first mode. And so Boethius's explanation of the third mode's difference from the previous two seems inadequate or even inapplicable. The best that can be said, I think, is just that there is a difference in external form among the first three argument forms. In the first mode the minor premiss is the antecedent and the conclusion is the consequent of the conditional in the first premiss. In the second mode the minor premiss is the negation of the consequent and the conclusion is the negation of the antecedent of the conditional in the first premiss. So according to Boethius, what makes the third mode distinct from the first two is that its minor premiss is the antecedent and its conclusion is the denial of the consequent of the conditional in the first premiss.

When Boethius discusses Cicero's example for the third argument form, Boethius gives that example in this formulation:

(B3)   (i) It is not the case that if the silver was bequeathed, the coin was not bequeathed.
    (ii) But the silver was bequeathed.
    (iii) Therefore, the coin was bequeathed.

But he goes on to say:

Cicero himself, however, formulated the proposition in this way: 'It is not the case that the silver was bequeathed and the coin was not bequeathed'; but we added the causal conjunction 'if' in order to show the genus of such a proposition. For an incompatible arises from a connected proposition with the addition of a negation. But no conjunction can show a connected proposition as well as 'if' can, although even a copulative conjunction might produce the same proposition since things that are connected are also understood to be conjoined.[56]

So Boethius understands Cicero's version of the third argument form to be what the Kneales suggest it was, the version Martianus Ca-

---

56. ICT, pp. 362–63 (PL 1140). "M. vero Tullius propositionem ita formavit: *Non et legatum argentum est, et non est legata numerata pecunia.* Sed nos idcirco causalem coniunctionem apposuimus eam, quae est *si*, ut, ex quo esset genere talis propositio, monstraremus. Namque ex connexo negatione addita fit repugnans. Connexum vero nulla

pella gives, (MC3). On Boethius's account he has formulated the initial premiss of the third mode as a conditional rather than as a conjunction in order to make manifest the sort of proposition from which a proposition containing incompatibles arises, since such a proposition is in general produced by negating the consequent of a true conditional, not by denying the second conjunct of a conjunction. He apparently thinks that

(1) It is not the case that if p, then not-q

is equivalent not only to

(2) If p, then q

but also to

(3) It is not the case that p and not-q.

I suggested earlier that to understand why Boethius thinks (1) and (2) equivalent we might read (1) as 'No p-world is a not-q-world' and (2) as 'Every p-world is a q-world'. If we suppose that for Boethius (3) is also modalized in this way:

(3') Necessarily, it is not the case that p and not-q,

then on Boethius's views (3) says that there is no possible world which is both a p-world and a not-q-world; and this does seem equivalent to my suggested Boethian readings of (1) and (2). The justification for reading (3) as modalized is that this mode is understood to be the mode for incompatibles, and incompatibles are generated from true conditionals, which are modal conditionals on Boethius's views. So p and not-q can be used in the third mode only if they are incompatibles; and they are incompatibles just in case 'if p, then q' is a necessarily true conditional. On these readings the logical form of the third mode as Boethius generally presents it is roughly of this sort: 'No p-world is a not-q-world; but this is a p-world; therefore, this is a q-world'.

So according to Boethius Cicero has a formulation of the third mode in which the major premiss is a negated conjunction with one negated conjunct, but Boethius has reformulated that premiss in a way which strikes him as logically equivalent, as a negated conditional with a negated consequent, in order to bring out the character of the

---

aeque ut *si* coniunctio posset ostendere: quamquam idem efficiat etiam copulativa coniunctio. Nam, quae connexa sunt, etiam coniuncta esse intelliguntur. . . ."

proposition containing incompatibles which is being negated in the major premiss.

From Boethius's examples for and discussion of the fourth and fifth modes it is clear that he understands disjunction as exclusive disjunction. That point is important to keep in mind because Boethius explicitly associates the sixth and seventh modes, whose major premisses are conjunctions, with disjunction:

> The sixth and seventh modes are derived from the disjunctive proposition of the fourth and fifth modes by adjoining a negation, withdrawing the disjunction from the proposition, and adding a conjunction to those propositions which were asserted previously in the disjunctive proposition, in the following way. 'It is not the case that it is day and that it is night'; this was formerly a disjunction of this sort: 'Either it is day or it is night'. When the conjunction 'or' was removed from this proposition which was disjunctive, we added 'and', which is copulative, and we asserted a negation. In this way from the united parts of a disjunctive proposition with the addition of a negation we made a proposition of the sixth and seventh modes, and it is this: 'It is not the case that it is day and that it is night'.[57]

Here Boethius indicates that he considers the sixth and seventh modes derivable from the fourth and fifth modes. And the point of deriving the conjunction of the sixth and seventh modes from the disjunction of the fourth and fifth modes is apparently that then for the negated conjunction to be true it must be the case that the two conjuncts cannot be true together but that at least one of them must be true, since one and only one disjunct can and must be true. Boethius emphasizes this condition for validity when he presents the seventh mode. He formulates the seventh mode as Cicero does:

> The seventh mode occurs when the first part of the proposition is taken negatively in the minor premiss so that the latter part may follow in this way: 'It is not the case that it is day and that it is night; but it is not day; therefore, it is night'.[58]

And he makes this comment on it: "This mode of propositions can be found only in those cases in which one or the other must be, as, for

---

57. ICT, p. 358 (PL 1135). "Sextus vero modus ac septimus ex quarti et quinti modi disiunctiva propositione deducuntur, una negatione scilicet adiuncta et disiunctiva propositione detracta additaque coniunctiva iis propositionibus, quae superius in disiunctione sunt positae, hoc modo: *Non et dies est, et nox est*. Dudum igitur in disiunctiva ita fuit, ut: *aut dies est, aut nox est*. Ex hac igitur propositione sublata *aut* coniunctione, quae erat disiunctiva, adiecimus *et*, quae copulativa est, proposuimusque negationem. Itaque fecimus ex partibus disiunctivae propositionis copulatis addita negatione propositionem sexti atque septimi modi, quae est: *Non et dies est et nox est*."

58. ICT, p. 358 (PL 1135). "Septimus vero modus est, quum prima pars propositionis negando assumitur, ut posterior subsequatur, hoc modo: *Non et dies est et nox est; atqui dies non est: nox igitur est*."

example, day or night, sickness or health, and whatever does not have an intermediate."[59] A little later in summarizing the sixth mode he says, "The sixth mode occurs when a negation is prefixed to the things which can enter into a disjunction (that is, to contraries or incompatibles lacking an intermediate)."[60] And finally, in analyzing the example for the seventh mode, Boethius ends with the following warning:

> These propositions cannot have a confirmed conclusion except with regard to things which are disjoined and which lack an intermediate. For suppose we were to speak in this way: 'It is not the case that it is white and that it is black'; and suppose we assert that it is not white. It does not follow that it is black, for there can be an intermediate. Hence, a proposition of this sort, made (as Cicero says) by the negation of a conjunction, should be applied to things which are disjoined and which lack an intermediate if it is going to confirm the conclusion; otherwise the conclusion will not be confirmed.[61]

So whether or not Boethius knows about subdisjunction, what he says about the sixth and seventh modes makes it clear that on his interpretation the major premisses of these modes cannot be subdisjunctions. On the contrary, he explicitly associates these major premisses with the exclusive disjunctions in the two preceding modes. And the stipulations he places on propositions which can serve as the conjuncts in the last two modes show that the conjuncts on his view meet the conditions not for subdisjuncts but rather for exclusive disjuncts: one and only one of those conjuncts can and must be true at a time.

Thus Boethius is here a witness both *against* the Kneales, who suggest that the Ciceronian text presenting the seventh mode is corrupt, and *against* Frede, who maintains the correctness of the text but interprets the sixth and seventh modes as involving subdisjunctions; and he is also a witness *for* the older editions of Cicero, which take Cicero's formulation of the third mode as (MC3), involving a negated conjunction with one negated conjunct, rather than as the formulation we now have in our text in passage (C). Furthermore, Boethius's understanding of the seven argument forms presents us with a reasonable and consistent interpretation of them, very different from the major interpretations offered by contemporary historians of philosophy.

---

59. Ibid. "Atque hic modus propositionum in solis iis inveniri potest, quorum alterum esse necesse est, ut diem vel noctem, aegritudinem vel salutem, et quidquid medium non habet."

60. ICT, p. 359 (PL 1136). "Sextus modus est, quum iis rebus, quae in disiunctionem venire possunt, id est, contrariis vel repugnantibus medietate carentibus, negatio praeponitur."

61. ICT, p. 366 (PL 1145). "Quae propositiones nisi in disiunctis medioque carentibus rebus ratam conclusionem habere non poterunt. Age enim ita dicamus: *Non et*

Cicero's list of Stoic argument forms presents us with three puzzles. The third and sixth forms seem equivalent; the seventh form seems invalid; and the ordering of the list appears jumbled. The Kneales suggest that our text of Cicero's seventh form is corrupt and that although our text of Cicero's third form is correct, Cicero himself was confused in the formulation of it. Frede argues that our current text of both Cicero's third and his seventh forms is correct, but that the sixth and seventh forms are subdisjunctions. Boethius's *In Ciceronis Topica* presents a different but consistent solution to the puzzles of Cicero's list.

On Boethius's presentation the grouping of the modes is orderly; the first three are conditional, the next two are disjunctive, and the last two are conjunctive. The third mode is:

(B3) (i) It is not the case that if p, then not-q.
 (ii) But p.
 (iii) Therefore q.

And the sixth mode is:

(B6) (i) Not both p and q.
 (ii) But p.
 (iii) Therefore, not-q.

Clearly, then, on Boethius's presentation the sixth mode is not a redundant re-expression of the third mode. And the constraint Boethius places on the sixth and seventh modes explains why on his views the seventh mode is not obviously invalid. On his constraint, the particular propositions substituted for p and q in modes six and seven must be mutually exclusive; with that constraint added, the seventh mode:

(B7) (i) Not both p and q.
 (ii) But not-p.
 (iii) Therefore, q.

is valid. And the added constraint is not an *ad hoc* attempt to validate this mode but rather a consequence of the recognition of the conjunction in these modes as derived from disjunctions and a view of disjunction as exclusive. If we take

---

album est, et nigrum; ponamusque non esse album; non consequitur, ut sit nigrum. Potest enim esse, quod medium est. Huiusmodi igitur per negationem coniunctionum (ut Tullius ait) propositio, si ratas factura est conclusiones, in disiunctis rebus medioque carentibus accommodetur; alias non erit rata conclusio."

(10) p or q

as a true exclusive disjunction, then either p or q but not both must be true. From the truth of this disjunction we can derive

(11) Not both p and q,

where p and q are mutually exclusive. On this interpretation of 'not both p and q' with the addition of the premiss 'not-p', we can legitimately conclude 'q', as the seventh mode requires.

I myself find Boethius's understanding of the Stoic argument forms more plausible, more likely to be historically accurate, than its current competitors. But what I want to say by way of conclusion is about Boethius's *In Ciceronis Topica* and not about Stoic logic. Boethius is only one—and a late one at that—of a number of sources we have for Stoic logic, and it would be unconscionable to frame a definite theory about the nature of Stoic logic or even just about Cicero's views of Stoic logic on the basis of Boethius's witness alone. What I hope to have shown instead is that in *In Ciceronis Topica* we have a philosophically sophisticated witness to Stoic logic which is well worth attending to, which should form part of the basis on which we reconstruct Stoic logic, but which has been almost entirely neglected by contemporary scholars. And the portion of *In Ciceronis Topica* which deals with Stoic logic is only a small part of the text. I am convinced that when *In Ciceronis Topica* begins to receive the attention it deserves, it will be found to be an equally powerful and interesting witness in a great variety of areas ranging from Roman law and rhetoric to Stoic and Peripatetic theories of causation and chance.[62]

Virginia Polytechnic Institute and State University

62. I owe thanks to Alan McMichael for help with certain portions of the Stoic logic in this paper, and I am grateful to Norman Kretzmann for numerous helpful comments and suggestions.

2   Al-Farabi and Emanationism
THÉRÈSE-ANNE DRUART

In 1981 Barry Sherman Kogan showed that emanationism had been a very controversial doctrine in Arabic philosophy.[1] In *The Incoherence of the Philosophers* al-Ghazali relentlessly criticizes al-Farabi and Avicenna for adopting it.[2] The *Epitome of Metaphysics* attributed to Averroes upholds emanationism but understands that it is not an Aristotelian tenet.[3] In *The Incoherence of the Incoherence*, his point-by-point reply to al-Ghazali, and in his *Commentary on Metaphysics* XII, Averroes concurs with al-Ghazali in rejecting emanationism.[4]

Both al-Ghazali and Averroes hold that emanationism is one of al-Farabi's views. Yet some scholars doubt the seriousness of al-Farabi's emanationism. Shlomo Pines contends that al-Farabi believes knowledge of separate substances to be impossible. If this is true then of course al-Farabi cannot defend emanationism.[5] In his two prefaces to

---

I would like to thank Professor Thomas P. McTighe for his helpful comments on this paper.

1. "Averroes and the Theory of Emanation," *Mediaeval Studies* 43 (1981), pp. 384–404. Cf. also the section "Did Averroes Subscribe to the Theory of Emanation?" in his *Averroes and the Metaphysics of Causation* (Albany, 1985), pp. 248–55.

2. Cf. *The Incoherence of the Philosophers*, discussions 3 and 17. These discussions and Averroes' replies to them can be found in Averroes' *Tahafot at-Tahafot*. Arabic edition by Maurice Bouyges, S.J. (Beirut, 1930), pp. 147–262 and 517–42; English translation by Simon Van Den Bergh, *Averroes' Tahafut al-Tahafut (The Incoherence of the Incoherence)*, vol. 1 (London, 1969), pp. 87–155 and 316–33.

3. B. S. Kogan, "Averroes and the Theory of Emanation," pp. 387–92. Averroes' *Epitome* has been edited by Uthman Amin (Cairo, 1958) and had been previously translated into German by Simon Van Den Bergh (Leiden, 1924). Kogan takes it as an early work of Averroes, who subsequently changed his mind about emanationism and rejected it. Yet its authenticity has long been disputed. About the question of authenticity, see *Ibn Rushd's Metaphysics. A Translation with Introduction of Ibn Rushd's Commentary on Aristotle's Metaphysics, Book Lam* by Charles Genequand (Leiden, 1984), pp. 10–11. Genequand considers it inauthentic.

4. B. S. Kogan, "Averroes and the Theory of Emanation," pp. 392–403, and C. Genequand, *Ibn Rushd's Metaphysics*, pp. 36–37 and 42–48.

5. "Les limites de la métaphysique selon al-Farabi, Ibn Bajja et Maïmonide: sources et antithèses de ces doctrines chez Alexandre d'Aphrodise et chez Thémistius," in *Sprache und Erkenntnis im Mittelalter*, 1. Halbband, *Miscellanea Mediaevalia*, Bd. 13/1

his translation of *The Attainment of Happiness, The Philosophy of Plato,* and *The Philosophy of Aristotle,* Muhsin Mahdi argues that, since emanationism is only in al-Farabi's popular works and not in his serious texts, it is not a true Farabian tenet.⁶ He also maintains that, in his serious works, al-Farabi does not consider metaphysics "as an urgent order of business" and excludes metaphysical and divine beings from the structure of the world to which he compares the structure of the city.⁷ Popular works, such as *The Political Regime,* present emanationism but only as a way of assuaging the religious feelings of the unenlightened. Mahdi's approach emphasizes a contrast between the popular and serious works of al-Farabi. The popular works are designed to disguise al-Farabi's own views.

I acknowledge that indeed al-Farabi is completely silent about emanationism in some texts and yet presents a rather complex emanationist scheme in others. But this curious feature does not presuppose a sharp contrast between popular and serious works. In fact, I think that al-Farabi offers much more continuity and consistency on this issue than meets the eye. What explains the discrepancies in the different works is simply the amount of Aristotelian loyalty al-Farabi wants to show in different contexts. Al-Farabi knows that emanationism is un-Aristotelian but wishes to adopt it in his own views because he thinks that Aristotle's *Metaphysics* is rather unsatisfactory and needs to be supplemented. Like the author of the *Epitome* attributed to Averroes, al-Farabi is aware that there is no place for emanationism in a faithfully Aristotelian metaphysics. Already Miriam Galston and Rafael Ramón Guerrero have suggested this theory.⁸

But let us now briefly state the problems involved in al-Farabi's presentation of emanationism.⁹

(Berlin, 1981), pp. 211–25. Pines grounds his claim wholly on accounts of al-Farabi's lost commentary on the *Nicomachean Ethics.* As these accounts are very obscure and not necessarily reliable and no explanation is provided why al-Farabi in this lost text would have contradicted positions held in the extant texts, it seems to me that Pines' claims lack foundation.

6. *Alfarabi's Philosophy of Plato and Aristotle,* trans. with an introduction by Muhsin Mahdi (Cornell Paperbacks, 2d ed., Ithaca, N.Y., 1969). This edition includes also the preface to the first edition of 1962. See 1962 preface, pp. 3–4, 5–6, and 9.

7. 1969 preface, pp. xix–xx and xvi.

8. Miriam Galston, "A Re-examination of al-Farabi's Neoplatonism," *Journal of the History of Philosophy* 15 (1977), pp. 13–32; Rafael Ramón Guerrero, "Al-Farabi y la 'Metafísica' de Aristóteles," *La Ciudad de Dios* 196 (1983), pp. 211–40.

9. I have excluded from consideration metaphysical texts the authenticity of which is not certain, i.e.: (1) *The Seals* [or *Gems*] *of Wisdom* or *Fusus* (cf. S. Pines, "Ibn Sina et l'auteur de la *Risalat al-fusus fi'l-hikma:* quelques données du problème," *Revue des Études islamiques* 19 [1951], pp. 121–24); (2) *The Main Questions* or *Fontes quaestionum* in

First, in what I shall call his "Aristotelian" texts, i.e., the texts in which he claims to report Aristotle's own views, al-Farabi keeps silent about emanation and leaves it aside from his presentation of metaphysics. The very brief *Aims of Aristotle's "Metaphysics"* focuses on the study of what is common to all beings.[10] It considers divine science—which examines God as principle of being in general and not as principle of any particular being—to be only one of the parts of metaphysics. *The Philosophy of Aristotle* emphasizes the necessity for a metaphysical inquiry but barely touches upon the *Metaphysics* itself.[11] The last two sections of the *Letter concerning the Intellect*, i.e., the sections dealing with Aristotle's *On the Soul* and *Metaphysics*, again do not speak of emanation.[12] Yet, in the *Harmonization of the Opinions of the two Sages, Plato and Aristotle*, al-Farabi quotes the spurious emanationist *Theology of Aristotle* but also indicates that its authenticity is disputed.[13] I have

---

its two versions, i.e., *ʿUyun al-masaʾil* and *Tajrid risalat al-da ʿawa al-qalbiyya*; about the relationship between the two Arabic versions, cf. Miguel Cruz Hernandez, "El Fontes quaestionum (ʿuyun al-masaʾil) de Abu Nasr al-Farabi," *Archives d'Histoire doctrinale et littéraire du Moyen Âge* 25–26 (1950–51), pp. 303–5; about the authenticity of this text, see again M. Cruz Hernandez, pp. 304–5, and Fazlur Rahman, *Prophecy in Islam: Philosophy and Orthodoxy* (repr. Chicago, 1979), pp. 21–22, n. 2; (3) *Commentary on the Treatise of the Greek Zeno the Great* or *Zinun al-Kabir* (cf. Franz Rosenthal, "Arabische Nachrichten ueber Zenon den Eleaten," n.s. *Orientalia* 6 [1937], pp. 63–64 and particularly, p. 64, n. 1); (4) *The Demonstration of Immaterial Things* or *Fi ʾithbat al-mufariqat* (cf. Ibrahim Madkour in his chapter on al-Farabi in *A History of Muslim Philosophy*, ed. M. M. Sharif, vol. I [Wiesbaden, 1963], p. 452, n. 10); (5) *Explanatory Remarks on Wisdom* or *Taʿliqat fiʾl-hikmah* (cf. Jean Michot, "Tables de correspondance des *Taʿliqat* d'al-Farabi, des *Taʿliqat* d'Avicenne et du *Liber Aphorismorum* d'Andrea Alpago," *MIDEO* 15 [1982], pp. 231–50).

10. *Fi ʾAghrad*, Arabic edition (1) by F. Dieterici in *Alfarabi's Philosophische Abhandlungen* (Leiden, 1890), pp. 34–38; (2) anonymously in Hyderabad, H. 1349. French translation and study by Thérèse-Anne Druart, "Le traité d'al-Farabi sur les buts de la Métaphysique d'Aristote," *Bulletin de Philosophie médiévale* 24 (1982), pp. 38–43. Spanish translation and study by Rafael Ramón Guerrero, "Al-Farabi y la 'Metafísica' de Aristóteles," pp. 225–40. English presentation by M. Galston, "A Re-examination of al-Farabi's Neoplatonism," pp. 18–19.

11. Arabic edition by Muhsin Mahdi, *Alfarabi's Philosophy of Aristotle (Falsafat Aristutalis)* (Beirut, 1961); English translation by Muhsin Mahdi, *Alfarabi's Philosophy of Plato and Aristotle*, 2d ed., pp. 71–130.

12. Arabic edition by Maurice Bouyges, S.J.: Al-Farabi, *Risalat fiʾl-ʿAql* (Beirut, 1938). English translation of the relevant sections by Arthur Hyman in *Philosophy in the Middle Ages: The Christian, Islamic, and Jewish Traditions*, ed. Arthur Hyman and James J. Walsh (New York, 1973), pp. 215–21. Full Italian translation with excellent notes by Francesca Lucchetta: Farabi, *Epistola sull'intelletto* (Padova, 1974).

13. Arabic edition (1) by F. Dieterici, *Alfarabi's Philosophische Abhandlungen* (Leiden, 1890), pp. 1–33 and particularly pp. 27–32; (2) by Albert Nader, *Al-Djamʿbayn al-Hakimayn* (Beirut, 1968), pp. 105–9. German translation by F. Dieterici, *Alfarabi's Philosophische Abhandlungen* (Leiden, 1892), pp. 1–53 and particularly pp. 43–51. French translation by Elie Abdel-Massih, *Melto* 5 (1969), pp. 305–58 and particularly pp. 347–

suggested elsewhere that al-Farabi, though officially accepting the authenticity of the *Theology*, has in fact reached the conclusion that it is not truly Aristotelian but supplements well Aristotle's own metaphysics.[14] If this interpretation is correct, then one can understand why al-Farabi, when he claims to present Aristotle's own views, is rather careful to avoid speaking of emanationism and to play down the divine-science aspect of metaphysics, i.e., the study of eternal and immaterial beings.

Second, in texts in which al-Farabi offers his own views but still in close reference to the framework of the traditional Aristotelian corpus, the focus of metaphysics shifts from the study of being as universal to divine science. *The Attainment of Happiness* emphasizes the place of metaphysics and focuses its presentation upon the study of immaterial beings, i.e., divine science.[15] *The Enumeration of the Sciences* substitutes a study of beings qua beings for the study of being qua universal and develops a lengthy program for metaphysics, which is then called divine science.[16] These two texts I shall call "programmatic," since they explain what al-Farabi thinks metaphysics should accomplish, but present only an outline.

Third, the main so-called political works, i.e., *The Opinions of the People of the Virtuous City*[17] and *The Political Regime*,[18] offer in their first half an extensive presentation of emanationism.[19] These texts I shall call "emanationist."

---

52. English presentation by Majid Fakhry, "Al-Farabi and the Reconciliation of Plato and Aristotle," *Journal of the History of Ideas* 26 (1965), pp. 469–78.

14. "Al-Farabi, Emanation and Metaphysics," in *Neoplatonism and Islamic Thought*, ed. Parviz Morewedge, Studies in Neoplatonism: Ancient and Modern (The International Society for Neoplatonic Studies, forthcoming). See also M. Galston, "A Re-examination of al-Farabi's Neoplatonism," pp. 14–19.

15. Anonymous Arabic edition, *Tahsil al-saʿadah* (Hyderabad, H. 1345). English translation by Muhsin Mahdi in *Alfarabi's Philosophy of Plato and Aristotle*, pp. 13–67.

16. Main Arabic edition by Uthman Amin (2d ed., Cairo, 1949). Other Arabic edition along with a Spanish translation and the edition of two Latin versions by Angel Gonzalez Palencia: Al-Farabi, *Catálogo de las ciencias*, 2d ed. (Madrid, 1953).

17. Arabic edition and English translation with commentary by Richard Walzer, *Al-Farabi on the Perfect State. Abu Nasr al-Farabi's Mabadiʾ Araʾ Ahl al-Madina al-Fadila* (Oxford, 1985).

18. Arabic edition by Fauzi M. Najjar, *Alfarabi's Political Regime (Al-Siyasa al-madaniyya also known as The Treatise on the Principles of Beings)* (Beirut, 1964). There is a full German translation by F. Dieterici, but it is based on a poor and incomplete text: *Die Staatsleitung von Alfarabi* (Leiden, 1904). English translation of nearly the whole political part by Fauzi M. Najjar in *Medieval Political Philosophy*, ed. Ralph Lerner and Muhsin Mahdi (Ithaca, N.Y., 1963), pp. 31–57. There is a full English translation available at the Translation Clearing House, Department of Philosophy, Oklahoma State University, Stillwater (ref. A-30-50 d), by Thérèse-Anne Druart, *The Political Regime or The Principles of Beings*.

19. *The Selected Aphorisms*, which presents al-Farabi's own views though purporting to

Fourth, *The Book of Letters*[20] analyzes some basic concepts, such as being, and is closely linked to the *Categories*. Though the expression "Book of Letters" is sometimes used as one of the ways to refer to Aristotle's *Metaphysics*, it is not so used here. In fact this text abundantly refers to the *Categories* and to other logical texts but does not directly refer to the *Metaphysics*. Yet some of al-Farabi's own metaphysical views are hinted at in the chapter on interrogative particles.[21] I shall refer to these passages when appropriate.

One could at once object to two aspects of my division into three basic kinds of texts.

First, one could argue that the inconsistencies in the texts can be explained by an evolution in al-Farabi's positions. Chronological dating of al-Farabi's works is extremely difficult. If one accepts Dunlop's general attempt[22]—even though its precise details are very shaky—or that of Walzer,[23] one has to conclude that al-Farabi's final position was essentially emanationist, since both claim that al-Farabi's emanationist works are his last ones.

Second, I have included *The Philosophy of Aristotle*, the third part of a trilogy, under the "Aristotelian" texts whereas I have classified its first part, *The Attainment of Happiness*, among the "programmatic" texts. It is clear that in *The Attainment*, al-Farabi offers his own conception of

---

offer selected aphorisms from the ancients, does not use technical emanationist language but provides a metaphysical outlook consonant with the emanationist texts. Arabic edition by Fauzi M. Najjar, *Al-Farabi's Fusul Muntaza'ah (Selected Aphorisms)* (Beirut, 1971). English translation from an earlier incomplete Arabic edition by D. M. Dunlop: Al-Farabi, *Fusul al-madani. Aphorisms of the Stateman* (Cambridge, 1961). For my purpose paragraphs 68–75 and 94 of Najjar's edition, corresponding to paragraphs 64–70 and 89 of Dunlop's translation, are particularly relevant.

20. Arabic edition by Muhsin Mahdi, *Alfarabi's Book of Letters* (Beirut, 1970). There is an interesting discussion of the meaning of the title *Book of Letters* by Rafael Ramón Guerrero, "Al-Farabi y la 'Metafísica' de Aristóteles," pp. 212–25. The chapter on being analyzes shades of meaning but does not refer to the first cause or to a cause of existence. A good summary of the content of this chapter is presented by Amina Rachid under the rather misleading title "Dieu et l'être selon al-Farabi: le chapitre de 'l'être' dans le Livre des Lettres," in *Dieu et l'être. Exégèse d'Exode 3, 14 et de Coran 20, 11–24* (Paris, 1978), pp. 180–90. At the end Rachid concludes: "this ontological and logical analysis of being in which the first cause appears *only discreetly and by allusion* will be taken over and expanded by Ibn Sina" (p. 190; my emphasis).

21. Cf. ch. 32, nn. 238–43, pp. 217–20. This passage wonders how the question "Does it exist?" or "Is it an existent?" can be answered when asked about the divinity. Al-Farabi then contrasts the way one answers these questions about the divinity with the way one would answer them if they were asked about natural beings. This passage contains interesting views on the uncaused cause's essence and attributes but nothing about emanationism.

22. Cf. his edition and translation of al-Farabi's *Fusul al-madani. Aphorisms of the Stateman*, pp. 9–17.

23. *Al-Farabi on the Perfect State*, pp. 1 and 20.

the philosophical enterprise but wants to give it authority in claiming that it reflects the old tradition of Plato and Aristotle. Yet *The Attainment* presents many un-Aristotelian features, in political matters for instance. Its Aristotelian character is limited. But in *The Philosophy of Aristotle* al-Farabi offers a fairly traditional presentation of the *corpus aristotelicum* and is much more faithful to Aristotle.

The hypothesis I want to explore is the following: since he is aware that emanation is not truly Aristotelian, al-Farabi thinks that Aristotle's own *Metaphysics* limits itself to the first task of divine science, i.e., the order of investigation and discovery of principles. Yet already in the order of discovery al-Farabi finds Aristotle unsatisfactory. He expresses this dissatisfaction in the "Aristotelian" texts. The "programmatic" texts show that al-Farabi asks metaphysics to go beyond the order of discovery, i.e., the ascent to principles, to reach the order of exposition, i.e., the descent from the principles previously discovered. He carries out such a descent, i.e., the second task of divine science, in his own "emanationist" texts.

Testing this hypothesis requires three steps. The first elaborates the order of discovery of the principles. Already the "Aristotelian" texts argue for the necessity of positing immaterial principles of being or existence. The second step examines al-Farabi's elaboration of a program for metaphysics. In the third and last step, I show how this program is realized in the "emanationist" works.

I. THE "ARISTOTELIAN" TEXTS

The Aims of Aristotle's "Metaphysics" is quite sketchy. A rather lengthy introduction states that Aristotle's *Metaphysics* does not essentially deal with God, the intellect, and the soul. This distinguishes metaphysics from Kalam (*'ilm al-tawhid* or Islamic Theology).[24] The reader will note that it also distinguishes it sharply from the pseudo *Theology of Aristotle*.[25] The extremely brief summary of each book of the *Metaphysics* is rather faithful to Aristotle. Yet his summary of book XII (called XI by al-Farabi) substitutes existence for the Greek *kinesis*, i.e., change. It speaks not of a prime mover but of a principle of existence.[26] This is

---

24. Dieterici's ed., p. 34, ll. 6–13.
25. An English version of the Arabic version of this text may be found in *Plotini Opera*, vol. II, ed. Paul Henry and Hans-Rudolf Schwyzer. The translation of the Arabic version is by Geoffrey Lewis (Paris, 1959).
26. Dieterici's ed., p. 38, ll. 2–4.

very un-Aristotelian even if it does not imply emanationism. Al-Farabi is not satisfied with a principle of change and a mere final cause.[27]

The Philosophy of Aristotle takes more liberties with Aristotle's own views. The first liberty taken by al-Farabi is the presentation of an Aristotle who carefully lays down his principles one by one through the traditional order of the corpus. To explain natural bodies and nature Aristotle posits form and matter, which he calls principles of existence.[28] He then shows the necessity for adding another principle, soul, to account for animate beings.[29] Later on, to explain the activities of the human intellect and particularly the acquisition of the first intelligibles, he posits a further principle, the Agent Intellect, which is not a body or in a body, since it is always in act.[30] He also requires an immaterial mover—the famous prime mover—to explain the circular motion of the heavenly bodies,[31] which themselves are active principles for the interactions between the four elements.[32] Al-Farabi confronts us with an unusual Aristotle who carefully distinguishes different kinds of principles of being, i.e., form and matter, and of change, i.e., soul, the Agent Intellect, the immaterial movers of the heavenly bodies, and the heavenly bodies themselves. The existence of these principles and of immaterial beings is discovered through natural philosophy.

Al-Farabi takes a second liberty. He claims that discovering the existence of these principles and beings is not enough. Their very existence raises new questions. So two further tasks need to be accomplished: first, to determine whether soul, the Agent Intellect, the celestial bodies, and the immaterial mover are not only principles of change but also principles of existence; and second, to clarify the relationships between these principles.

The true Aristotle limited himself to principles of change. Al-

---

27. Hellenistic commentators too had not been very satisfied with Aristotle's prime mover. Charles Genequand shows this in "L'objet de la métaphysique selon Alexandre d'Aphrodise," *Museum Helveticum* 36 (1979), pp. 48–57.
28. Mahdi's trans., n. 20, p. 99; Arabic, p. 92.
29. Trans., n. 74, p. 115; Arabic, pp. 112–13.
30. Trans., nn. 97–98, pp. 126–28; Arabic, pp. 127–29. *The Opinions*, section VI, ch. 13, also claims that it is the Agent Intellect which gives the first intelligibles and explains what these first intelligibles are (pp. 198–207). See also *The Political Regime*, p. 71, l. 14–p. 72, l. 4. In the same way he had claimed in n. 87, p. 121 (Arabic, p. 121) that the soul and nature, i.e., form and matter, are "insufficient to explain the dream-vision that warns of future events. This requires other principles with a rank of being higher than that of the soul." (Note the expression "rank of being.") In *The Opinions*, this principle is the Agent Intellect. Cf. Walzer's edition and translation, section IV, ch. 14, nn. 6–11, pp. 218–27.
31. Trans., n. 34, p. 103; Arabic, p. 97.   32. Trans., n. 49, p. 107; Arabic, p. 103.

Farabi's Aristotle, on the other hand, feels a great need for tackling the question of the cause of existence. In his presentation of the *Posterior Analytics*, al-Farabi argues that true science looks not only for principles of instruction, i.e., principles showing that a thing exists, but also for the causes of the thing's existence, i.e., its principles of being.[33] Therefore al-Farabi thinks that Aristotle failed to provide a truly scientific physics, since he did not determine the cause of existence of natural beings. For instance, at the end of his presentation of the natural sciences he complains that "up till now it had not become evident that the heavenly bodies supplied the natural bodies with anything besides motion."[34] He also asks whether the Agent Intellect too is a cause of existence and what are the relationships between Agent Intellect, soul, heavenly bodies, and nature, i.e., form and matter.[35] The Farabian Aristotle is much more inquisitive than the Greek one. He even begins wondering whether higher principles, conceived as immaterial *beings*, such as the Agent Intellect, can explain the existence of lower principles, such as soul, form, and matter.

Having expressed his need for further inquiries he confesses that such "matters are beyond the scope of natural theory. For natural theory includes only what is included in the categories;[36] and it has become evident that there are other instances of beings not encompassed by the categories: that is, the Agent Intellect and the thing that supplies the heavenly bodies with perpetual circular motion."[37] "Natural theory terminates in the Agent Intellect and the mover of the heavenly bodies, and then stands still."[38] All these questions should be resolved in metaphysics, but as they are neither resolved nor really considered in Aristotle's own *Metaphysics*, the reader is not surprised that al-Farabi claims that "we do not possess metaphysical science"[39]—at least if one limits oneself to Aristotle's *Metaphysics*, which hints at divine science but does not really develop it. So al-Farabi ends by simply stating that metaphysics is an investigation of beings (not being

---

33. Trans., n. 7, pp. 84–85; Arabic, p. 75. One can find an application of this theory to natural science and metaphysics in *The Selected Aphorisms*, Dunlop's trans., n. 89, pp. 72–74; Arabic, n. 94, pp. 95–98, l. 8.

34. Trans., n. 99, p. 128; Arabic, p. 130.

35. "Whether the Agent Intellect is also the cause of the existence of nature and natural beings and of the soul and animate things" (n. 99, p. 128; Arabic, p. 129).

36. That the categories limit themselves to natural beings which are attested by sense perception has already been affirmed in n. 4, pp. 82–83; Arabic, pp. 72–73. The need for a cause which is a being of a kind not included in the categories is also expressed in *The Book of Letters*, n. 17, p. 69; n. 72, pp. 104–5; and n. 92, p. 119.

37. Trans., n. 99, p. 129; Arabic, p. 130. 38. Trans., n. 99, p. 129; Arabic, p. 130.

39. Trans., n. 99, p. 130; Arabic, p. 133.

qua universal) in a manner different from natural inquiry and of the beings that are above things material in their *rank of existence*.⁴⁰

Such inquiries are missing from Aristotle's genuine texts but can be found in al-Farabi's own emanationism in which the question of existence and of ranking are of utmost importance. This is why al-Farabi concludes his *Philosophy of Aristotle* with the following sentence: "Therefore philosophy must necessarily come into being in every man in the way possible for him."⁴¹ The only possible way for al-Farabi is emanationism, even though he knows it not to be Aristotelian and therefore avoids foisting it on Aristotle.

The third and last "Aristotelian" text I want to examine is the last part of the *Letter concerning the Intellect*, i.e., the sections about the meaning of intellect in Aristotle's *On the Soul* and *Metaphysics*. Whereas *The Philosophy of Aristotle* raises questions and determines lines of investigation without pursuing any, the *Letter concerning the Intellect* makes these investigations and provides answers. It offers a long presentation of the Agent Intellect and of its thinking (both topics rather ignored in Aristotle's *On the Soul*) and explores the Agent Intellect's relationship to another principle and to the celestial bodies. The move to the celestial bodies leads to affirming the existence of a series of immaterial movers which culminates in an immaterial non-mover equated with the intellect of *Metaphysics*, book Lambda or XII.⁴² The text presents an ascent to principles and immaterial separate beings. It uses ascent language too.

The first stage of the ascent is the rank of the Agent Intellect, which is a separate form.⁴³ At first the Agent Intellect's role is presented in Aristotelian terms of actualizing the potential intellect as well as the potential intelligibles.⁴⁴ The *Posterior Analytics* has shown that human beings ascend from that which is less perfect but better known to them, to that which is more perfect but previously less known to them. By contrast, the Agent Intellect thinks first the most perfect beings. Again, whereas we acquire most intelligibles by abstracting them from

---

40. Trans., n. 99, p. 130; Arabic, p. 131.   41. Trans., n. 99, p. 130; Arabic, p. 133.
42. Hyman's trans., p. 221; Arabic, pp. 35–36.
43. Trans., p. 218; Arabic, p. 24. It is curious that al-Farabi here calls an immaterial being a separate "form." In *The Political Regime*, he refuses to use such a terminology and reserves this word for an enmattered form, i.e., form as correlative to matter in natural beings (p. 37, l. 4–p. 38, l. 1).
44. Trans., p. 218; Arabic, pp. 24–25. Note that previously (trans., p. 216; Arabic, pp. 16–17) al-Farabi had explained that the categories do not apply very well to intelligibles. He wonders whether the categories when applied to intelligibles are meaningless or simply used metaphorically. Here again we find the theme that there is something beyond the categories, since they deal only with sensible beings.

matter, the Agent Intellect does not do so. The intelligible forms which it thinks originally exist in it qua indivisible. It is the Agent Intellect which puts these forms, in divisible mode, in matter. Thus the material divisible forms imitate the forms in the Agent Intellect, which thereby gives to matter images of what is in its substance.[45] The reader wonders what exactly al-Farabi means by these forms. They seem to be exemplars of the natural forms. But does the Agent Intellect really give forms to all natural beings or only to souls or human intellects? The text seems first to imply the former but later states that the Agent Intellect "brings [these forms] closer to that which is immaterial little by little until there comes to be the acquired intellect."[46] So it seems that the main function of the Agent Intellect is to provide souls or intellects with forms.[47]

Once al-Farabi has delineated the function and thinking activity of the Agent Intellect in what concerns lower beings, he explains that the Agent Intellect is not self-sufficient for its task of imparting intelligible forms. This task requires that the celestial bodies provide matter and substrates for these forms and that there be no impediment. Hence the Agent Intellect needs the help of the celestial bodies in order to exercise its own activity.[48] This need for help is a sign of deficiency. The Agent Intellect's deficiency prevents it from producing the totality of existing things and from being its own cause of existence. Therefore its existence requires another principle whose name is not given.[49]

The Agent Intellect's need for the celestial bodies leads al-Farabi to

45. Hyman's English trans., p. 219; Lucchetta's Italian trans., pp. 103–4; Arabic, pp. 28–30. The passage is very obscure. I have preferred Lucchetta's translation to Hyman's. Herbert A. Davidson, "Alfarabi and Avicenna on the Active Intellect," *Viator* 3 (1972), pp. 150–51, underlines the obscurity of this passage and tries to interpret it.

46. Trans., p. 219; Arabic, p. 31.

47. Lucchetta interprets this passage as meaning that the Agent Intellect is a *dator formarum* but points to the ambiguities of al-Farabi's philosophy of mind, pp. 68–79 (about the Agent Intellect as *dator formarum*, see particularly pp. 71–73). This interpretation runs counter to what al-Farabi says in other texts, particularly the popular political ones, which are probably late. In those texts al-Farabi claims that the natural forms are given by the celestial bodies. The Agent Intellect's only function is to bring man's intellect from potentiality to actuality (cf. Thérèse-Anne Druart, "Al-Farabi's Causation of the Heavenly Bodies," in *Islamic Philosophy and Mysticism*, ed. Parviz Morewedge [Delmar, N.Y., 1981], pp. 35–45). Herbert A. Davidson had already noticed this discrepancy, pp. 136–37. The eventual discrepancies between al-Farabi's views in this text and his views in the late emanationist works could be explained by J. Finnegan's hypothesis that this is an early text (cf. "Al-Farabi et le 'Peri Nou' d'Alexandre d'Aphrodise," in *Mélanges Louis Massignon*, II [Damascus, 1957], p. 136; Bouyges, p. vii, and Lucchetta, p. 16, on the other hand, suggest that this text is a "mature" work).

48. Trans., pp. 220–21; Arabic, pp. 32–34.

49. Trans., p. 220; Arabic, p. 33.

investigate such bodies. He argues that each one of them has a mover which is the cause of its existence. The more perfect the body the more perfect the mover. The most perfect celestial body is the first heaven, whose mover has a double nature which is grounded in its intellectual activity. The inferior nature thinks of itself and thereby produces the sphere of the first heaven; the superior one by thinking its principle produces the mover of the next lower sphere, i.e., the mover of the sphere of the fixed stars. Because of its dual nature, the mover of the first heaven cannot be the first principle of all beings and must have a principle which is the ultimate one. This ultimate principle, too, is an intellect, but it is one in all respects. This is why it is called "the principle of all principles and the first principle of all beings."[50] Al-Farabi daringly equates this first principle, which for him is not a mover, with the intellect Aristotle speaks of in *Metaphysics* XII, i.e., the unmoved mover. All the others (which are movers) are also intellects but become so only from the first intellect, who is also the first being, the first one, and the first true.[51] The other pure intellects exist according to ranks, and as I indicated at the very beginning, the Agent Intellect occupies the lowest rank.[52]

So in the *Letter concerning the Intellect* al-Farabi pursues the investigations adumbrated in *The Philosophy of Aristotle*. The cause of existence for all principles and beings is discovered. There is an ascent from the lower pure intellect, the Agent Intellect, through the movers of the celestial bodies to the first principle, which itself is not a mover. All these principles are neatly ranked. At each step of the ascent al-Farabi justifies why a new principle needs to be assumed. Each principle derives its existence from a higher one. The relationship between the Agent Intellect and the celestial bodies is determined. In this ascent al-Farabi makes some use of *On the Soul* but very little of the *Metaphysics* and adds a lot of his own. His sole reference to the *Metaphysics* is to book XII, the only one dealing with divine science. Al-Farabi claims that his ultimate principle, which is not a mover, corresponds to Aristotle's unmoved mover. The emphasis is no longer on a cause or principle for motion but on a cause or principle of existence for all principles and all beings. The arguments set forth to justify the existence of all these principles are Neoplatonic. It seems that al-Farabi

---

50. Trans., p. 221; Arabic, p. 35. Cf. also *The Book of Letters*, n. 242, pp. 219–20.
51. Trans., p. 221; Arabic, p. 36. The description of divine science in *The Enumeration of the Sciences* gives the same attributes to the First or ultimate principle.
52. The number of pure intelligences is not given. The "emanationist" *Opinions*, section II, pp. 100–105, tells us that from the First emanate ten intelligences, including the Agent Intellect.

uses Aristotle as a springboard for an elaboration of his own metaphysics. While dealing with Aristotle's own views al-Farabi simply reports them, but when he goes beyond them he argues rather carefully. This ascent smacks of Neoplatonism yet it does not include any technical emanationist term.

II. THE "PROGRAMMATIC" TEXTS

The views offered in the "programmatic" texts are al-Farabi's own but are still couched in an Aristotelian framework. The first part of *The Attainment of Happiness* presents the theoretical virtues necessary for obtaining happiness. "[These] virtues consist in the sciences whose ultimate purpose is only to make the beings and what they contain intelligible with certainty."[53] The presentation of these virtues or sciences follows the order of the Aristotelian corpus: logic, mathematics, natural science, metaphysics, ethics and politics. In his description of logic, al-Farabi states at once that what interests him in every science is the attempt to know the principles of existence.[54] These principles are the four causes, and there are three kinds of beings. The first kind of being has no cause for its existence but "is the ultimate principle for the existence of all other beings."[55] This principle is the First or the divinity.[56] The second kind, which consists of the natural beings, has the four causes. The third kind, which covers the "metaphysical" beings,[57] except for the First, has only three of the four principles, since it does not need a material cause. The methodology of going from principles of instruction, i.e., primary cognitions, to the principles of existence is an ascent. Once these principles of existence have been discovered, they become principles of instruction for a descent towards unknown inferior beings originating from these principles.[58]

Having explained the methodology, al-Farabi applies it to the study of natural beings. The ascent to the principles of existence for the celestial bodies and for the soul and intellect leads to the discovery that such principles are metaphysical, i.e., immaterial, beings.[59] Therefore metaphysics is "the science of what is beyond material things in the order of investigation and instruction and above them in the order of

---

53. Mahdi's trans., n. 2, p. 13; Arabic, p. 2.
54. Trans., n. 5, p. 15; Arabic, pp. 4–5.   55. Trans., n. 16, p. 15; Arabic, p. 5.
56. Trans., n. 19, p. 24; Arabic, p. 15.
57. Trans., n. 6, pp. 15–16, and n. 16, p. 21; Arabic, pp. 5 and 12.
58. Trans., nn. 8–9, pp. 17–18, and n. 15, p. 21; Arabic, pp. 6–8 and pp. 11–12.
59. Trans., nn. 16–17, pp. 21–22; Arabic, pp. 12–13. Note the term "metaphysical" applied to beings and meaning immaterial.

existence."⁶⁰ The metaphysical inquiry, too, proceeds by means of an ascent from beings that are immaterial but caused to a perfect uncaused being.⁶¹ This, in turn, "is itself the first principle of all the aforementioned beings,"⁶² since it is their formal, efficient, and final cause. The *Letter concerning the Intellect* presents such an ascent.⁶³ In it, as in *The Philosophy of Aristotle*, investigation of both the celestial bodies and the intellect causes the ascent.

According to the methodology a descent should follow the ascent. Al-Farabi considers such a descent as soon as the ultimate principle has been discovered. "Having understood this [i.e., the existence of the ultimate principle and its attributes], one should investigate next what properties the other beings necessarily possess as a consequence of their having *this* being as their principle and the cause of their existence."⁶⁴ The descent should proceed in orderly fashion from the higher being to the lower. Such an orderly descent is carried out in the "emanationist" texts. *The Attainment of Happiness* calls the metaphysical ascent and descent the divine inquiry.⁶⁵

The Attainment of Happiness designs a program for metaphysics which includes ascent and descent. It also ends in claiming that the philosophy which answers such a program is Greek philosophy, but only as transmitted by Plato and Aristotle.⁶⁶ Yet *The Philosophy of Aristotle*, which, as we have seen, completes *The Attainment of Happiness*, barely alludes to the *Metaphysics*, though it emphasizes the need for a metaphysical inquiry. It even claims that "we do not possess metaphysical science."⁶⁷ Instead it offers a rather extensive presentation of natural science. On the other hand, *The Attainment of Happiness* delineates a careful program for mathematics—which is not included in the corpus—and metaphysics but gives short shrift to natural science. *The Philosophy of Aristotle* focuses on what Aristotle accomplished but suggests that more has to be done. *The Attainment of Happiness*, on the other hand, emphasizes what philosophy now needs to investigate because Aristotle failed to do so, and drafts a program for further research.

The Enumeration of the Sciences presents a more extended metaphysical program. The whole text offers an overview of the sciences which basically follows the order of the corpus. The section on metaphysics

---

60. Trans., n. 16, p. 22; Arabic, pp. 12–13.
61. *The Book of Letters* also claims that the divinity is uncaused, n. 239, p. 218.
62. Trans., n. 19, p. 23; Arabic, pp. 12–13.
63. *The Selected Aphorisms* speaks of this same ascent in n. 94, p. 95–p. 98, l. 8; Dunlop's trans., n. 89, pp. 72–74.
64. Trans., n. 19, p. 24; Arabic, p. 15.   65. Ibid.
66. Trans., n. 63, p. 49; Arabic, p. 47.   67. Trans., n. 99, p. 130; Arabic, p. 133.

is entitled "Divine Science" and comes at the completion of the section on natural science. At once it is stated that divine science is divided into three parts according to Aristotle's own presentation in *Metaphysics* VI, 1.

The content of the first part is stated in one sentence only: it "investigates the beings and their accidents qua beings."[68]

The second part investigates the principles of demonstration in the particular theoretical sciences: logic, mathematics, and natural science. It also refutes false views on such topics.

The third part is a study of beings that are neither bodies nor in bodies. Al-Farabi tells us that one should first investigate whether such bodies exist and maintains that one can demonstrate that they do. Divine science then shows that these immaterial beings are many and finite in number, and that their ranks of order differ with respect to perfection. Consideration of these ranks of perfection leads to the investigation of an absolutely perfect being which is the most perfect, cannot share its rank with any other, has no like or contrary, and is fully prior. The other beings are posterior to its existence, and it is this first being which bestows on each of them being, oneness, and truth. Thus the First is that which is the most deserving of the name and meaning of one, being, and true. These three attributes were exactly the ones given to the first intellect at the end of the *Letter concerning the Intellect*.[69] The *Enumeration of the Sciences* no longer highlights the fact that the first being is an intellect, but uses another terminology and says that such a being "ought to be believed to be god" and that one should investigate all its attributes or names.[70]

This description of the first cause differs from Aristotle's presentation of the prime mover. Most of the attributes of al-Farabi's first cause

---

68. The Arabic text for the whole section can be found in Amin's edition, pp. 99–101; Spanish translation in Gonzalez Palencia, pp. 63–65; Medieval Latin version by Gerard of Cremona also in Gonzalez Palencia, pp. 163–66. The formulation "beings qua beings," instead of the more common Aristotelian "being qua being," is typical of *Metaphysics* VI, 1. In his *Commentary on the "De Interpretatione"* (ed. Wilhelm Kutsch, S.J., and Stanley Marrow, S.J. [Beirut, 1960]), p. 84, 14f., al-Farabi makes the point that the study of beings qua beings is no part of logic but rather part of metaphysics. See F. W. Zimmermann's English translation and introduction, *Al-Farabi's Commentary and Short Treatise on Aristotle's "De Interpretatione,"* Classical and Medieval Logic Texts, III (Oxford, 1981), pp. xxxix and 78. This work again refers us back to the claim that metaphysics deals with what is beyond the categories. Yet al-Farabi does not hesitate to study the meaning of "being" as a concept in his reflections on the categories in ch. XV of his *Book of Letters*, pp. 110–28.

69. See supra, text at note 51.

70. That the First is an intellect is also emphasized in the *Book of Letters*, n. 242, p. 220. One should keep in mind that discussion of God's attributes is a very important theme in Islamic Theology (Kalam).

are missing in Aristotle, since the prime mover is a final cause of motion but does not bestow being, oneness, and truth on any other being.

So divine science begins with an ascent leading to the discovery of the first cause, its activity and its attributes. There follows a descent which explains how other beings receive their existence from the first cause, and how they are ranked. It also shows that the immaterial beings are interconnected and ordered in relation to each other. This descent is nowhere to be found in Aristotle's *Metaphysics*, but is certainly typical of emanationism, even if al-Farabi does not use proper emanationist terminology.

The program for the third part of divine science is much more elaborate and expanded than the program for the other parts. It is carried out in *The Political Regime* and in *The Opinions of the People of the Virtuous City*. The double task of ascent and descent was already adumbrated in *The Attainment of Happiness* and applies the program set out for every science in which principles of discovery and principles of beings do not coincide, i.e., all theoretical sciences save mathematics and logic.[71]

Al-Farabi concludes his program for the third part of divine science by a refutation of false views of the acts of God which claim that in these acts there is some defect. *The Political Regime*, which ends rather abruptly, contains some exposition of false views among the "Weeds," i.e., the nonconformists. *The Opinions* ends with a presentation of false metaphysical views of different kinds.[72] One can find an exposé and refutation of views implying a defect in the acts of God—if one understands these acts broadly—in *The Selected Aphorisms*.[73] There al-Farabi claims that evil has no absolute existence. Both *The Opinions* and *The Selected Aphorisms* are probably late works. The un-Aristotelian aspect of, and the emphasis on, the program for the third part of divine science may explain a puzzling feature. At the very beginning of the chapter on metaphysics, some Arabic manuscripts add a line which claims: "the whole of divine science is in his [Aristotle's] book on metaphysics." This sentence is the only one which does not appear in all Arabic manuscripts of this section. Amin's edition does not consider it as part of the text. If I am right in thinking that al-Farabi had a pretty good grasp of the genuine Aristotelian metaphysics and of its limitations, then this sentence can be understood as simply a gloss by an

---

71. See supra, text at note 33.
72. *The Political Regime*, Najjar's trans., pp. 53–56; Arabic, p. 104, l. 7–p. 108, l. 19. *The Opinions*, section VI, chs. 18–19.
73. Arabic by Najjar, nn. 72–75, pp. 79–82; English by Dunlop, nn. 67–70, pp. 59–61.

overzealous scribe. In the section on natural science, al-Farabi usually indicates the name of the Aristotelian work in which each of its subdivisions was studied. Some scribe, knowing of Aristotle's *Metaphysics*, inserted this sentence thinking it had been inadvertently omitted. Al-Farabi omitted it deliberately. He is aware that most of what he is suggesting has not been realized by Aristotle even if he hinted at it.

Obviously *The Enumeration of the Sciences* expands the program barely alluded to in *The Attainment of Happiness*. The task of ascent is realized in the *Letter concerning the Intellect*. The first half of the so-called *Political Regime* carries out the descent.

III. THE "EMANATIONIST" TEXTS

In this last section I want to show how *The Political Regime* accomplishes the second and third parts of this program for divine science. In it al-Farabi uses emanationism to explain the existence of the beings. My hypothesis that *The Political Regime* realizes this program explains its subtitle, its abrupt beginning, and the structure of its first half, which is purely metaphysical. In it al-Farabi presents the descent about which he had spoken. When useful I shall indicate parallel passages or additions in the other main emanationist text, *The Opinions of the People of the Virtuous City*.

First, let us look at the title of *The Political Regime*. In many manuscripts this text is subtitled *The Principles of the Beings*,[74] i.e., the principles of natural science as well as the principles of immaterial beings. Old listings of al-Farabi's works report this subtitle.[75] Maimonides recommended to Ibn Tibbon the reading of al-Farabi's *Principles of the Beings*.[76] This subtitle reminds us of the beginning of *Metaphysics* VI, 1: "We are seeking the principles and causes of the beings qua beings." This subtitle was rather popular because it gives a good account of the work's strong metaphysical character.

Second, the abrupt beginning of the text can be understood only if one assumes that the inquiry about and discovery of such principles has already been accomplished. It begins by listing the principles of the beings: "The principles by means of which bodies and their accidents subsist are of six kinds, and have six main ranks. Each rank em-

---

74. Cf. Najjar's ed., pp. 13–16; 24–25; 31, n. 1.
75. Cf. Moritz Steinschneider, *Al-Farabi. Des Arabischen Philosophen Leben und Schriften* (Saint-Petersburg, 1869; repr., Amsterdam, 1966), p. 217.
76. Cf. S. Munk, *Mélanges de philosophie juive et arabe*, last ed. (Paris, 1955), p. 344.

braces one of the kinds."[77] This is an immediate listing of the number of principles of natural science and of the number of their ranks. This general statement is then somewhat expanded: "The first cause in the first rank; the second causes in the second rank; the Agent Intellect in the third; soul in the fourth; form in the fifth and matter in the sixth."[78] Again these principles are simply listed and ranked. Al-Farabi offers no justification whatsoever for his choice of principles or for their ranking. Obviously he considers the discovery of the principles as settled. In the *Letter concerning the Intellect,* he had argued for the existence and nature of the highest principles. Aristotle himself had already shown the necessity of positing the lower principles—matter, form, and soul—as we saw in *The Philosophy of Aristotle.*

The next step for al-Farabi is to claim that the first cause is one and unique whereas all other principles are multiple: "That which is in the first rank cannot be multiple but is only one and unique. But that which is in each of the other ranks is multiple."[79] This highlights the Neoplatonic contrast between the one and the many. He then presents a second contrast: "Three of these principles are neither bodies nor in bodies. These are: the first cause, the second causes, and the Agent Intellect. Three are in bodies but are not themselves bodies. Those are: soul, form, and matter."[80] The former are the immaterial beings that Aristotle wanted to study in divine science or theology.[81] The latter are the basic principles of natural science.[82]

Finally, al-Farabi lists in descending order the six kinds of bodies: "celestial body, rational animal, irrational animal, plants, minerals, and the four elements. The totality constituted by these six kinds of bodies is the universe."[83] As the celestial bodies are not really part of natural science, al-Farabi argued in *The Philosophy of Aristotle* for the necessity of determining their substance.[84] *The Political Regime* shows that they are not subject to the hylomorphic composition of natural bodies, since their souls are always in actuality and have a substrate instead of matter.[85]

This abrupt introduction assumes that the principles of natural science and the principles of these principles, be they material or not,

---

77. Najjar's ed., p. 31, ll. 2–3.
78. Arabic, p. 31, ll. 3–5.
79. Arabic, p. 31, ll. 5–7.
80. Arabic, p. 31, ll. 7–9.
81. *Metaphysics* VI, 1, 1026a8–32.
82. In *The Enumeration of the Sciences,* the study of the principles of other sciences, such as natural science, is the second division of metaphysics or divine science.
83. Arabic, p. 31, ll. 9–11.
84. Trans., n. 99, pp. 128–29; Arabic, pp. 129–30.
85. Arabic, p. 34, ll. 1–3, and p. 41, ll. 3–6.

have already been discovered and partially ranked. One striking feature of this presentation as well as of the *Letter concerning the Intellect* is that the Agent Intellect is assigned a rank inferior to the second causes though it too is a pure intelligence. This inferior rank is explained by the Agent Intellect's need for an intermediary, i.e., the celestial bodies, for its activity of providing intelligibles to human beings and actualizing their intellect. On the other hand, the second causes are superior, since they do not need any intermediary for their own activity of giving rise to the existence of these celestial bodies.[86] In *The Opinions of the People of the Virtuous City*, a less complex text, there is not so much refinement in assigning ranks, and the Agent Intellect there is viewed mainly as the last of the second causes.[87]

From this compact introduction al-Farabi goes on to accomplish two tasks: (1) a brief study of each of the principles he has just listed; and (2) an account of how all beings derive from the first cause. Both studies proceed rank by rank in descending order.

(1) The study of the six principles (p. 31, l. 12–p. 42, l. 13) carries out the task assigned to the second part of divine science. The principles are briefly described.

First, there is a presentation of the first cause (p. 31, ll. 12–13). "The First is the one which ought to be believed to be god [this is nearly word for word a repetition of a formula in *The Enumeration of the Sciences*[88]] and it is the proximate cause of the existence of the second causes and of the Agent Intellect."

Second (p. 31, l. 13–p. 32, l. 5), the second causes are described as the causes for the existence of the celestial bodies and so must be as many in number as the celestial spheres. As in the *Letter concerning the Intellect* their exact number is not given.[89] Again, al-Farabi assumes this has already been determined. In *The Opinions*, he tells us that there are nine celestial spheres and therefore nine movers, i.e., a number very different from the fifty-five or forty-seven movers of Aristotle's *Metaphysics* XII, 8.[90]

Third, al-Farabi explains the Agent Intellect's role (p. 32, ll. 6–12). It takes care of man instead of a celestial sphere. "The essence of the

---

86. *The Political Regime*, Arabic, p. 55, ll. 5–12; The *Letter concerning the Intellect*, Hyman's trans., pp. 220–21; Arabic, p. 32, l. 8–p. 34, l. 3.
87. Section II, ch. 3 and ch. 4, n. 1, pp. 100–107; section III, ch. 6, pp. 112–19.
88. Arabic, p. 34, l. 4–p. 35, l. 11; cf. supra, text at note 70.
89. Hyman's trans., p. 221; Arabic, p. 34, l. 4–p. 35, l. 11.
90. Section II, ch. 3, pp. 100–105. Al-Farabi substitutes for Aristotle's Eudoxean multiplication of spheres the more recent and economical scheme of Ptolemy. Cf. Walzer's commentary on this chapter, pp. 364–66.

Agent Intellect is one, but its rank includes the rational animals who have purified themselves and attained happiness."[91]

Fourth, the different kinds of souls, i.e., celestial, rational, and irrational, are ranked (p. 32, l. 13–p. 36, l. 5).

Fifth, form is explained in correlation with prime matter and ranks are assigned to the different forms, whereas ranks are denied to matter (p. 36, l. 6–p. 39, l. 13).

Finally, al-Farabi concludes this first part by contrasting the imperfection belonging to hylomorphic bodies with the perfection of the incorporeal substances (p. 39, l. 14–p. 42, l. 13). The inferior ranks among the latter are assigned in accordance with the degree of multiplicity of their objects of thought. It is only to the first cause that there attaches no multiplicity whatsoever. Al-Farabi then speaks of souls and particularly of the celestial souls. As the celestial bodies are not subject to hylomorphic composition but are still corporeal, their degree of perfection is intermediate between the hylomorphic beings and the incorporeal substances.

(2) The account of how all beings and principles derive from the first cause (p. 42, l. 14–p. 69, l. 14) covers at least twice as many pages as the study of the principles; it corresponds to the third division of divine science and matches its greater length. To show how all beings derive from the First, al-Farabi proceeds no longer principle by principle, but rather according to the ranks of the beings. Hence he investigates first the beings that are not bodies or in bodies, then the celestial bodies, and finally the hylomorphic bodies, which he now calls possible beings to contrast them with all the other beings, which are necessary. Thanks to this structure, al-Farabi can study all the beings in descending order. Nearly the same structure is used for the first four sections of *The Opinions*.

First, there is a rather intricate study of the first cause (p. 42, l. 14–p. 52, l. 4; *Opinions*, section I). This study shows its absolute perfection. It has no like, no contrary, and is indivisible. It is more entitled than anything else to the name of the one and its meaning, and is intelligence. The First causes all natural beings in bestowing existence to them. This emanation (*faydh*) does not add anything to it. Finally its names and attributes are discussed. All these points are carefully argued, fulfill more or less chronologically the program designed in *The Enumeration of the Sciences*, and match its length.

Second, the study of the second causes explains how they give exis-

---

91. About al-Farabi's conception of the Agent Intellect, see Herbert A. Davidson's detailed account, "Alfarabi and Avicenna on the Active Intellect," pp. 134–54.

tence by emanation to each other and to the celestial bodies (p. 52, l. 5–p. 55, l. 5).

Third, only a few lines are assigned to the Agent Intellect (p. 55, ll. 5–12). These last two themes are grouped under section II of *The Opinions*. This concludes the study of the beings that are not bodies nor in bodies.

Fourth, the study of the celestial bodies (p. 55, l. 13–p. 56, l. 12) explains how prime matter proceeds from the common motion of the first heaven. The other various celestial motions give rise to the various forms. This corresponds to chs. 4–7 of the third section of *The Opinions*. Thus al-Farabi has discovered a cause for the existence of the two basic principles of Aristotle's hylomorphism, i.e., form and matter.

Finally, al-Farabi studies the possible beings, i.e., the hylomorphic substances (p. 56, l. 13–p. 69, l. 14; *Opinions*, chs. 8–9 of section III and section IV). Their ranks are explained and justified, but in ascending order this time, i.e., first the elements, then minerals, plants, irrational animals, and, finally, rational animals. The possible beings are carefully ranked according to their degree of subordination to each other. The same basic structure of presentation is used in *The Opinions*.

In the metaphysical half of the so-called political works, the interconnections between the actions of the different principles and the interactions between principles and the different beings are explored, such as the interaction between form and matter; between the celestial bodies and the Agent Intellect (this was one of the unanswered queries in *The Philosophy of Aristotle*)[92]; and between superior and inferior bodies. This metaphysical part carries out the program delineated in *The Enumeration of the Sciences* and answers all the questions raised in *The Philosophy of Aristotle* and therefore supplements it in completing it.

The emanationist texts offer a detailed account of emanation and even use technical emanationist terms of the root *faydh*.[93] They alone use such technical language because they do not claim to present in any way Aristotle's own views.

---

92. Trans., n. 99, p. 128; Arabic, p. 130.
93. Najjar's index to his edition of *The Political Regime* curiously omits such terms: p. 40, l. 4; p. 41, ll. 10 and 14; p. 42, ll. 7 and 12; p. 47, ll. 13 and 14; p. 48, ll. 11, 14, and 15; p. 50, l. 3; p. 52, ll. 7 and 8; p. 53, ll. 5 and 15; p. 57, l. 2; p. 65, l. 1; p. 79, ll. 15 and 17; p. 80, l. 1. In *The Opinions* such terms are found: p. 88, ll. 15 and 16; p. 92, ll. 8 and 16; p. 94, ll. 2, 4, 7, 8, and 16; p. 100, l. 11; p. 220, l. 2; p. 244, ll. 10 (twice), 12, and 13; p. 278, l. 1. See also Walzer's commentary on these terms, pp. 354–55. About specific

The emanationist texts are consonant with the "programmatic" and the "Aristotelian" works. The "Aristotelian" texts do not directly speak of emanation but raise questions that Aristotle did not answer in his *Metaphysics*. They also show the need for a quest for principles of existence instead of the Aristotelian mere final cause for motion. This explains why al-Farabi is rather silent about Aristotle's *Metaphysics* while insisting on the need for a metaphysical science. Somehow Aristotle had not accomplished what should have been done. The "programmatic" texts advocate al-Farabi's own conception of metaphysics as fundamentally a divine science, including an order of descent explaining how the existence of all beings proceeds from the First. Yet as the program is still somehow linked to the traditional Aristotelian corpus, he is careful not to use technical emanationist terms since he knows that emanationism is not to be found in the true Aristotle. In the "emanationist" texts, al-Farabi shakes off fully the fetters imposed by the limitations of Aristotle's *Metaphysics* and presents a complex descending emanationist scheme. This scheme answers all the questions raised by Aristotle's *Metaphysics*. In such texts he does not hesitate to use technical emanationist language.

Al-Farabi tries to be faithful to Aristotle's letter in avoiding direct emanationism when he purports to present Aristotle's own views. He knows that emanationism is not compatible with true Aristotelianism. Yet he is also convinced that Aristotle's *Metaphysics* is unsatisfactory and needs to be supplemented. In the *Posterior Analytics,* Aristotle's conception of science reveals the incompleteness of the *Metaphysics*. Faithful to the spirit of his master, al-Farabi undertakes to complete and expand Aristotelian metaphysics by adding to the order of inquiry and by providing an order of exposition or descent. Emanationism allows him to deal with the principles and causes of existence and to explain how all beings and principles, including the principles of hylomorphism, proceed from the First.

Georgetown University

---

and original features of al-Farabi's emanationist scheme, see Herbert A. Davidson, "Alfarabi and Avicenna on the Active Intellect," p. 136.

3 Maimonides on Creation and Emanation
ARTHUR HYMAN

Maimonides, as one would expect of an adherent of biblical religion and its interpreter, devoted a substantial section of his *Guide of the Perplexed* to a discussion of creation. How important this subject was for him can be seen from a passage in the *Guide*[1] in which he writes that belief in creation "is undoubtedly a fundamental principle of the Law of Moses our teacher, peace be upon him, and is second to the fundamental principle of belief in the unity of God."

Maimonides' discussion is divisible into two basic parts: (1) his critique of the opinions of the dialectical theologians, the Mutakallimūn,[2] and (2) the presentation of his own views, as part of which he develops a critique of the Aristotelian opinion that the world is eternal. Against the Mutakallimūn he argues that their proofs for the creation of the world are philosophically unsound, and more than that, he holds that there are no demonstrative proofs for the creation of the world or its eternity.

Maimonides begins the presentation of his own views by enumerating three opinions concerning creation that are worthy of consideration,[3] proceeding to a critique of the position of Aristotle and his followers—a critique developed in two stages: textual and philosophical. In the textual part he sets out to show that a careful examination of the relevant Aristotelian texts, which he had in Arabic translation, discloses that Aristotle was well aware that he had no demonstrative

---

Research for this paper was done under a Category A fellowship that I held from the National Endowment for the Humanities during 1980–81. I gratefully acknowledge this support from NEH.

1. *Guide of the Perplexed*, II, 13 (Arabic: p. 197, Hebrew: p. 246, English: p. 228). Cf. *Guide*, II, 30 (A: p. 245, H: pp. 206–7, E: pp. 349–50). The following texts were used: Arabic: ed. I. Joel (Jerusalem, 1930–31); Hebrew: trans. Samuel ibn Tibbon, ed. Y. Even Shemu'el (Jerusalem, 1981–82); English: trans. S. Pines (Chicago, 1963).
2. *Guide*, I, 73–74. Cf. II, 16, beginning.
3. *Guide*, II, 13.

proof for the eternity of the world and that his account was only an opinion.[4] In the philosophic part Maimonides sets out to support the same point by means of arguments.

Developing his own position, Maimonides offers two reasons for his belief in creation: philosophical and methodological. Philosophically he argues that creation can be supported only by dialectical arguments, not demonstrations, and that the evidence for creation is more persuasive than that for the eternity of the world.[5] Methodologically he holds that in the case of apparent conflict between the literal meaning of Scripture and demonstrated truth, the former must be interpreted to yield the latter. But if there is no demonstration for the philosophic claim, then, in case of conflict, the literal meaning of Scripture is to be accepted. Since there are no demonstrative proofs for the creation of the world or its eternity, the biblical teaching that the world has been created must be accepted.[6]

Maimonides' discussion in the *Guide* is complex, part of the complexity being occasioned by the method he uses in the work. Concerned that philosophic discussions should not disturb the faith of ordinary believers, Maimonides informs his reader that he will use an esoteric method. Listing in the Introduction to the *Guide* seven causes for contradictions appearing in treatises and books, he states explicitly that he will make use of two of them in his work. One of these is the use of contradictions for pedagogic reasons, the other is the use of contradictions to conceal his true opinions.[7] Concerning the latter he writes:[8]

In speaking of very obscure matters it is necessary to conceal some parts and to disclose others. Sometimes in the case of certain dicta this necessity requires that the discussion proceed on the basis of a certain premise, whereas in another place necessity requires that the discussion proceed on the basis of another premise contradicting the first one. In such cases the vulgar must in no way be aware of the contradiction; the author accordingly uses some device to conceal it by all means.

This methodological principle gave rise to Maimonides interpretations devoted to the discovery of his esoteric views. Already current during the Middle Ages, they received a new impetus through the re-

4. *Guide*, II, 15. For a similar view, see Thomas Aquinas, *Summa Theologiae*, I, qu. 46, a. 1.
5. *Guide*, II, 16. Cf. II, 22.
6. *Guide*, II, 17 and 25. For a similar view, see Aquinas, *Summa Theologiae*, I, qu. 46, a. 2.
7. *Guide*, I, Introduction (A: p. 13, H: p. 18, E: p. 20).
8. Ibid. (A: p. 12, H: p. 16, E: p. 18).

searches of Leo Strauss.[9] It is probably fair to say that a good deal of contemporary Maimonides scholarship is influenced by Strauss's views. For the case of creation, at least some of the followers of this method hold that Maimonides' professed belief in creation by the divine will and out of nothing is a concession to the understanding of the masses, while esoterically he agrees with Aristotle that the world is eternal.[10] It has similarly been maintained that the careful analysis of the Maimonidean texts discloses that he believed in creation out of a preexistent matter.[11]

While no responsible scholar can bypass Maimonides' explicit statement concerning his use of an esoteric method, nor, for that matter, ignore the findings of those who claim to have discovered his esoteric views, I have set myself a different task. Proceeding on the assumption that Maimonides is an informed, acute, and responsible philosopher who uses recognizable concepts and arguments, I shall attempt to discover what philosophic sense one can make out of his overt claim that he believes in creation. However, the issue is not so much his acceptance of this belief, but how he understands it. I shall argue that Maimonides' theory of creation consists of four propositions, each of

---

9. L. Strauss, *Persecution and the Art of Writing* (Glencoe, Ill., 1952), pp. 38–94; "How to Begin to Study *The Guide of the Perplexed*," in *Guide*, trans. S. Pines, pp. xi–lvi.

10. Among those who have defended this interpretation are: J. Becker, *The Secret of the Guide of the Perplexed* (Tel Aviv, 1956) [in Hebrew]; L. Berman, "Ibn Bājjah and Maimonides" (unpublished dissertation, Hebrew University, 1959), pp. 156–63 [in Hebrew]; J. Glücker, "Modality in Maimonides' *Guide of the Perplexed*," *Iyyun* 10 (1959), pp. 177–91 [in Hebrew]; W. Z. Harvey, "A Third Approach to Maimonides' Cosmogony-Prophetology Puzzle," *Harvard Theological Review* 74 (1981), pp. 287–301; S. Klein-Braslavy, *Maimonides' Interpretation of the Story of Creation* (Jerusalem, 1978), p. 256 [in Hebrew]; A. Nuriel, "The Question of a Created or Primordial World in the Philosophy of Maimonides," *Tarbiz* 33 (1964), pp. 372–78 (repr. in *Likkutei Tarbiz*, 5: Studies in Maimonides [Jerusalem, 1985], pp. 338–53) [in Hebrew]; S. Pines, "Translator's Introduction," *Guide*, pp. cxxviii–cxxx.

For the names of some medievals who subscribed to this interpretation, see L. Kaplan, "Maimonides on the Miraculous Element in Prophecy," *Harvard Theological Review* 70 (1977), p. 240, nn. 25 and 26.

Among those who accepted that Maimonides was of the opinion that the world was created by the divine will and out of nothing are: J. Guttmann, *Philosophies of Judaism*, trans. D. W. Silverman (New York, 1964), pp. 165–69; I. Husik, *A History of Medieval Jewish Philosophy* (New York, 1966), pp. 269–76; L. Kaplan, "Maimonides on the Miraculous Element in Prophecy," p. 253; I. Ravitzky, "The Question of a Created or Primordial World in the Philosophy of Maimonides," *Tarbiz* 35 (1966), pp. 333–48 (repr. in *Likkutei Tarbiz*, 5, pp. 354–69) [in Hebrew]; H. A. Wolfson, "The Platonic, Aristotelian and Stoic Theories of Creation in Hallevi and Maimonides," *Studies in the History of Philosophy and Religion*, ed. I. Twersky and G. H. Williams (Cambridge, Mass., 1973), I, 234–39, esp. pp. 235 and 247–48.

11. This interpretation has been proposed by H. Davidson in "Maimonides' Secret Position on Creation," in *Studies in Medieval Jewish History and Literature*, ed. I. Twersky (Cambridge, Mass., 1979), pp. 16–40.

which I shall examine in turn. Central to these is the proposition that God created the world by "His will and volition." But there are also passages in which he states that the creation of the world is the result of divine wisdom, no less than divine will. Here I shall attempt to show that will and wisdom, according to Maimonides, cannot refer to positive attributes predicated of God, but can refer only to effects of God's causal agency. Maimonides' theory of creation is, therefore, a description not of God as creator, but rather of certain features of the created order. In the final section of this paper I shall briefly consider Maimonides' attitude toward emanation as a cosmogonic theory.

I

Maimonides begins his discussion of creation, in *Guide*, II, 13, by enumerating and analyzing three views worthy of consideration: (1) that of all who believe in the Law of Moses, (2) that of an unnamed group of philosophers to whom Plato belongs (I shall refer to this as the Platonic view), and (3) that of Aristotle and his followers. Two other views are not included in the enumeration: (1) that of the Epicureans, who deny the existence of God and hold that the world came to be by chance and (2) that of the emanationists,[12] who maintain that the world came to be from God by necessity. He rejects the opinion of the Epicureans because the existence of God has been established by demonstrative proofs (and more generally because their system has been shown to be philosophically unsound),[13] and that of the emanationists because he considers it equivalent to Aristotle's view that the world is eternal. Hence, whatever he has to say against Aristotle applies to the emanationists as well.

Maimonides describes the opinion of all who believe in the Law of Moses at length, but the following excerpt contains the salient points:

> ... the world as a whole—I mean to say, every existent other than God, may He be exalted—was brought into existence by God after having been purely and absolutely nonexistent and ... God, may He be exalted, had existed alone and nothing else.... Afterwards, through His will and volition He brought into existence out of nothing all the beings as they are, time itself being one of the created things.... Accordingly one's saying: God "was" before He created the world—where the word "was" is indicative of time—and similarly all the

---

12. Those I have called emanationists are described by Maimonides as followers of Aristotle.

13. *Guide*, II, 13 (A: pp. 198–99, H: p. 248, E: pp. 284–85). Cf. *Guide*, II, 32, beginning and III, 17, beginning.

thoughts that are carried along in the mind regarding the infinite duration of His existence before the creation of the world, are all of them due to a supposition regarding time or to an imagining of time and not due to the true reality of time.

Reflection on this passage discloses that there are four propositions which make up Maimonides' view:

(1) God brought the world into existence after absolute nonexistence;

(2) He brought everything into existence through His will and volition (though, as has already been noticed, His wisdom was operative as well);

(3) He brought everything into existence out of nothing; and

(4) time is created, so that, whatever one's theory, creation must be considered as atemporal.

These propositions require a number of comments. In the opening passage Maimonides uses the rather neutral term "brought into existence" (*'awjada, himṣi'*)[14] rather than the more technical terms "create" (*khalaqa, bara'*) or "create in time" (*ḥadatha, ḥiddesh*). This suggests that he is interested in God as the cause of the world, keeping it open at this point how divine causality is to be understood. It appears that there is little difference between holding that the world came into being "out of nothing"[15] and holding that it came into being "after absolute nonexistence (privation)." In fact, H. A. Wolfson has maintained that the two expressions are identical in meaning.[16] However, if a distinction is to be made, it can be argued that the two expressions form part of Maimonides' denial that Aristotle's account of change provides a model for creation. In that case, to hold that the world was created "out of nothing" would be to deny that there existed some matter out of which the world came to be, while the expression "after *absolute* nonexistence (privation)" would deny that the nonexistence (privation) of the world prior to creation was the kind of nonexistence (privation) of which Aristotle had spoken in his analysis of change— the kind of nonexistence (privation) which belongs to matter.[17]

In holding that the world was created through the divine will,

---

14. Cf. the rather neutral terminology in *Mishneh Torah*, ed. and trans. M. Hyamson (Jerusalem, 1962), *Book of Knowledge*, Laws concerning the Basic Principles of the Torah, I, 1, p. 34a, and *Book of Commandments*, Positive Commandments, 1.

15. Literally, the text reads: "not from a thing (something) [*lā min shay, lo midabar*]."

16. H. A. Wolfson, "The Meaning of *Ex Nihilo* in the Church Fathers, Arabic and Hebrew Philosophy, and St. Thomas," *Studies in the History of Philosophy and Religion*, I, p. 215.

17. Aristotle, *Physics*, I, 7. Cf. Sir D. Ross, *Aristotle* (London, 1964), pp. 63–66.

Maimonides disagrees with Aristotle, who held that the world was eternal, as well as with the emanationists, who affirmed that the world emanated from God by necessity. He also distances himself from the Mutakallimūn, who held that the world was created by the undetermined will of God and that everything within the world is determined directly by the same will. This he does by holding that at least the sublunar world functions according to necessary laws (as Aristotle had correctly stated) and by maintaining that divine wisdom no less than divine will is operative in creation.

Finally, creation is atemporal. Following Aristotle, Maimonides defines time as an accident of motion, so that there cannot be time unless there is motion.[18] But motion is "subsequent" to creation, so that time can only exist once the world has been created. "God's bringing the world into existence," writes Maimonides in *Guide*, II, 13,[19] "does not have a temporal beginning, for time is one of the created things." To be sure, there are people who identify eternity with infinite time, but they are subject to the vagaries of the imagination. For while the imagination can picture a time prior to any given time, this construct has no physical interpretation. The case is similar to Aristotle's opinion that the world is finite. For while one can imagine place or bodies outside the existent world, this construct of the imagination does not have a physical interpretation and is not intelligible to the mind.[20] A belief in eternal time also commits one to the eternity of the world, for eternal time requires eternal motion and eternal motion requires some eternal substance that is moved. Eternity, then, cannot be understood as some positive existent, but rather can be understood only as a denial of temporality. "God is eternal" means that time and temporal categories cannot be predicated of God, not that God exists in infinite time. From all this it follows that there is no temporal process that yields a model for creation.

The second opinion, that associated with Plato, consists, according to Maimonides, of the following major points:

... it is absurd that God would bring a thing into existence out of nothing ... they [the proponents of this view] believe that there exists a certain matter that is eternal as the deity is eternal; and that He does not exist without it, nor

---

18. Aristotle, *Physics*, IV, 11. Cf. Ross, *Aristotle*, pp. 89–91. *Guide*, II, 13, beginning; II, 14 (A: p. 199, H: p. 249, E: p. 286).
19. A: p. 197, top, H: p. 245, E: p. 282.
20. This argument is mentioned by Algazali in *Tahāfut al-Falāsifah*, I (A: ed. M. Bouyges [Beirut, 1927], pp. 55–56; E: in *Averroes' Tahāfut al-Tahāfut*, trans. S. van den Bergh [London, 1954], pp. 41–42). Cf. Aquinas, *Summa Theologiae*, I, qu. 46, a. 1, obj. 8 and ad 8.

does it exist without Him. They do not believe that it has the same rank in what exists as He, may He be exalted, but that He is the cause of its existence; and that it has the same relation toward Him as, for instance, clay has toward the potter.... But he [Plato] does not believe what we believe, as is thought by him who does not examine opinions and is not precise in speculation....

The focus of Maimonides' account of the Platonic position is the creation of the world out of some preexistent matter rather than out of nothing. Plotting the Platonic account against the four propositions which make up the opinion of the believers in the Law of Moses, it can be seen that Plato and his followers accept that God brought the world into existence, but deny that this occurred after absolute nonexistence (prop. 1). The second proposition, that God created the world through His will, is not addressed, but it would appear that Plato accepted necessary creation. The third is denied, since God created the world out of a preexistent matter. Finally, Plato did not commit himself on the temporality of creation, but it appears that creation, for him, is eternal.[21]

Maimonides explains that Plato came to his opinion because he thought that it is impossible that something can come to be out of nothing, just as it is impossible—to cite two of his examples[22]—that God should create another being like Himself or that He should create a square whose diagonal is commensurate with its sides. What is impossible in itself is also impossible for God, and this impossibility does not indicate lack of power in Him. Maimonides does not counter this argument in the present passage, but he argues later on that creation is not a kind of generation, so that, even if the Platonic principle would apply to generation in the created world, it would not apply to creation. In fact, were the Platonic account of creation correct, it would be similar to Aristotle's opinion that the world is eternal. Writes Maimonides in *Guide*, II, 13:[23] "there is in our opinion no difference between those who believe that the heaven must of necessity be generated from a thing [preexistent matter] ... or the belief of Aristotle who believed that it is not subject to generation and corruption." But having taken this rather firm position in the present passage, he is more lenient later on, when he writes in *Guide*, II, 25, that Plato's opinion does not undermine the foundations of the Law, while Aristotle's does. One can only speculate about Maimonides' reason. It

21. Maimonides writes concerning the opinion of those who believe in creation out of a preexistent matter: "For they believe in eternity." *Guide*, II, 13. For the continuation of this passage, see below, at n. 24.
22. *Guide*, II, 13 (A: p. 197, H: p. 246, E: p. 283).
23. Ibid. (A: p. 199, H: p. 248, E: p. 285).

might be that if the Platonic view is understood as creation by the divine will rather than by necessity, at least one basic principle of the correct theory is preserved.[24]

Aristotle's opinion is straightforward: the world is eternal and hence creation is false. This leads to the denial of all of Maimonides' propositions: the world is not created; it exists by necessity, not by will; matter is contemporaneous with the world; and time is eternal.

II

That creation is to be conceived in atemporal terms is one of the main features of Maimonides' account. From this it follows that the Aristotelian analysis of change or motion is inapplicable to creation. To illustrate this point, Maimonides constructs, in *Guide*, II, 17, what might, somewhat anachronistically, be called a Robinson Crusoe example. Imagine, he states, a small child whose mother had died a short time after he was born and who was taken by his father to an isolated island where there were no women or females of any other species. When the child is grown, he inquires how he came to be. The father explains how human beings are conceived, exist inside the body of their mother for a certain time, and finally are born through an opening of the mother's body. The father's explanation seems to be impossible to the child. He asks: how can anyone live inside the body of another without suffocating? How can anyone live without eating and drinking as we do? How can anyone live without excreting wastes? And how can the mother's body open without resulting in her death? Yet, however implausible to the child, the father's explanation is correct.

Maimonides uses this picturesque story to illustrate that from Aristotle's account of change and motion, derived from our experience of the world as it exists, no inference can be drawn about its origin. (To put it somewhat differently, from laws operative within a physical system, it cannot be inferred that these same laws are applicable to its origin.) It follows that creation cannot be understood through such

24. It might also be the case that Maimonides permits this opinion as a concession to the understanding of the masses who might find it difficult to conceive of creation "out of nothing." This would be similar to his holding that the masses must be taught that anthropopathic terms are not applicable to God (*Guide*, I, 35, beginning) and yet allowing such terms as "necessary opinions" required to provide sanctions for obeying the Law (*Guide*, III, 28). Still another reason might be that he wants to take account of certain midrashic statements that speak of creation "out of something." Cf., however, *Guide*, II, 26 and 30. For other discussions of this issue, see Judah Halevi, *Kuzari*, I, 67, and J. Albo, *Ikkarim*, ed. and trans. I. Husik (Philadelphia, 1946), I, 1, pp. 47–48; 12.

Aristotelian notions as potentiality and actuality, and the temporal priority of an efficient cause to its effect. In fact, states Maimonides, were the Aristotelian analysis applicable, it would follow that the world is eternal.

To hold that the Aristotelian analysis of change or motion is inapplicable to creation and that creation is atemporal entails a sharp distinction between the temporal and the atemporal realms. To attempt to understand the latter through the former is to commit a category mistake. For example, to ascribe time to God, even supposed infinite time, is to maintain falsely that there is some similarity between the temporal and the atemporal realm. It is similar to ascribing color to number (what color is the number one?) or weight to taste (how much does sweet weigh?).

With this sharp distinction between the temporal and the atemporal realms, a number of questions that have traditionally been raised against creation begin to disappear. If God exists apart from time, it makes no sense to ask: "what did God do before He created the world?" or "why did God create the world at one time rather than another?"[25] To be sure, human language requires temporal terms—"was," "is," "will be," "before," "after"—but, strictly speaking, temporal terms are not applicable to God. However God's creative activity is to be described, it cannot be described in temporal terms.

From this negative discussion of creation, we must now turn to its more positive aspects. Here it should be recalled that the second of Maimonides' four propositions affirms that God created the world through His will and His volition. In fact, Maimonides considers it the fundamental difference between his own view and that of Aristotle and the emanationists. Aristotle and the emanationists believed that the world existed through necessity (either eternally or through the necessary causal agency of God), while Maimonides holds that it was created through the divine will. The issue then is the relation between necessary and volitional causes. Aristotle, to be sure, recognizes volitional causes for the limited case of human volitional acts—for example, Socrates who is now sitting may decide to stand at a future time—[26] but he denies that volitional causes are operative in the sublunar natural order, in the movement of the celestial spheres, or in the relation between the prime mover and the universe. Maimonides

---

25. This is one of the three objections that Maimonides raises on behalf of those who oppose creation because it would require affirming of God what cannot be affirmed of Him (*Guide*, II, 14 [A: pp. 200–201, H: pp. 250–51, E: pp. 287–88]). For Maimonides' reply to these objections, see *Guide*, II, 18.

26. Aristotle, *Metaphysics*, IX, 2 and 5.

agrees with Aristotle that necessary causes are operative within the sublunar world, but he differs from him in holding that the supralunar world provides some evidence that divine volition is at work. Yet how divine volition is to be understood requires further investigation. Two interpretations present themselves: (1) God possesses the attribute of will, which, however different from human will, shows some similarity to it, and (2) the world possesses certain features which cannot be explained through necessary causation, but only by invoking a volitional cause, in this case the divine will. To discover which of these two propositions Maimonides accepts, we must next turn to his account of divine attributes.

III

An underlying principle of Maimonides' discussion of divine attributes is that no attribute predicated of God can introduce ontological multiplicity into Him.[27] Distinguishing between essential attributes which describe some essential property of God, such as God exists or is one, and accidental attributes which describe some affect, habit, or disposition in Him, such as God is merciful, Maimonides accepts the generally held position that accidental attributes introduce ontological multiplicity in Him. Agreeing with Avicenna, he holds that essential attributes introduce ontological multiplicity as well. It follows that neither essential nor accidental attributes can be predicated positively of God, from which, in turn, it follows that attributes cannot signify metaphorically or eminently. For the case of essential attributes Maimonides holds that they must be predicated according to complete equivocation and that they signify by "negation of privation." For example, "God is wise" must be understood as "God is not ignorant." For the case of accidental attributes he holds that they must be understood as attributes of action. For example, "God is merciful" must be understood as "God causes actions that can be described as merciful."

To affirm that "will" is predicated of God and man according to complete equivocation disposes of certain objections that opponents of creation had raised. Among these are the following: If God created the world by will and if the divine will is similar to the human will, then prior to creation God must have been a potential creator who

27. For a discussion of what follows, see my article "Maimonides on Religious Language," in *Studies in Maimonides' Thought and Environment*, ed. J. Kramer (in press).

became actual when He created the world. But that God should change from a potential to an actual state is incompatible with His immutability.[28] Again, to maintain that God acts through will would imply that He desired to create the world before He actually created it. But to ascribe desire to God conflicts with His perfection, for one only desires something that one does not possess.[29]

Maimonides counters objections such as these by holding that "will" is predicated of God and man according to complete equivocation. And if there is no similarity between the divine and human wills, then characteristics found in the human will do not apply to the will of God. For example, while the human will changes from potentiality to actuality, the divine will does not; and while the human will desires something that it does not possess, the divine will does not. It follows then that if the proposition "God created the world through His will" has any meaning at all, it can refer only to some effect, that is, feature of the world, of which God is the cause, not to some positive attribute of God. Since Maimonides also holds that there can be causes that are totally dissimilar to their effects, God can be the creator of the world without sharing any of its features. By a similar argument it can be established that the proposition "God created the world through His wisdom" refers to some feature of the world, not to a positive attribute predicated of Him.

While in the first part of the *Guide* Maimonides had launched a grand attack on the dialectical theologians, the Mutakallimūn, and while he had rejected their arguments for creation, he found some of their views useful for his own account. He writes in *Guide*, II, 19:[30]

My purpose in this chapter is to explain to you, by means of arguments that come close to being demonstrations, that what exists indicates to us of necessity that it exists in virtue of the purpose of One who purposed, and to do this without having to take upon myself what the Mutakallimūn have undertaken. . . . On the other hand, there is no doubt that they wished what I wished.

The last phrase suggests that Maimonides wanted to find some meaning for creation by the divine will, but without having to resort to the Kalāmic account.

Two Kalāmic discussions are of importance: the nature of the divine will and the principle of particularization (*takhṣīṣ*). How the Mutakallimūn understood the divine will can be seen from Algazali's *Incoherence of the Philosophers*, a work in which, as part of his exposition,

---

28. See above, n. 25.
29. *Guide*, II, 18 (A: p. 210, H: p. 262, E: p. 301).
30. A: pp. 211–12, H: p. 263, E: pp. 303–4.

he argues against the existence of necessary causes.[31] Using as one of his examples the common experience that fire will burn cotton when in contact with it, Algazali denies that there is any necessary connection between the fire and the cotton's burning. We know only that there is fire in contact with cotton and the cotton which burns, but there is no evidence of any necessary connection between the two. For Algazali the only cause of the cotton's burning is the undetermined will of God. If God so wills, the cotton will burn; if God wills the contrary, the cotton will not burn. Algazali does not deny that in the ordinary course of events cotton in the proximity of fire will burn, but this is a matter of habit ('ādah), not necessity. Similarly, there are no necessary causes operative in the celestial world, and the creation of the world occurs solely through the undetermined will of God. According to Algazali, there exists only one cause, namely, the undetermined will of God.

In developing his doctrine of will, Algazali takes issue with the Aristotelians, who had argued that volitional acts can take place only when there is some cause or reason that determines the will. According to the Aristotelians a totally undetermined act is an impossibility; if there is no reason for acting, the act will not occur. By contrast, Algazali defends the possibility of acts that are the product of an undetermined will. To support this view he brings the following example. Imagine, he states,[32] a man who has a strong desire for two dates which are in front of him and of which he can take only one. The dates are similar in all respects, so that he has no reason for taking one rather than the other. Were a reason for choice required, he would never take either. Yet experience discloses that he will arbitrarily take one. It follows that there can be undetermined volitional acts, that is, acts of which will is the sole cause. Writes Algazali:[33] ". . . will is a quality which has the faculty of differentiating one thing from another."

Closely related to this conception of the undetermined will is Algazali's understanding of "possibility." For the case of God it means that, while God cannot do what is logically impossible, he can do everything else. For example, He could have created a world other than the one He did in fact create, or He could not have created a world at all. Within the world, he can keep fire from burning and heavy objects from falling, and he could have created human beings

31. Algazali, *Tahāfut*, XVII (A: pp. 277 ff., E: in A. Hyman and J. J. Walsh, eds., *Philosophy in the Middle Ages*, 2d ed. [Indianapolis, 1984], pp. 283 ff.).
32. Ibid., I (A: pp. 40–41, E: in *Averroes' Tahāfut al-Tahāfut*, p. 21).
33. Ibid., I (A: p. 37, ll. 10–11, E: in *Averroes' Tahāfut al-Tahāfut*, p. 19).

that have the size of mountains. However, in order that one or some of the many possibilities come to be, a "differentiating principle" is required, and this principle is the will of God.

Maimonides shows an affinity to the Kalāmic analysis of volition, at least as far as the human will is concerned. In fact he echoes Algazali when he writes:[34] ". . . the true reality and the quiddity of will means: to will and not to will." The will then is an independent cause that can choose between two or more equally possible alternatives. From the drift of the discussion it appears, however, that Maimonides distinguishes between two kinds of volitional acts: those that have some reason, and those that do not, that is, those which are arbitrary. It is this distinction that distances him from the Mutakallimūn. For while he agrees with them that the world was created by the divine will, he disagrees with them in holding that divine wisdom was operative as well. To hold that the world was created solely by the undetermined will of God makes God capricious, and this cannot be admitted of God.

To support this view, Maimonides invokes a classification of actions into four kinds:[35] futile, frivolous, vain, and good. Futile actions are those by which no end is sought, frivolous actions those by which an end is sought but not achieved, vain actions those by which a low end is sought, and good actions those "that are accomplished by an agent aiming at a noble end." Since futile, frivolous, and vain actions cannot be ascribed to God, it remains that God's actions are good, that is, they are in conformity with His wisdom.

Since, as we have seen earlier, Maimonides rejects Aristotle's opinion that the world is eternal as well as the view of the emanationists that the world has been created by necessity, it becomes clear that he subscribes to creation by the divine will. And since creation is atemporal, it follows that creation must be an instantaneous atemporal volitional act. (If a miracle is an act not in conformity with the laws of nature, creation can also be described as miraculous.) How divine will and wisdom are operative in creation remains, however, still to be explained.

As we have seen earlier, Maimonides holds that "will" and "wisdom" are predicated of God according to complete equivocation, so that "creation by will" and "creation by wisdom" can refer only to effects produced by God, that is properties of the world. Since for Maimonides order and regularity seems to be a sign of wisdom, disorder

---

34. *Guide*, II, 18 (A: p. 210, ll. 4–5, H: p. 262, E: p. 301).
35. *Guide*, III, 25. Cf. *Guide*, II, 19 (A: p. 216, H: pp. 269–70, E: p. 310).

and irregularity a sign of will, it is the order and disorder appearing in the world that yield the interpretations of divine wisdom and will.

To develop this thesis, Maimonides points to observed differences between the sublunar and translunar worlds. Within the sublunar world, events manifest order and regularity and occur according to necessary causes: acorns, for example, become oak trees through necessary causes, not through chance or the direct intervention of God. And it was Aristotle who had given the correct account of what occurs in the sublunar world. Writes Maimonides:[36]

> Everything that Aristotle has said about all that exists from beneath the sphere of the moon to the center of the earth is indubitably correct, and no one will deviate from it unless he does not understand it or unless he has a preconceived opinion that he wishes to defend or that leads him to a denial of a thing that is manifest.

It is this order in the sublunar world that is the effect of divine wisdom. Since, as we have seen, the world was created by the divine will, creation may best be described as creation by the divine will informed by divine wisdom. In terms of the previously made distinction between two kinds of volitional acts, it may be said that the creation of the sublunar world is a volitional act that has reasons.

By contrast, observation discloses that, while there is some order in the translunar world (for example, celestial spheres move with uniform circular motion), some disorder also exists and, here, Aristotle is not an infallible guide. Writes Maimonides in the continuation of the just-quoted passage:

> On the other hand, everything that Aristotle expounds with regard to the sphere of the moon and that which is above it, except for certain things, is something analogous to guessing and conjecturing.

Two astronomical observations in particular provide a serious challenge to Aristotle's necessitarian cosmological scheme.[37] One of these is the velocity of the planets. Observation discloses that the varying velocities of the planets have no apparent order. In some instances a sphere moving with greater velocity is above one moving more slowly, while in other instances the reverse is seen to be the case. In still other instances two spheres differing in location have the same velocity. Another challenge to the Aristotelian scheme is provided by the difference between stars and planets and the spheres in which they are set.

36. *Guide*, II, 22 (A: p. 223, H: pp. 278–79, E: pp. 319–20). Cf. II, 19 (A: p. 217, H: pp. 270–71, E: p. 311).
37. *Guide*, II, 19. Cf. *Guide*, II, 24.

From the uniformity of celestial motion Aristotle had concluded that the heavens consist of only one element, the so-called fifth element, of which stars, planets, and the celestial spheres are composed. Yet observation seems to contradict this conclusion, since it can be seen that, while the spheres move with uniform circular motion, the stars and planets set within them have no motion of their own, but are at rest. In terms of the previously made distinction between two kinds of volitional acts, it may be said that the creation of the celestial world (at least of the disorders within it) is a volitional act that has no reasons. It appears, however, that this conclusion is not wholly satisfactory to Maimonides, since it seems to be based on the previously rejected notion that God can act in arbitrary fashion. God's wisdom is manifest even in the disorder in the world. But here the wisdom of God accounts not for the particular disorder that exists, but for why there should be disorder at all. The question is no different from the one asking: why does God permit evil? and similar ones. The answer that Maimonides provides is that these occurrences are the result of the inscrutable wisdom of God.[38]

By way of summary it may then be said that Maimonides holds that the creation of the world is the result of an instantaneous atemporal volitional act of God, but a volitional act informed by His wisdom as well. For the case of the sublunar world this wisdom is manifest in its functioning in accordance with necessary laws which are intelligible to man. For the case of the translunar world, divine will is manifest in the disorder that exists, but even this disorder has behind it the wisdom of God; but why there should be disorder cannot be known by man.

IV

In the final section of this paper I shall briefly turn to Maimonides' attitude toward emanation. While it is not certain that Maimonides knew such works as the *Theology of Aristotle* or the *Liber De Causis*, it is clear that he was familiar with emanation as a cosmogonic theory through the writings of Avicenna.[39] In its Avicennian form this theory held that from God there emanated a first intellect which, similar to

38. *Guide*, II, 18 (A: p. 210, H: pp. 262–63, E: pp. 301–2), 19 (A: p. 215, H: p. 268, E: pp. 308–9 and A: p. 216, H: pp. 269–70, E: p. 310), 22 (A: p. 223, H: p. 278, E: p. 319), 25 (A: p. 230, H: p. 287, E: p. 329).

39. For accounts of Avicenna's view on emanation, see S. M. Afnan, *Avicenna: His Life and Works* (London, 1958), pp. 126–35; A.-M. Goichon, *La distinction de l'essence et de l'existence d'après Ibn Sīnā (Avicenne)* (Paris, 1937), pp. 201–59. Cf. *Guide*, II, 4.

God, is one and simple. Reflecting upon its source the first intellect gives forth a second intellect, reflecting upon itself as necessary it gives forth a soul, and reflecting upon itself as contingent it gives forth a celestial sphere, that responsible for the daily rotation of the heavens. From the second intellect there emanates the intellect, soul, and body of the second celestial sphere (that of the fixed stars) until the tenth intellect—the Agent Intellect—and the sublunar world are reached. Emanation, as has been noted earlier, takes place by necessity, not will.

Maimonides' critique of emanationist necessitarianism is directed primarily against one of its basic propositions. In Maimonides' formulation in *Guide*, II, 22, it reads:[40]

It is impossible that anything but a single simple thing should proceed from a simple thing. If the thing is composite, there may proceed from it several things according to the number of simple things of which the compound is composed.

If this proposition is accepted, it can be seen how a simple first intellect can emanate from God or even how simple intellects can emanate from other simple intellects, but it is impossible that a composite celestial sphere can emanate from intellects that are simple. Asks Maimonides:[41]

How does a sphere proceed from the one simple thing from which [according to the emanationists] it proceeds? A sphere is composed of two kinds of matter and two forms: the matter and the form of the sphere itself and the matter and the form of the star fixed in the sphere. Now if this comes about in virtue of a procession [emanation], we cannot but require for this compound a composite cause, the procession of the body of the sphere being occasioned by one of its parts and that of the body of the star by another!

The difficulty occasioned by emanationism is resolved by another principle that Maimonides cites:[42]

Every agent, acting in virtue of purpose and will, not by virtue of its nature, accomplishes many different acts.

If it is the nature of will to produce multiple effects, then it is possible that God, though simple, can produce a world of multiplicity through his will.

While Maimonides rejects emanation as an explanation of creation, he finds it useful for explaining one kind of causality operative in the

---

40. *Guide*, II, 22 (A: p. 221, H: p. 276, E: p. 317).
41. Ibid. (A: p. 222, H: p. 277, E: p. 318).
42. Ibid. (A: p. 221, H: p. 276, E: p. 317).

world.[43] For the case of bodies, efficient causality requires contact, direct or indirect. One body moves another body only if it is in direct contact with it or with some intermediate body. For example, fire will light a candle only if it is in contact with it or the air surrounding it. But there are other cases in which efficient causality cannot be explained by contact: forms can be caused only by other forms, and corporeal celestial spheres are moved by incorporeal intelligences, not by other spheres. To explain causality of this kind, Maimonides finds emanation of help. As he writes in *Guide*, II, 12:[44]

Considering that the effects produced by the separate intellect are clear and manifest in that which exists . . . it is necessarily known that this agent does not act either through immediate contact or at some particular distance, for it is not a body. Hence the action of the separate intellect is always designated as an overflow [emanation], being likened to a source of water that overflows in all directions and does not have one particular direction from which it draws while giving its bounty to others.

And finally, while emanation does not provide a theory of creation it is of help in describing God's causal agency within the world, once it has been created. Writes Maimonides in *Guide*, II, 12:[45]

This term, I mean "overflow," is sometimes applied in Hebrew to God, may He be exalted, with a view to likening Him to an overflowing spring of water. . . . For nothing is more fitting as a simile to the action of one that is separate from matter than this expression, I mean "overflow."[46]

Yeshiva University

---

43. *Guide*, II, 12.
44. Ibid. (A: p. 195, H: p. 243, E: p. 279).
45. Ibid. (A: p. 194, H: p. 243, E: p. 279). For an application of this account of emanation to prophecy, see *Guide*, II, 36; to providence, see *Guide*, III, 17–18.
46. There is an additional problem that is important for our investigation, but it cannot be considered within the confines of this paper. It is: On the opinion that the world is created, was it "possible" before it came to be? This, in turn, requires an investigation of the role of possibility in Maimonides' philosophy. For literature on this topic, see: E. Fackenheim, "The Possibility of the Universe in Al-Farabi, Ibn Sina and Maimonides," *Proceedings of the American Academy for Jewish Research* 16 (1947), pp. 40–70 (repr. A. Hyman, ed., *Essays in Medieval Jewish and Islamic Philosophy* [New York, 1977], pp. 303–34); J. Guttmann, "Das Problem der Kontingenz in der Philosophie Maimonides," *Monatsschrift für Geschichte und Wissenschaft des Judentums* 83 (1939), pp. 406–30 (Hebrew trans. in Guttmann, *Dat u-Madda'*, trans. S. Esh [Jerusalem, 1955], pp. 119–35); A. Ivry, "Maimonides on Possibility," in *Mystics, Philosophers, and Politicians: Essays in Jewish Intellectual History in Honor of Alexander Altmann*, ed. J. Reinharz et al. (Durham, N.C., 1982), pp. 67–84; N. Rabinowitz, "The Concept of Possibility in Maimonides," *Tarbiz* 44 (1975), pp. 159–71 (repr. in *Likkutei Tarbiz*, 5, pp. 403–15) [in Hebrew].

4   Plato or Aristotle—a Real Alternative in Medieval Philosophy?

GEORG WIELAND

Medieval philosophy develops far more intensively than other periods in the history of philosophy through receiving, interpreting, and coming to terms with ancient authors and their works. It would be a mistake to see in this a lack of originality. First of all, this period, even by modern standards, has its original thinkers. The originality of Eriugena, Meister Eckhart, or Nicholas Cusanus has never been in question. Nor can the uniqueness of Thomas Aquinas or Duns Scotus or William of Ockham be seriously doubted if we examine their scholastically expressed thought in its application to the questions they raise and the solutions they propose. Moreover, medieval thinking is interested not in originality as such, but in discovering "what is the truth concerning things."[1] And it is this interest which assigns in some way to the answers of tradition an advance for truth, since these answers have established their effectiveness over a long period of time. Herein also lies the reason why philosophy can comply with authorities, not because they are authorities, but because they are representatives of truth.[2]

We could say—in fact it has been said[3]—that medieval thought until the twelfth century lives essentially on the unity of reason and authority. I would like to call this conjunction "Christian doctrine"; it is frequently called wisdom (*sapientia*) or also philosophy (*philosophia*) by contemporaries.[4] And this usage is not completely incorrect, since it is

---

1. Thomas Aquinas, *In I De caelo*, lect. 22.
2. On the role of authorities in medieval authors cf. M.-D. Chenu, *Das Werk des hl. Thomas von Aquin* (Heidelberg, 1960), pp. 138–73.
3. M. Grabmann, *Die Geschichte der scholastischen Methode*, Bd. I (Freiburg, 1909), pp. 178–92, 224 ff., 269–84 and passim.
4. Cf. F. Van Steenberghen, *La philosophie au XIIIe siècle* (Louvain, 1966), pp. 50–58; G. Wieland, "Weisheit, Dialektik, Wissenschaft," in W. Kluxen, ed., *Thomas von Aquin im philosophischen Gespräch* (Freiburg, 1975), pp. 204 ff.

an interpretation of the universe which has in common with philosophy taken strictly the claim of being a comprehensive interpretation. Of course this wisdom or Christian doctrine justifies its claim to universality by having recourse to the validity of the Christian tradition whose insights form the kernel of wisdom or philosophy. This also applies to rationally constructed works such as the *Periphyseon* of Eriugena[5] or the *De docta ignorantia* of Cusanus. The Christian tradition with elements of biblical history and nonderivable "facticity" is, roughly speaking, the authoritative side of this philosophy. Its rational side is nurtured through different resources. The basic elements of Aristotelian logic belong to it as much as do certain elements of Platonic and Neoplatonic origin. The latter take on very different accents depending upon whether it is the influence of Augustine, Pseudo-Dionysius, or Boethius which predominates, not to mention that of the later Arab Neoplatonism.

It is now evident that philosophy—in the sense here indicated—oriented itself mainly if not exclusively on Platonism until the twelfth century. This was so even though Latins of the twelfth century had direct access only to parts of the *Timaeus*, and from ca. 1156 to the *Meno* and *Phaedo*. The reasons for Platonism's dominant position are most clearly understood in the case of Augustine. In his *Confessions* he stresses the agreement of Platonic (= Plotinian) philosophy with the beginning of St. John's Gospel, which mentions the Word of God, the origin of the world, and the illumination of souls.[6] However, in the same context Augustine also emphasizes what he does not find in the "books of the Platonists," namely, the Incarnation, humiliation, and death of the Divine Word, i.e., the decisive data concerning the Passion and Salvation of Christ as presented in the Gospel. The limits are thereby delineated, but above all, the possibilities offered by Platonism for an interpretation of the world by means of Christian tradition and sanctioned at the same time by the foremost theological authority of the Middle Ages. Correspondingly high during this period is esteem for Plato. *Maximus* or *summus philosophorum* (Abelard), *princeps philosophorum* (John of Salisbury), *magnus theologus* (Isaac of Stella), are customary designations for him in the twelfth century.[7] The

---

5. G. Schrimpf, *Das Werk des Johannes Scottus Eriugena im Rahmen des Wissenschaftsverständnisses seiner Zeit. Eine Hinführung zu Periphyseon* (Münster, 1982), p. 137.
6. *Conf.* VII 9, 12; cf. E. Gilson, "Le christianisme et la tradition philosophique," *Revue des sciences philosophiques et théologiques* 30 (1941–42), pp. 249–66.
7. A. Schneider, *Die abendländische Spekulation des zwölften Jahrhunderts in ihrem Verhältnis zur aristotelischen und jüdisch-arabischen Philosophie* (Münster, 1915); M.-D. Chenu, *La théologie au douzième siècle* (Paris, ²1966), p. 109, n. 1.

main reason for this high regard is mentioned by William of Conches: "For he is more in agreement with our faith."[8] The Platonic material which the Latins had at their disposition proved to be extremely fruitful in speculation concerning creation and the Trinity. This becomes clear, for instance, in the well-known *Metrum* III, 9, in the *Consolatio* of Boethius, according to which the world was made according to God's image and likeness, and continues to be effective up to the teaching on creation by Thierry of Chartres or by Clarembald of Arras. In interpreting the Trinity as *unitas, aequalitas,* and *connexio* the Masters of Chartres and Alan of Lille take up a patristic motif which, for its part, refers to Plato's *Parmenides*.[9]

It cannot be our task here to develop more fully the general theme of Platonism in the Middle Ages. Decisive, however, is the fact that Platonism in its different forms, transmissions, and variations is until the twelfth century an obvious and basically little doubted part of what we call Christian doctrine or Christian wisdom. If Bernard of Clairvaux not only carries on a controversy against the cleverness of Aristotle, but advises against reading Plato,[10] he expresses something of the tension between Platonism and Christianity; but we cannot seriously regard him as representative of the intellectual development of the twelfth century.

Why could Platonism and Christianity—in spite of their inner tensions—blend to such an extent? To this we may offer a general answer. The philosophy influenced by Platonism—at least we may understand it in that way—informs us about the origin of the world. It offers an insight not only into the origin but also into the present situation and the final destination of mankind. In sum, we can say that it is especially suited to express religious and Christian ideas and values. The later Henry of Ghent puts it this way: "Plato thought much better . . . than Aristotle and things more in accord with faith."[11] It is therefore easy to understand that it is Plato and not Aristotle who dominates the thinking of the Christian world so effectively and for so long a time.

It is far more complicated to answer the question why, in spite of

8. *Dragmaticon philosophiae* I (ed. G. Gratarolus, Strassburg, 1567), p. 13.
9. N. Häring, "The Creation and Creator of the World according to Thierry of Chartres and Clarenbaldus of Arras," *Archives d'histoire doctrinale et littéraire du moyen âge* 30 (1955), pp. 162–242.
10. *Serm. in festo Apostoli Petri* 1,3 (*Sancti Bernardi Opera* V: *Sermones* II, rec. J. Leclerq et H. Rochais [Romae, 1968], p. 190): "non Platonem legere, non Aristotelis versutias inversare."
11. *Summae quaestionum ordinariarum*, a. 25, qu. 3 (reprint of the 1520 edition, Franciscan Institute Publications 5 [St. Bonaventure, 1953]), fol. 154.

the congruity of Platonism and Christianity, Aristotelianism dominated speculation and scholarship beginning with the thirteenth century. This is so even though religious enthusiasm is almost completely lacking to Aristotelianism. Furthermore, we must remember that through Cicero and Ambrose the Aristotelian theory of the "eternity" of the world was known to the Middle Ages and that, at least since John of Salisbury, Aristotle was known as a representative of psychological determinism.[12] In spite of this and other theologically dubious points (following Chalcidius the Aristotelian concept of the soul was interpreted into the twelfth century as involving an accidental relation to the body),[13] Aristotle already appears in the work of John of Salisbury as the one to whom the name "Philosopher" belongs in the true and preeminent sense. As the reason for this John cites Aristotle's universality in scope; he had treated of all the parts of philosophy including physics, ethics, and logic.[14] In other words, Aristotle was no longer only the logician, though he continued to be known for this as well by the Middle Ages.

This new assessment could take place, of course, only because in the meantime—owing to the various translations—it was possible to get a more precise and comprehensive grasp of the Aristotelian corpus. Viewed in this way, the question raised in the preceding paragraph finds a simple answer. Because the complete Aristotelian corpus became available, Aristotle gained acceptance as the Philosopher for the Middle Ages. This answer is certainly not wrong. Without knowledge of his natural science, metaphysics, and ethics, Aristotle would have never been able to reach this status. Not his logic but above all his physical and metaphysical works won for him an importance which far surpassed that of Plato. However, considered as a whole, this answer is quite unsatisfying. Was in fact the translation of the Aristotelian works from Greek and Arabic the real reason for this reorientation in thinking? This would explain far too little. The mere availability of texts does not of itself account for their influence. There must rather be clear interest on the part of the recipients to account sufficiently for the great impact of the respective texts.

To answer the question why in the thirteenth century Aristotelianism rises to its leading position whereas previous development had inclined toward Platonism, one must look for a change in interest on the part of the Latin world. And this change must above all appear within

---

12. Cicero, *Acad.* pr. II 38,119; Ambrosius, *In Hexaem.* I 1 (CSEL 32,1:4); John of Salisbury, *Entheticus*, v. 833–34 (PL 199,983).
13. Cf. A. Schneider (note 7), pp. 54 ff.
14. *Policraticus* VII 6 (ed. Webb II, pp. 111 ff.).

that broad system of interpreting the world which, as Christian wisdom, contains all the elements established by tradition and by reason in understanding reality.

In historical abstraction several possibilities can be conceived in which Christian wisdom or doctrine might further develop. It might maintain its elements from tradition and from reason in a tolerable balance and therefore be able to answer questions arising in a given period of time adequately and in an existentially satisfying way. I would interpret the work of Hugh of St. Victor in this sense. Nevertheless, it became obviously more and more difficult in the twelfth century to maintain the balance within Christian wisdom. Otherwise the change— the subject matter of this study—would not have taken place.

A second possibility might be to emphasize the moment of tradition against that of reason. This possibility was worked out historically, for instance, by Bernard of Clairvaux, and in the mysticism of the School of St. Victor. A third possibility might be a strong emphasis on the moment of reason in opposition to that of tradition, as one may observe in the School of Chartres.

Of all three models it can be said that they assume a claim to universality in interpretation and explanation. This is true, for example, of a position such as that held by Bernard of Clairvaux, who from his "philosophy"—"to know Jesus and him crucified"—claims competence for every form of rationality insofar as he assigns to it a serving function. Science for its own sake is condemned as the "windy babbling of the philosophers."[15] This position does not admit of any independent form of rationality and in a time of growing acceptance of science necessarily becomes a limited conception. This seems to me to be a rather important development in itself, but less important as regards the reasons for the shift from Plato to Aristotle.

More significant for our question is the third position, which is frequently found in the speculation of the School of Chartres. Thus Thierry explicitly explains the *rationabilitas* of his method when considering the Trinity, which he attempts to derive by means of the well-known triad *unitas, aequalitas, connexio*.[16] Thus the universe is explained according to natural science, and this in significantly different fashion from the traditional allegorical and moral interpretation.[17]

15. *Serm. sup. cant.* 43,4 (*Sancti Bernardi Opera* II: *Sermones super Cantica canticorum*, rec. J. Leclerq, C. H. Talbot, H. M. Rochais [Romae, 1958], p. 43): "haec mea subtilior, interior philosophia, scire Iesum et hunc crucifixum."—*Serm. sup. cant.* 58,7 (ibid., p. 131): "philosophorum ventosa loquacitas."
16. *De sex dierum operibus*, ed. N. Häring (note 9), pp. 194 ff.
17. Ibid., p. 184,1: ". . . primam Geneseos partem secundum phisicam et ad litteram

Plato is—so far as I can determine—not even mentioned in Thierry's three commentaries on the *De Trinitate* of Boethius. Nevertheless, everything there is imbued with the spirit of a still polymorphous Platonism. This appears clearly, for example, when Thierry identifies God's wisdom as the formal cause of the world, saying that "the form of all things emanates from the simple divine form."[18] However, it is not the individual Platonic or Neoplatonic teaching which is decisive for our context, but the universal rationality, established in Platonism, which is concerned with the origin of the world and of mankind as well as with human destiny. To that extent the Platonism of the twelfth century, when considered in terms of its tendency and its claim, is not a limited but a universal position, which offers decisive insights for understanding the world and mankind.

Nevertheless, objections are raised against such tendencies, and not merely from the side of traditional theology. To me John of Salisbury's criticism of the "number speculation" of the followers of Chartres is significant: he who entertains true unity would have to disregard mathematical consideration and move his heart and senses towards the simplicity of insight.[19] This is a judgment made not by an enemy of rationality, but by one who says that he is a friend of the sciences. However, it becomes clear that the speculations which are being criticized do not square with the existential self-understanding of the time. If this is so, even the Platonically inspired universal rationality of the School of Chartres turns out to be of only particular significance; for it is unable to incorporate given contemporary problems into its system of universal interpretation. I submit that it is in this way that we can understand John of Salisbury's criticism.

Before applying these suggestions to our question, we must note that the second and third positions, that is, those of Bernard of Clairvaux and of the School of Chartres, are genuine possibilities for the realization of Christian wisdom or doctrine. It is self-evident that this applies to Bernard and others like him. But the rationality of the School of Chartres likewise is not an unfamiliar feature of the Chris-

---

ego expositurus. . . . Postea vero . . . allegoricam et moralem lectionem quas sancti expositores aperte executi sunt ex toto praetermittam."

18. *In Boeth. De Trin.* (ed. N. Häring, "Two Commentaries on Boethius [*De Trinitate* and *De Hebdomadibus*] by Thierry of Chartres," *Archives d'histoire doctrinale et littéraire du moyen âge* 27 [1960], p. 103,41): "merito ergo ab illa simplici forma divina rerum omnium formae emanare dicuntur, quia iuxta formam illam divinam unaquaque res suam habet essendi aequalitatem."

19. *De septem septenis* (PL 199,961): "qui illam veram unitatem considerare desiderat, mathematica consideratione praetermissa, necesse est ad intelligentiae simplicitatem animus sese erigat."—There are, to be sure, doubts about the authenticity of this work.

tian legacy. On the contrary, the increase of rationality in the twelfth century is an authentic event, to be explained in terms of the means traditionally available. Moreover, the turn to previously unknown texts and sciences would be an expression of interest which is in the main to be looked for within the development of Christian wisdom or Christian doctrine itself.

Our topic is now taking on more precise outlines. Of course it is a genuine Christian attitude to maintain the presence of the historical events of the Redemption as such, without trying to derive or explain them from a rational context. Bernard of Clairvaux may be considered as representative of such a Christian directness. As soon as this thinking is more strongly emphasized, as soon as the realism of Christian history and the personalism of grace are more clearly perceived, the Platonically inspired interpretation of the metaphysical triad of God, the world, and man proves to be insufficient. This interpretation can uphold its rational claim only at the expense of historical reality. There is no place in this system of interpretation for the history of sinful man and the reality of the Incarnation. In other words, the universal unity of Christian tradition and rational interpretation—established within the conception of Christian wisdom or Christian doctrine—falls apart as soon as one or both elements are considered with their full claims.

Moreover, I wish to point out that the conception of Christian wisdom or doctrine—in spite of its fundamental crisis in the twelfth century—has again and again experienced new renaissances, although by increasingly distancing itself from the respective intellectual movements and by tending toward a growing "aestheticism." In my opinion the initial steps in this direction were already taken by St. Bonaventure. Roughly speaking, this is a tendency which credits categorial rationality with only limited possibilities of interpretation and which deals with current questions in a way which lies beyond the recognized and institutionalized rationality.

Besides holding on to the old conception or taking it up again, there are two additional possible reactions to the crisis for Christian wisdom or Christian doctrine. First, one might give up the concept completely and leave the elements to develop on their own independently from one another. This would mean that Christianity and intellectual development would walk separate paths and that the former would give up being a cultural force at all. Yet this was not a real medieval possibility, as was the opposite situation where the religious tradition forcibly puts an end to rationality in its own world. Such was the solution not in the West, but in the oriental world of Islam. There, owing to overriding traditionalism, rationality would lose its legitimate cultural place. The second possible reaction to the crisis for Christian wisdom or doctrine must be investigated more closely, for here lies the key to our question.

First of all, it must be shown more clearly why the old model of Christian wisdom (or Christian doctrine) cannot simply be renewed under new conditions which are not favorable to continuing the old model. Here we must turn to the previously mentioned concept of increased rationality during the transition from the eleventh to the twelfth centuries. There seems to be no good reason we can offer for this development. At the moment, at least, we are unaware of any external causes.[20] It would be wrong to assert that direct knowledge of Islamic culture will furnish us with the appropriate explanation; for its cultural complex was far too little known within the Latin world. Moreover, the procedure in question is realized first and foremost in dialectics, that is to say, in that discipline which deals with the formal structure of reason. It becomes clearer now than before that rationality is to be realized in notions which have the character of universality. The more philosophy becomes aware of this fact, the more "unhistorical" it becomes. In other words, philosophy will no longer be able to retain the singular and the individual as its object.

This new form of rationality leads, on the one hand, to the crisis of Christian wisdom or Christian doctrine and, on the other, opens up new possibilities. This applies before all else to what can be called the "discovery of nature."[21] If in fact our speech and understanding should be abstract and universal in character, symbolical or allegorical interpretations must be eliminated; for these interpretations are connected with traditional presuppositions which are not directly accessible to universal reason. This is why the writers of the School of Chartres, when explaining Genesis, do so according to physics (*secundum physicam*) and are well aware that in doing this they must use general arguments which everyone can understand.[22] It is typical for them to use the Platonic *Timaeus* as their guide. Owing to this concern

---

20. Cf. W. Kluxen, "Der Begriff der Wissenschaft," in P. Weimar, ed., *Die Renaissance der Wissenschaften im 12. Jahrhundert* (Zürich-München, 1981), pp. 282f.

21. M.-D. Chenu (note 7): "L'homme maître de la nature. Ars et natura" (pp. 44–51); T. Gregory, "La nouvelle idée de la nature et de savoir scientifique au XIIe siècle," in J. E. Murdoch and E. D. Sylla, eds., *The Cultural Context of Medieval Learning* (Dordrecht-Boston, 1975), pp. 193–212.

22. Cf. note 17 and Clarembaldus of Arras, *Tractatulus super librum Genesis* (ed. N. Häring, *Life and Work of Clarembaldus of Arras* [Toronto, 1965], p. 229): "ex creatione enim mundi adeo certa argumenta sumi possunt ut etiam paganis et incredulis probari possit mundum habuisse conditorem . . ."

with universal reason, the works of Arabic science are also noted and received. This becomes possible because by now Arabic science is viewed no longer as the expression of an alien culture but as a work of reason. And reason is a common property.

What is indicated formally with the development of dialectics and realized in terms of content with the discovery of nature and the reception of Arabic science does not stop short of theology. Theology too becomes dialectical.[23] Owing to the predominant position of Christianity, it is here that the decision is made concerning whether or not the increase of rationality will be only a passing episode. If Christian teaching should oppose the influence of dialectics, the increasing rationality would have to consider Christian teaching as an alien dimension and turn away from it. The result would have probably been similar to what happened in the Islamic world. Though we are all familiar with the development in the Latin world, the whole procedure is anything but obvious. How does a theology which accepts the abstractness and universality of science deal with the nondeducible, we might even say, the unseemly facts of the economy of salvation? This is one of the major problems for the new theology. Either it deals with singular facts and follows a poetical, historical, or dialectical method; or it is science in the sense of the universality of this conception.[24]

It seems to me that it is in connection with this problem that we will find an essential reason for the turn from Plato to Aristotle. This surmise requires closer explanation. A kind of rationality which universally neutralizes the central Christian truth, i.e., by stripping it of its worldly and concrete meaning, is hardly suited to foster the tendency of theology towards science if this theology is to remain an interpretation of the revealed truth handed down by tradition and accepted on faith. A philosophy inspired by the spirit of Platonism is inclined to neutralize the history of salvation as well as history in general, and to interpret the concrete drama of the fall of man, the Incarnation, and Redemption as a mere fall into diversity and return to the One, or to reduce the influence of the Divine Spirit in the world to mere cosmic evolution.[25] Behind these attempts and temptations stands a tendency—not yet fully developed in the twelfth century but perceptible in its first beginnings and consequences—to test and realize the human mind in all its possibilities down to its foundations.

23. Cf. L. Hödl, "Die dialektische Theologie des 12. Jahrhunderts," in *Arts libéraux et philosophie au moyen âge* (Montréal-Paris, 1969), pp. 137–47.
24. See the problem formulated, for example, by Alexander of Hales, *Summa* I, tr. introd., qu. 1, c. 1, arg. 2, and c. 4, a. 1, arg. 1.
25. Cf. M.-D. Chenu (note 7): "Les platonismes au XIIe siècle," pp. 122 and 133.

Here it may be sufficient to remind you of Anselm's idea of the human mind understood as a likeness of the divine spirit, or to draw your attention to the common concept of *intellectibilitas*, employed in the School of Chartres, which makes man see the divine form *pure, simpliciter et presentarie*.[26] This thinking includes a full rehabilitation of reason—at least in fact if not in intention—which tends to resolve speculatively the paradoxes of revelation. This means that a rationality nourished by the spirit of Plato is well suited intellectually to express Christian attitudes. With respect to the medieval situation, especially during the eleventh and twelfth centuries, this means that so long as Christian doctrine remains within the limits of the seven liberal arts it will undoubtedly retain a Platonic hue. But as soon as Christian theology is asked whether it will be prepared to become involved methodically in the universality of science, Platonism becomes a problem.

With this background in mind, it seems to me that the development of theology into a rigorous, i.e., scientific, discipline is an important reason why the Latin world switched its allegiance from Plato to Aristotle. At first sight this statement may surprise you. Even if the previously mentioned difficulties with Plato are acknowledged, it is not easy to understand why the problems with Aristotle should be any less. In the final analysis it was Aristotle who, having his effect for centuries, directed science to the universal and thereby caused the dilemma with which theology was confronted on its way to becoming a science. The various attempts to explain how theology, in spite of its scientific character, could lay hold of the individual fact, result from the turn to Aristotle. On the whole these attempts cannot be regarded as convincing. Whether we take Alexander of Hales, for whom the individual fact serves as a sign of the universal, or Thomas Aquinas, who admits the individual fact as an example for life or as a confirmation of Christian authority, this is obviously a dilemma caused by the Aristotelian conception of science.[27] In sum, what makes Aristotelianism suitable to serve as sponsor for the development of theology as a science? The characteristics of science developed in the *Posterior Analytics*, which besides dealing with abstract universality also mentions its principles and methods, cannot be particularly attractive to theology; for many of the Aristotelian determinations tend to increase the difficulties. Why, therefore, does Aristotelianism prevail nonetheless?

26. On *intellectibilitas* cf. N. Häring (note 22), p. 48, and W. Jansen, *Der Kommentar des Clarenbaldus von Arras zu Boethius' De Trinitate* (Breslau, 1926), p. 55.

27. Cf. G. Wieland, *Ethica—Scientia practica. Die Anfänge der philosophischen Ethik im 13. Jahrhundert* (Münster, 1981), pp. 72–77.

Here we must mention first of all reasons which are internal to theology. Theology is becoming increasingly aware of the uniqueness and singularity of its specific principles. The "topical" theology[28] of the twelfth century leaves its principles largely undetermined. Its elements from reason and from authority are merging, so that under the common roof of Christian teaching bold speculation and pious devotion find their respective places. The clearer awareness of theology's grounding in faith apparently confronts theology with this alternative. Either theology becomes pious without taking into account the emphasis on universal rationality of the period (which would mean that theology is excluded from the field of culture-determining forces and becomes merely a devotional aspect of Christian life), or it becomes rational without taking into account the uniqueness of its foundations. This dilemma does not arise by accident but results from the process of trying to give to theology a scientific character. The whole process may be understood as a kind of compensation. Inasmuch as theology understands itself scientifically, it must, if it is to remain theology and not become metaphysics, emphasize its nonscientific principles even more. Concerning this dilemma Plato remains silent, that is, the Plato and Platonism of the twelfth century. And achievements of that time in the spirit of Plato—I have mentioned the cosmogony of Thierry of Chartres—rather show a tendency not to consider the nonscientific principles or to minimize their importance.

In this situation the Aristotelian theory of science offers a suitable way out. It is not without reason that the reception of Aristotle (the so-called second reception) begins already before the middle of the twelfth century with the *logica nova*, which includes the *Analytics*.[29] The first book of the *Posterior Analytics* deals, as you will recall, with science as an axiomatic-deductive structure, based on evident first principles. The prospect included in this determination is only too willingly grasped by the theologians, who render fruitful for their discipline the Aristotelian distinction between principles and levels of argumentation. By identifying theological principles with articles of faith (beginning with William of Auxerre),[30] they secure the founda-

---

28. A. Lang, *Die theologische Prinzipienlehre der mittelalterlichen Scholastik* (II. Abschnitt: "Die theologische Prinzipienlehre der Frühscholastik unter dem Einfluss der aristotelischen Topik") (Freiburg-Basel-Wien, 1964), pp. 41–105.

29. Cf. M. Y. Congar, "Théologie," in *Dictionnaire de théologie catholique* 15, pp. 375–78; B. G. Dod, "Aristoteles latinus," in N. Kretzmann, A. Kenny, and J. Pinborg, eds., *The Cambridge History of Later Medieval Philosophy* (Cambridge, 1982), p. 46; C. H. Lohr, "The Medieval Interpretation of Aristotle," ibid., pp. 81 ff.

30. U. Köpf, *Die Anfänge der theologischen Wissenschaftstheorie im 13. Jahrhundert* (Tübingen, 1974), p. 140.

tions for theology against other sciences. Through acknowledgment of its argumentative structure, theology remains within the context of universal rationality.

Still another thought in the *Posterior Analytics* could prove to be useful for the theology of the twelfth and thirteenth centuries. At the end of the first book Aristotle indicates that the Platonic idea of considering all knowledge as one single science cannot be maintained. On the contrary, he stresses the self-sufficiency of the different sciences.[31] This may be seen as a justification for the scientific situation in the twelfth and thirteenth centuries, and this in two respects. First of all, this applies to the de facto plurality of sciences which were now entering into the consciousness of the Latin world as well as to those which were newly emerging, such as canon law and theology. Although we might unite medicine, theology, astronomy, canon law, jurisprudence, and natural science under one common idea—that of scientific rationality which uses conceptual means and aims at general statements—a general conception regarding contents can no longer be established for the variety we find here.

This already brings us to the second aspect. Christian wisdom or doctrine, as the sum total of what man can know about God, the world, and man himself, is unable to absorb the new development into itself; for an important part of the above-mentioned disciplines falls outside the unifying focus of Christian doctrine or wisdom. Neither as preparatory nor as serving instrument can they be immediately subordinated to a Christian general conception. From an overall Christian viewpoint this growth of the secular may be given a negative interpretation. But for scientific theology this development involves a concentration on its own real task, to reflect on faith in a suitable way, and at the same time theology is freed from various less rational undertakings.

With the Aristotle of the *Posterior Analytics* theology can consider itself as a science among other sciences. Therefore theology, justified by a recognized theory of the sciences, can be prepared for its limited task. In light of tradition and the claims of Christian doctrine or wisdom, acknowledgment of its limitation and recognition of the growth of the profane disciplines is certainly a kind of resignation for theology. By this I mean a rejection of universal direction in the realm of study and teaching. Of course theology remains highest among the

---

31. *Anal. Post.* I 27 and 28 (87a31–b4); see I. Düring, *Aristoteles. Darstellung und Interpretation seines Denkens* (Heidelberg, 1966), p. 100.

high-ranking faculties of the medieval university, but it is only one faculty among the three superior faculties. Nevertheless, I wish to emphasize once more: corresponding to this renunciation from cultural universality is a deeper understanding of theology's specific principles.

It may be useful to illustrate historically these general remarks about the development of theology and its turn toward Aristotle. For two reasons Abelard strikes me as the best example: first, because he does not yet know the *logica nova* and therefore the Aristotelian doctrine of science in detail; second, because through a more precise distinction between faith and knowledge it is he who brings theology to the path we have so far sketched.

Here it is essential to observe that this work of theological clarification is already under way before the reception of the *Posterior Analytics*. This means that it was not Aristotelianism that initiated the theological process, but that this process, once begun, makes use of Aristotelian categories and methods. The decisive insight of Abelard which is relevant to our discussion consists in the fact that he regards the human knowing power as limited in principle and judges comprehensive knowledge (*comprehendere*) of the central contents of faith completely impossible.[32]

It is therefore completely inappropriate to speak of rationalism in Abelard. This would be possible only if we understood it to be something like a critique of reason. With Abelard we see for the first time signs of what later on will become increasingly significant for rationality: to the extent that the universal claim of science becomes accepted, so does awareness of the subjective conditions of this form of universality. Already at the very beginnings of scholastic rationality there is insight into the limitations of man's ability to know. At the end it becomes even clearer that scholasticism—owing to increasing rationality—cannot refrain from making the question concerning the range of human reason a subject of its considerations. Ockham's philosophy makes this sufficiently clear. This implies a new and extremely important aspect. While Platonic philosophy—of no matter what variety—is much inclined to examine the structures of cognition as such, Aristotelian philosophy aims at judging and criticizing the possibilities of human reason in its concrete situation. If the above-mentioned point is correct, that in the twelfth century the process of

---

32. *Theologia Summi boni* II (ed. H. Ostlender, *Peter Abaelards Theologia Summi boni* [Münster, 1939], p. 34): "quae etiam maior indignatio fidelibus habenda esset, quam eum se habere deum profiteri, quem ratiuncula humana posset comprehendere aut mortalium lingua disserere."

rationalization already takes two directions, one universal and one subjective and critical, then under medieval conditions Aristotelianism is better suited than Platonism to give an answer to this new view of the problem. For Aristotelian philosophy may be understood as a philosophy of the finiteness and infirmity of human existence, thereby answering to the critical consciousness of that time; and it is critical of the extreme tendencies of Platonism.[33]

Although the points mentioned—the aspect of science and the aspect of knowledge—may help us better understand the turn from Plato to Aristotle, I do not think they can sufficiently explain the scope and duration of this turn. Only reflection on the Aristotelian metaphysics makes this turn fully intelligible. We must always be aware that according to Aristotle this discipline—at least in its results—is fundamentally quite modest. To be sure, it is the most universal and at the same time the first science; but the study of being as such and its essential attributes—measured against the insights of the particular sciences—remains at a level of generality which is unable to satisfy our intellectual striving for final knowledge. Even the study of the highest being remains always related to the starting point of this reflection, i.e., to physics, and this regardless of whether we accept the position of Avicenna, who reserves the proof of God's existence for metaphysics, or the position of Averroes, who viewed this proof as a task for physics.[34] In any event, for the metaphysics inspired by Aristotelianism, there is no possibility of reaching a knowledge of God which leaves no questions open. In other words, the most that man can know, according to Aristotle, falls short of that at which man actually aims. We might again reflect on the difference between real and absolute human possibilities and reproach Aristotle for not having decisively enough settled the philosophical question. However, with this another problem arises which touches directly on philosophy's self-understanding: Is philosophical reflection about what is or about what is supposed to be?

It is not our task here to answer this question. But we must answer another one: Did the thirteenth-century theologians—those who had before them the complete Aristotelian philosophy—recognize and understand its finiteness? In fact we find in Thomas Aquinas that well-known statement regarding the anxiety (*Angst*) of philosophers

---

33. It is obvious that the Dionysian Neoplatonism subdues rational optimism; it is, on the other hand, not properly qualified to establish the required continuity with the other sciences.

34. Cf. J. C. Doig, *Aquinas on Metaphysics* (The Hague, 1972), pp. 23–46.

when faced with the human situation and therefore the limited possibilities of human existence.[35] This is clear evidence that Aquinas understands Aristotelian philosophy as a philosophy of finiteness.

He can do this because this philosophy taken in its entirety as well as in its parts starts in fact from man's concrete situation and never disregards this. The Aristotelian doctrine of science begins with the plurality and self-sufficiency of the different sciences, without seriously considering the idea of a single, united science. Nor can we regard metaphysics as a science of that type. Although it is focused on all being, this is done from a perspective which does not allow for a deduction of the contents of the other sciences. There is quite a distance between Aristotelian metaphysics and the claims of modern rationalism. Moreover, the doctrine of cognition takes the human condition into account, as a connection with sensible reality remains fundamental for all intellectual cognition. In spite of occasional hints at the permanent actuality of *Nous*,[36] Aristotle does not assign these considerations to individual human cognition. An immediate self-knowledge of the intellect cannot be derived from Aristotelian premises. Similar recognition of the finite can be shown in Aristotle's ethics.

In general it may be said that the theology of the twelfth and thirteenth centuries turns to Aristotle because he offers a philosophy which leaves open the differences between this-worldly and absolute possibilities for man and at the same time permits theology to take its place among the sciences, a place which is legitimated by these sciences themselves.

The opposite is true of Platonism. Here there is a tendency to dissolve such differences in favor of an absolute position, so that theology as a distinct speculative discipline really becomes superfluous. Therefore, I believe, theologians seized the alternative presented by Aristotelian philosophy. If I am correct about this, it would explain quite plausibly the turn from Plato to Aristotle. For it is historically and philosophically unsatisfying to understand this merely as the result of external factors, that is, of translations and the reception of the translated works. My thesis, on the contrary, explains the reception of Aristotle as itself resulting from a fundamental reorientation of intellectual life in the twelfth century. However, no unambiguous and convincing reasons can be offered for this reorientation itself, unless we turn to the rational tendencies present in Christian doctrine itself which might develop and intensify under favorable conditions.

35. SCG III, cc. 25–50, esp. c. 48.   36. *De an.* III, c. 5 (430a19–22).

The reasons I have offered for the turn from Plato to Aristotle should not be misunderstood. This process does not take place in a radical or abrupt way. It lasts for many decades, in fact for a full century. From the institutional side it comes to a certain conclusion with the Statutes of the Arts Faculty at Paris in 1255.[37] From the systematic side it ends, in a way, with the system of St. Thomas Aquinas. It is well known that much resistance had to be overcome along the way. Unlike Plato, Aristotle is not one who is spontaneously loved but a stranger who knows no religious enthusiasm, and who therefore lacks the direct proximity with Christianity which distinguishes Platonism. Without certain, shall we say, "mitigating circumstances," the resistance against Aristotle would probably have been even stronger and more effective. From the vantage point of history we are able to judge positively theology's transition from Christian doctrine to science; for in this process theology manages to maintain or to establish its continuity with the developing scientific disciplines of its time and at the same time recognizes its specifying principles of faith more clearly than ever before. While we can see this clearly from afar, contemporary players experienced the whole movement as a path into an uncertain future. Papal warnings to the theologians at Paris telling them to tend to their business and to occupy themselves not with worldly knowledge but with theological purity speak clearly enough.[38]

I wish to single out two circumstances which favored the entry of Aristotelianism. First of all, certain works were attributed to Aristotle which moderate somewhat the impression of foreignness—that the corpus of his work leaves no place for religious feeling. This is especially true of the *Liber de causis*, which, as is well known, is an extract from the *Elementatio theologica* of Proclus, in which the Neoplatonic emanation system is transformed into a genuine doctrine of creation. In the thirteenth century this work was seen as a supplement to the Aristotelian metaphysics and was also generally attributed to Aristotle. Thereby Aristotle's philosophy of finiteness receives a conclusion which is conciliatory to theology. The *Liber de pomo*—an imitation of Plato's *Phaedo*—contains a conversation between the dying Aristotle and his disciples. This work, translated into Latin in the mid-thirteenth century, corrects the refusal to acknowledge personal immortality or the silence concerning the same of the Aristotelian corpus. More important than such corrections of the Aristotelian image, however, is

---

37. *Chartularium Universitatis Parisiensis* I, ed. H. Denifle and A. Chatelain (Paris, 1899), n. 246.
38. Ibid., n. 59.

another well-known circumstance. The Aristotelianism of the early thirteenth century, with its deficiencies and dark spots, is furnished through Avicenna's interpretation with a Neoplatonic cast which makes a turn from Plato to Aristotle less radical.

While the transition to the new paradigm is long lasting and favored by various circumstances, a systematic acceptance of the new philosophy, taken as a whole, does not occur in the most fundamental sense. Even the radical Aristotelians of the thirteenth century cannot possibly manage without Neoplatonic additions. However, I wish to disregard this subject completely, as it merely serves to document the systematic and institutional self-reliance of philosophy which was initiated by the turn. But another question should be considered more closely. How is it possible that from the soil of Aristotelianism a radical heterodoxy can grow, while the systems of Eriugena, Thierry of Chartres, Eckhart, or Cusanus—developed in the spirit of Platonism, and no less radical—in spite of ecclesiastical condemnations or at least suspicions, give the impression rather of a contingency-free theology than of decisive this-worldliness? This is owing to the religious character which is immanent in Platonism. Its assertions regarding the origin and destiny of the world and of man refer—speaking in modern terms—to a deeper meaning which transcends the empirical world and promises to overcome the contingencies of human life. Not without reason does Marsiglio Ficino describe Plato in a letter as follows: "Our Plato united into one in wonderful fashion the two ways [the philosophical and the priestly], and everywhere he is equally the religious person and the philosopher."[39] In contrast Aristotelianism remains decidedly secular. Compared with modern empiricism Aristotelianism is, undoubtedly, an open system, which does not identify the world of sensible experience with being as a whole. But its reference to transcendence has the character more of a hint than of fulfillment. As a matter of fact, Aristotelian philosophy—given its premises and its claims—cannot offer satisfying answers to questions concerning human contingency, i.e., problems of suffering, illness, and death.

With Aristotle philosophy renounces any competence for redemption and final fulfillment. Even the happiness of this life, as it is developed in the *Nicomachean Ethics*, is no more than a hint of the real happiness which is beyond all philosophy. In this respect Aristotelianism is not the friend of theology, to whom theology would feel spon-

---

39. "Responsio petenti Platonicam instructionem et librorum numerum" (ed. R. Klibansky, *The Continuity of the Platonic Tradition during the Middle Ages* [London, ¹1981], p. 45).

taneously attracted. Signs of such distance are to be found all over. Whereas in the anonymous *Summa philosophiae*, Plato is known as an amiable thinker, open to human problems, Aristotle—though fully appreciated for his rational achievement—is regarded as decidedly arrogant.[40] For instance, there are two widely circulated medieval legends which assign to Plato the dignity of a true philosopher, while Aristotle—the authority of the schools—"falls a victim to the arts of a coquettish woman": "Car la femme tout seurmonta."[41] Aristotle is considered only as representing an authentic secularism, which theology will not renounce because of its rationality and cultural effectiveness. Therefore we may see in the turn towards Aristotle a recognition of this secularism which finds excellent expression in philosophy and the sciences.

Against this background, how are we to judge the relationship of the thirteenth and fourteenth centuries to Platonism—taken here in the broader sense? In order to answer this question it is not enough to look at the sources and analyze them. This is important, of course, but it leads to problematic results if we restrict ourselves to this method. Thomas Aquinas, for instance, depending upon what sources one uses, represents a more or less pure Aristotelianism, or a Neoplatonic Aristotelianism, or even a Platonism with some Aristotelian characteristics. Against such labeling I wish to make some methodological and factual points, no matter whether or not they describe correctly the source of the individual philosophical currents. The decisive process in this period is the discovery of universal rationality; this first appears in dialectics, then in the various sciences and in philosophy. Universal rationality now includes the possibility of taking a critical attitude towards tradition, and this in contrast to the tradition-directed rationality of Christian wisdom. Here a moment of freedom makes its appearance, which can be verified historically at least since the thirteenth century. I would like to illustrate this with three examples, which also tell something about the relationship of the thirteenth century to Platonism.

Example One: Thomas Aquinas develops his own philosophy on the foundations of the reception of Aristotle. His philosophy above all in metaphysics and theory of knowledge picks up Platonic motifs.[42] His

---

40. *Summa philosophiae*, tr. I, c. 3 (ed. L. Baur, *Die philosophischen Werke des Robert Grosseteste, Bischofs von Lincoln* [Münster, 1912], p. 278).
41. R. Klibansky, *The Continuity* (note 39), Supplement: *The Schools and the Vernacular Literatures in the Thirteenth and Fourteenth Centuries*, p. 65.
42. Cf. for example K. Kremer, *Die neuplatonische Seinsphilosophie und ihre Wirkung auf Thomas von Aquin* (Leiden, ²1971).

metaphysics does have a "physical" starting point, and here it follows the Aristotelian pattern and the interpretation by Averroes. However, Aquinas discovers that in its core a being is dependent, and that it only participates in that which makes a being a being. The Platonic concept of participation is thereby rehabilitated.[43] How shall we interpret this and other similar procedures? Thomas surpasses the scope of his historical sources and thereby creates something new in the field of philosophy, something that cannot be explained by the mere addition of two or more sources. In fact philosophical speculation and scholarship always proceed so that from a contemporary posing of a question historical material is transformed and reorganized. Thomas does this consciously. We should see this not merely as an expression of his personal genius, but as a historical possibility given to him through new conditions either to accept or to reject traditions, to select traditions and to reorganize them—in brief, to display a critical attitude with respect to traditions.

Example Two: The situation is much more apparent in late thirteenth-century Augustinianism. This movement should be viewed not as a naturally compelled recourse to old traditions but as a deliberate revival which is in no way identical with the original Augustinian teaching. Universal hylemorphism, the doctrine of *rationes seminales,* the introduction of a proper *forma corporeitatis,* the theory of illumination, and other particular positions serve mainly to refute a philosophy which had become presentable through the work of Albert the Great and Thomas Aquinas. However, the central point of controversy is to be found not in these various theories, but in the claim of a "profane" philosophy to be regarded as independent from theology. John Peckham accepts the study of philosophy so long as it is of service to theological mysteries; but he strongly criticizes *prophanas novitates,* i.e., "profane innovations," which are aimed against "philosophical" truth and against Christian tradition.[44] With striking clarity the old model of Christian doctrine appears again, which does not accept an independent and "profane" rationality, and which advances the

---

43. Cf. W. Kluxen, "Thomas von Aquin: Das Seiende und seine Prinzipien," in J. Speck, ed., *Grundprobleme der grossen Philosophen. Philosophie des Altertums und des Mittelalters* (Göttingen, ⁸1978), pp. 210–16.

44. Letter of John Peckham to the bishop of Lincoln from 1285 (ed. F. Ehrle, "John Peckham über den Kampf des Augustinismus und Aristotelismus in der zweiten Hälfte des 13. Jahrhunderts," *Zeitschr. für kath. Theologie* 13 [1889], p. 186): "philosophorum studia minime reprobamus, quatenus mysteriis theologicis famulantur, sed prophanas vocum novitates, quae contra philosophicam veritatem sunt in sanctorum iniuriam citra viginti annos in altitudines theologicas introductae . . . illa novella quasi tota contraria, quae quidquid docet Augustinus de regulis aeternis . . ."

theological authority of St. Augustine against philosophical claims. It is remarkable that this theological "integralism" uses on decisive points means which originate from a Platonic context—taken in the broadest sense. The choice of these means is, however, determined less by tradition than by the intellectual requirements of the late thirteenth century. Therefore the Platonically colored Augustinianism of these decades should first and foremost be understood not as the continuous living-on of "Christian doctrine," but as a deliberate use of proven means in a dangerous situation. What is intimated in the case of Thomas Aquinas becomes evident here: Platonic material does not serve to enable one to visualize the past, but is a helpful means in a contemporary discussion.

Example Three: The third example shows how little the intellectual dispute of the thirteenth and fourteenth centuries follows a traditional course. Dietrich of Freiberg consciously refers more forcefully than other authors of the declining thirteenth century to Neoplatonism, especially to Proclus.[45] However, differing in this from the representatives of Neo-Augustinianism at his time, Dietrich does not intend to come to the aid of the endangered precedence of theology. With respect to this he even seems to force an increase of "profane" rationality. Dietrich's interest seems to be far more to discover and overcome systematic inconsistencies in the philosophy of Thomas Aquinas. Platonic motifs are used for critical and systematic purposes and applied to contemporary discussions. Another study would be required to determine whether and to what extent the systematization of the Platonic material again puts into question the contingent starting point of theology. However, this does not seem to be felt immediately as a problem; at least I see no corresponding reaction.

These three examples of deliberate recourse to Platonic motifs point to completely different interests. Thomas Aquinas develops his own philosophy on an Aristotelian base. Because he regards this base as insufficient in certain respects and as in need of completion, he turns back to Platonic material. Yet he maintains the finiteness of Aristotelianism. Neo-Augustinianism attempts to keep "profane" rationality within narrow limits, while Dietrich of Freiberg designs a new system, which hardly seems to take notice of the contingent structure of theology. All intellectual efforts of this time, whether positively or negatively, are related to this rationality. Whether it is our three examples, or Bonaventure and Siger of Brabant, or Henry of Ghent and

---

45. Cf. K. Flasch, "Einleitung" to *Dietrich von Freiberg, Opera omnia* I: *Schriften zur Intellekttheorie,* ed. B. Mojsisch (Hamburg, 1977), pp. ix–xxvi.

Godfrey of Fontaines, all know what they are speaking about. Knowing this, they can understand one another even when really opposed to one another. In contrast, there is no common language for Bernard of Clairvaux and Abelard in the twelfth century. It seems especially important to me that this community in the thirteenth century is gained not through renewing a common tradition, but through recognition of the validity of reason.

In summarizing I wish to emphasize that rational community is always possible in principle, and has been realized in fact on many occasions. What is special about the thirteenth century is the explicit will for such community; even opponents of "profane" rationality could not withdraw from it. On this soil different systems of Aristotelian but also of Platonic character can develop. Even the system of Nicholas Cusanus remains bound to this common rationality. In contrast, a change of interest takes place in the Renaissance. Petrarch, for instance, sees in Plato not the representative of a universal rationality, but an ideal personality in whose life he wishes to recognize himself, and this in religious as well as in aesthetic respects.[46] From the religious and aesthetical sides, Aristotelianism has little to offer. And yet herein lies the reason why the theology of the twelfth and thirteenth centuries chooses Aristotelianism instead of Platonism as its intellectual guide; for Aristotelianism leaves to theology its own field for scientific activity, something which Platonism cannot offer without difficulties.

University of Trier

46. See R. Klibansky, *The Continuity* (note 39), Supplement: *Petrarch*, p. 69.

5   The Divine as the Measure of Being in Platonic and Scholastic Thought

JAMES McEVOY

I became interested in the constellation of themes clustering around the term "measure" when reading Robert Grosseteste, for the number of his references to Wisdom 11 : 21 is high, and it seems to me that the speculative and mathematical aspect of his cosmology, in particular the designation of God as *mensurator* and *numerator primus*, marks a significant new modulation of that Augustinian interpretation of creation *in mensura, numero et pondere* ("in measure, number, and weight") which was to prove so attractive to medieval exegetes and theologians. When, in turn, I approached St. Augustine's book on time and its measurement (*Confessions*, book XI),[1] I expected to find there an exploration of a quite different side of the concept of measure; and while that expectation was indeed fulfilled, the inquiry led me in a new and unexpected direction, one that pointed back less to the Wisdom theme than to Plato's discussion of the transcendence of the soul over the material; for the more I tried to comprehend the capacity of the Augustinian soul to measure the passing of time, motion, sound, and even silence, the more I became aware that this ability to measure is a revelation of the spirituality of the soul and of its transcendence with regard to physical being. Augustine has two terms of comparison for the experience of time, the one below the level of the mind, the other transcendent to it: the mind has a permanence not found in matter, but it has also a mutability that is not there in God. The mind itself cannot, therefore, be the absolute term of reference for being, since it

---

I should like to take this opportunity of thanking the Alexander von Humboldt–Stiftung (Bonn) for their generous financial and scholarly support, from April to August 1985, which enabled me to extend and rewrite this paper. I offer my sincere thanks to Dr. G. L. Huxley and Mr. James Daly, for their critical and helpful reading of an earlier draft of the paper, and to Mrs. S. Smyth for her patient help in the preparation of the typescript.

1. J. McEvoy, "St. Augustine's Account of Time and Wittgenstein's Criticisms," *Review of Metaphysics* 38 (1984), pp. 547–77; pp. 570, 573.

is God alone who is the measure without measure, and the creative ideas contained in the Word "provide a measure for every being." The present study will take up that train of thought once more and will work back along the links of the Platonic chain, the great chain of ontology of classical and Hellenistic philosophy.

The earliest appearance of μέτρον (measure) in Greek philosophy is found in Fragments 30 and 31 of Heracleitus, preserved by St. Clement of Alexandria:[2]

30   This world-order [the same of all] did none of gods or men make, but it always was and is and shall be: an ever-living fire, kindling in measures and going out in measures.

31   Fire's turnings: first sea, and of sea the half is earth, the half 'burner' . . . ⟨earth⟩ is dispersed as sea, and is measured so as to form the same proportion as existed before it became earth.

The world order is a lasting thing without beginning or end, yet change is a continuous process. "Eternal" fire embraces the diversity of things in a unity: not all of the cosmos is being consumed at the same time, but parts "according to measure" are being kindled and other parts extinguished. The force of "measure" is brought out in the second fragment, when the balance of earth and sea is said to be governed or measured by a λόγος, or intelligible relationship. The eternal fire (equated with the λόγος) is not the same as the element of fire, but something divine and eternal and regulative (as in the thunderbolt). Kirk and Raven have this to say, by way of elucidation:

All fire (even the lower, mundane sort), by the regularity with which it absorbs fuel and emits smoke, while maintaining a kind of stability between them, patently embodies the rule of measure in change which inheres in the world process, and of which the Logos is an expression. Thus it is naturally conceived as the very constituent of things which actively determines their structure and behaviour—which ensures not only the opposition of opposites, but also their unity through 'strife'.[3]

It is in Solon, the lawgiver of Athens, that we first find the notion of measure given a profound political and religious sense, one which roots the human struggle to be just within the cosmic-divine order,

---

2. G. S. Kirk and J. E. Raven, *The Presocratic Philosophers* (Cambridge, 1957), p. 199; translation slightly modified. Frag. 94, preserved by Plutarch, reads: "Sun will not overstep his measures [μέτρα]; otherwise the Erinyes, ministers of Justice, will find him out" (Kirk and Raven, p. 203). The sun holds the balance of the seasons, giving to each what is its due, whence it is an agent of cosmic justice.

3. Ibid., p. 200.

over which the justice of Zeus presides, silently but always effectively, in the long run. In his long meditative *Elegy*, Solon places the responsibility for the disorder of the polis upon men, not gods.[4] The citizens must blame only themselves for the cowardice which permits the rise of tyrannical rule. The polis is not the stage for the exhibition of aristocratic "heroism," for citizenship requires a certain moderation and restraint, if exploitation and factionalism are not to devour the whole substance of community. True human excellence (ἀρετή) cannot in any case take visible possessions or wealth as the measure of successful living, for therein lies private delusion (δόξα), not right order (εὐνομία). "It is very hard to know the unseen measure of right judgement; and yet it alone contains the right limits of all things." Real human excellence results from placing faith in the "mind of the immortals, all unseen to men." Solon claims to have done that: "At the behest of the gods have I done what I said."

Solon marked the life of Athens in a way that no political figure after him ever managed to do. Plato undoubtedly drew a definite strand of inspiration from the man whom he revered for his wisdom, garnered through travel in Egypt[5] and left as a precious legacy to his fellow-citizens, under the sacred form of city law. Plato claimed descent from Solon on his mother's side; there can be no doubt concerning the kinship of their mental outlook, for in the Platonic *Laws* the "invisible measure" of Solon is reproduced as the "divine measure of all things."[6]

Reflection on the art of measurement occupies an important place in a number of the Platonic dialogues, being interwoven with such themes as the relativity of knowledge; the mathematically based arts; the measurement of pleasure and pain; the critique of the Protagorean dictum; form and limit as expressions of being, truth, and goodness; and, finally, the Good as the measure of all things. If I am not to devote this entire discussion to Plato, I must risk a certain breathlessness and incoherence, in attempting to mention the various heads

---

4. γνωμοσύνης δ' ἀφανὲς χαλεπώτατόν ἐστι νοῆσαι / μέτρον, ὃ δὴ πάντων πείρατα μοῦνον ἔχει. This fragment of Solon, *Elegy*, is preserved by Clement of Alexandria, *Stromata* 5, 81, 1, who introduces it by saying, σοφώτατα τοίνυν γέγραπται τῷ Σόλωνι ταῦτα περὶ θεοῦ ("Now these most wise thoughts about God have been written by Solon"); *Elegy and Iambus*, ed. J. M. Edmonds, vol. 1, The Loeb Classical Library (London–New York, 1931), p. 132. For a comment, see E. Voegelin, *The World of the Polis, Order and History*, vol. 2 (1957), pp. 194–99.

5. J. McEvoy, "Plato and the Wisdom of Egypt," *Irish Philosophical Journal* 1 (1984), pp. 1–24.

6. "The work of Plato is hardly conceivable, and certainly not intelligible, without the paradigmatic life of Solon." Voegelin, op. cit., p. 199.

under which "measure" appears and to say something of the relevant contexts. In doing so I run the risk of tearing the web of Platonic dialectic. Five works of Plato appear to be of particular significance: *Protagoras, Statesman, Philebus, Theaetetus,* and *Laws.*

The young Socrates, meeting the most learned of the Sophists (τὸν σοφώτατον, "the wisest of his generation": that is ironic, of course), comes with two questions: What does a Sophist teach? and Can virtue be taught, in the way that the arts can be?[7] Plato makes play with the cohort around Protagoras, who is walking up and down as he discourses; his hearers wheel at the end of each straight and turn like a well-drilled company. When, however, the image changes to Protagoras as Orpheus, enchanting his listeners, the reader who ponders the scene must ask whether these men are alive at all: are they not shades of the underworld, or even beasts? That underlying seriousness which is encountered here becomes evident, once more, when Socrates describes going to a teacher of wisdom in terms of giving the soul into care, or risking a treasure at the throw of dice (312C–314). Protagoras blandly claims that he leaves each pupil a better man for each day's tuition. What he teaches his pupil is εὐβουλία (318D)—good judgement in his private affairs, and power in speech and action over the affairs of the city (319A). Such μάθημα is, he suggests, cheap at the price he charges.

When Plato addresses the question "How are we to live?" we can generally expect that the life of pleasure will be taken up and considered, as a dialectical starting point. Socrates leads the discussion from the idea that it is good to live pleasureably, towards a disjunction between pleasure and pain, on the one hand, and good and evil, on the other, as quite different sets of scales for the weighing of experience. If we go by pleasure and pain, admitting no other criterion, then questions of worth (ἀξία-ἀνάξια, 356A) are replaced by excess and defect in comparison, or greater and less: "Like a practised weigher, put pleasant things and painful in the scales, and with them the nearness and the remoteness, and tell me which count for more. . . ."[8] Socrates at once moves away from this calculus, to the relativity of objects of sight and sound, of thickness and number, depending upon their nearness to and distance from the perceiver, and asks whether, if the safety (σωτηρία) of our life lay in choosing, say, large things rather than small, we would choose to rely upon the art of measurement (μετρητικὴ τέχνη), or upon the perceptual impact of appearances (ἡ τοῦ φαινομένου δύναμις, 356D). The force of truth is poured into the

---

7. Plato, *Protagoras* 304D.   8. Ibid., 356.

discussion, for true measurement annuls perceptual relativity and ends the confusion which that engenders; in that case our salvation would be assured by ἐπιστήμη—measurement, and the numbering on which that is based. The point of the parable, needless to say, is that life does depend upon right choices in the area of pleasure and pain; and that there must be an art and science (τέχνη καὶ ἐπιστήμη) which guides us truly, "the nature of which we will consider on a future occasion."

Where that further discussion is to be located is a subject of dispute. The most thorough exploration of measurement is found in *Philebus*, but the theme also turns up in *Statesman*, and it is to that dialogue that we briefly turn.

In what is essentially a digression, interjected between discussion of the art of weaving and the art of ruling, the Eleatic Stranger affirms that the difference between good and bad men is found in excess or deficiency over against the standard of the mean (τὴν τοῦ μετρίου φύσιν).[9] Comparative terms (such as great and small) are defined, not by simple relativity, but by reference to the mean (πρὸς τὸ μέτριον), which determines goodness and beauty in all the arts: "If this exists they exist, but neither can ever exist without the other" (284D). Advancing upon that, the Stranger divides μετρητική into two, the arts of measuring dimensions and numbers (a relative art, which has an obscure term of comparison in τὸ ἐναντίον, the opposite) and arts which measure the same objects, though by reference to τὸ μέτριον καὶ τὸ πρέπον καὶ τὸν καιρὸν καὶ τὸ δέον, and all standards which are at home in the mean between extremes. In this exercise in dialectic division, the contrast seems to lie between a kind of measurement which applies to "all things which come into being" and the nonrelative or absolute art of measurement, which invokes "what ought to be," "the true form of accuracy"; for Plato passes to the things that are accessible only to reason, in an unmistakeable reference to the forms (286A). And we know from the mouth of the Stranger that we will need the true standard of the measure at some time (ποτε, 284D) for the demonstration of the most exact truth.[10]

The much more lengthy discussion of measurement given in *Philebus* 55–65 cannot be summarized here; I can at most set out a series of points.

(1) *Philebus* is linked with *Protagoras* (and even more with *Gorgias*)

---

9. Plato, *Statesman* 283E.
10. Cf. Paul Friedlaender, *Plato*, vol. 3: *The Dialogues. Second and Third Periods* (Princeton, 1969), pp. 292–93, on the critique of the Pythagoreans, to whom Plato nevertheless owed so much.

by the discussion concerning pleasure and the true good of life. The question "How should we live?" brings up a conflict between pleasure (represented by Protarchus) and goodness, reason, wisdom (Socrates). An insuperable difficulty lies in discussing the two at all, for discussion takes place through reason, in language, but the pleasure principle cannot win in rational discussion: if it enters there at all, it is lost. Philebus, its representative, remains lying down and is silent in protest against all reasonable assessment; he cannot be forced into dialogue. Protarchus, however, can be, since he "represents the average view, the one that is inclined toward hedonism without—in contrast to Philebus—shutting off all other powers in life."[11] Having been brought to speak, however, he cannot win.

(2) Pure pleasure is opposed to any limit; like pain, it is limitless. If, however, the good life consists in a mixture of pleasure and reason, supposing that pleasure has a part in reason, as Socrates maintains it does, then knowledge must be given a place in human life. We come back, then, to the place of "numbering, measuring, and weighing" in the arts (55E) and must distinguish between arts which, like building, are more mathematical and accurate, using instruments of measurement, and those like music, on the other hand, which have less accuracy in them. We must also distinguish between pure mathematics (which is exact) and applied (which is less so).

(3) The inference which Socrates draws is that there is a hierarchy in knowledge just as there is in pleasures, some knowledge being clearer and purer than other kinds (57C). The truest art is that of the philosopher, and knowledge "which has to do with being, reality, and eternal immutability is the truest kind of knowledge" (58A). Protarchus evokes Gorgias in protest; but Socrates appeals to the capacity to distinguish between the perception of utility (and rhetoric—closely associated by Plato with pleasure and the will to power), and the ability to "love truth and do all things for the sake of truth," an ability which he terms νοῦς καὶ φρόνησις. The dialectic suddenly seems to pierce through the human reality—"the thought of you and me and Gorgias and Philebus" (59C)—to "what is firm [βέβαιον] and pure [καθαρόν] and true [ἀληθές] and unalloyed [εἰλικρινές], and has to do with things eternally the same without change or mixture . . . all other things being regarded as secondary and inferior."

(4) In the life mixed of contemplation and pleasure, the highest pleasure attaches to the highest knowledge (63). The nature of mixture naturally reintroduces measure and proportion (μέτρον καὶ συμ-

---

11. Friedlaender, vol. 3, p. 310.

μέτρον), which are at once allied with beauty (κάλλος) and virtue (ἀρετή) and with "the power of the good." The good can be made visible only through beauty (συμμετρία) and truth (ἀλήθεια); μετριότης, measure, forsakes once and for all the limitless and immoderate (ἄμετρον) nature of pleasure, since measure is internal to mind and knowledge. The passage which I summarize here would merit full quotation, for it is replete with compounds and derivatives of μέτρον. The crowning accolade of measure follows it at once (66A): the eternal nature has chosen μέτρον and the moderation and balance which it confers (τὸ μέτριον), together with τὸ καίριον, the fitting, and all such terms as the very first of goods (κτῆμα), after which, in second place, come proportion (σύμμετρον, the effect of measure), beauty, perfection, etc.; in the third place are νοῦς and φρόνησις, and in the fourth, the arts and sciences. The highest pleasures follow this hierarchy faithfully. All are the offspring of the *Agathon*, which in itself remains invisible.[12]

If I have left the *Theaetetus* until now, that is because it is there that Plato confronts, in its sharpest delineation and formulation, that relativism which he always (as we have seen) attributes to Protagoras, and seeks to draw out its last baneful consequence; for the dialogue, often referred to as epistemological, is concerned as much with moral norms and with identity, with the nature of the true philosopher, and with education, as it is with knowledge. The identity of αἴσθησις with ἐπιστήμη is "the description which Protagoras used to give" (151E). However, his own formulation in the celebrated dictum is more general: "Man is the measure of all things, of those that are, that they are, and of those that are not, that they are not."[13] The statement is interpreted by the Platonic Socrates to mean that "individual things are for me such as they appear to me, and for you in turn such as they appear to you—you and I (each) being 'man'" (152B). In the discussion which follows, the thrust of dialectic moves through sensory and perceptual differences to the thesis which Plato attributes to all those philosophers who were the objects of his disapprobation, to Protagoras and Heracleitus, Empedocles, and the poets too—that nothing ever is (= is one), but everything is always becoming. We may well doubt whether the historical Protagoras put forward his views with the strictly metaphysical sense that Plato finds in them; perhaps Marrou is closer to the truth than many historians of philosophy when he remarks:

---

12. Ibid., p. 349.
13. Plato, *Theaetetus* 152A: φησὶ (i.e., Protagoras) γάρ που πάντων χρημάτων μέτρον ἄνθρωπον εἶναι, τῶν μὲν ὄντων, ὡς ἔστι, τῶν δὲ μὴ ὄντων, ὡς οὐκ ἔστιν.

A great deal of mischief has been done by trying to give this a metaphysical significance, turning its author into the fountainhead of phenomenalist empiricism, a forerunner of modern subjectivism. . . . This is a gross exaggeration of the meaning of the passages concerned, which were intended to be taken at their face-value: neither Protagoras nor Gorgias had any intention of creating a system; both were simply concerned to formulate a number of practical rules. They never taught their pupils any truths about being or man, but merely how to be always, and in any kind of circumstances, right. . . . This education developed in the direction of a relativistic humanism.[14]

What we may not gainsay, however, is Plato's right to explore, in depth and generality and in all its consequences, the import of a view that was admittedly more banal than philosophical in its first coining. In any case, Plato leaves us in no doubt of his loathing for Protagoras, as he pours quite unaccustomed sarcasms upon his wisdom, plays cruelly with the title of his book ("Truth"), and even suggests that Protagoras may have spoken tongue in cheek (161C–162). If each man is the measure of his own wisdom, if a pig, or a baboon endowed with sensation, is the measure of all, then Protagoras should have talked to tadpoles; but tadpoles evidently do not repay the educational investment, in the way humans are prepared to do.

I have just two remarks to add here. (1) Knowing what we by now do of Plato, we expect him to invoke the art of measurement, which promises rescue from the power of appearance; and so he does, although briefly and not without some obscurity (154B). (2) The opposition of two kinds of existence, sophistic and Socratic, englobes the discussion of relativism in a wider tension between the uninitiated, playfully excluded by Socrates (155E), and a kind of becoming over which the divine power is invoked, namely, coming to be wise. Socratic midwifery is indissociable from the god, for the origin of life and of wisdom, it is hinted, is the same. There are four allusions to the divine in the maieutic passage: "it is the god who compels me to act as midwife" (μαιεύεσθαι με ὁ θεὸς ἀναγκάζει; 150C); the delivery of the soul is done by "the god and me" (ὁ θεός τε καὶ ἐγὼ αἴτιος; 150D); Socrates acting σὺν θεῷ sends some away who are not really pregnant—a playful, ironic note: a hidden reference, perhaps, to Alkibiades (151B); if god wills it, Theaetetus will be able to find what knowledge is (151D). Throughout this passage, the dictum of Protagoras the Wise (as Plato always calls him) is undermined, hollowed out in advance by the fulness of the Socratic profession which precedes it, and which strongly suggests that the human cannot be the ultimate

14. H.-I. Marrou, *A History of Education in Antiquity* (London–New York, 1956), p. 51.

measure of anything, but that a higher kind of weighing and measuring has always the last word. As Socrates says to the youth, Theaetetus,

> Tell me, with reference to the doctrine just expounded, do you not share my amazement at being suddenly exalted to an equality with the wisest man, or even god? Or do you think Protagoras's "measure" applies any less to gods than to men? (162C)

It is only in the *Laws* that the opposition of the human and the divine measure becomes fully articulate.

The Athenian Stranger preludes his imaginary address to the immigrants to the new colony with the claim that age brings keenness of vision with regard to the salvation (σωτηρία) of the state and the blessings the gods have it in their power to bestow.[15] The address opens with the acknowledgement that "the god holds the beginning and end and middle of all things that exist."[16] That is the god's nature and that of divine *Dikē*, which is the criterion for human life, whether in its folly and abandonment by the god (Plato appears yet again to have Alkibiades in mind) or in that likeness to god which is the aim and achievement of those who are his acolytes, since only what follows the measure can be "dear" or "like" to what has the measure within it (ἐμμέτροις), "but let the god be for us the measure of all things, in the highest degree, much more than any man they talk of."[17] One commentator on this passage summarizes its message thus: "Thus the man who is temperate and ordered (*sophron*) will be loved by God, for his measure is attuned to God's measure; while the disordered (*me sophron*) man is unlike God."[18]

A brief remark may be permitted me, to draw into unity the lines of association which run between this passage and some other themes of *Laws*.

First, the opposition of seriousness and play. Human affairs, the Stranger suggests, should not be taken too seriously, for the truly serious matters concern the most serious realities, which by nature are

---

15. Plato, *Laws* IV, 715D.
16. Ibid., 715E: ΑΘ. Ἄνδρες τοίνυν φῶμεν πρὸς αὐτούς, ὁ μὲν δὴ θεός, ὥσπερ καὶ ὁ παλαιὸς λόγος, ἀρχήν τε καὶ τελευτὴν καὶ μέσα τῶν ὄντων ἁπάντων ἔχων, εὐθείᾳ περαίνει κατὰ φύσιν περιπορευόμενος. The old tradition referred to is probably Orphic: the Scholiast preserves the lines Ζεὺς ἀρχή, Ζεὺς μέσσα, Διὸς δ'ἐκ πάντα τέτυκται. See art. "Orphism," in *The Oxford Classicial Dictionary* (Oxford, 1970²), 759–60.
17. Ibid., 716C: Τίς οὖν δὴ πρᾶξις φίλη καὶ ἀκόλουθος θεῷ; μία, καὶ ἕνα λόγον ἔχουσα ἀρχαῖον, ὅτι τῷ μὲν ὁμοίῳ τὸ ὅμοιον ὄντι μετρίῳ φίλον ἂν εἴη, τὰ δ' ἄμετρα οὔτ' ἀλλήλοις οὔτε τοῖς ἐμμέτροις. ὁ δὴ θεὸς ἡμῖν πάντων χρημάτων μέτρον ἂν εἴη μάλιστα, καὶ πολὺ μᾶλλον ἤ πού τις, ὥς φασιν, ἄνθρωπος.
18. E. Voegelin, *Order and History*, vol. 3: *Plato and Aristotle*, p. 254.

the divine. Only the corrupt state of things "in our time" obliges us to take human affairs seriously, because men have forgotten that humans are the playthings of the gods and have inverted the true order of reality; we are puppets for the most part, though having a little of ἀλήθεια too.[19]

Second, the structure of the soul is imaged by Plato in the parable of god as the puppet player (644D–645C). The instinctual and passional pulls within us are controlled by strong and unbreakable cords of iron and metal that pull us in different ways; but the cord attached to the λογισμός, or rational part, is of gold, and goes back to the finger of the god. Being of gold, of course, it is easily snapped by wilful movement, and to be preserved it requires the cooperative, reflective movement of the puppet. It is a poetic and religious symbol of great beauty; and we are reminded by the sun symbolism of the *Laws* (which relays that of *Republic*) that the golden cord, sharing in the colour of the sun, is the symbol of balanced and beautiful nature, of what is most of value within us, the λογισμός, which is kingly and is destined to govern the passions in measured harmony, as divine reason orders the universe.

Plato's faith in the divine measure is the flowering of his Socratic education. It gives impressive articulation to that opposition of divine wisdom and human folly in which the Delphic oracle first instructed Socrates. It takes up into itself the theme of listening to the δαιμόνιον, or existing in obedience to the God. It rejoins the symbol of the divine judgement of souls, which began to be symbolized in the judgement of Socrates by his fellow citizens and was lovingly elaborated by Plato in numerous myths; and the acknowledgement by Plato that the divine is the measure of all leaves the last word on all human things to the god, as Socrates did at the close of his trial. Eric Voegelin writes:

> The *Apology* concludes with the great theme that will run through the work of Plato: "And now it is time for us to go, I to die, and you to live." The philosopher's life toward death and the judgment in eternity separates from the life of the dead souls. And then the pathos of the moment is relieved by the last irony of Socratic ignorance: "Who of us takes the better way, is hidden to all, except to the God."[20]

If I have little to say about the theme of measure in the writings of Aristotle, that is due, not to any paucity of references, but to the inclination of this lecture in the direction of Platonism. Four contexts in

19. Plato, *Laws* 804B; cf. Voegelin, op. cit., vol. 3, p. 232.
20. Voegelin, op. cit., vol. 3, p. 10.

which Aristotle considers μέτρον come easily to mind, and I will say, here, just a word about each of these, in view both of their interest and of their enormous influence.

In a fragment of the lost dialogue *Politicus*, preserved by Syrianus, Aristotle is reported as saying that "the good is the most accurate measure of all things" (πάντων γὰρ ἀκριβέστατον μέτρον τἀγαθόν ἐστιν). This rings very Platonically. No doubt it is a vital testimony to his assimilation and personal formulation of the Platonic measure doctrine while he was a member of the Academy. Cicero tells us that in this dialogue Aristotle included himself as one of the interlocutors; Syrianus implies that he placed this remark on his own lips.[21]

In *Physics* IV Aristotle defines time as "the number of motion according to before and after."[22] This idea roots time in the objectivity of the physical and suggests an absolute time, the measure of the absolute motion, or that of the first sphere. It makes, however, a reference to soul as that which measures the "before" and "after" of movement. This strict attachment of time to motion will be taken over by Averroës, Albert the Great, and Aquinas, and will prove influential throughout the history of Aristoteleanism.

In his ethical thought, Aristotle defines each moral virtue as a mean between extremes, or corresponding vices. Virtue is a rational or intellectual principle of unity which induces form upon the limitless, shapeless thing which is passion or instinct, and the acquisition of moral virtue is the presupposition of the fullest unfolding of the natural teleology of human life, of the rational power in its openness to eternal truth. In the notion of the mean as a measure achieved by the intellect on its path towards the contemplation of the unchanging structure of the cosmos and of the truly first being, we may legitimately find a development of the Platonic μέτρον. This element is a very central part of the Aristotelean heritage.[23]

In a passage of the *Metaphysics* which was to attract the attention of Avicenna and Averroës, as well as Albert the Great, Thomas Aquinas, and Nicholas of Cusa, Aristotle rejects the relativism of Protagoras in Platonic fashion and states that each knowing capacity is measured by its object, so that the ontological basis of our knowledge is secured.[24] He adds that the greatest in a genre is the measure of all, a doctrine of

---

21. The reference is to Aristotle, *Politicus*, Frag. 2, ed. W. D. Ross, p. 64. See also the translation by Ross of the surviving *testimonia: The Works of Aristotle Translated into English*, vol. XII: *Selected Fragments*, pp. 68–71, and the introduction to that work.
22. Aristotle, *Physics* IV, 220a4.
23. Aristotle, *Nicomachean Ethics* II, 2–9.
24. Aristotle, *Metaphysics* X, 1, 1053a30–33.

which St. Thomas was to make use (very much on his own terms), in
the fourth argument for the existence of God.

If we leave aside the Stoic discussions of μέτρον,[25] in order to arrive
(rather breathlessly) at the Neoplatonic, we find that Plotinus has little
to say, whereas Proclus, in the *Elements of Theology*, has a large number
of interesting developments to make.

It is in Plotinus, as one might expect, that the Platonic thought concerning the invisible divine measure of all things finds an eminently
dialectical expression. Immanent to the thought of Plato is the implication that the divine measure of being is the highest causal agency,
the framer of the universe (*Laws* X), the one who allots to each kind of
thing a share in the good. This thought is made explicit by Plotinus:
the One is the first principle and the universal cause of being, the absolute measure of all that exists (μέτρον οὐ μετρούμενον; *Enneads* V, 5,
4, 13). In *Enneads* I, 8, 2, 5, the One is μέτρον πάντων καὶ πέρας.[26]

In *Enneads* II, 4, 8, Plotinus seeks to establish that the underlying
matter must be without form and magnitude, since form and all that
follows upon it must come from the *Idea* through the work of the Reason principle. About the absence of quality there can be no doubt, but
we should not be surprised that quantity also is the work of an outside
power; it is of the nature of measure and number. All that comes
from number and from the νοητόν is on the side of limit, and bestows
limit and settlement and order upon all else, even upon matter, which
is the sheer, unimaginable, unthinkable opposite of limit and defi-
niteness. Yet even illimitableness is generated by the One (II, 4, 15). In

---

25. See art. "Mass," in *Historisches Wörterbuch der Philosophie*, Bd. 5, pp. 807–26;
p. 810: Epicurus, Zeno, and Chrysippus understood the μέτρον doctrine in its ethical
meaning, as referring to the harmony that enters reason through its exclusion of the
emotions (ἀταραξία; ἀπάθεια; αὐτάρκεια). See also W. Kullmann, "Zur Nachwirkung
des *homo-mensura*-Satzes des Protagoras bei Democrit und Epikur," *Archiv für Geschichte
der Philosophie* 51 (1969), pp. 128–44. Cicero proposes *mensura*, not indeed as the highest virtue, for it is not in his thinking the rival of *iustitia* or *sapientia*, but as the expression, in and through the four cardinal virtues, of the agreement of man with nature: *De
officiis* I, xxvii–xxviii, 101–2.

The general articles on the concept "measure" which I have consulted all avoid the
metaphysical dimension of the theme and concentrate upon the ethical, in ancient
times, and the aesthetical in modern (*Historisches Wörterbuch der Philosophie*, Bd. 5,
pp. 807–26); or the geometrical-physical in both ("Misura," *Enciclopedia Filosofica*, vol. 5
[Florence, 1982], 804–9); or the practise and logic of measurement—scales, procedures, numerical laws ("Measurement," in *The Encyclopedia of Philosophy*, ed. P. Edwards,
vol. 5 [1967], pp. 241–50).

26. W. Beierwaltes comments on this idea as follows: "Alles Gestaltete (εἶδος, μορφή)
ist 'gemessen'; das Eine ist gestalt-los (ἀνείδεον), weil Nicht-Etwas, deshalb auch nicht
'gemessen'" (referring to *Enneads* VI, 7, 33, 16 ff.) ("Augustins Interpretation von *Sapientia* 11. 21," *Revue des Études augustiniennes* 15 [1969], pp. 51–61).

genuinely Platonic fashion, Plotinus draws the notion of measure towards form, limit, and intelligibility, the work of reason, allying it with number as a principle of order in the universe.

It is in Proclus, however, that the Platonic theme of the measure finds its most systematic expression in Greek.[27] Gone is the dramatic contest between dialogue and sophistic ἐπίδειξις, between Socratic existence and relativism, for Proclus is intent upon the systematization of the truth in the supremely epistemic form of the theorem. His thoughts on measure are drawn by the very movement of procession and reversion into a meditation upon that causality of higher beings which measures their products by unity and number, and upon the participation of the effects in the causes, according to the μέτρον of their being and their place within the whole hierarchical order of the cosmos. To discuss the twelve or so relevant passages would require an entire lecture.[28] I must be content to set the ideas of Proclus on μέτρον together in rough juxtaposition, in order to convey an impression of his purpose. I shall stay as close to the language of the *Elements* as I can manage.

Perhaps the governing statement occurs in the explanation of the following proposition:

Prop. 39: All that exists reverts, either in respect of its existence only, or in respect of its life, or by way of knowledge also.[29]

Proclus explains: "For as it proceeds, so it reverts; and the μέτρον of its reversion is determined by the μέτρον of its procession."

The three typically Neoplatonic categories of existence, life, and intellect are invoked; and the general law which governs all things in their πρόοδος and their ἐπιστροφή, when applied to intellect, determines that the intellectual creature makes its return through consciousness of the goodness of its cause.

Prop. 52: All that is eternal is a simultaneous whole.[30]

Since the measure of being is also that of activity (ἐνέργεια), the activity of what is eternal will likewise be simultaneous and whole, fixed in the same μέτρον of perfection as its being.

---

27. Proclus, *The Elements of Theology. A Revised Text, with Translation, Introduction and Commentary* by E. R. Dodds (Oxford, 1963¹).
28. For a general philosophical study of the metaphysics of Proclus see W. Beierwaltes, *Proklos. Grundzüge seiner Metaphysik* (Frankfurt am M., 1965). See also the same writer's "Augustins Interpretation von *Sapientia* 11. 21" (referred to in note 26), pp. 54–55.
29. Πᾶν τὸ ὂν ἢ οὐσιωδῶς ἐπιστρέφει μόνον, ἢ ζωτικῶς, ἢ καὶ γνωστικῶς.
30. Πᾶν τὸ αἰώνιον ὅλον ἅμα ἐστίν.

Prop. 117: Each god is a measure of the beings.[31]

The reason is that unity defines and measures all the manifold of existent things, bestowing unity where there would be mere indetermination; that which possesses unity tends of its nature to measure and determine the things in which it is present, as cause.

Prop. 75: Every cause properly so called transcends its effect.[32]

Every cause in the true sense, in as much as it is both more perfect than the effect which comes forth from it, and itself furnishes the μέτρον to the production, transcends whatever it employs in producing, as well as what it produces.

Prop. 136: Of any two gods the more universal, who stands closer to the One, is participated in by a more universal genus of existents.

In commenting on the proposition, Proclus reiterates the truth that all effects receive from their being-causes their unity and their appropriate measure (τὸ ἕν καὶ τὸ οἰκεῖον μέτρον), as an irradiation from those as sources.

Prop. 142: The gods are present alike to all things.[33]

The variation in beings produced is due, not to the unchanging divine natures present to all things, but to the different ways and degrees in which the effects are present to the gods, each order according to its capacity, for participation (μεθέξις) is according to the μέτρον of the presence of the different orders to the divine.

In the explanation of Prop. 156, Proclus affirms that "In the gods, all the unitary measures of all the good things are preexistent and nothing is found in secondary beings which is not preexistent in the divine."[34]

Propositions 198, 199, and 200 concern the different measures of time in (a) things moving perpetually (periods); (b) souls (reincarnation); (c) the first soul, which has the whole of time for its measure.

Prop. 54: Every eternity is a μέτρον of things eternal, and every time of things in time; and these two are the only measures of life and movement in things.[35]

31. Πᾶς θεὸς μέτρον ἐστὶ τῶν ὄντων.
32. Πᾶν τὸ κυρίως αἴτιον λεγόμενον ἐξῄρηται τοῦ ἀποτελέσματος.
33. Πᾶσι μὲν οἱ θεοὶ πάρεισιν ὡσαύτως.
34. καὶ ὅλως πάντων τῶν ἀγαθῶν τὰ ἑνοειδῆ μέτρα παρ' ἐκείνοις προείληπται.
35. Πᾶς αἰὼν μέτρον ἐστὶ τῶν αἰωνίων καὶ πᾶς χρόνος τῶν ἐν χρόνῳ· καὶ δύο ταῦτα μέτρα μόνα ἐστὶν ἐν τοῖς οὖσι τῆς ζωῆς καὶ τῆς κινήσεως.

The Divine as the Measure of Being   99

Turning now from Proclus in the direction of one who assimilated his thought and relayed it silently to the Greek Christian world, I choose only one passage from the Pseudo-Areopagite in order to illuminate the absorption of pagan Neoplatonism and its constitutive part in the legacy of antiquity to the Middle Ages.

Chapter 4 of the *Divine Names* is a contemplation of the name "*Agathon*" and the names closely associated with it—"light" and "beauty," among others.[36] Plotinus's image of the Good as pouring forth a multiplicity of rays into being is adopted and the variety of the receptions of being-light are enumerated, beginning with the pure intellects in their different orders. Human souls participate according to their measure in the illuminations of the good, as in their different ways do living things and material, unsouled things. This is the same hierarchy as that of Proclus. Measurement and order are given to the visible cosmos by the sun, the image of the archetypal good that is the source and creator of all order; and Pseudo-Dionysius gathers into a single phrase the Platonic and Neoplatonic symbols of the transcendence of the Source over the product: the Good "is the μέτρον of the universe and its eternity, its numerical principle, its order, its power, its cause, and its end."[37] All creatures in time are measured by eternity (X, 3) and participate in unity and being, according to the ἀναλογία or receptive capacity of their being, which likewise ensures their place in the hierarchical outpouring of things, their activity, and the way of their turning back towards their source. God is the μέτρον of being (V, 8): all that is, is measured through him, the one universal μέτρον; but He himself, being superessential, is unmeasurable.[38]

It is a matter of recurrent interest and delight to the historian of medieval thought to trace the distributaries of Greek Neoplatonic philosophy in their passing into Latin, to study the differences of nuance brought to the themes by the translation of Greek terms into Latin, and to view the interweaving of thoughts, which flow variously through the Pseudo-Dionysius, Boethius, Augustine, the *Liber de causis*, and many lesser channels, always with the same fundamental thrusts, but

---

36. Καὶ ὅτι τῷ εἶναι τὸ ἀγαθὸν, ὡς οὐσιῶδες ἀγαθὸν, εἰς πάντα τὰ ὄντα διατείνει τὴν ἀγαθότητα. Καὶ γὰρ ὥσπερ ὁ καθ'ἡμᾶς ἥλιος, . . . πᾶσι τοῖς οὖσιν ἀναλόγως ἐφίησι τὰς τῆς ὅλης ἀγαθότητος ἀκτῖνας. Pseudo–Dionysius Areopagita, *De Div. Nom.*, c. 4, 1, PG 3, 693B.

37. Καὶ μέτρον ἐστὶ τῶν ὄντων, καὶ αἰών, καὶ ἀριθμὸς, καὶ τάξις, καὶ περιοχὴ, καὶ αἰτία, καὶ τέλος. Ibid., c. 4, 4, 697C.

38. Καὶ ἐν αὐτῷ ἐστι τὸ εἶναι, καὶ οὐκ αὐτὸς ἐν τῷ εἶναι· Καὶ αὐτός ἐστι τοῦ εἶναι καὶ αἰὼν, καὶ ἀρχὴ, καὶ μέτρον, πρὸ οὐσίας ὢν καὶ ὄντος, καὶ αἰῶνος, καὶ πάντων οὐσιοποιὸς ἀρχὴ, καὶ μεσότης, καὶ τελευτή. Ibid., V, 8, 824A.

variegated, as the thought passes through the more or less refractive medium of the individual thinker, often to rejoin and reinforce in writings of the Latin Middle Ages an inspiration derived from a parallel distributary. In a number of important medieval thinkers, the ideas of Proclus concerning μέτρον, coming through the Pseudo-Dionysius, rejoined the theme of *mensura* and *modus*, which the very different and individual Neoplatonism of St. Augustine had transmitted to the Latin Church and to its schools. We can thus study in the *mensura* theme a process of transmission and reception which has parallels in ideas such as participation, illumination, and light.

But first a philological note.

The Greek μετρεῖν and Latin *metiri* had a common root in Sanskrit *MA*, measure. In classical Latin, *metior* had a number of senses: to mete out or deal out (food, etc.); to measure a distance or area; metaphorically and poetically, to travel a distance; and again, metaphorically, to judge one thing by another, to estimate.[39] The noun *mensus* came to mean a norm. From *mensura* derived nouns, adjectives, and adverbs: *mensuratio, mensurabilis, mensuralis, mensuraliter*, and, in late Latin, *mensurator* (first occurrence in St. Jerome, on Ps. 44), the new verbal form *mensurare*, and the resulting adverb *mensurate*. *Metrum*, or metre, was the measure of verse, exactly parallel to the "metrical" meaning of Greek μέτρον, which is akin to *modus* in music; and *modus* and its forms and derivatives likewise appear to originate from the same root. This metrical sense allows a natural and easy affiliation between the idea of measure and that of consonance, harmony, agreement; a great deal of St. Augustine's discussion of time as well as of the examples he develops, of measuring time by a movement of the soul, are made possible by just this close alliance of meanings. And we can read in Aquinas that "the truth of our intellect is measured by the thing which is outside the soul, for our intellect is said to be true because it is in agreement with the thing."[40] When Aquinas recurs to the idea of measure, it is often to make a *glissement* to *proportio, consonatio, adaequatio,* and *comparatio*.

Finally, the derivative forms of *modus*—*moderatio, modestia,* and *moderare*—taken in an ethical sense, are found in Augustine. *Dimensio*

---

39. Lewis and Short, *A Latin Dictionary* (Oxford, 1975); A. Forcellini, *Lexicon totius Latinitatis* (Padova, 1913); A. Blaise, *Dictionnaire latin-français des auteurs chrétiens* (Strasbourg, 1954; reprinted with one fasc. of *Addenda*, Brepols, Turnhout, 1962, 1975); idem, *Lexicon Latinitatis Medii Aevi* (Corp. Christ. Contin. Mediaevalis) (Brepols, Turnhout, 1975).

40. St. Thomas Aquinas, *Summa contra gentiles* I, c. 62: "Veritas enim nostri intellectus mensuratur a re quae est extra animam, ex hoc enim intellectus noster verus dicitur quod *consonat* rei."

comes from *mensura;* however, *mens* does not, *pace* St. Albert, St. Thomas, Giles of Rome, and many other writers of the Middle Ages.[41]

A German scholar, Krings, has claimed that Augustine made of Wisdom 11:21 something that became "ein Grundsatz einer Ontologie des Mittelalters."[42] The legitimacy of this claim depends upon the basic qualification of order which the idea of creation *in mensura, numero et pondere* constitutes; and we know just how important that notion of order was for Augustine, from the early and programmatic *De ordine* right up until the *De civitate Dei*.[43] When we begin to follow the reminiscences of Wisdom 11:21 in Augustine's writings, taken in chronological order, the profusion of associated notions produces an effect of bewilderment, and the difficulty of attempting to draw out the single strand of *mensura* from the rich tapestry of interwoven motifs becomes almost oppressive.[44] I can do no more than enumerate

41. St. Thomas Aquinas, *De veritate* X, 1, resp.: "Nomen mentis a mensurando est sumptum." Cf. *In I Sent.*, d. 3, q. 5, a. 1, solutio; *Summa theol.* I, q. 79, a. 9, ad 4; *In Matth.* 22 (Parma 10, 204). Albert the Great frequently repeats the false etymology "mens a mensura dicitur." Wéber ("*Commensuratio* de l'agir par l'objet d'activité et par le sujet agent chez Albert le Grand, Thomas d'Aquin et Maître Eckhart," in *Miscellanea Mediaevalia* 16/1, pp. 43 ff.; see note 53) suggests that Albert may have relied upon the Burgundio version of Damascene, *De fide orthodoxa:* "mens diiudicans opinionem sive vera est, sive falsa, iudicat veritatem. Unde et mens dicitur a metiendo et excogitando et diiudicando. Quod igitur iudicatum est et determinatum vere, intellectus dicitur" (ed. E. Buytaert, 134, 45 ff.). Wéber has noticed that the corresponding passage in the Greek text (PG 94, 941C–D) speaks of διάνοια. Peri, in the same volume of *Miscell. Med.*, p. 20, reports an alternative source: the *Epitomies* of Virgilius Maro Grammaticus (7th cent.): "mens de metiendo dicta, quando subtiliorum sensuum mensuram aperit animae." *Mens* appears to be related to *mentio, memini,* and even *mentior;* but none of these comes from the same root as μέτρον, μετρεῖν/metrum, metiri, mensura (etc.), namely, the Indo-European *metro-m (= earlier form) and *med-tro-m (later form; both conjectural reconstructions of F. de Saussure). Brugmann attached μέτρον directly to the Sanskrit *mātram mātrā* (= measure). The difference between these two etymologies is slight and is due to analysis only; see Émile Boisacq, *Dictionnaire étymologique de la langue grecque* (Heidelberg, 1950³), pp. 630–31.
42. H. Krings, "Das Sein und die Ordnung. Eine Skizze zur Ontologie des Mittelalters," *Deutsche Vierteljahrsschrift für Literaturwissenschaft und Geistesgeschichte* 18 (1940), pp. 237–49; p. 238.
43. J. Rief, *Der Ordobegriff des jungen Augustinus,* Abhandlungen zur Moraltheologie, Tübingen (Paderborn, 1962), 372 pp.
44. W. Beierwaltes, in the article referred to in note 26. W. J. Roche ("Measure, Number and Weight in Saint Augustine," *The New Scholasticism* 15 [1941], pp. 350–76) collects and paraphrases the main texts of Augustine which refer to Wis. 11:21. O. Du Roy explains the meaning of the triad for the trinitarian structure of the creation: *L'intelligence de la foi en la Trinité selon saint Augustin* (Paris, 1966), pp. 279–81.
The major Augustinian passages are as follows: *De natura boni* I; *De Trinitate* III, 9, 18; *De Genesi ad litt.* IV, 3 ff.; V, 22, 43; *De civitate Dei* V, 11; XI, 28, 30 ff., 35; XII, 19, 20; *De libero arbitrio* II, 20; *De Genesi contra Manichaeos* I, 16, 26, 31, 32; *Enarr. in Psalmos* CXVIII, 20, 2, 14; CXLVI, 11, 24; *Contra Faustum* XX, 7; XXI, 6; *In Iohann. tractatus* I, 13.

those associations, in order to evoke the affiliations of the term, and must rest content with three remarks of a more general kind, the very inadequacy of which may suggest the latent fertility of the nexus. Like the thought of St. Bonaventure, his great medieval disciple, that of St. Augustine is a circular universe, in which each significant theme may be taken in turn as a relative centre, around which the others may be viewed as moving in constellations; each time the exercise is done, the admiration of the student for the intellectual and spiritual fertility of the great doctor grows that much greater.

Mensura, numerus, pondus: each of these has a definite kernel of meaning in Augustine's thought, together with a rich series of cognate notions. Taken together as a triad, they call forth that series of triadic formulae through which, in *De Trinitate*, Augustine seeks to point to the mysterious life of God and to the triadic structure of *mens*, made in his image. The terms of the triad vary, almost (one is tempted to suggest) systematically, even in the early works:[45]

De Genesi contra Manichaeos I, 15, 26:

mensura	numerus	pondus
mensura	numerus	ordo
summa mensura	summus numerus	summus ordo

In *De libero arbitrio* III, 12, 25, *naturae moderatae* takes the place of *mensura*, *naturae formatae* of *numerus*, and of course *naturae ordinatae* of *ordo/pondus*. Elsewhere, in *De vera religione*, the triad has become

esse   speciem habere   ordinatissime administrari

or even

unum (unitas)   species   ordo

Ordo can be replaced by *caritas*, a possibility replete with the development of Augustine's intellectual and spiritual life. *De Genesi ad litteram* and *De civitate Dei* will show further variations. The coordinates for the *ordo* concept, in turn, involve practically every significant term in the early thought of Augustine, as Josef Rief has patiently and ably demonstrated: *ratio; species; numerus; sapientia; mensura; modus; modulatio; unitas; esse; bonum.*

I propose to take the second group (*mensura* and *modus*) and to glance briefly and illustratively at part I of the *De natura boni*, to gather the thrust of thought which they carry.[46]

In this brief, carefully finished and metaphysically profound treatise

---

45. Rief, op. cit., pp. 176 ff.   46. Augustine, *De natura boni* I, 1–25.

against Manichaean dualism, Augustine relies upon the *modus, species,* and *ordo* of creation as the guideline of his thought, and these words and synonyms for them recur on almost every page. Whatever is, is good, for every nature, in so far as it is a nature, is good and cannot but come from the sovereign and true God; unequal participation in the divine nature does not compare with the good of being, since all are alike created. This fundamental statement is worked out in a series of contexts (grades of creation; whole and part; mutability; evil). From God is every measure, great or small, every form, great or small, every order, great or small, and the degree of measure, of form-beauty, and of order it possesses, within the grades of creation. *Modus, species, ordo* (which we may regard as a triad that encloses *mensura, numerus,* and *pondus*), are "tamquam generalia bona ... in rebus a Deo factis" (III, 3); hence God is above all measure, species, or order, from whom all measure, species, and order come. Where, however, this triad does not exist we find, not some residual evil that must be traced back to an evil principle, but nothing at all; if corruption or mutability removes this triad, then nothing remains of what was, and was good for as long as it was. The beauty of each thing and of the whole of creation is designated by the triad; and even matter does not proceed from a dark power of evil, for as it represents only the barest capacity for being (and we know how Augustine came back again and again to meditate on the place of this *informis materia* in God's productive work), it certainly is a good, if it is anything at all. Augustine continues through physical and moral evil, to vindicate the goodness of being against what had for years been his own belief, and closes the first part of his work with praise of God, who has no limit, no opposite, no measure (I, 22).

Rief, whom I mentioned earlier, has well said:

As likeness of the highest measure, the measure of the creature signifies immediately to be a unity, and by being a unity, to be *esse.* This *esse,* which is interchangeable with the concept of *modus,* will be understood by Augustine as a reference to the cause activating the being. Since finally only a single cause can be named for all being, the concept of *modus* also contains always the ordination of the many to unity. In other words, "modus est pater ordinis."[47]

In *De Genesi ad litteram* IV, 7, Augustine will say that *mensura, numerus,* and *pondus* are not created as such, but are in the divine nature, "qui terminat omnia et ordinat omnia," being *mensura sine mensura.*[48]

Even in the early *De beata vita,* Augustine is already turning the

---

47. Rief, op. cit., p. 223.   48. *De genesi ad litteram* IV, 3, 7.

creationist metaphysics into ethics.[49] All things have their measure; from that comes the ethical demand to measure the attention and the love given to things, in terms of the measure of being present in them, or according to the ontological intensity of each thing. In the dialogue, it is Monica who enunciates the principle "It will not be . . . by these things that he is happy but by moderation of his soul," since happiness comes, not from excess of things, but from a limit and moderation of desire, a *modus* that includes *moderatio*. *Modus* is given the sense of a limitation over against excess and deficiency, both of which appear as *egestas*, by comparison with the fulness found in the wise existence. A *mensura* is allotted to each reality, bodily or spiritual, through its participation in the divine measure, which is measureless, the absolute fulness, *summus modus*.

We noted above that *pondus* can be replaced by *caritas* in the triadic ordering of terms. Now, when we read the triad *mensura, numerus, pondus* in this way, giving each word its weight (*mensura*, as limit defined by the cause, *ipsum esse; numerus*, meaning above all the unity of a being, but referring also to the transcendent One; and *pondus*, in the rich Augustinian sense of the gravitation of each thing to its natural place of rest), we can begin to understand the significance of the symbol as a whole for Augustine's reflections upon love. According to what we may call the realism of Augustine's doctrine, this order (for the triad always denotes order), the order of love, is given in being itself, in its diversity and interconnectedness: "the disposition of things equal and unequal, which grants its place to each."[50]

Human love, that gravitational force which moves us ineluctably in search of rest, is an inexhaustible source of action. Its capacity is unfailing, but ambivalent, for love is cause of crime as well as of heroism. To become ordered love, it must be unified by a will which has taken the true order of reality, as it is, to be its own internal ordering principle and which then accords to each thing of the varied objects of our experience only so much of desire and love as is that thing's due, granted the measure of its participation in being. Ordered love loves material things for their intrinsic goodness, usefulness, and place within the entire order of goodness and beauty, which is creation; spiritual beings on a plane equal to oneself, in ideal equality and unity; and God, the unmeasured measure of all that is, without mea-

---

49. *De beata vita* II, 11: "Non ergo . . . illis rebus, sed animi sui moderatione beatus est."

50. *De civitate Dei* XIX, 13: "parium dispariumque rerum sua cuique tribuens loca dispositio."

sure. "Each is such as that which he loves. Do you love the earth? You will be earth. Do you love God? What am I to say, you will be God."[51]

"There the measure is to love without measure [*Ipse ibi modus est sine modo amare*]." This is the way in which Augustine took up a spiritual seed that was latent in Plato's reverence for the divine measure, and poured it into his own interpretation of the evangelical precept. "Delight is like a weight for the soul. Therefore delight orders the soul ... where delight is, there is the treasure; but where the heart is, there is happiness or misery."[52]

The development given by Augustine to the Platonic theme of the measure is eminently dialectical, in agreement with the whole style of his thought. Against the Manichaean belief that the two principles of good and evil somehow limit and measure each other, Augustine argues that Good has no opposite, any more than Being has an opposite, and he expresses this insight in the paradoxical concept of a "measureless measure of all measures." In his most mature work on creation, the great literal commentary on Genesis, Augustine's thinking rises methodically from the outer material order, through the interior life of reason, to the superior—from the "measure in the things we measure, the number in the things we number, the weight in the things we weigh," upwards in being through the measure of our ordered, conscious rationality, shown in the principle of orderliness that guides action, in judgement, and in love, attempting, as it were, to rise above all things that can be measured, in order to glimpse with the mind the measure with which all created realities are measured, but which is itself without measure, having no origin. That measure without measure is also number without number, since it forms all things without itself being formed, and weight without weight, since it draws all things to itself without being drawn to any other being. This "rising in the mind," as Augustine calls it, recalls all the other applications of dialectic in his writings, notably the dialectical movement of the mind from external change, through internal temporal measurement of that change, to the eternally present measure of all self-presence in duration.

*

51. Quoted by É. Gilson, *The Christian Philosophy of St. Augustine* (London, 1961), p. 139 n.: "Talis est quisque qualis eius dilectio est. Terram diligis? Terra eris. Deum diligis? Quid dicam, Deus eris."
52. *De musica* VI, 11, 29: "Delectatio quippe quasi pondus est animae. Delectatio ergo ordinat animam ... ubi delectatio, ibi thesaurus: ubi autem cor, ibi beatitudo aut miseria."

Only in relatively recent years have studies begun to build up concerning the measure theme in writers of the Middle Ages.[53] It has become apparent that we are dealing with a strand of thought of major importance, and one that is represented in some way or other in almost every significant theologian and philosopher of the period between Augustine and Nicholas of Cusa. The presence of the triad *mensura, numerus, pondus* has been noted, for instance, in the thought of Claudianus Mamertus, where it is invoked to underline the orderliness of creation and the difference between the material order and the spiritual soul.[54] Cassiodorus connects the power of arithmetic with the work of the creator as described in Wisdom 11:21, and Isidore of Seville makes the same connection.[55] These seminal authors assured the widespread diffusion of the measure theme in subsequent centuries, reinforcing in this way the decisive influence of St. Augustine. Rhabanus Maurus, the first Latin commentator on the Book of Wisdom, saw in the famous verse a statement of the justice of the creator and of the orderliness of the universe.[56] The presence of the same triad in *De natura corporis et animae* of William of St. Thierry has been noted, but as yet no overall treatment of its development by authors of the twelfth century has been given. When we turn to the thirteenth century, on the other hand, studies become more abundant: of Robert Grosseteste, who gave a distinctively mathematical sense to Wisdom 11:21 and praised God as *numerator primus et certissimus*, and as *mensurator*;[57] of Albert the Great, in whose thought the active measuring power of the human mind receives such special importance and appears to prefigure the Neoplatonic idealism of his German successors Thierry of Freiberg and Meister Eckhart;[58] and above all of St. Thomas Aquinas, to whose thought we will turn in a moment.

The interest of a good number of historians of fourteenth-century Scholasticism has been directed for many years to the efforts of Aristotelean commentators and of the *Mertonenses*, in particular, to measure qualitative change, or the intension and remission of forms.[59] In

---

53. See especially the studies contained in *Mensura. Mass, Zahl, Zahlensymbolik im Mittelalter*, ed. A. Zimmermann, *Miscellanea Mediaevalia* 16/2 (Berlin–New York, 1983–84).

54. I. Peri, "*Omnia mensura et numero et pondere disposuisti:* Die Auslegung von Weish. 11, 20 in der lateinischen Patristik," in *Miscell. Med.* 16/1, pp. 1–21; p. 16.

55. Ibid., p. 17.

56. *Commentarium in librum Sapientiae* 2, 10, PL 109, 723.

57. J. McEvoy, *The Philosophy of Robert Grosseteste* (Oxford, 1982), pp. 176–79, 214–15.

58. E.-H. Wéber, in article referred to in note 41; pp. 41–64.

59. J. A. Weisheipl, "Ockham and the Mertonians," ch. 16 in *The History of the Univer-*

the fifteenth century, it was above all by the towering dialectical genius of Cardinal Nicholas of Cusa that the various traditional Neoplatonic ideas on measure were revivified; they became in fact one of the focal points of his effort to think consistently the relationships of the mind to all objects of understanding and of the creation to the absolute being of God.[60]

To return now to St. Thomas Aquinas: the central importance of the idea of measure for both his metaphysics and his psychology, or knowledge theory, has recently been studied.[61] The development made by Aquinas of the measure theme offers an irreplaceable point of view from which the ontological basis of his epistemological teaching can be grasped. As we might expect, Aquinas relies heavily on Aristotle in matters of epistemology (e.g., that question as to whether knowledge measures its objects, or is measured by these), while at the metaphysical level (the discussion of the divine intellect as the measure of all created things) his thought is very close to that of his Neoplatonic sources, especially perhaps to the Pseudo-Dionysius and the *Liber de causis*.[62]

The computerized concordance of the works of Aquinas has made it at last possible, in principle, to disclose the omnipresence of "mea-

---

sity of Oxford, vol. 1: *The Early Oxford Schools*, ed. J. I. Catto (Oxford, 1984), pp. 607–58; see also the literature he cites there.

60. In the thought of Cusanus, the Proclean designation of God as *mensura omnium* is tightly interlocked with the themes of divine infinity, of God as *magnitudo maxima et minima*, and of God as *supra coincidentiam oppositorum*. Oddly enough, the enormous secondary literature on Cusanus in the German language does not appear to have highlighted the importance of the *mensura* theme in his thinking. There can be no doubt that the study of his discussions of the Protagorean dictum alone would prove of great interest; for instance, *De Beryllo*, ch. V: "Tertio notabis dictum Protagorae hominem esse rerum mensuram." Nicholas can accept that without difficulty, since "in se homo reperit quasi in ratione mensurante omnia creata." Cf. chs. XI, XVIII, XXXVII–XXXIX. The only useful relevant studies known to me are: M. Stadler, "Zum Begriff der *mensuratio* bei Cusanus. Ein Beitrag zur Ortung der cusanischen Erkenntnislehre," in *Miscell. Med.* 16/1, pp. 118–31; M. Alvarez-Gomez, *Die verborgene Gegenwart des Unendlichen bei Nikolaus von Kues*, Epimeleia. Beiträge zur Philosophie 10 (Munich-Salzburg, 1968), pp. 52–53.

61. H. Seidl, "Bemerkungen zu Erkenntnis als Massverhältnis bei Aristoteles und Thomas von Aquin," in *Miscell. Med.* 16/1, pp. 32–42; G. Isaye, *La théorie de la mesure et l'existence d'un maximum selon saint Thomas*, Archives de philosophie 16/1 (Paris, 1940; not available to me).

62. E. P. Mahoney, "Metaphysical Foundations of the Hierarchy of Being according to Some Late-Medieval and Renaissance Philosophers," pp. 165–257 in P. Morewedge, ed., *Philosophies of Existence Ancient and Medieval* (New York, 1982). The footnotes of this wide-ranging article are of exceptional richness.

sure" and its cognate and derivative forms in his thought.[63] A very great quantity of these references accompany and derive from his reading of Aristotle. The present essay addresses itself principally to the Platonic origin and meaning of the measure theme, rather than to the Aristotelean (which, admittedly, both in its ethical side and in the discussion of knowledge derives from Plato); despite that emphasis and the selection of material which it imposes, however, the epistemological relevance of the *mensura* theme in Aquinas must be summarized here, because of its relevance to his metaphysical doctrine concerning the relationship of creation to the divine intellect, in which the basis of both being and knowledge for the whole of creation is to be located.

In *Metaphysics* Iota, 1, Aristotle remarks that knowledge and perception are called the measure of things, because through their agency we come to know something.[64] In fact, however, knowledge and perception are measured by other things, rather than being their measure; for when we know something, it is as if someone else measured us and we came to know how big or small we are, by seeing that the measure was applied so-and-so many times to us. In his commentary on this portion of the *Metaphysics*, St. Thomas develops this rather dialectical thought of Aristotle.[65] He grants that knowledge is in some way akin to measuring, since it results in the making known of some object, but he maintains at the same time that in a truer sense the mind is dependent upon the object of knowledge and hence is measured by that object: "for every thing is measured by that upon which it depends."[66] In coming to know objects, whether through the senses or through the intellect, it is more the case that we are measured by those objects than that we measure them, because the objects of knowledge are like a measuring instrument which is applied to us from without. Just as when we want to know our height we make use of a measure and apply it so many times, so knowledge is more like being measured by having a measure applied to us from outside, than actively measuring. In agreement with Aristotle, Aquinas wishes to restrict the sense of the Protagorean dictum and give it a meaning that is fully acceptable within his own framework of thought.[67] In the per-

---

63. *Index Thomisticus*, ed. R. Busa (Stuttgart, 1975), Sectio II, *Concordantia Prima*, vol. 13, pp. 851–77.
64. Aristotle, *Metaphysics* Iota 1, 1053b31.
65. St. Thomas, *Comm. in X Met.*, lect. 2 (Marietti ed., n. 1937).
66. Ibid. *In V Met.*, lect. 17 (Marietti ed., n. 1027): "nam ab eo quaelibet res mensuratur, a quo ipsa dependet."
67. Aristotle, loc. cit.; cf. 1062b11; Aquinas, *In X Met.*, nn. 1956–59.

spective of his realist epistemology, human knowledge cannot be the measure of things in an absolute or unrestricted sense, but only in the very general metaphysical sense which he is prepared to allow.[68] It is only in the case of artistic creation that man's knowledge is in the truest sense the measure of the production.[69]

Aquinas seeks to reconcile the two Aristotelean statements (concerning knowledge as the measure of things, and things as the measure of knowing), in the following manner, in order to safeguard the roles of object and subject of knowing. Each of them applies legitimately to one aspect of the process of knowing. The things do serve as the measure for the knowing subject, but they are known *ad modum cognoscentis*, or *per modum recipientis*. In the first place, the objectivity of knowledge is secured by the doctrine that things are in no way dependent in their being upon the knowing subject, but are independent beings which determine our knowledge, without being taken up into it and losing their ontologically independent status.[70]

When, however, we consider knowledge no longer from the side of the object but from the psychological aspect, the measuring relationship between thing and soul is reversed. The soul, of course, in its knowing is passive before the object, for as a spiritual power it exerts no physical operation upon that object: the action itself of knowing, whether taken at the sensible or taken at the intellectual level, remains within the soul as an immanent act—one, therefore, which leaves the external reality unchanged. The passivity of the soul with regard to the objects of knowledge is, of course, in no way a physical passivity, as is the case with purely material things, but a specifically psychic receptivity, consisting in the passing of the soul from its first act to a second act or activity. From this point of view, therefore, the relationship between object and subject in knowledge is not that of an active to a purely passive capacity, but more a relationship between two active agents. Nevertheless, the passing of the soul from potentiality, as a first act, to the act of knowledge, as a second act, is made possible only through its dependence upon the object of cognition. The relationship between

---

68. "Et sic sicut cubitus exterius appositus est mensura quantitatis corporalis nostrae, ita res scitae, vel per sensum apprehensae, sunt mensurae per quas potest sciri utrum vere cognoscamus aliquid per sensum vel per intellectum." Ibid., n. 1958.

69. "Si qua vero scientia est quae est causa rei scitae, oportebit quod sit eius mensura. Ut scientia artificis est mensura artificiatorum." Ibid., n. 1959.

70. "Non enim quia nos aliquid sentimus aut scimus, ideo sic est in rerum natura. Sed quia sic est in rerum natura, ideo vere aliquid scimus aut sentimus, ut dicitur in nono Metaphysicorum. Et sic accidit nobis, quod in sentiendo et sciendo mensuramur per res quae extra nos sunt." Ibid., n. 1956.

object and subject is a one-sided relationship of measuring and being measured, since the object is best thought of as a measure, which itself remains unchanged by the soul's active reception of it.

When we turn from the psychological to the ontological domain and consider the relationship of created realities to the divine intellect, that is to say, to absolute being, bearing in mind that in the simplicity of the divine nature being and knowing are wholly identical, we find we can best define the relationship of creatures to God as a one-sided one of knowing and measuring. In the *Sentences* commentary already, Aquinas says the following: "Therefore the divine intellect is, as the first measure, not measured; a thing is a second measure, (which is) measured; but our intellect is measured and does not measure."[71] This is a very fundamental statement of his thinking about the relationship of infinite being to creation and of the human subject to both. The finite or proportionate objects of the human mind are placed into existence by the divine measure, and the entirety of creation thus stands as an intermediary between the divine, universal measure and the human mind, revealing the divine origin of all finite reality to the human subject. The divine understanding (*intelligere*) is elsewhere described as "the measure and cause of every other being and every other intellect [*mensura et causa omnis alterius esse et omnis alterius intellectus*]."[72] This thought is of a piece with the foregoing: Aquinas concludes from his statement of the universal divine causality that just as knowledge at our level consists in the conformity of the mind with its principle, namely, its objects, those objects or realities are, in turn, conformed to their principle, the divine mind. He is then enabled to employ the relationship of the human knowing capacities to their proportionate objects as an analogy for thinking the relationship of creatures to their originating cause. The one-sided relationship between the mind and its objects, whereby those objects are the active measure of the mind, without being affected or changed in their own being by being known, serves as an analogy for the absolutely one-sided relationship between the divine intellect, as the ontological basis of all created being and intelligibility, and the things which God has brought forth into existence. Of course, the analogy is incomplete, for the one-sidedness of the relationship between the ob-

---

71. "Sic ergo intellectus divinus est ut mensura prima, non mensurata; res autem est mensura secunda, mensurata; intellectus autem noster est mensuratus et non mensurans." *In Sent.*, d. 19, q. 5, a. 2; cf. *De veritate*, q. 1, a. 2, in corp., where almost the same words are used. Cf. *Summa theol.* I, q. 16, aa. 1–7.

72. *Summa theol.* I, q. 16, a. 5, in corp. and ad 2.

jects of knowledge and the mind must be qualified, as was said above, by the acknowledgement that the human intellect is an active recipient of the forms impressed upon it by the objects of knowledge, whereas there is no preexistent, active recipient of the act of creation. With this qualification, however, the analogy between the human intellect and its objects of knowledge provides a partial metaphysical understanding of the dependence of finite beings upon the infinite act of being, upon which they depend for existence and for intelligibility.

The ontological relationship between creation and God must be conceived as a real relationship when it is taken from the side of the creation, since apart from God nothing is or can be; from the side of absolute being, however, the relationship is constituted purely by our thinking, since God and creation are not proportionate partners in being, and the fulness of all that is, *ipsum esse subsistens* as Aquinas terms it, is not added to nor subtracted from, nor intrinsically qualified by the production of finite beings.[73] The divine plenitude is determinant of the finite beings which God freely posits in being without any precondition, but those finite participations cannot correlatively determine or modify the fulness from which they come, any more than human knowledge, which is determined and brought into act by its objects, could be conceived as codeterminant of the structure of those objects, taken in themselves. The subject-object relationship, therefore, suggests itself to St. Thomas as a privileged analogical model for understanding (in so far as we can understand it) the asymmetrical nature of that relationship, which is really constitutive of creation, while being purely logical or rational, when it is considered as holding between finite being and its infinite cause.

It is, then, in taking his cue from Aristotle that Aquinas initiates his development of the *mensura* theme. However, here as elsewhere in his thought, when he comes to the strictly metaphysical domain he leaves Aristotle far behind and rejoins a series of reflections that derive from his Neoplatonic sources: the hierarchy of being; God as the measure of the whole scale of being; participation and causality. Even when Aquinas uses ideas taken from Aristotle, such as, for instance, that the unit is the true measure in the realm of quantity, he does so in ways that Aristotle himself could not have recognized, for he speaks, just as

73. *Summa theol.* I, q. 45, a. 3: "Utrum creatio sit aliquid in creatura," in corp.: "Unde relinquitur quod creatio in creatura non sit nisi relatio quaedam ad creatorem, ut ad principium sui esse." Ibid., ad 1: "dicendum quod creatio active significata significat actionem divinam, quae est eius essentia cum relatione ad creaturam. Sed relatio in Deo ad creaturam non est realis, sed secundum rationem tantum. Relatio vero creaturae ad Deum est relatio realis."

any Neoplatonist would, of the One as the measure of all that is: the One is present to each thing or reality, analogously as unity is present in every number.[74]

In the *Sentences* commentary, Aquinas claims that the term *mensura* can be transferred (*transsumptum*) to all *genera*, so that what is first, most simple, and most perfect in each genus is said to be the measure of everything else in that genus.[75] It is according as a thing "magis accedit ad ipsum [i.e., to the measure] vel recedit" that it has more or less of being. Now, in the genus of substances it is God who is the most perfect and simple being and who is, therefore, the measure of all substances, and hence of the entire realm of being, including accidental being. These key ideas of Aquinas turn up in a number of his works. The *quarta via*, for instance, invokes the idea just now outlined, even though one will look there in vain for the actual term *mensura*.[76]

If the term *genus* is understood strictly, then, of course, God is not in any genus: the absolute measure of being measures all finite beings from beyond. Aquinas does indeed attempt to express the varied participation of the different grades of being in God through the two ideas of God as the measure and of the approach of the thing in greater or lesser degree to the divine perfection, that is, to being itself. The *modus essendi* of each creature is a contracted participation in the divine being; in this sense, the finite *modus* is the causal effect of the infinite *mensura*. However, the language of closer and more remote approximation does not imply that the measure of all being is to be thought of as the highest in a proportionate series or in a genus, because there is an *infinita distantia* between God and every creature. God is the measure of all things, simply by the fact that a thing approaches the divine nature in the measure that it has being, and creatures imitate or participate in being in different ways and degrees. God is not in any genus, nor can he be reduced to any genus as its principle, since he is not a measure proportionate to something or other (*mensura proportionata mensuratis*).[77]

---

74. *In I Sent.*, d. 8, q. 4, a. 2, ad 3: cf. *QQ. Disp. De potentia Dei*, q. 7, a. 3, in corp. and ad 7: "licet Deus non pertineat ad genus substantiae quasi in genere contentum, sicut species vel individuum sub genere continentur, potest tamen dici quod sit in genere substantiae per reductionem, sicut principium, et sicut punctum est in genere quantitatis continuae, et unitas in genere numeri; et per hunc modum est mensura substantiarum omnium, sicut unitas numerorum."

75. *In I Sent.*, Prol., q. 2, a. 2, ad 2; cf. d. 8, q. 4, a. 1.

76. V. De Couesnongle, "Mesure et causalité dans la *quarta via*," *Revue Thomiste* 58 (1958), pp. 55–75, 244–84.

77. *Summa theol.* I, q. 3, a. 5, in corp.; cf. ad 2: "obiectio illa procedit de mensura proportionata: hanc enim oportet esse homogeneam mensurato. Deus autem non est men-

The doctrine of God as the measure of all substances, when it is properly understood and is combined with the analogy of the presence of unity in every number, allows both the transcendence and the immanence of God to come to an adequate metaphysical expression, in so far as that is possible, for it emphasizes at once the transcendence of the divine measure, in which alone the total simplicity of being is found, and the immanence of the divine measure within each participated grade of being and each individual reality, in the same way that unity is in each number, yet at the same time each number is itself and not some other.

It is clear that the Platonic thought of the divine measure is present in an eminent way in St. Thomas and that it receives an enormous development at the very centre of his metaphysics. In fact, we are entitled to regard his thoughts on *mensura* as a synthesis of practically all the traditional themes associated with that fertile idea, in both its Platonic and its Aristotelean form: the critique of the Protagorean exaltation of man, as the measure of all things; the orderliness of creation, *in mensura, numero et pondere*;[78] the Aristotelean epistemological realism, expressed in the idea that knowing and understanding are measured by their objects, rather than measuring those; the doctrine of God as the measure of all things (the strictly Platonic teaching), which permeates the metaphysical thinking of Aquinas; the Augustinian teaching on the *modus* or measure of loving God, which is to love God *sine modo*;[79] and finally, the ethical theme of the virtuous man as the measure of all action, and of virtue itself as a mean.

To explore the reflections on *mensura* that are to be found in other thinkers of the great period of Scholastic metaphysics would take us

---

sura proportionata alicui. Dicitur tamen mensura omnium, ex eo quod unumquodque tantum habet de esse, quantum ei appropinquat." Cf. I, q. 13, a. 5, ad 3. The principle involved comes, of course, from Aristotle, *Metaphysics* 1053a24–28.

78. *In I Sent.*, d. 3, q. 2. Here Aquinas places the triad *numerus-pondus-mensura* in parallel with *modus-species-ordo*, in a very Augustinian way.

79. *Summa theol.* II-II, q. 27, a. 6: "Utrum divinae dilectionis sit aliquis modus habendus?": "*Sed contra est* quod Bernardus dicit, in libro *De diligendo Deo*, quod causa diligendi Deum Deus est; modus, sine modo diligere." In his response, Aquinas appeals to Augustine, *De natura boni*, for the idea that "modus importat quandam mensurae determinationem," on the basis of which he analyses the relationship between *mensura* and *mensuratum*, and concludes: "sicut invenitur modus in mensura, in qua non potest esse excessus, sed quanto plus attingitur regula, tanto melius est. Et ita quanto plus Deus diligitur, tanto est dilectio melior." Cf. St. Bernard, *De diligendo Deo*, c. 1, n. 1 (*Opera* [Rome, 1963], vol. 3, 119, 19). Wéber (in the article cited in note 41, pp. 62–64) gives a comment on the above article of Aquinas.

far afield, but mention of a few outstanding names should not be omitted here.[80] In the treatise of Giles of Rome *De mensura angelorum*, we are presented with a comprehensive synthesis of the measure theme, a synthesis which clearly reflects the influence of St. Thomas, and which sets out with admirable clarity the Aristotelean ideas of the unit as the measure of quantity, and the measuring of qualities by analogy with quantities (e.g., of the colours in terms of their relative proximity to the most simple and pure colour, light); and then the Neoplatonic conception of the various grades of created being (material, human, and angelic), as so many different participations in the purely simple and incomposite being of God.[81] Henry of Ghent and Godfrey of Fontaines in their different ways retained the metaphysical doctrine of participation, as expressed in the idea of God as *mensura omnium*.[82] Somewhat more surprisingly, perhaps, Siger of Brabant placed emphasis on this same doctrine in his metaphysical thought, under the influence, apparently, of the traditional Neoplatonic sources.[83]

It was proverbial in the Greek language to admire and to advocate measure and moderation in action (μηδὲν ἄγαν; μέτρον ἄριστον). Since the ideal of moderate and balanced action is an expression of right judgement, it bears implicit reference—even in its earliest forms—to the nature of man and to the order or disorder that is brought about by action. Solon was the first Greek thinker to place the true measure in the unseen mind of the immortals and thus to open the metaphor to religious and philosophical development. Plato sought to establish the measure as an important, even an indispensable, term of dialectic. He interwove it with mind and knowledge, ἐπιστήμη being of what is definite and formed, the opposite of the illimitable; with ἀρετή and the power of the *Agathon*, which shun the bad infinity of limitless pleasure seeking; and with beauty, symmetry, and perfec-

80. Consult the invaluable pages of Mahoney, in the article referred to in note 62, where the teaching on the participation of creatures in the divine simplicity (*mensura omnium*) is examined (pp. 174–82) in relation to such authors as Giles of Rome, Henry of Ghent, Godfrey of Fontaines, Siger of Brabant, and Duns Scotus.
81. B. Faes de Mottoni, "*Mensura* im Werk *De mensura angelorum* des Aegidius Romanus," in *Miscell. Med.* 16/1, pp. 86—102. The substance of the first of the ten questions of which *De mensura* consists is given in the footnotes to this article, the text of the Venice 1503 edition being corrected from several trustworthy MSS. The author has undertaken the critical edition of the work.
82. On Godfrey, and especially on his doctrine concerning the divine simplicity, see the recent work of J. F. Wippel, *The Metaphysical Thought of Godfrey of Fontaines: A Study in Late Thirteenth-century Philosophy* (Washington, D.C., 1981), pp. 91–99.
83. On participation, divine simplicity, and allied questions in this author, see F. Van Steenberghen, *Maître Siger de Brabant*, Philosophes Médiévaux XXI (London-Paris, 1977), pp. 289–302.

tion, those unmistakeable effects of reason in nature, thought, and action. The epistemological, moral, aesthetic, and metaphysical senses of measure were fused into unity by Plato, who thus determined the shape which the entire discussion of measure was to take in metaphysical thought. It can be said with confidence that whenever a metaphysical thinker of the Hellenistic, patristic, or Scholastic centuries invoked the theme of measure in its wholeness, he did so in conscious or unconscious dependence upon Plato, and that the discussions of the mean and measure which derived more proximately from the Aristotelean μεσότης and μέτρον were never wholly to lose that reference to the totality with which Plato had stamped the measure theme.

In Neoplatonism, metaphysical causality and measure came to be drawn together into inseparability: the One is the measure of number and multiplicity, of emanation and reversion, and is the immanent source of form, unity, and being within each thing, without itself being measurable or finite (the *unmeasured* measure) and without being relative to any particular reality, or indeed to the sum of beings. If *mensura* and *ordo* are drawn very close together by St. Augustine, measure nevertheless retained its specific metaphysical value and was not simply swallowed up, for, quite uniquely among the heirs of Plato, Augustine recovered the theme in its wholeness, that is to say, in its moral (*modus; moderatio; modulatio; modestia*), aesthetic (*species; forma; metrum*), and metaphysical range (God, as *mensura non mensurata*, has no limit and no opposite).

With regard to the measure theme, St. Thomas was the continuator of both Augustine and Aristotle. It is of central importance in his metaphysics of infinite and finite being, when he seeks to relate the creation and the human intellect dialectically back to the unity of the creative *intellectus*. The Platonic dialectical movement of thought ascending to unity, which was so powerfully accomplished in the metaphysics of Aquinas, found its apogee in the reflections of Nicholas of Cusa, who employed the *mensura* theme to think both the finality of the intelligible creation with reference to man the knower, and the infinity of the immeasurable, hidden God, in whom the fullest expression of all that is or could be is present before creation and without any intrinsic reference to the number, weight, and measure of finite beings.

Whatever remained of philosophy after it had been largely evacuated of the truly metaphysical, dialectical impulse could indeed still employ the motif of measure, but only in a fragmentary way, using the term "measure" anthropomorphically, with reference to the judgement of artistic quality; the other dimensions of μέτρον scarcely resonate any longer through the *Mass, Angemessen,* and *Symmetrie* of German Enlightenment aesthetics.[84] Even the Romantic Idealists do not appear to have recovered the metaphysical dimension of the Platonic theme: Hegel admittedly did regard the measure that indwells the dialectic as the opposite of the bad infinity of *Reflektionsphilosophie* and of modern subjectivity in general,[85] but his own conception of the dialectical self-constitution of the Absolute inclined more to pantheism than to the affirmation of the unmeasured measure of all measures. The Nietzschean celebration of the Apollonian measure in its singular Greek combination with Dionysian life-power was aimed at the forging of a weapon against Platonic metaphysics and Christianity,[86] but carried with it the message of a debased vitalism. Somewhat surprisingly, Neo-Scholastic metaphysics neglected the theme of measure. Relatively few historical studies of it have appeared, so that there remains a great deal more to be discovered before the theme lies before us in its wholeness; no doubt there are still many surprises in store.

The Queen's University of Belfast

84. Winckelmann, Lessing, Herder; see art. "Mass," in *Hist. Wört. der Phil.*, Bd. 5, p. 816.
85. Hegel, *Glauben und Wissen* I, 422 ff.
86. F. Nietzsche, *Die Geburt der Tragödie* 1, 33 ff.; cf. *Nachlass der Achtzigerjahre* 3, 425.

6   Thomas Aquinas and Participation
JOHN F. WIPPEL

During the intensive revival of interest in the philosophical thought of Thomas Aquinas which marked the closing decades of the nineteenth century and the first six decades or so of the twentieth century, various points have been singled out by Thomistic scholars as offering a key or even *the* key to his metaphysical thought. Thus his theory of real distinction between essence and existence in creatures, his metaphysics of act and potency, his views concerning analogy of being, and his stress on the primacy of the act of existing (*actus essendi*), all have been emphasized in due course. And each in fact has an important place within Thomas's metaphysics.[1] But at about the time of the outbreak of World War II, and continuing on within Thomistic studies down to the present, another significant aspect of Thomas's metaphysical thought has come to be recognized. At about that time important books were produced by C. Fabro, writing in Italy, and L. Geiger, writing in French, on the role of participation in Thomas's metaphysics.[2] More or less at about the same time another interesting study, if not all that reliable, was written in Ireland by Arthur Little, *The Platonic Heritage of Thomism*. And not too long thereafter Robert

---

1. For works which have stressed each of these points in turn see, for instance, N. Del Prado, *De veritate fundamentali philosophiae christianae* (Fribourg, 1911); G. M. Manser, *Das Wesen des Thomismus*, 3d ed. (Fribourg, 1949); M. T. Penido, *Le rôle de l'analogie en théologie dogmatique* (Paris, 1931), which has been completely superseded by the more recent study by B. Montagnes, *La doctrine de l'analogie de l'être d'après saint Thomas d'Aquin* (Louvain-Paris, 1963); and the many studies by Gilson emphasizing the primacy of existence in Thomas's metaphysics including, for instance, *Being and Some Philosophers*, 2d ed. (Toronto, 1952); *The Christian Philosophy of St. Thomas Aquinas* (New York, 1956); *Elements of Christian Philosophy* (Garden City, N.Y., 1960); *Introduction à la philosophie chrétienne* (Paris, 1960); *Le thomisme*, 6th ed. (Paris, 1965). This line of interpretation has been developed by many of Gilson's followers, especially by J. Owens.

2. C. Fabro, *La nozione metafisica di partecipazione secondo S. Tommaso d'Aquino* (Milan, 1939). Here I shall cite from the 2d revised edition (Turin, 1950). L. Geiger, *La participation dans la philosophie de S. Thomas d'Aquin* (Paris, 1942), 2d ed. in 1953. Here I shall use the 1953 edition.

Henle published a collection of texts drawn from Thomas's writings which contain his explicit references to Plato.[3]

In this study I shall concentrate on this issue, the meaning and role assigned by Thomas to participation in his metaphysics. With this in mind, (1) I shall attempt to explain what Thomas understands by participation in general, and then what he understands by the most important case of this, that of beings in *esse*. (2) Then I shall concentrate on an aspect of Thomas's theory which has received too little attention until now. If, as we shall see, Thomas often refers to creatures or to created natures as participating in being (*esse*), to what does that *esse* refer in which they are said to participate? Does it mean that creatures participate in self-subsisting *esse* (God)? Or does it mean that they participate in some general form of being (*esse commune*)? Or does it have some other meaning? (3) Finally, I shall turn to another issue which has sharply divided the leading students of participation in Aquinas, Fabro and Geiger, that is, the relationship between participation, composition, and limitation in created beings.

I

First, then, what does Thomas understand by participation? We are familiar with Aristotle's obvious impatience with both the Pythagoreans and the Platonists when they appealed to participation and imitation. "The Pythagoreans," comments Aristotle, "say that beings are by imitating numbers. Plato, on the other hand, by simply changing the term, holds that they are by participation. Both Plato and the Pythagoreans have failed to examine the nature of participation in the Ideas [Forms], and of imitation."[4] As Geiger has pointed out, Thomas's commentary on this particular passage from *Metaphysics* I is instructive. "The Pythagoreans," writes Aquinas, "while affirming participation or imitation, have not investigated how a common species is participated in by sensible individuals, or imitated by them, as the Platonists teach."[5]

---

3. See A. Little, *The Platonic Heritage of Thomism* (Dublin, 1949). As Little indicates, his book "was projected before the war and written immediately after it" (p. xiv). See the sympathetic but critical review article by W. N. Clarke, "The Platonic Heritage of Thomism," *The Review of Metaphysics* 8 (1954), pp. 105–24. Also see R. J. Henle, *Saint Thomas and Platonism* (The Hague, 1956).
4. *Met.* I, ch. 6 (987b11–14).
5. "Sed tamen est sciendum, quod Pythagorici, licet ponerent participationem, aut imitationem, non tamen perscrutati sunt qualiter species communis participetur ab individuis sensibilibus, sive ab eis imitetur, quod Platonici tradiderunt." *In I Met.*, lect. 10 (Cathala-Spiazzi ed., n. 156, p. 46). For Geiger see *La participation*, pp. 10–11.

Thomas, at least in this text, does not reject every kind of participation, nor does he here even directly criticize the Platonists. And Plato himself seems to have recognized this same difficulty, as we can surely conclude from the first part of his *Parmenides*.[6]

In this paper, however, I shall bypass such questions concerning earlier versions of participation, and concentrate on Thomas Aquinas himself. What does he understand by participation? At times he offers a kind of etymological explanation. "To participate is, as it were, to take a part of something." However, already in this same early writing, his Commentary on the *De Hebdomadibus*, he goes considerably beyond this appeal to etymology. "And therefore, when something receives in particular fashion that which belongs to another in universal [or total] fashion, the former is said to participate in the latter."[7] In other words, when we find a quality or characteristic possessed by a given subject in only partial rather than total fashion, such a subject is said to participate in that perfection. If in fact other subjects also do or even can share in that same perfection, it is because each of them only participates in it. None is identical with it. Thus, appeal to a participation structure is also a way of accounting for the fact that a given kind of characteristic or perfection can be shared in by many different subjects, or of addressing oneself to the problem of the One and the Many.

Thomas immediately goes on to observe that participation can take place in different orders and in different ways. Thus (I) man is said to participate in animal because man does not possess the intelligible content of animal according to its full universality (*secundum totam communitatem*). So too, Socrates is said to participate in man, and appar-

---

6. Without pausing to go into this issue here, I would simply refer the reader to two excellent studies by R. E. Allen: *Plato's Parmenides: Translation and Analysis* (Minneapolis, 1983); "Participation and Predication in Plato's Middle Dialogues," in *Plato: A Collection of Critical Essays*, vol. 1: *Metaphysics and Epistemology*, G. Vlastos, ed. (Garden City, N.Y., 1971), pp. 167–83.

7. "Est autem participare quasi partem capere; et ideo quando aliquid particulariter recipit id quod ad alterum pertinet universaliter, [punctuation changed] dicitur participare illud." *In De Hebdomadibus*, ed. by M. Calcaterra, in *S. Thomae Aquinatis Opuscula Theologica*, vol. 2 (Turin-Rome: Marietti, 1954), lect. 2, p. 396, n. 24. For other general descriptions of participation see: *In I Met.*, lect. 10, n. 154, p. 46: "Quod enim totaliter est aliquid, non participat illud, sed est per essentiam idem illi. Quod vero non totaliter est aliquid habens aliquid aliud adiunctum, proprie participare dicitur. Sicut si calor esset calor per se existens, non diceretur participare calorem, quia nihil esset in eo nisi calor. Ignis vero quia est aliquid aliud quam calor, dicitur participare calorem." *In II De caelo*, ed. by R. M. Spiazzi (Turin-Rome: Marietti, 1952), lect. 18, p. 233, n. 463: ". . . dicit autem *participat*, propter inferiores substantias separatas, quae esse et bonum habent ex alio: nam *participare* nihil aliud est quam ab alio partialiter accipere." Also see Fabro, *La nozione metafisica*, pp. 316–17.

ently for the same reason. My understanding of Socrates taken as this individual human being does not exhaust the intelligible content expressed by man in its full universality. In like fashion, continues Thomas, (II) a subject participates in an accident, and matter in form; for a substantial or an accidental form, while being general or universal in terms of its intelligible content, is restricted to this or that subject in which it is received. Thomas concludes this general description of the kinds of participation by noting (III) that in like fashion an effect is said to participate in its cause, and especially when it is not equal to the power of that cause.[8]

In sum, Thomas has here singled out three major kinds of participation. The first type is represented both by the way a specific notion such as man shares in a generic notion such as animal, and by the way my understanding of an individual such as Socrates shares in my notion of the species of man as such. In each of these examples we are dealing with a less extended intelligibility which is said to share in a more universal or more extended intelligible content. Since in each of these instances we are dealing with the fact that one intelligible content shares in another without exhausting it, we may describe this as a case of participation; but since we are dealing only with intelligible contents, the participation is logical or intentional, not real or ontological.[9]

8. "... sicut homo dicitur participare animal, quia non habet rationem animalis secundum totam communitatem; et eadem ratione Socrates participat hominem; similiter etiam subiectum participat accidens, et materia formam, quia forma substantialis vel accidentalis, quae de sui ratione communis est, determinatur ad hoc vel ad illud subiectum; et similiter effectus dicitur participare suam causam, et praecipue quando non adaequat virtutem suae causae; puta, si dicamus quod aër participat lucem solis, quia non recipit eam in ea claritate qua est in sole" (loc. cit., pp. 396–97, n. 24).

9. For discussion of this see Fabro, *La nozione metafisica*, pp. 27–28, 145–46, 149–50; Geiger, *La participation*, pp. 48–49. On this second general type of participation also see SCG I, ch. 32: "Amplius. Omne quod de pluribus praedicatur univoce, secundum participationem cuilibet eorum convenit de quo praedicatur: nam *species participare dicitur genus*, et *individuum speciem*. De Deo autem nihil dicitur per participationem: nam omne quod participatur determinatur ad modum participati [participantis?], et sic partialiter habetur et non secundum omnem perfectionis modum" (Leonine manual ed. [Rome, 1934], p. 33; italics mine). Thomas's point here is to reject univocal predication of anything of God and creatures. Also note near the end of this same chapter: "... de aliis autem praedicationes fiunt per participationem, sicut Sortes dicitur homo non quia sit ipsa humanitas, sed *humanitatem habens*" (italics mine). But compare this with the following remark from *In VII Met.*, lect. 3, p. 329, n. 1328: "Genus autem non praedicatur de speciebus per participationem, sed per essentiam. Homo enim est animal essentialiter, non solum aliquid animalis participans. Homo enim est quod verum est animal." For discussion of this difficulty, see below, note 30. For other texts where Thomas reaffirms the point that an individual may be described as participating in a species see, for instance, ST I, qu. 44, art. 3, ad 2: "Licet igitur hic homo sit per participationem speciei, non tamen potest reduci ad aliquid existens per se in eadem specie; sed ad speciem

The second major division is represented by two examples as well, that of a subject or substance participating in an accident, and that of matter participating in substantial form. In each of these cases, Thomas has indicated, the forms in question, whether substantial or accidental, simply considered in themselves, are still common. I take this to mean that, simply viewed in themselves, such forms can be shared in by any number of different subjects or instances of matter. It is only when a given accidental or substantial form is actually received in its appropriate substantial subject or its appropriate matter that it is thereby limited and restricted to the same. Hence the receiving principle, whether matter or a substantial subject, may be said to participate in the received form. In each of these cases the result is a real or ontological composition of a receiving subject and the perfection which is received in that same subject, that is, of substance and its given accident, or of matter and its given substantial form. Hence we may describe this kind of participation as real or as ontological. Here we are no longer dealing merely with a less extended concept which shares in one that is more extended.[10]

Rather than develop the third major kind of participation which he has singled out here (that of an effect in its cause), Thomas immediately returns to the first two. He does this in order to show that in neither of these first two ways can *esse* itself be said to participate in anything.[11] Here it should be noted that Thomas has been commenting on an axiom proposed by Boethius at the beginning of his *De Hebdomadibus* to this effect, that being (*esse*) and "that which is" are diverse. Thomas had noted that at this stage in his treatise Boethius is not yet discussing a diversity that applies to things or which is real, but diversity in the order of intentions.[12] As Aquinas interprets him, Boethius here distinguishes between *esse* and "that which is" as between that which is signified abstractly, for instance by expressions

---

superexcedentem, sicut sunt substantiae separatae" (P. Caramello ed. [Turin-Rome, 1950], p. 226); ST I, qu. 45, art. 5, ad 1: "Sed sicut hic homo participat humanam naturam, ita quodcumque ens creatum participat, ut ita dixerim, naturam essendi. . . ." (ed. cit., p. 231).

10. C. Fabro has referred to both of these major kinds of participation as instances of predicamental participation. By this he means that both terms of the participation relationship, the participant and the participated characteristic, remain within the field of finite being and finite substance (predicamental). See *La nozione metafisica*, pp. 145 ff.

11. "Praetermisso autem hoc tertio modo participandi, impossibile est quod secundum duos primos modos ipsum esse participet aliquid" (p. 397, n. 24).

12. See p. 396, n. 22: "Dicit ergo primo, quod diversum est esse, et id quod est. Quae quidem diversitas non est hic referenda ad res, de quibus adhuc non loquitur, sed ad ipsas rationes seu intentiones."

such as to run or whiteness, and the same thing when it is signified concretely, as by terms such as a runner (*currens*) or a white thing (*album*). Thus while *esse* is signified abstractly, "that which is" or being (*ens*) is signified concretely.[13] Nonetheless, Thomas also finds Boethius spelling out the distinction between these two, that is, between *esse* and "that which is," in three ways, each of which Thomas develops far more fully than does Boethius.

First of all, *esse* is not signified as the subject of being, just as the act of running ("to run") is not signified as if it were the subject which runs. Just as we cannot say that the act of running ("to run") itself runs, neither can we say that *esse* itself exists. And if "that which runs" is signified as the subject of running, so do we signify "that which is" as the subject of existing (*subiectum essendi*). And if we can say of one who runs that he does so insofar as he is subject to running and participates in it, so can we say that a being, or "that which is," exists insofar as it participates in the act of existing (*inquantum participat actum essendi*).[14]

Secondly, Boethius states that "that which is" can participate in something, but *esse* itself cannot. It is in explaining this second difference that Thomas introduces the description and divisions of participation we have been considering. Thomas immediately turns from

---

13. "Aliud autem significamus per hoc quod dicimus esse, et aliud: *per hoc quod dicimus id quod est; sicut et aliud* significamus cum dicimus currere, et aliud per hoc quod dicitur currens. Nam currere et esse significantur in abstracto, sicut et albedo; sed quod est, idest ens et currens, significantur sicut in concreto, velut album" (ibid.).

14. See p. 396, n. 23. Note in particular: ". . . unde, sicut non possumus dicere quod ipsum currere currat, ita non possumus dicere quod ipsum esse sit: sed sicut id ipsum quod est, significatur sicut subiectum essendi, sic id quod currit significatur sicut subiectum currendi: et ideo sicut possumus dicere de eo quod currit, sive de currente, quod currat, inquantum subiicitur cursui et participat ipsum; ita possumus dicere quod ens, sive id quod est, sit, inquantum participat actum essendi. . . ." As Fabro points out, Thomas here introduces one of his most original insights into his Commentary on the Boethian text, and one which is completely missing from Boethius himself, that is, his identification of *esse* as it is realized in a creature as the *actus essendi:* ". . . sed *id quod est, accepta essendi forma,* scilicet suscipiendo ipsum actum essendi, *est, atque consistit,* idest in seipso subsistit" (ibid.). For Fabro see *Participation et causalité* (Louvain-Paris, 1961), p. 270. For different medieval and contemporary ways of understanding the meaning of *esse* in Boethius himself see Fabro, *La nozione metafisica*, pp. 100–103. Also see Geiger, *La participation*, pp. 36–45; P. Hadot, "La distinction de l'être et de l'étant dans le *De Hebdomadibus* de Boèce," *Miscellanea Mediaevalia* 2 (1963), pp. 147–53; G. Schrimpf, *Die Axiomenschrift des Boethius (De Hebdomadibus) als philosophisches Lehrbuch des Mittelalters* (Leiden, 1966), The general (if not universal) consensus is that, however Boethius may have understood and contrasted *esse* and *id quod est*, he did not distinguish them in Thomistic fashion as existence and essence. Also cf. R. McInerny, "Boethius and Saint Thomas Aquinas," *Rivista di Filosofia neo-scolastica* 66 (1974), pp. 219–45.

this description of participation to explain why *esse* itself cannot participate in anything else even though "that which is" or the subject which exists can. Precisely because *esse* is signified in abstract fashion, it cannot participate in anything else in the second general way Thomas has singled out, that is, as a substance participates in its accident or as matter participates in form. This is so, we may presume, because both a substantial subject and matter are signified concretely, and, as we have seen, *esse* is signified abstractly.[15]

Neither, continues Thomas, can *esse* participate in anything else in the first general way, that is, as a less universal concept participates in one which is more universal. (Thomas does acknowledge in passing that in this general way some things which are signified abstractly may be said to participate in others, for instance, whiteness in color.) This kind of participation will not apply in the case of *esse* itself because there is nothing more general than *esse* in which it could participate. *Esse* itself is most universal (*communissimum*). Therefore *esse* is participated in by other things, but cannot itself participate in anything else.[16] On the other hand, being (*ens*), even though it too is most universal, is expressed in concrete fashion. Therefore while being cannot participate in anything in the way the less universal participates in the more universal, it does participate in *esse* in the way something concrete participates in something abstract.[17]

We shall pass over Thomas's discussion of the third difference between *esse* and "that which is" as he finds this in Boethius's text. Of greater interest for our immediate purposes is Thomas's acknowledgment that being (*ens*) can participate in *esse* in the way in which something taken concretely participates in something taken abstractly. If we were to stop at this point, we would not yet be justified in thinking that he here defends any kind of real diversity or real composition of *esse* and "that which is" within participating beings. We should note that in the following context Thomas writes that for something to be a subject in the unqualified sense, that is, a substance, it must partici-

15. "Non enim potest participare aliquid per modum quo materia vel subiectum participat formam vel accidens: quia, ut dictum est, ipsum esse significatur ut quiddam abstractum" (p. 397, n. 24).
16. "Similiter autem nec potest aliquid participare per modum quo particulare participat universale: sic enim etiam ea quae in abstracto dicuntur, participare aliquid possunt, sicut albedo colorem; sed ipsum esse est communissimum: unde ipsum quidem participatur in aliis, non autem participat aliquid aliud" (ibid.).
17. "Sed id quod est, sive ens, quamvis sit communissimum, tamen concretive dicitur; et ideo participat ipsum esse, non per modum quo magis commune participatur a minus communi, sed participat ipsum esse per modum quo concretum participat abstractum" (ibid.).

pate in *esse* itself.[18] This is important because it indicates that if something is to serve as a subject for an accident, it must first of all exist. And in order for it to exist, it must participate in existence (*esse*), or as Thomas also puts it, in the *actus essendi*. Here, then, we find Thomas very deftly inserting his own metaphysics of *esse* into his Commentary on Boethius.[19] This becomes even clearer as Thomas turns to another Boethian axiom: in every composite, *esse* and the composite itself which participates in *esse* differ. At this point, comments Thomas, Boethius has shifted from diversity in the order of intentions to diversity in the order of reality. "Just as *esse* and 'that which is' differ in simple entities in the order of intentions, in composite entities they differ really [*realiter*]."[20]

In order to prove this, Thomas first recalls a point which we have already considered—that *esse* itself does not participate in anything else. He also recalls another point which we have not mentioned— that *esse* does not admit of the addition of anything extraneous to its formal content. Therefore, he quickly concludes, *esse* itself is not composed. But if it is not, then it cannot be identified with a composite or composed entity.[21] Here, then, we have an argument for the real dis-

18. "... ubi dicit, quod ad hoc quod aliquid sit simpliciter subiectum, participat ipsum esse; sed ad hoc quod sit aliquid, oportet quod participet alio aliquo; sicut homo ad hoc quod sit albus, participat non solum esse substantiale, sed etiam albedinem.... Nam aliquid est simpliciter per hoc quod participat ipsum esse; sed quando iam est, scilicet per participationem ipsius esse, restat ut participet quocumque alio, ad hoc scilicet quod sit aliquid" (p. 398, nn. 29, 30). This indicates that when Thomas refers to being (*ens*) as participating in *esse*, he ultimately has in mind the fact that a given concrete being must participate in substantial *esse* (existence) if it is to exist in actuality.

19. In addition to other passages from the Commentary on the *De Hebdomadibus* (see note 14 above), one may consider a much later text such as *Quaest. Disp. de anima*, qu. 6, ad 2: "Ad secundum dicendum quod ipsum esse est actus ultimus qui participabilis est ab omnibus; ipsum autem non participat. Unde si sit aliquid quod sit ipsum esse subsistens, sicut de Deo dicimus, ipsum nihil participare dicimus. Non est autem similis ratio de aliis formis subsistentibus, quas necesse est participare ipsum esse et comparari ad ipsum ut potentiam ad actum" (Robb ed. [Toronto, 1968], p. 112). Here we have in outline form most of the elements of Thomas's mature doctrine of participation of beings in being (*esse*): *esse* is the ultimate act which can be participated in by all; *esse* itself does not participate in anything; if there is a subsisting *esse*—God—this participates in nothing; other subsisting forms (angels) must participate in *esse* and be related to it as potency to act. In other words, their essence is in potency with respect to their act of existence. This text seems to date from early 1269. See J. A. Weisheipl, *Friar Thomas D'Aquino: His Life, Thought, and Works* (Garden City, N.Y., 1974), p. 365.

20. "Deinde cum dicit, *Omni composito*, ponit conceptiones de composito et simplici, quae pertinent ad rationem unius. Est autem considerandum, quod ea quae supra dicta sunt de diversitate ipsius esse et eius quod est, est secundum ipsas intentiones; hic autem ostendit quomodo applicetur ad res" (p. 398, n. 31). "Est ergo primo considerandum, quod sicut esse et quod est differunt in simplicibus secundum intentiones, ita in compositis differunt realiter" (n. 32).

21. "... dictum est enim supra, quod ipsum esse neque participat aliquid, ut eius

tinction between essence and existence (*esse*) in composite entities, though not one of Thomas's more usual arguments for that conclusion, I would add.

One might immediately ask, however, about created simple entities. Will essence and *esse* be distinct in them? It seems that some other kind of argumentation will be necessary to establish this. In seeming anticipation of our query, Thomas insists that in any simple entity, *esse* and "that which is" are really identical. Otherwise the entity would not really be simple. In explaining this Thomas notes that something is simple insofar as it lacks composition. Since something may lack a given kind of composition without lacking all composition, it may be simple in a qualified sense without being completely simple. Thus fire and water, two of the elements for Thomas and his contemporaries, are called simple bodies because they are not composed of contraries, as are mixtures. But each is still composed both of quantitative parts and of matter and form. If we find certain forms which do not exist in matter and which are simple in the sense that they lack matter-form composition and quantitative parts, it will not immediately follow that they are perfectly simple. Since any such form must still determine its *esse*, it follows that no such form is its *esse*. It simply has *esse*.[22]

In fact, in an interesting thought experiment, Thomas suggests that even if, for the sake of discussion, we grant with Plato that there are certain subsisting immaterial forms or ideas such as a form for men and another for horses, every such form will still be determined with respect to its kind or species. Hence no such subsisting form could be identified with existence in general (*esse commune*). Each such form would only participate in *esse commune*. The same will hold, continues Thomas, if with Aristotle we defend the existence of separate and immaterial substances above the world of sensible things, as Thomas himself does. Each of these, insofar as it is distinct from the others, is a given kind of form and therefore participates in *esse*. No such substance, whether it be a Platonic form or an Aristotelian separate sub-

---

ratio constituatur ex multis; neque habet aliquid extraneum admixtum, ut sit in eo compositio accidentis; et ideo ipsum esse non est compositum. Res ergo composita non est suum esse. . . ." (p. 398, n. 32). For the point that *esse* admits nothing extrinsic into its formal content see p. 397, n. 25.

22. See p. 398, n. 34. Note in particular: ". . . nihil prohibet aliquid esse secundum quid simplex, inquantum caret aliqua compositione, quod tamen non est omnino simplex. . . . Si ergo inveniantur aliquae formae non in materia, unaquaeque earum est quidem simplex quantum ad hoc quod caret materia, et per consequens quantitate, quae est dispositio materiae; quia tamen quaelibet forma est determinativa ipsius esse, nulla earum est ipsum esse, sed est habens esse."

stance, will be perfectly simple.²³ Each will be composed of itself—form, or essence if you will—and of the *esse* in which it participates. There can be only one completely simple being, continues Thomas, and this does not participate in *esse*, but is subsisting *esse*. This, of course, is God.²⁴ Given all of this, we may now ask, how does participation of beings in *esse* fit into Thomas's threefold division of participation?

We may immediately conclude from the above that the participation of beings in *esse* cannot be reduced to the first kind of participation singled out by Aquinas, whereby a less universal notion or concept participates in one that is more general or universal. Such participation belongs to the logical or intentional order, and does not entail real distinction between the participant and that in which it participates. But, as we have now seen, participation of beings in *esse* is not restricted to the logical or intentional order. And it clearly does entail real distinction and composition of the participating nature and that in which it participates.²⁵

What, then, of the second general kind of participation, wherein a subject participates in its accidents, or a given instance of matter participates in substantial form? This, too, evidently involves real participation and real diversity between the participating subject and the participated perfection, that is, between substance and accident, or between prime matter and substantial form. Nonetheless, it seems clear enough that for Thomas, participation of beings in being (*esse*)

---

23. "... manifestum erit quod ipsa forma immaterialis subsistens [a Platonic form], cum sit quiddam determinatum ad speciem, non est ipsum esse commune, sed participat illud ... unaquaeque illarum [Aristotelian separate substances], inquantum distinguitur ab alia, quaedam specialis forma est participans ipsum esse; et sic nulla earum erit vere simplex" (ibid.).

24. See p. 398, n. 35. Note Thomas's reason here for saying that such a being can only be one: "... quia si ipsum esse nihil aliud habet admixtum praeter id quod est esse, ut dictum est, impossibile est id quod est ipsum esse, multiplicari per aliquid diversificans. . . ."

25. See the text cited in note 23 above. There Thomas reasons that every such form, by reason of the fact that it is different from every other, is a given (*specialis*) form which participates in *esse* itself. From this he concludes that no such form is truly simple (which is to say that it is composed). On the other hand, in the text cited above in note 22 Thomas reasons that since every such separated form determines *esse* itself, no such form is *esse* itself; it simply has *esse*. Here Thomas seems to move from the claim that no such substance is *esse* (distinction between essence and *esse*), to participation of every such form in *esse*. For another text where he seems to reason in both ways, that is, from distinction in a creature of essence and *esse* to participation in *esse*, and farther on in the same context from participation to distinction of essence and *esse*, see Quodlibet 2, qu. 2, art. 1. For discussion see Wippel, *Metaphysical Themes in Thomas Aquinas* (Washington, D.C., 1984), p. 150, n. 42.

cannot be reduced to this kind of participation any more than to the first kind.

First of all, in order for a subject to participate in its accidents, Thomas has noted, the subject must first exist. And it exists only insofar as it participates in *esse*.[26] Participation in *esse* is clearly more fundamental than that of a substance in its accidents. The same may be said of participation of matter in form. According to Aquinas, if a matter-form composite is to exist, it must participate in *esse* (see, for instance, *De substantiis separatis*, ch. 8).

Moreover, in the case where matter is said to participate in form, a third thing (*res*) or a *tertium quid* results, that is, the essence of the material thing which includes both its form and its matter. However, as Thomas brings out on other occasions, for instance in his considerably later and very full discussion of participation in Quodlibet 2, qu. 2, art. 1 of 1269, it is not in this way that essence and *esse* unite in a creature. No *tertium quid* results from their union. Essence and *esse* do not unite in a created separate substance—an angel—as if they were two different parts of the angelic substance. "If, therefore, in an angel there is a composition as of essence and *esse*, this is a composition not as of parts of a substance, but rather as of a substance and of that which unites with the substance [*adhaeret substantiae*]."[27]

And in replying to the first objection Thomas notes that in some cases a third thing (*res tertia*) does result from things which are joined together, as humanity or man results from the union of soul and body. But on other occasions this is not so. Rather something is composed of itself and of something else. Hence, we may conclude, in the case of an angel we have a composition of the angelic essence and of a distinct *esse*, which itself is neither an essence or "thing" nor even a part of the essence.[28]

Still another difference has been pointed out between matter-form composition and the union of essence and *esse* in Thomas's metaphys-

26. See note 14 above.
27. Quodlibet 2, qu. 2, art. 1, is addressed to this question: "Utrum angelus substantialiter sit compositus ex essentia et esse." See *Quaestiones Quodlibetales*, R. Spiazzi, ed. (Turin-Rome: Marietti, 1956), pp. 23–24. Note in particular: "Si ergo in angelo est compositio sicut ex essentia et esse, non tamen est compositio sicut ex partibus substantiae, sed sicut ex substantia et eo quod adhaeret substantiae."
28. The first objection reasons that the essence of an angel is the angel itself. If, therefore, an angel were composed of essence and *esse*, it would be composed of itself and something else. This is rejected by the objection as unfitting. Note from Thomas's reply: "Aliquando autem ex his quae simul iunguntur, non resultat res tertia, sed resultat quaedam ratio composita, sicut ratio hominis albi resolvitur in rationem hominis et in rationem albi; et in talibus aliquid componitur ex seipso et alio, sicut album componitur ex eo quod est album et ex albedine." Ed. cit., p. 24.

ics,²⁹ and therefore, one may conclude, between the kinds of participation involved in each. In the case of matter-form union, the specification of the kind of being enjoyed by the composite essence, human being or canine being, for instance, is determined by the act principle within the essence, that is, by the substantial form. But in the composition of essence and *esse* within any created entity, the specification or determination of the kind of being comes not from the side of the act principle—the *actus essendi*—but from the side of the potency principle, that is, from the essence. This is not surprising, of course, since that very essence principle itself either is or at least includes a substantial form.

Another important difference between the first kind of participation, that of a species in its genus or of an individual in its species, and other kinds of participation including that of beings in *esse* is brought out in Thomas's Commentary on the *De Hebdomadibus* and in Quodlibet 2, qu. 2, art. 1. In lectio 3 of the former text Thomas comments that Boethius has assumed that to be something essentially is diametrically opposed to being something by participation. Thomas concedes that this is true according to the second major kind of participation he has distinguished (that of a substance in an accident, or of matter in form). This follows because an accident is not included within the very nature of its substantial subject, and form is not included within the very nature of matter. But this does not apply to the first kind of participation, at least not according to Aristotle, though it would if, with Plato, we defended distinct forms or ideas for man, for instance, as well as for animal. According to Aristotle, whom Thomas here follows, a man is truly that same thing which is an animal. Hence animal does not exist apart from the difference man, or some other difference. Therefore, what is said by participation in this first major way can also be predicated substantially of something at the same time. For instance, man is said to participate in animal, just as a species participates in its genus. But because animal is included within the nature of man, animal may be predicated of man substantially as well.³⁰

---

29. See Geiger, *La participation*, pp. 198–99, n. 2; Fabro, *Participation et causalité*, p. 65. For a general comparison and contrast between the essence (*substantia*) and *esse* relationship and that of matter and form, see SCG II, ch. 54. There Thomas concludes by noting that the composition of act and potency is broader in extension than that of matter and form. While the latter is restricted to physical (*naturalem*) entities, the former extends to the entire realm of being in general: ". . . potentia autem et actus dividunt ens commune." Ed. cit., p. 147.

30. Ed. cit., p. 401, nn. 44, 45. Note in particular: "Sed secundum sententiam Aristotelis, qui posuit quod homo vere est id quod est animal, quasi essentia animalis non existente praeter differentiam hominis; nihil prohibet, id quod per participationem di-

Evidently Thomas would deny that *esse* is predicated of any creature in this way, substantially or essentially, if you will.

In Quodlibet 2, qu. 2, art. 1, Thomas explicitly makes this final point. There he has commented that something can be predicated of something either essentially or else by participation. Being (*ens*) is predicated of God alone essentially, and of every creature only by participation; for no creature is its *esse*, but every creature merely has *esse*. But when anything is predicated of something by participation, something else must be present there in addition to that which is participated. Therefore, in every creature there is a distinction between the creature which has *esse*, and *esse* itself.³¹

But, continues Thomas, something may be participated in two different ways. On the one hand, what is participated may be included within the very essence (*substantia*) of the participant, as when a genus is participated in by its species. *Esse*, however, is not participated in by a creature in this fashion, for what is included within the essence of a thing falls within its definition. Being (*ens*) is not included within the definition of a creature. Therefore *esse* is participated only in the second way, as something which is not included within the essence of the participant. Given this, we have to distinguish the question "is it?" (*an est*) from the question "what is it?" (*quid est*). In fact, Thomas even goes so far here as to say that if anything not included within the essence of a thing may be described as an accident, the *esse* which answers to the question *an est* may also be referred to as an accident. He means by this not that *esse* or existence is a predicamental accident, but only that it is not part of the essence of any creature. This he clarifies with all desired precision in other contexts, for instance, in his Commentary on *Metaphysics* IV and in his Quodlibet 12.³²

---

citur, substantialiter praedicari" (n. 45). Hence in the text from *In VII Met.* (see note 9 above) Thomas must be using participation only in the second way, so that the participated characteristic is not included within the essence of the participant. A species does not participate in a genus in this way.

31. Ed. cit., p. 24. Note in particular: "Secundum ergo hoc dicendum est, quod ens praedicatur de solo Deo essentialiter, eo quod esse divinum est esse subsistens et absolutum; de qualibet autem creatura praedicatur per participationem: nulla enim creatura est suum esse, sed est habens esse."

32. Ibid. "Uno modo quasi existens de substantia participantis, sicut genus participatur a specie. Hoc autem modo esse non participatur a creatura. Id enim est de substantia rei quod cadit in eius definitione. Ens autem non ponitur in definitione creaturae, quia nec est genus nec differentia. Unde participatur sicut aliquid non existens de essentia rei; et ideo alia quaestio est *an est* et *quid est*. Unde, cum omne quod est praeter essentiam rei, dicatur accidens; esse quod pertinet ad quaestionem *an est*, est accidens." See Thomas's reply to objection 2: ". . . esse est accidens, non quasi per accidens se habens, sed quasi actualitas cuiuslibet substantiae." Cf. Quodlibet 12, qu. 5, art. 1: "Et sic dico quod esse substantiale rei non est accidens, sed actualitas cuiuslibet

In comparing participation in *esse* with the first two major kinds singled out by Thomas in his Commentary on the *De Hebdomadibus*, we should also note that each of the other kinds allows for univocal predication of the participated perfection. According to Aquinas, this is not true of *esse*. It can be predicated only analogically of whatever participates in it. As regards univocal predication of genera and species, Thomas correlates this with participation in an important text from *Summa contra gentiles* I, ch. 32. There he is attempting to show that nothing can be predicated univocally of God and creatures. "Everything which is predicated of many things univocally pertains to each of those things of which it is predicated only by participation. For a species is said to participate in a genus, and an individual in a species."[33] If these are cases of participation, as Thomas has again reminded us here, they are also paradigms for univocal predication.

As Thomas also explains within this same chapter, what is predicated of different things in terms of priority and posteriority is not predicated of them univocally. Thus being (*ens*) is not predicated univocally of substance and accidents. This is not, of course, for Thomas to deny that an accident itself is predicated univocally as it is realized in and participated in by different substances. And, as Thomas continues, nothing can be said of God and creatures as if they were on the same level, but everything must be said of them only according to priority and posteriority. Therefore, while names such as being and goodness are said of God essentially, they are predicated of all else only by participation. Hence, Thomas concludes once more, nothing can be said univocally of God and of other things.[34]

---

formae existentis, sive sine materia sive cum materia. . . . Et quod Hilarius dicit, dico quod accidens dicitur large omne quod non est pars essentiae; et sic est esse in rebus creatis, quia in solo Deo esse est eius essentia." Ed. cit., p. 227. Cf. *In IV Met.*, lect. 2, p. 155, n. 558.

33. "Amplius. Omne quod de pluribus praedicatur univoce, secundum participationem cuilibet eorum convenit de quo praedicatur: nam species participare dicitur genus, et individuum speciem. De Deo autem nihil dicitur per participationem: nam omne quod participatur determinatur ad modum participati, et sic partialiter habetur et non secundum omnem perfectionis modum. Oportet igitur nihil de Deo et rebus aliis univoce praedicari." Ed. cit., p. 33.

34. Ibid. See in particular: "Adhuc. Quod praedicatur de aliquibus secundum prius et posterius, certum est univoce non praedicari. . . ." If, as I am implying, a given kind of substantial form will also be predicated univocally of the individual instances of matter which participate in it, and, it would seem, a given kind of accidental form of the different substances which participate in it, this is because, considered in itself, every such substantial or accidental form will fall into its proper predicament or genus. However, this is not to imply that *esse* (or being) is predicated univocally of the different individuals within a given class or species. On this see Fabro's critique of John of St. Thomas, *La nozione metafisica*, pp. 172–73. Note the text he cites from *In I Sent.*, d. 35,

Before leaving this general discussion of Thomas's understanding of participation, we should refer to another aspect of his theory. Participation evidently entails composition in the participant of a receiving and limiting principle, and of that which is received and participated. This has already emerged from our analysis of Thomas's Commentary on the *De Hebdomadibus*, and is reinforced by his discussion in Quodlibet 2. But going hand in hand with this is another part of Thomas's theory. In cases of real or ontological participation, the participating principle or subject is related to the participated perfection as potency to act. The participated perfection is the act of the subject which receives it as its corresponding potential principle. As Thomas explains in *Summa theologiae* I, qu. 75, art. 5, ad 1: "Since potency is that which receives act, a potency must be proportioned to its act. Received acts, however, which proceed from the first and infinite act and are certain participations of it, are diverse."[35]

Very frequently Thomas also applies this thinking to the participation of beings in *esse*. That essence is related to existence (*esse*) as potency to act in every finite being is a position defended by Thomas from his earliest writings, and even in contexts where he is not using the language of participation, as for instance, in certain passages in his Commentary on I *Sentences*, or in ch. 4 of his *De ente et essentia*.[36]

---

qu. 1, art. 4: "... unde habitus humanitatis non est secundum idem esse in duobus hominibus; et ideo quandocumque forma significata per nomen est ipsum esse, non potest univoce convenire, propter quod etiam ens non univoce praedicatur." Mandonnet ed., vol. 1, p. 819. Note Thomas's reply to objection 3: "... dicendum, quod magis et minus nunquam univocationem vel speciei unitatem auferunt; sed ea ex quibus magis et minus causantur possunt differentiam speciei facere, et univocationem auferre: et hoc contingit quando magis et minus causantur non ex diversa participatione unius naturae, sed ex gradu diversarum naturarum; sicut angelus homine intellectualior dicitur" (p. 820). Also see SCG II, ch. 81, reply to the second argument: "Non enim quaelibet formarum diversitas facit diversitatem secundum speciem, sed solum illa quae est secundum principia formalia, vel secundum diversam rationem formae: constat enim quod alia est essentia formae huius ignis et illius, nec tamen est alius ignis neque alia forma secundum speciem" (ed. cit., p. 191). Hence numerical distinction between forms of the same kind does not destroy identity in species; therefore, we may conclude, it does not militate against univocal predication of the species of its individuals, or of a specific kind of form of the different instances of matter which participate in it. Cf. *Super librum de causis*, prop. 4a, Saffrey ed., p. 31. Note the reference there to different subjects (possibly) participating *aequaliter* in whiteness.

35. "... dicendum quod primus actus est universale principium omnium actuum, quia est infinitum, virtualiter *in se omnia praehabens*, ut dicit Dionysius. Unde participatur a rebus, non sicut pars, sed secundum diffusionem processionis ipsius. Potentia autem, cum sit receptiva actus, oportet quod actui proportionetur. Actus vero recepti, qui procedunt a primo actu infinito et sunt quaedam participationes eius, sunt diversi" (ed. cit., p. 354).

36. See, for instance, *In I Sent.*, d. 8, qu. 5, art. 2: "Si vero non sit ipsum esse, oportet quod habeat esse acquisitum ab alio, sicut est omnis quidditas creata. Et quia haec quid-

The conjoining of the potency-act relationship between essence and *esse* with the metaphysics of participation seems to be emphasized ever more frequently from the time of the *Summa contra gentiles* onward.[37] One may recall the following text from SCG II, ch. 53: "Everything which participates in something is related to that which is participated as potency to act. Through that which is participated the participant becomes actually such. But it has been shown above that God alone is being essentially, and that all others participate *ipsum esse*. Therefore every created essence [*substantia*] is related to its *esse* as potency to act."[38] Here we have the general point that whatever participates in something is related to that in which it participates as potency to act. And this is followed by the particular application to created essences as participating in and being related to *esse* as potency to act.

If the act-potency relationship applies to the participation of beings in *esse*, it also holds in other instances of real participation. According to Aquinas, matter participates in form and is related to it as potency to act. A substance participates in its accidents and is related to them as a receiving potency to its received albeit secondary acts. But most

---

ditas posita est non subsistere in materia, non acquiretur sibi esse in altero, sicut quidditatibus compositis, immo acquiretur sibi esse in se; et ita ipsa quidditas erit hoc 'quod est', et ipsum esse suum erit 'quo est'. Et quia omne quod non habet aliquid a se, est possibile respectu illius; huiusmodi quidditas cum habeat esse ab alio, erit possibilis respectu illius esse, et respectu ejus a quo esse habet, in quo nulla cadit potentia; et ita in tali quidditate invenietur potentia et actus, secundum quod ipsa quidditas est possibilis, et esse suum est actus ejus. Et hoc modo intelligo in angelis compositionem potentiae et actus, et de 'quo est' et 'quod est', et similiter in anima." Ed. cit., vol. 1, pp. 229–30. In the *De ente* it is only after having completed his argumentation for the essence-*esse* distinction in non-divine simple entities and after having reasoned from their caused character to the existence of God that Thomas establishes act-potency composition within them. "Omne autem quod recipit aliquid ab aliquo [Leonine: alio] est in potentia respectu illius, et hoc quod receptum [Leonine: est] in eo est est [Leonine: omit] actus eius. Ergo oportet quod ipsa quiditas vel forma que est intelligencia sit in potentia respectu esse quod a Deo recipit, et illud esse receptum est per modum actus" (Roland-Gosselin ed., p. 35/Leonine ed., vol. 43, p. 377).

37. See W. N. Clarke, "The Limitation of Act by Potency: Aristotelianism or Neoplatonism," *The New Scholasticism* 26 (1952), pp. 167–94. Clarke concentrates on one aspect of the potency-act doctrine in Aquinas, the view that act is limited only by a receiving potency. This he finds joined with the act-potency theory from the *Summa contra Gentiles* onward. See pp. 192–93. Also see B. Montagnes, *La doctrine de l'analogie de l'être*, p. 58.

38. "Omne participans aliquid comparatur ad ipsum quod participatur ut potentia ad actum: per id enim quod participatur fit participans actu tale. Ostensum autem est supra quod solus Deus est essentialiter ens, omnia autem alia participant ipsum esse. Comparatur igitur substantia omnis creata ad suum esse sicut potentia ad actum" (ed. cit., p. 146). The whole of ch. 53 is devoted to proving that there is act-potency composition in created intellectual substances, that is, of *substantia* and *esse*. In ch. 52 Thomas had offered a series of arguments to prove that there is diversity of *quod est* (essence) and *esse* in such entities.

important for our purposes is Thomas's repeated application of this to participation in being. As he puts it in his even later *Treatise on Separate Substances:* "Everything which is has *esse*. Therefore, in everything apart from the first, there is both *esse* itself as act, and the substance of the thing which has *esse* as the potency which receives this act which is *esse*."[39]

At this point it may be helpful for us to sum up the various features of Thomas's understanding of the participation of beings in being (*esse*) which have so far emerged from our discussion. The participa-

---

39. See Thomas's *De virtutibus in communi*, art. 3, where he comments that a subject is related to an accident in three ways: (1) as offering a support to it; (2) as potency to act, since the subject stands under the accident; (3) as a cause to its effect, insofar as the principles of the subject are the per se principles of the accident. See *Quaestiones disputatae*, vol. 2 (Turin-Rome, 1953), p. 715. Here Thomas is seeking to determine whether a power of the soul can be the subject of a virtue. On the causality of a substance with respect to its proper accidents, and especially with respect to the powers of the soul, see ST I, qu. 77, art. 6, and ad 2. That Thomas relates prime matter to substantial form as potency to act is too well known to need documentation here. For the text from the *Treatise on Separate Substances* see: "Omne autem quod est esse habet. Est igitur in quocumque praeter primum et ipsum esse tamquam actus et substantia rei habens esse tamquam potentia receptiva hujus actus qui [with Lescoe instead of Leonine: quod] est esse" (Lescoe ed., p. 79, n. 42/Leonine ed., vol. 40, p. D55). That the expression "esse habet" as used here means to participate in *esse* becomes abundantly clear from the immediately following context. For other equally explicit texts see Quodlibet 3, qu. 8, art. 1: "Oportet ergo quod quaelibet alia res [other than *esse subsistens*] sit ens participative, ita quod aliud sit in eo substantia participans esse, et aliud ipsum esse participatum. Omne autem participans se habet ad participatum, sicut potentia ad actum; unde substantia cuiuslibet rei creatae se habet ad suum esse, sicut potentia ad actum. Sic ergo omnis substantia creata est composita ex potentia et actu, id est ex eo quod est et esse, ut Boëtius dicit in lib. *de Hebd.*, sicut album componitur ex eo quod est album, et albedine" (ed. cit., p. 61). Here Thomas is rejecting matter-form composition in the human soul. Also see *De spiritualibus creaturis*, art. 1, where Thomas is rejecting matter-form composition of spiritual substances. Note from this extremely important discussion the following: "Omne igitur quod est post primum ens, cum non sit suum esse, habet esse in aliquo receptum, per quod ipsum esse contrahitur; et sic in quolibet creato aliud est natura rei quae participat esse, et aliud ipsum esse participatum. Et cum quaelibet res participet per assimilationem primum actum in quantum habet esse, necesse est quod esse participatum in unoquoque comparetur ad naturam participantem ipsum, sicut actus ad potentiam." See *Quaestiones disputatae*, ed. cit., vol. 2, p. 371. Here Thomas also explicitly refers to the fact that when *esse* is received in something, that is, nature or essence, *esse* itself is limited thereby. Also see *In VIII Physic.*, lect. 21, where Thomas is criticizing Averroes for rejecting true matter-form composition in heavenly bodies. Even if one conceded this position to Averroes, there would still be a potency for being (*potentia essendi*) in heavenly bodies. "Omnis ergo substantia quae est post primam substantiam simplicem, participat esse. Omne autem participans componitur ex participante et participato, et participans est in potentia ad participatum . . ." (ed. Maggiòlo [Turin-Rome, 1954], p. 615, n. 1153). Quodlibet 3 dates from Easter 1270; *De substantiis separatis* from 1271–73; *De spiritualibus creaturis* ca. 1267–68; *In Physic.* from 1270–71. In other words, all are relatively late works. Also see W. N. Clarke, "The Meaning of Participation in St. Thomas," in *Proceedings of the American Catholic Philosophical Association* 26 (1952), pp. 147–57, esp. pp. 154–55.

tion of beings in *esse* is more fundamental than the other kinds, for it alone accounts for the fact that a given entity actually exists. No *tertium quid* or third thing results from the union of the participating principle (essence) and that in which it participates (*esse*). The participated perfection—*esse*—cannot be predicated univocally of the various subjects which participate in it, but only analogically. The participating principle, or essence, specifies the kind of *esse* which is received, and therefore also establishes the kind of entity which results from this participation. The participating principle also limits *esse*, although as yet we have not developed this point. The participated perfection is not included in the nature or essence which participates in it, but is really distinct from that essence. Therefore essence and *esse* can only enter into composition with one another. If on occasion Aquinas describes *esse* as accidental insofar as it is not included within the essence of the participating subject, he refuses to regard it as if it were a predicamental accident. The participated perfection (*esse*) unites with the participating subject as act with potency, so as to result in a being which is not merely accidentally but essentially one, an *unum per se*.

Granting all of this, however, one may still wonder how Thomas's view of the participation of beings in *esse* can be fitted into his threefold division of participation. Since it is not reducible either to logical participation or to the kind of real participation whereby matter participates in form or a subject in its accidents, what remains? It seems that the only possible remaining member of that division is that wherein an effect participates in its cause, and especially if it is not equal to the power of its cause. As is well known, Thomas often refers to created beings as participating in *esse*. On some occasions he means by this that they participate in *esse commune*, as we have seen from his Commentary on the *De Hebdomadibus*. On other occasions, however, he seems to mean that creatures participate in self-subsisting *esse*, or in God.[40] How are we to understand each of these usages, and can we fit them together? This brings us to the next major part of this study.

II

In an interesting passage in *Summa theologiae* I, qu. 45, art. 5, ad 1, Thomas draws a comparison between the way an individual partici-

---

40. See L. Dümpelmann, *Kreation als ontisch-ontologisches Verhältnis* (Munich, 1969), p. 24. While my presentation will differ in many ways from his, he has seen the need

pates in human nature, and the way any created being participates in the "nature of being." "Just as this man participates in human nature, so does any created being [*ens*] participate, if I may so speak, in the nature of being."⁴¹ His qualifying remark suggests that we should not simply identify the "nature of being" (*natura essendi*) with another abstract and universal concept.

In fact, as Thomas explains in *Summa contra gentiles* II, ch. 52, *esse* is not divided in the way a genus is divided by differences into its species. If *esse* were so divided, it would already follow from this that there can only be one self-subsisting *esse*. But *esse* is rather divided by reason of the fact that it is received in this or in that subject. Hence it follows with even greater force that *esse subsistens* or any separate *esse* can only be one.⁴² For our immediate purposes, the point to be stressed is this. Thomas is keenly aware of the difference between *esse commune* and any abstract and universal generic or specific notion.⁴³

---

to raise this question about the meaning of the *esse* in which creatures are said to participate.

41. "Sed sicut hic homo participat humanam naturam, ita quodcumque ens creatum participat, ut ita dixerim, naturam essendi: quia solus Deus est suum esse, ut supra dictum est" (ed. cit., p. 231). In this article Thomas is addressing the question "Utrum solius Dei sit creare."

42. "Sic igitur, si hoc ipsum quod est esse sit commune sicut genus, esse separatum per se subsistens non potest esse nisi unum. Si vero non dividatur differentiis, sicut genus, sed per hoc quod est huius vel illius esse, ut veritas habet; magis est manifestum quod non potest esse per se existens nisi unum" (ed. cit., p. 145). By way of contrast, Thomas concludes that nothing other than God can be its own *esse*.

43. Thomas makes the point that *esse* is not divided like a genus through differences in many different contexts, some of which will be noted below. Here one is also reminded of the procedure used by Thomas in the *De ente*, ch. 4, in what I have called the second phase of his complex argumentation for real distinction of essence and *esse* in separate entities other than God. If something can be multiplied (1) by the addition of some difference, as a generic nature is, or (2) by reason of the fact that the same kind of form is received in different instances of matter, or (3) by reason of the fact that in one case it exists in separation and in all others is received in something else, Thomas there argues that only the third will account for the multiplication of *esse*. On this basis he concludes that there can only be one self-subsisting *esse*, since this alternative in effect concedes this very point. While not there explicitly referring to *esse commune*, the similarity in procedure is worth noting. See my *Metaphysical Themes*, ch. 5. Also see *In I Sent.*, d. 8, qu. 4, art. 1, ad 2, although the third way is expressed differently (see ed. cit., vol. 1, pp. 219–20). For a simplified approach see *Compendium theologiae*, ch. 15 (*Opuscula theologica*, vol. 1, p. 17/Leonine ed., vol. 42, p. 87). See Fabro, *La nozione metafisica*, p. 220. One is also tempted to draw a parallel between the three ways of multiplying something proposed in the *De ente*, and the three main divisions of participation already considered above from lect. 2 of the *De Hebdomadibus*. It is true, of course, that the contexts differ and that there is no explicit reference to participation in the text at issue in the *De ente*. On this see S. MacDonald, "The *Esse/Essentia* Argument in Aquinas's *De ente et essentia*," *Journal of the History of Philosophy* 22 (1984), p. 163, n. 14. I would, however, interpret the *text* which he cites from the Boethian Commentary (p. 397) as indicating that Thomas wishes to show that it is impossible for *esse* to partici-

Still, one might be tempted to identify *esse commune* with self-subsisting being or God as one recent writer, Klaus Kremer, has done.[44] Thomas strongly rejects any such suggestion. For instance, in *Summa contra gentiles* I, ch. 26, he attempts to show that God is not the formal *esse* for other things, or the *esse* whereby each of them exists.[45] One of his arguments runs this way. What is common to many things does not exist as such apart from the many except in the order of thought alone. Thus animal is not something which exists apart from Socrates and Plato and other animals except in the intellect. The intellect can grasp the form of animal by abstracting it from all individuating and specifying characteristics. Much less, continues Thomas, is *esse commune* to be regarded as something which exists apart from individual existent things, except in the order of thought. If, Thomas concludes, God were to be identified with *esse commune*, then God too would exist only in the order of thought or in the intellect.[46]

It is important to bear this in mind lest one misinterpret a passage such as this one from Thomas's very late *Treatise on Separate Substances*, ch. 8, of 1272–73. There he is attempting to show against Avicebron that one need not postulate matter-form composition in created separate substances in order to avoid identifying them with God. Some po-

---

pate in anything in the first two ways rather than that it is impossible for something to participate in *esse* in these ways. But I would agree, as has already been indicated, that Thomas likewise refuses to reduce participation of beings in *esse* to either the first or the second type.

44. *Die Neuplatonische Seinsphilosophie und ihre Wirkung auf Thomas von Aquin* (Leiden, 1966), especially pp. 356–72. As my remarks in the following paragraphs will indicate, I find Kremer's interpretation of Aquinas on this point both forced and unjustified by the texts. For a long and critical review see Fabro, "Platonism, Neo-Platonism and Thomism: Convergencies and Divergencies," *The New Scholasticism* 44 (1970), pp. 69–100, especially from p. 80 onward (on Kremer's identification of *esse commune* and *ipsum esse subsistens* in Thomas, and the implications he draws from this).

45. This entire chapter bears reading, for it offers a host of arguments against any such pantheistic understanding of God, and concludes by considering and criticizing a series of reasons or motives which may have led some to accept it. One interesting possible source for such is a misinterpretation of a remark in ch. 4 of Pseudo-Dionysius's *Celestial Hierarchy:* "Esse omnium est super-essentialis divinitas." For Thomas any attempt to interpret this as implying that God is the formal *esse* of all things is offset by the text itself, for then God would be not *above* (*super*) all things but in (*inter*) all things or even something of all things. See ed. cit., p. 28.

46. "Adhuc. Quod est commune multis, non est aliquid praeter multa nisi sola ratione: sicut *animal* non est aliud praeter Socratem et Platonem et alia animalia nisi intellectu, qui apprehendit formam animalis exspoliatam ab omnibus individuantibus et specificantibus; homo enim est quod vere est animal; alia sequeretur quod in Socrate et Platone essent plura animalia, scilicet ipsum animal commune, et homo communis, et ipse Plato. Multo igitur minus et ipsum esse commune est aliquid praeter omnes res existentes nisi in intellectu solum. Si igitur Deus sit esse commune, Deus non erit aliqua res nisi quae sit in intellectu tantum." Ed. cit., p. 27.

tency is present in such substances precisely because they are not *ipsum esse* but only participate in *esse*. Thomas then reasons that there can only be one subsisting *esse*, just as any form, when it is considered in itself and as separate, can only be one. So it is that things which differ in number are one in species, since the nature of the species simply considered in itself is one. If such a specific nature could exist in itself, then it would also be one in the order of reality. The same holds, continues Thomas, for a genus in reference to its species, until we reach *esse* itself, which is most common. That is, if any genus could exist apart from its species, it could only be one. But in the case of *esse*, Thomas implies, there is a self-subsisting *esse*. Therefore he concludes that this self-subsisting *esse* can only be one, and that in addition to it no other subsisting entity can be pure *esse*.[47]

One should not infer from this, however, either that Thomas regards *esse commune* as another genus, albeit the most general one, or that he is identifying *esse commune* with God. His purpose is rather to show that if, *per impossibile*, a genus or species could subsist in itself, it could only be one. So too, since there is a self-subsisting *esse*, it can only be one.

In other contexts Thomas brings out the difference between *esse commune* and self-subsisting *esse* in still another way. For instance, in *De potentia*, qu. 7, art. 2, ad 4, he explicitly makes the point that the divine *esse* which is identical with the divine essence (*substantia*) is not *esse commune* and is distinct from every other instance of *esse*. Hence through his very *esse* God differs from every other being. And in replying to the sixth objection Thomas acknowledges that being in general (*ens commune*) is such that nothing is added to it, but not in such a way that no addition can be made to it. On the other hand, the divine *esse* is such that nothing is added to it and nothing can be added to it. Therefore, he concludes, the divine *esse* is not *esse commune*.[48] In

---

47. Note in particular: "sublata omni potentialitate materiae, remanet in eis potentia quaedam inquantum non sunt ipsum esse sed esse participant. Nihil autem per se subsistens quod sit ipsum esse potest inveniri nisi unum solum, sicut nec aliqua forma si separata consideretur potest esse nisi una; inde est enim quod ea quae sunt diversa numero sunt unum specie quia natura speciei secundum se considerata est una: sicut igitur est una secundum considerationem dum per se consideratur, ita esset una secundum esse si per se existeret. Eademque ratio est de genere per comparationem ad species, quousque perveniatur ad ipsum esse quod est communissimum." In contrast with the unique *ipsum esse subsistens*, Thomas concludes that in everything else there is both *ipsum esse*, as act, and the substance (or essence) of the thing, which has *esse* and receives it as potency. (Lescoe ed., p. 79/Leonine ed., vol. 40, p. D55.)

48. "Ad quartum dicendum, quod esse divinum, quod est eius substantia, non est esse commune, sed est esse distinctum a quolibet alio esse. Unde per ipsum suum esse Deus differt a quolibet alio ente. . . . Ad sextum dicendum, quod ens commune est

other words, being in general is neutral with respect to such addition. Self-subsisting *esse* excludes the possibility of any kind of addition.[49]

In *Summa theologiae* I, qu. 3, art. 4, ad 1, Thomas makes this very same point. To be without addition in the sense that all addition is positively excluded is true of the divine *esse*. To be without addition in the neutral sense is true of *esse commune*. The only difference between the two discussions is that in the text from the *Summa* Thomas speaks of *esse commune* rather than of *ens commune*, as he does in his reply to objection 6 in the text from the *De potentia*. Even in the *De potentia*, however, he then refers to *esse commune* just as he had done in the corpus and in his reply to objection 4.[50]

In his late Commentary on the *Liber de causis* of 1271–72 Thomas finds its unknown author considering the following objection. Someone might argue that if the first cause is pure *esse* (*esse tantum*), it is *esse commune* which is predicated of all things; therefore it is not a given

---

cui non fit additio, de cuius tamen ratione non est ut ei additio fieri non possit; sed esse divinum est esse cui non fit additio, et de eius ratione est ut ei additio fieri non possit; unde divinum esse non est esse commune. . . ." (in *Quaestiones disputatae*, ed. cit., vol. 2, p. 192).

49. To illustrate the kind of "neutrality" he is here assigning to *ens commune* (and then, apparently, to *esse commune*), Thomas concludes his reply to objection 6 by drawing a comparison with animal taken in general (*animal commune*). If animal considered as such does not include the difference rational, neither does it exclude the possibility of its being added to animal. One should not conclude from this that Thomas has therefore identified *ens commune* as another albeit most universal genus. He is simply drawing this comparison in order to illustrate the kind of neutrality to addition which he finds in *ens commune*. Nor need this be taken to mean that something can be added to *ens commune* the way rational, for instance, is added to animal. Cf. *De veritate*, qu. 1, art. 1, where in speaking of being (*ens*) rather than explicitly of *ens commune* he had reasoned that if all other conceptions on the part of the intellect involve some addition to being (*ens*), still nothing can be added to being from without in the way a difference is added to a genus or an accident to a subject. We may assume that in the present context (*De potentia*, qu. 7, art. 2, ad 6) he is not contradicting this position but is, to repeat our point, merely illustrating the neutrality of *ens commune* and of *esse commune*, and contrasting this with *esse subsistens*. Given Kremer's insistence on identifying *esse commune* and *esse subsistens*, he understandably finds this text and its parallels difficult (op. cit., p. 361).

50. "Ad primum ergo dicendum quod *aliquid cui non fit additio* potest intelligi dupliciter. Uno modo, ut de ratione eius sit quod non fiat ei additio; sicut de ratione animalis irrationalis est, ut sit sine ratione. Alio modo intelligitur aliquid cui non fit additio, quia non est de ratione eius quod sibi fiat additio: sicut animal commune est sine ratione, quia non est de ratione animalis communis ut habeat rationem; sed nec de ratione eius est ut careat ratione. Primo igitur modo, esse sine additione, est esse divinum: secundo modo, esse sine additione est esse commune" (ed. cit., p. 17). Here he is answering an objection which would identify God with *esse commune* or *ens commune* if one maintains that in God essence and *esse* are the same. Thomas's reply to objection 6 in *De potentia*, qu. 7, art. 2, is addressed to essentially the same objection. Cf. *In I Sent.*, d. 8, qu. 4, art. 1, ad 1, where the same objection and Thomas's reply are expressed in terms of *ens commune* (vol. 1, p. 219).

being which is distinct from all others. That which is common is not rendered individual except by being received in something. Since the first cause is, in fact, a given individual which is distinct from all others, it seems necessary to conclude that it has *yliatim*, that is, something which receives its *esse*.[51]

Thomas comments that to this the *Liber de causis* replies that the very infinity of the divine *esse*, insofar as it is not restricted by any receiving principle, plays the role in the first cause which *yliatim* exercises in other things. This is so because the divine goodness and the divine *esse* are rendered individual by reason of their very purity, that is, by reason of the fact that they are not received in anything else. In commenting on this Thomas explains that something is said to be an individual because it is not its nature to be found in many things. But this may happen in two ways. It may be owing to the fact that the thing in question is determined to some one subject in which it is received. Or it may simply be owing to the fact that the thing in question is not of such a nature as to be received in something, and therefore is an individual of itself. Thus, if there were a separated whiteness which could exist apart from any receiving subject, it would be individual of itself. This kind of individuation in fact obtains in the case of created separate substances which are forms which have *esse*. In other words, such entities are not individuated by being received in matter. This explanation also applies, concludes Thomas, to the first cause which is

---

51. "Posset enim aliquis dicere quod, si causa prima sit esse tantum, videtur quod sit esse commune quod de omnibus praedicatur et quod non sit aliquid individualiter ens ab aliis distinctum; id enim quod est commune non individuatur nisi per hoc quod in aliquo recipitur. Causa autem prima est aliquid individuale distinctum ab omnibus aliis, alioquin non haberet operationem aliquam; universalium enim non est neque agere neque pati. Ergo videtur quod *necesse* sit dicere causam primam habere *yliatim*, id est aliquid recipiens esse." See *Sancti Thomae de Aquino super Librum de causis expositio*, ed. H. D. Saffrey (Fribourg-Louvain, 1954), pp. 64–65. Thomas has greatly expanded upon a brief statement of this objection by the author of the *Liber de causis* (see prop. 9), and seems to have read into it his own concern about not identifying the first cause with *esse commune*. The original objection reads: "Quod si dixerit aliquis: necesse est ut sit ⟨habens⟩ *yliatim*, dicemus. . . ." (p. 57). Thomas had attempted an etymological explanation of the rather mysterious expression *yliatim* in the immediately preceding context, by tracing it back to the Greek term for matter: "Nam *intelligentia habet yliatim*, id est aliquid materiale vel ad modum materiae se habens; dicitur enim *yliatim* ab *yle*, quod est materia" (p. 64). In fact, it seems that the Arabic original from which the corrupted Latin transliteration was taken really meant form in this context. See R. Taylor, "St. Thomas and the *Liber de causis* on the Hylomorphic Composition of Separate Substances," *Mediaeval Studies* 41 (1979), pp. 510–11. As Taylor also points out, while being mistaken in thinking that *yliatim* is derived from the Greek term for matter, "he was quite correct in maintaining that in the *De causis* the intelligences do not have matter." At the same time, Taylor correctly also notes that in relating form to *esse* as potency to act Thomas was reading his own position into his explanation of the *De causis* (pp. 512–13).

subsisting *esse* itself. Most important for our immediate purposes, however, is Thomas's continuing refusal to identify *esse commune* with *esse subsistens*.[52]

If this is granted, it must also be acknowledged that there are other passages where Thomas refers to beings or to created beings as participating in self-subsisting *esse* or in their cause. How is this to be reconciled with his view that finite entities participate in *esse commune*? An extremely important discussion of this is contained in Thomas's Commentary on the *Divine Names*, ch. V, lect. 2, dating from 1265–67. Here Thomas finds Dionysius drawing out certain implications from his conclusion that God is the universal cause of being, that is, by showing that he is the cause of all particular beings (*entium*), including the various levels or degrees of beings. These levels include, continues Thomas, angelic substances in their various degrees; substances which are not bodies but are united to bodies, i.e., souls; corporeal substances themselves; accidents insofar as they fall into the nine supreme genera of predicaments; and finally, things which exist not in the nature of things but only in thought and which are called *entia rationis*, such as genera, species, mental states (here illustrated by opinion), and others of this kind.[53]

Shortly thereafter Pseudo-Dionysius shows that God is the cause of *esse commune* itself. As Thomas interprets this, Pseudo-Dionysius first indicates that *esse* is common to all things; then he explains how *esse*

---

52. Saffrey ed., pp. 65–66. Note in particular: "Sed ad hoc respondet quod ipsa *infinitas* divini *esse*, in quantum scilicet non est terminatum per aliquod recipiens, habet in causa prima vicem *yliatim* quod est in aliis rebus. . . . ita divina *bonitas* et esse individuatur ex ipsa sui puritate per hoc scilicet quod ipsa non est recepta in aliquo. . . . Quod autem aliquid non sit natum esse in multis hoc potest contingere dupliciter. Uno modo per hoc quod est determinatum ad aliquid unum in quo est, sicut . . . haec albedo quae est recepta in hoc subiecto, non potest esse nisi in hoc. . . . et hic est secundus modus quo aliquid non est natum esse in multis, quia scilicet non est natum esse in aliquo, sicut, si albedo esset separata sine subiecto existens, esset per hunc modum individua. Et hoc modo est individuatio in substantiis separatis quae sunt formae habentes esse, et in ipsa causa prima quae est ipsum esse subsistens."

53. *In librum beati Dionysii De divinis nominibus expositio*, ed. C. Pera (Turin-Rome, 1950), p. 244, n. 655. Earlier in his Commentary (see ch. V, lect. 1) Thomas had commented on Dionysius's view that God is the universal cause of being. See in particular n. 629 (p. 234), where Thomas explains that all things other than God have "esse receptum et participatum et ideo non habent esse secundum totam virtutem essendi, sed solus Deus, qui est ipsum esse subsistens, secundum totam virtutem essendi, esse habet"; n. 630 (pp. 234–35), where he warns that Dionysius's statement about God's being the *esse* for existents (*ipse est esse existentibus*) should not be taken to mean that God himself is the formal *esse* of existents, but rather in a causal sense; n. 631 (p. 235), where Thomas comments: "*et iterum omnia Ipso participant*, sicut prima forma exemplari; *et* non solum est causa quantum ad fieri rerum, sed et quantum ad totum esse et durationem." Also see n. 634 for an interesting discussion of the ways Dionysius agrees and disagrees with the Platonic doctrine of separate forms.

commune stands in relation to God. Granted the diversity in levels of beings, Thomas concludes his discussion of the first step by noting that nothing can be described as an existent unless it has *esse*. This is what he means, therefore, by referring to *esse* as common. It is that intrinsic principle found in every being, that is, every substance, which accounts for the fact that it exists. As regards the second step, Thomas comments that *esse commune* is related to God and to other existents in very different fashion. In fact, Thomas spells out three such differences.[54]

First of all, other existents depend on *esse commune*, but God does not. Rather, *esse commune* itself depends on God. If we wonder how this can be, this becomes clearer as Thomas develops the second and third differences. Secondly, therefore, all other existents are contained under *esse commune* itself, but God is not. *Esse commune* itself rather falls under God's power. For God's power is more extended than is created *esse*. By this Thomas must mean that God can create many things which he does not actually create and to which *esse commune* does not actually extend.[55]

As a third difference Thomas explains that all other existents participate in *esse*, but that God does not. On the contrary, created *esse* or *esse commune* is a kind of participation in God and a likeness of God. So it is that Pseudo-Dionysius can say that *esse commune* has God, meaning that it participates in a likeness of God, and that God does not have *esse*, meaning that God does not participate in it. Thomas goes on to explain that God is an existent before every other substance and every other being and before every *aevum*, not only in terms of duration or order, but also in terms of causality. God is the cause of existence (*causa subsistendi*) for all other things, and their principle of being (*principium essendi*). He is also the end to which all things tend.[56]

54. See n. 658 (p. 245): ". . . ostendit quod Deus est causa ipsius esse communis; et circa hoc, duo facit: primo, ostendit quod ipsum esse est omnibus commune; secundo, ostendit qualiter ipsum esse commune se habeat ad Deum. . . ." Also see nn. 659–60: "Et licet huiusmodi *dignitates essendi* superioribus tantum substantiis conveniant, tamen hoc ipsum quod est *esse, ab omnibus existentibus* non *derelinquitur*, quia nihil potest dici existens nisi habeat esse. . . . ostendit quomodo esse se habeat ad Deum; et dicit quod *ipsum esse* commune *est ex* primo Ente, quod est Deus, et ex hoc sequitur quod esse commune aliter se habeat ad Deum quam alia existentia, quantum ad tria. . . ."

55. ". . . primo quidem, quantum ad hoc quod alia existentia dependent ab esse communi, non autem Deus, sed magis esse commune dependet a Deo; et hoc est quod dicit quod ipsum *esse* commune est *ipsius Dei*, tamquam ab Ipso dependens, *et non ipse* Deus *est esse*, idest ipsius esse communis, tamquam ab ipso dependens. Secundo, quantum ad hoc quod omnia existentia continentur sub ipso esse communi, non autem Deus, sed magis esse commune continetur sub eius virtute, quia virtus divina plus extenditur quam ipsum esse creatum. . . ." (ibid.).

56. Ibid. Note in particular: "Tertio, quantum ad hoc quod omnia alia existentia participant eo quod est esse, non autem Deus, sed magis ipsum esse creatum est quaedam

Two questions might be raised about this passage: How do other existents depend upon *esse commune*? And how does *esse commune* itself depend on God? As regards the first question, Thomas has indicated both that other existents are contained under *esse commune*, and that they participate in it. Here, then, we return to a theme we have already considered in other texts—other existents are said to participate in *esse commune*. This accounts for the fact that they are said to have *esse*, but are not identical with the *esse* which they have or in which they participate. This should not be taken to imply, of course, that *esse commune* actually subsists as such apart from individual existents. It rather means that every individual created existent may be viewed as only sharing in or participating in *esse*, with the consequence that the *esse* which is intrinsic to it is only a partial sharing in the fullness of *esse commune* when the latter is simply considered in itself.

As for our second question, in saying that *esse commune* depends upon God, Thomas has commented that it falls under God's power. I take him to mean by this that every individual existent exists only insofar as it is caused by God. Moreover, created *esse* has also now been described as a likeness of God. Hence, in participating in the *esse* which is efficiently communicated to it by God, the creature may also be said to participate in some way in God, that is, in his likeness. God is its exemplar cause as well as its efficient cause and its final cause.

With this we have rejoined the third member of Thomas's earlier division of participation, that whereby an effect may be said to participate in its cause, and especially if it is less perfect than its cause. In the case where a creature participates in God, its first cause, it is clear enough that the effect is less perfect than the cause. It is also clear that Thomas often draws a close connection between being by participation and being caused. Thus in *Summa theologiae* I, qu. 44, art. 1, he comments that if "something is found in some thing by participation,

---

participatio Dei et similitudo Ipsius; et hoc est quod dicit quod *esse* commune *habet Ipsum* scilicet Deum, ut participans similitudinem Eius, *non* autem *ipse* Deus *habet esse*, quasi participans ipso esse."

57. Ed. cit., p. 224. Note in particular: "Si enim aliquid invenitur in aliquo per participationem, necesse est quod causetur in ipso ab eo cui essentialiter convenit. . . . Relinquitur ergo quod omnia alia a Deo non sint suum esse, sed participant esse. Necesse est igitur omnia quae diversificantur secundum diversam participationem essendi, ut sint perfectius vel minus perfecte, causari ab uno primo ente, quod perfectissime est." Thomas's concluding remark in this discussion brings out two complementary features of his theory of participation, by turning both to Plato and to Aristotle, i.e., that one must posit some kind of unity to account for any multitude (the Platonic solution to the problem of the One and the Many); and that, according to Aristotle in *Metaphysics* II (993b24–31), that which is being to the maximum degree and true to the maximum degree is the cause of every being and every truth.

it must be caused in that thing by that to which it belongs essentially." He recalls that earlier in the *Summa* he has already shown that God is self-subsisting being (I, qu. 3, art. 4), and that *esse subsistens* can only be one. Therefore all things other than God are not identical with their *esse*, but participate in *esse*. But things which differ according to varying degrees of participation in *esse*, so as to be more or less perfectly, are caused by one first being, which is in most perfect fashion.[57] In replying to the first objection within this same article, Thomas comments that it follows from the fact that something is a being (*ens*) by participation that it is caused by something else.[58]

Thomas makes a similar point in ch. 3 of his *Treatise on Separate Substances*, where he is bringing out some points of agreement between Plato and Aristotle concerning separate substances: "Everything which participates [in] something receives that which it participates from that *from* which it participates, and with respect to this that from which it participates is its cause."[59] This text is interesting because it makes three points: (1) something may participate (in) some perfection (accusative case); (2) it then participates in that *from* something else (ablative case); (3) the source is identified as the cause which accounts for the presence of the participated perfection in the participant.[60]

On other occasions Thomas refers even more directly to the participant as participating in its source or in God rather than in *esse commune*. In these cases one is dealing with what Thomas at times refers

---

58. According to the objection, a relationship of effect to cause does not seem to be included in the intelligible content (*ratio*) of beings. Certain things can be understood without this relation, and therefore they can exist without it. To this Thomas replies that while relationship to a cause is not included in the definition of a being which is caused, it does follow from that which is included in its intelligibility: "quia ex hoc quod aliquid per participationem est ens sequitur quod sit causatum ab alio" (ibid.).

59. "omne autem participans aliquid accipit id quod participat ab eo a quo participat, et quantum ad hoc id a quo participat est causa ipsius: sicut aer habet lumen participatum a sole, qui [Leonine: quae] est causa illuminationis ipsius." Lescoe ed., p. 51/Leonine ed., vol. 40, p. D46. It is true that Thomas is here presenting this as Plato's opinion, but also as one with which Aristotle agrees. But there can be no doubt that it is also Thomas's personal view, in light of the texts we have seen, and in light of the fuller discussion in ch. 8 of this same treatise. For his remarks about Plato and Aristotle, see: "Sic igitur secundum Platonem summus Deus causa est omnibus immaterialibus substantiis quod unaquaeque earum et unum sit et bonum. Et hoc etiam Aristoteles posuit, quia, ut ipse dicit, necesse est quod id quod est maxime ens et maxime verum sit causa essendi et veritatis omnibus aliis." Ibid.

60. In this text the participated perfection is described as being in the participating subject. As will be seen below, this is one way in which Thomas refers to creatures as participating (in) *esse*, i.e., in the *actus essendi* which is intrinsic to them. As will be noted, however, at times it is difficult to determine whether Thomas is referring explicitly to the *esse* which is intrinsically present in the participating entity (see the *suum esse* in the text cited in note 57) or to *esse commune* when he refers to something as participating in *esse*.

to as an analogical cause or agent, and at times as one that is equivocal. His point is that the divine agent is not univocal with any creature.[61] As will be recalled, in the major text taken from his Commentary on the *Divine Names*, if a creature is said to participate in the divine *esse*, this is because a likeness or similitude of the divine is in some way produced in the creature.

We have an interesting illustration of this in a text taken from Thomas's Disputed Question *On Spiritual Creatures*, art. 1, of 1267–68:

> Everything which comes after the first being [*ens*], since it is not its *esse*, has an *esse* which is received in something by which the *esse* itself is limited; and thus in every creature the nature of the thing which participates *esse* is one, and the participated *esse* itself is something other. And since every thing participates in the First Act by assimilation insofar as it has *esse*, the participated *esse* in each thing must be related to the nature which participates [in] it as act to potency.[62]

In this text Thomas appeals to diversity of essence and *esse* in everything other than God. (Thomas has argued for this on the ground that there can only be one first being which is unlimited act and contains in itself the fullness of being.) From this diversity he concludes that the *esse* of such a being is received by a distinct principle which limits that *esse*. Here another important part of Thomas's views on participation of beings in *esse* is introduced, that is, that the participating and receiving principle also limits the participated act or *esse*.[63] Now Thomas goes on to express the diversity of essence and received

---

61. For this distinction in Thomas's Commentary on the *Sentences* see Montagnes, *La doctrine de l'analogie de l'être*, pp. 47–49. For this in some later writings see Fabro, *Partecipazione e causalità* (Turin, 1960), p. 452, n. 2. See especially ST I, qu. 13, art. 5, ad 1 (quoted by Fabro); *De potentia*, qu. 7, art. 7, ad 7: "... dicendum quod agens aequivocum oportet esse prius quam agens univocum, quia agens univocum non habet causalitatem super totam speciem, alias esset causa sui ipsius, sed solum super aliquod individuum speciei; agens autem aequivocum habet causalitatem super totam speciem; unde oportet primum agens esse aequivocum." Ed. cit., p. 205.

62. "Omne igitur quod est post primum ens, cum non sit suum esse, habet esse in aliquo receptum, per quod ipsum esse contrahitur; et sic in quolibet creato aliud est natura rei quae participat esse, et aliud ipsum esse participatum. Et cum quaelibet res participet per assimilationem primum actum in quantum habet esse, necesse est quod esse participatum in unoquoque comparetur ad naturam participantem ipsum, sicut actus ad potentiam." Ed. cit. (Calcaterra-Centi ed. in *Quaestiones disputatae*, vol. 2), p. 371. Here Thomas is again rejecting matter-form composition of spiritual substances. The corpus of his reply is a masterly statement of his general position concerning that issue, the essence-*esse* relationship within creatures, and, as can be seen from the passage cited here, his views on participation in *esse*.

63. This point is extremely important in connection with Thomas's understanding of the relationship between essence and *esse* in finite beings. Its importance will also emerge in the following section of our study when we turn to the issue of participation by composition and participation by assimilation.

esse in terms of participation. The nature which participates *esse* is one thing, and the participated *esse* something else. Until this point he has been speaking of the nature of the thing as participating (in) *esse*, where *esse* is expressed by the accusative case. But he goes on to explain that everything participates in the First Act (also in the accusative case) by assimilation, i.e., imitation, insofar as it has *esse*, and then applies act-potency composition to the participated *esse* and the participating nature.[64]

This is a helpful summarizing passage because here we find two usages of participation: (1) The essence or nature of the creature participates *esse*, taken here, presumably, as the *actus essendi* which is realized within this particular individual. (2) It participates in the First Act or God by imitation. Hence both composition and imitation are involved in participation. We shall return to this point below.

Similar language appears in ch. 8 of Thomas's *Treatise on Separate Substances*. There he notes that things which participate (in) *esse* (accusative case) from the First Being (ablative case) participate *esse* not according to the universal mode of being, i.e., the fullness of being, as it is present in the First Principle, but in particular fashion according to the determined mode of being which pertains to this or to that species.[65] And he notes that each and every thing is adapted to one determined mode of being in accord with the mode of its substance (essence). Thus the mode for a substance composed of matter and form will be in accord with its form by which it belongs to its given species. Therefore a thing composed of matter and form participates in *esse* through its form, from God, and according to its proper mode.[66]

Here again we find Thomas referring to things as participating (in) *esse* from the first cause. We may conclude from this that the *esse* in which they participate according to this passage is not the divine *esse*

---

64. As I shall point out below, it seems to me that in this text Thomas refers explicitly to the nature of the creature as participating not in *esse commune*, but in the *esse* which is intrinsic to the creature in that it is received and limited by the nature of the creature, and is related to the nature which participates in it (*esse*) as act to potency. This suggests that the *esse* in which the creature participates may be taken in three ways: (i) as *esse commune*; (ii) as the *actus essendi* which is intrinsic to the creature in that it is received by the creaturely nature; (iii) as *esse subsistens* or God, the unparticipated source.

65. "Sed considerandum est quod ea quae a primo ente esse participant non participant esse secundum universalem modum essendi, secundum quod est in primo principio, sed particulariter secundum quendam determinatum essendi modum qui convenit vel huic generi vel huic speciei." Lescoe ed., p. 80/Leonine ed., vol. 40, p. D55.

66. "Unaquaeque autem res adaptatur ad unum determinatum modum essendi secundum modum suae substantiae; modus autem uniuscuiusque substantiae compositae ex materia et forma est secundum formam per quam pertinet ad determinatam speciem: sic igitur res composita ex materia et forma per suam formam fit participativa ipsius esse a Deo secundum quendam proprium modum" (ibid.).

but *esse* insofar as it is realized in particular fashion in the given participants. They participate in *esse* from the first being, as Thomas phrases it this time. Again he singles out the important role assigned to essence, or to the form principle within the essence of a matter-form composite, that is, to determine the essence's appropriate mode or way of receiving *esse*. Shortly thereafter he refers to matter as, when it is simply considered in itself, having *esse* only in potency, and this, he continues, belongs to it because of its participation in (literally: of) the First Being.[67]

In another text from Quodlibet 12, qu. 5, art. 1, of 1270 Thomas refers to the fact that something which is in potency is actualized in that it participates in a higher act. And something is in act to the maximum degree in that it participates by likeness (in) the First and Pure Act (accusative case). This Thomas immediately identifies as *esse subsistens*. In short, here he is referring to a creature as participating by likeness or by imitation in subsisting *esse* or God.[68]

On some occasions Thomas describes this kind of participation—that of creatures in God—by reversing his perspective, that is, by looking at things from the side of God. For instance, in his Commentary on the *Divine Names* (n. 158) he contrasts the way in which the second and third persons of the Trinity proceed from the Father, and the way creatures come forth from God. In the procession of divine persons the divine essence itself is communicated to the persons which proceed; and so there are different persons which possess one and the same divine essence. But in the procession of creatures the divine essence itself is not communicated to the creatures which proceed from God. To admit this, of course, would be to fall into a pantheistic understanding of creation. The divine essence itself remains

---

67. "Invenitur igitur in substantia composita ex materia et forma duplex ordo: unus quidem ipsius materiae ad formam, alius autem ipsius rei iam compositae ad esse participatum; non enim est esse rei neque forma eius neque materia ipsius, sed aliquid adveniens rei per formam. Sic igitur in rebus ex materia et forma compositis materia quidem secundum se considerata secundum modum suae essentiae habet esse in potentia, et hoc ipsum est ei ex aliqua participatione primi entis, caret vero secundum se considerata forma per quam participat esse in actu secundum proprium modum." Lescoe ed., pp. 80–81/Leonine ed., vol. 40, p. D55.

68. "Sciendum ergo, quod unumquodque quod est in potentia et in actu, fit actu per hoc quod participat actum superiorem. Per hoc autem aliquid maxime fit actu quod participat per similitudinem primum et purum actum. Primus autem actus est esse subsistens per se." Spiazzi ed., p. 227. The text continues: ". . . unde completionem unumquodque recipit per hoc quod participat esse; unde esse est complementum omnis formae, quia per hoc completur quod habet esse, et habet esse cum est actu. . . ." Here again Thomas refers within the same context to something as participating in *esse subsistens* (God), and then to it as participating in *esse* where *esse* is that which perfects the thing's form, in other words, the intrinsic *actus essendi*.

uncommunicated, continues Thomas, or as he also phrases it, remains unparticipated; but its likeness, through those things which it communicates to creatures, is propagated and multiplied in creatures. In this way, therefore, divinity may be said to proceed into creatures and to be multiplied in them, that is, by likeness but not by its very essence.[69]

Thomas is evidently much concerned in this context about avoiding any semblance of a pantheistic interpretation of the procession of creatures from God. In fact, as he has implied, if one were to understand participation as meaning that the divine essence itself is communicated to creatures, this would involve a kind of pantheism. What Thomas does admit is that a likeness of the divine essence is communicated to creatures and multiplied in them. In fact, a bit farther on in this same Commentary (n. 178) he harks back to this same passage and explains that there he has shown that God is participated in by creatures in such fashion that he still remains unparticipated with respect to his own substance (or essence). In other words, God does not communicate his own substance or essence to creatures.[70]

In sum, it seems that Thomas refers to created beings as participating in *esse* in three different senses. (1) At times he means thereby that they participate in *esse commune*. This is to say that each creature merely shares in, without possessing in its fullness, the perfection signified by the term *esse*. It is not to imply that there is some kind of subsisting universal existence—*esse commune*—of which each creature would simply have a piece or a part. *Esse commune* does not exist as such apart from individual existents, except in the order of thought. (2) On other occasions Thomas refers to creatures as participating in the First Act, or the First *Esse*, or the First Being, by similitude or by imitation. This does not imply that creatures thereby have a part of God's being. It rather means that in each creature there is a partici-

---

69. See ch. II, lect. 3 (ed. cit., p. 51): "Nam in processione divinarum Personarum ipsa eadem divina Essentia communicatur Personae procedenti et sic sunt plures Personae habentes divinam Essentiam, sed in processione creaturarum, ipsa divina Essentia non communicatur creaturis procedentibus, sed remanet incommunicata seu imparticipata; sed similitudo eius, per ea quae dat creaturis, in creaturis propagatur et multiplicatur et sic quodammodo Divinitas per sui similitudinem non per essentiam, in creaturas procedit et in eis quodammodo multiplicatur. . . ."

70. See lect. 4 (pp. 56–57): "Ostensum est autem supra, quod Deus ita participatur a creaturis per similitudinem, quod tamen remanet imparticipatus super omnia per proprietatem suae substantiae." In this same context (n. 177) Thomas has referred to Dionysius's remark that divine things are known to us only by participation. Thomas comments that this participation is twofold: one insofar as our intellect participates in the intellectual power and the light of divine wisdom; another insofar as things which can be grasped by our intellect themselves participate in the divine, as things are good by participating in divine Goodness, and things are existent and living "per participationem divini Esse seu Vitae."

pated likeness or similitude of the divine being, that is, the *esse* which is intrinsically present to each created substance and which is efficiently caused in it by God. (3) On still other occasions, when Thomas refers to creatures as participating in *esse*, he seems to have in mind the *esse* which is intrinsic to the creature insofar as it is its act of existing (*actus essendi*).[71]

Even so, for Thomas to speak in this third way is also for him to indicate, at least by implication, that the creature simply has, or participates in, *esse commune* without exhausting it. The first usage, whereby creatures participate in *esse commune*, whether explicitly expressed or implied by the third usage, does not exclude the second major usage, whereby the created nature participates in self-subsisting *esse*. In fact, as we shall suggest below, in the order of philosophical discovery, the first usage should ultimately lead to the second. In the order of nature, on the other hand, the second usage is the ultimate metaphysical explanation for the first. If creatures do in fact participate in *esse commune*, this is ultimately because they participate in *esse subsistens*.[72]

71. For examples see ST I, qu. 44, art. 1 (cited above in note 57: "omnia alia a Deo non sint suum esse, sed participant esse"); *On Spiritual Creatures*, art. 1 (see note 62 and the English translation in the corresponding text, and note 64 for discussion); *De substantiis separatis* (cited in notes 65, 66, 67: while the passage cited in note 65 might leave one in doubt as to whether Thomas has in mind *esse commune* or the creature's intrinsic *actus essendi*, the latter interpretation is strongly suggested by the remainder of the text as quoted in notes 66 and 67); Quodlibet 12, qu. 5, art. 1 (see note 68). For an early text see *In I Sent.*, d. 19, qu. 5, art. 2 (Mandonnet ed., vol. 1, p. 491): ". . . quaelibet res participat suum esse creatum, quo formaliter est."

72. It is not always easy to determine which of these three usages of *esse* Thomas has in mind, and on occasion it is especially difficult to decide between the first and the third usages, i.e., between *esse commune* and *esse* taken as the *actus essendi* which is intrinsic to the creature. See, for instance, *Quaestiones de anima*, ed. J. Robb, p. 112: qu. 6, ad 2: ". . . dicendum quod ipsum esse est actus ultimus qui participabilis est ab omnibus; ipsum autem non participat. Unde si sit aliquid quod sit ipsum esse subsistens . . . , ipsum nihil participare dicimus. Non est autem similis ratio de aliis formis subsistentibus, quas necesse est participare ipsum esse et comparari ad ipsum ut potentiam ad actum." The first reference to *ipsum esse* would make one think of *esse commune;* but one wonders whether the final reference to *ipsum esse* may not rather be to the intrinsic *actus essendi*. This usage is clearly intended, at any rate, in the corpus of Thomas's reply (pp. 111–12): "Nam materia ex hoc quod recipit formam participat esse. Sic igitur esse consequitur ipsam formam, nec tamen forma est suum esse cum sit ejus principium. . . . Et ita in formis per se subsistentibus invenitur et potentia et actus, in quantum ipsum esse est actus formae subsistentis, quae non est suum esse." Also see SCG I, ch. 22 (ed. cit., p. 24): "Amplius. Omnis res est per hoc quod habet esse. Nulla igitur res cuius essentia non est suum esse [*actus essendi*, presumably], est per essentiam suam, sed participatione alicuius, scilicet ipsius esse [*esse commune* or *actus essendi?*]. . . ." For another clear reference to participation in *esse* in the sense of *actus essendi* see Quodlibet 3, qu. 8, art. 1 (cited above in note 39). Also see *In VIII Physic.*, lect. 21 (ed. P. M. Maggiòlo [Turin-Rome, 1954], n. 1153, p. 615): "Necesse est enim quod omnis substantia simplex subsistens, vel ipsa sit suum esse, vel participet esse. . . . Omnis ergo substantia quae est

This brings us to still another important difference between participation of beings in *esse* and the other major kinds singled out by Thomas in his Commentary on the *De Hebdomadibus*. If created entities participate in *esse commune*, this ultimately leads one to posit the existence of a self-subsisting source which is *esse*.[73] In other cases of real participation, Thomas will not permit us to conclude to the existence of a self-subsisting accidental form in which particular substances participate, or a self-subsisting substantial form in which individual instances of matter would participate. While Thomas stoutly resists any suggestion that *esse commune* subsists as such outside the mind apart from individual existents, self-subsisting *esse* does exist. It is his distinction between *esse commune* and self-subsisting *esse* which permits him to maintain this view, and yet to avoid any Platonic theory of subsisting universal forms.[74]

This also seems to go hand in hand with another distinctive Thomistic position, Aquinas's refusal to include God within the subject of metaphysics. For Thomas the subject of metaphysics is what he sometimes describes as *ens commune* (being in general), and sometimes as being as being or *ens inquantum ens*. He stands out among his contemporaries for refusing to admit that God himself falls under this notion of being which is the very subject of metaphysics. God can and indeed should be studied by the metaphysician, but only as the principle or cause of *ens commune* or of that which falls under *ens commune*. God himself is not included within *ens commune*.[75] If we may assume that

---

post primam substantiam simplicem participat esse. Omne autem participans componitur ex participante et participato, et participans est in potentia ad participatum." While such examples can be multiplied, enough have been offered to suggest that considerable care is needed in interpreting them.

73. See, for instance, ST I, qu. 44, art. 1, as cited above in note 57; *De substantiis separatis*, ch. 8, as cited above in notes 65, 67; Quodlibet 12, qu. 5, art. 1, as cited in note 68; *Quaestiones de anima*, qu. 6, art. 2 (cited in note 72). Arguments for God's existence based on participation also make this same point. See ST I, qu. 2, art. 3, for the fourth way. It is also clearly implied by the three arguments offered in *De potentia*, qu. 3, art. 5, to show that there can be nothing apart from God which is not created by him. See ed. cit., p. 49, especially arguments 2 (the way of Aristotle) and 3 (the way of Avicenna). See W. N. Clarke, "The Meaning of Participation in St. Thomas," *Proceedings of the American Catholic Philosophical Association* 26 (1952), pp. 152–54.

74. Cf. the texts cited above from SCG I, ch. 26 (note 46); *De potentia*, qu. 7, art. 2, ad 4 and ad 6 (notes 48, 49); ST I, qu. 3, art. 4, ad 1 (note 50).

75. See *In De Trinitate*, qu. 5, art. 1, ad 6 (Decker ed., p. 171:16–26), where *ens* is identified as the subject of metaphysics; qu. 5, art. 4 (Decker ed., pp. 194–95), where it is referred to as *ens in quantum est ens* (p. 194:26), and where *res divinae* are identified not as the subject of metaphysics, but as principles of the subject (p. 195:7–9); Prooemium to his Commentary on the *Metaphysics* (Cathala-Spiazzi ed., p. 2), where he identifies it as *ens commune* and refuses to include separate substances within the subject. These (God and intellectual substances) are rather studied by metaphysics as causes of

esse commune is coterminous in extension with *ens commune*, then we may conclude that the subject of metaphysics is limited to the kinds of being which participate in *esse*, and that it includes the *esse commune* in which they participate, but not the *esse subsistens* in which they also participate. As we have already seen from the important text from Thomas's Commentary on the *Divine Names*, there he excludes God from *esse commune*. If God does not fall under the *ens commune* which is the subject of metaphysics, no more does he fall under *esse commune*.⁷⁶

Perhaps a word should be said here about the precise relationship between *ens commune* and *esse commune*. Are they completely identical? As Thomas indicates in his Commentary on the *De Hebdomadibus*, they are most universal, and hence, they are equal in extension. But he had also noted there that while *esse* may be participated in by other things, *ens* may not be. When Thomas describes the subject of metaphysics as *ens commune* or as *ens inquantum est ens*, he is using *ens* in such fashion as to include both the essence principle and the existence (*esse*) principle found within any finite substance. Hence, strictly speaking, the subject of metaphysics for Aquinas is not the act of existing (*esse*) but being (*ens*), which includes, to repeat, both essence and act of existing (*esse*).⁷⁷ But, as we have now seen in many different contexts, Thomas constantly refers to creatures as participating in *esse*. Since he has denied that *ens* can be participated in, and since he has correlated the *esse* in which creatures participate with their nature or essence as act

---

its subject, i.e., *ens commune*. Also see *In IV Met.*, lect. 1, ed. cit., p. 151, n. 533: "ergo in hac scientia nos quaerimus principia entis inquantum est ens: ergo ens est subjectum huius scientiae, quia quaelibet scientia est quaerens causas proprias sui subiecti."

76. See above, note 55, for the text from the Commentary on the *Divine Names*.

77. In addition to the texts just cited (see note 75), see *In IV Met.*, lect. 2, p. 155, nn. 553, 558. There Thomas makes the point that if the name *res* is taken from quiddity, the name *ens* is taken from the *actus essendi*. Both designate the same reality, however, as Thomas repeats in n. 558: "Et ideo hoc nomen Ens quod imponitur ab ipso esse, significat idem cum nomine quod imponitur ab ipsa essentia." In short, both *res* and *ens* are convertible insofar as they designate the concrete entity, including both its essence and its *esse*. For the same see *De veritate*, qu. 1, art. 1, where Thomas offers his well-known derivation of what are often called the transcendental properties of being. For the explicit point that *ens* is that which has *esse* see, for instance, ST I-IIae, qu. 26, art. 4: "Sicut enim ens simpliciter est quod habet esse, ens autem secundum quid quod est in alio; ita bonum, quod convertitur cum ente, simpliciter quidem est quod ipsum habet bonitatem; quod autem est bonum alterius, est bonum secundum quid" (ed. P. Caramello, p. 130). Also see *In XII Met.*, lect. 1, p. 567, n. 2419: "Nam ens dicitur quasi esse habens, hoc autem solum est substantia, quae subsistit." See the text cited in note 17 above from Thomas's Commentary on the *De Hebdomadibus:* "Sed id quod est, sive ens, quamvis sit communissimum, tamen concretive dicitur; et ideo participat ipsum esse. . . ." (ed. cit., p. 397, n. 24). Cf. the text from the same cited in note 14 (p. 396, n. 23): ". . . quod ens, sive id quod est, sit, inquantum participat actum essendi. . . ."

and potency, it seems clear enough that *esse commune* also signifies the act principle (*actus essendi*) which is required for any concrete entity (*ens*) to be realized in actuality; but it signifies this act principle as considered in its fullness of perfection rather than as received in any given participant. It follows from this that while *ens commune* and *esse commune* are equal in extension, and while God is excluded from both of them, they are not completely identical nor are they perfectly convertible with one another.[78]

At the same time, it should also be noted that *esse* has been applied by Thomas to self-subsisting *esse* or God, in which creatures participate. When used in this way, of course, as *esse subsistens*, it is no longer included within *esse commune* or, for that matter, within *ens commune*. Confirmation for this is found in Thomas's Commentary on prop. 6 of the *Liber de causis*. There he is trying to explain what certain Platonists had in mind by stating that the First Cause is above being (*supra ens*). Rightly understood, says Thomas, this means that the First Cause is above being (*ens*) insofar as it (the First Cause) is unlimited or infinite *esse*. Being (*ens*), continues Thomas, is restricted to that which participates (in) *esse* in finite fashion. This in turn is proportioned to our intellect, whose object is quiddity (*quod quid est*), as is said in bk. III of the *De anima*. Therefore that alone can be grasped by our intellect which has a quiddity which participates in *esse*. Because God's quiddity is his very *esse*, he is beyond our understanding, that is, we cannot know him as he is in himself.[79] While Thomas is here commenting on a highly Neoplatonic source, he certainly agrees that we cannot arrive at quidditative knowledge of God in this life.[80] As we have noted, he also refuses to include self-subsisting *esse* within *ens commune*.

---

78. Thus while one can say that *ens commune* is the subject of metaphysics, one should not say this of *esse commune*. This is because *esse* here signifies the *actus essendi* rather than "that which is," which *ens* signifies and therefore which is also signified by *ens commune*.

79. *Super librum de causis*, ed. Saffrey, p. 47. Note in particular: "Sed secundum rei veritatem causa prima est supra ens in quantum est ipsum esse infinitum, ens autem dicitur id quod finite participat esse, et hoc est proportionatum intellectui nostro cuius obiectum est quod quid est ut dicitur in *III° De anima*, unde illud solum est capabile ab intellectu nostro quod habet quidditatem participantem esse; sed Dei quidditas est ipsum esse, unde est supra intellectum." For Aristotle see *De anima* III, ch. 4 (429b10ff.).

80. For fuller discussion of this, see my "Quidditative Knowledge of God," ch. 9 in *Metaphysical Themes*. See pp. 240–41, n. 80, for discussion of several remarks to this effect in Thomas's Commentary on this same prop. 6 of the *Liber de causis*.

III

With this we come to an issue which has divided Fabro and Geiger from the time when their two books on participation first appeared.[81] How does one ultimately account for the fact that finite beings are indeed finite or limited? Is it by appealing to the intrinsic composition within any such being of an essence principle which limits the *actus essendi* which it receives? Or is it rather by appealing to the fact that the *esse* of every such being is only a limited and deficient imitation of the divine being? In other words, when it comes to the ultimate explanation for the limitation of the many within the order of being, is this due to what Geiger calls participation by composition or to what he calls participation by similitude or formal hierarchy?

In accounting for the limited character of finite beings, Fabro assigns primacy to participation by composition, though he refuses to separate composition and imitation as sharply as he believes Geiger has done. Geiger, on the other hand, assigns primacy to participation by similitude in accounting for this. If the *esse* of a given being is limited, this is first and foremost because it imitates its divine source only to a limited degree, not because it is limited by the essence which receives it. Limitation is prior in nature to composition.[82]

This disagreement in interpretation centers in large measure on what Fabro calls transcendental participation rather than predicamental participation. By predicamental participation he means that all the participants have in themselves the same formality in terms of its essential content, and that the participated characteristic does not exist as such apart from its participants.[83] Here one has to do with "univocal formalities, such as genera with respect to species, and species with respect to individuals."[84] In other words, Fabro here has in mind the first two major kinds of participation distinguished by

---

81. Fabro's *La nozione metafisica di partecipazione secondo S. Tommaso d'Aquino* has appeared in three editions: (Milan: Vita e pensiero, 1939); revised (Turin: Società editrice internazionale, 1950; 1963). Here I am citing from the second edition. Geiger's *La participation dans la philosophie de S. Thomas d'Aquin* (Paris: Vrin, 1942), was reissued by the same publisher in 1953. Geiger notes at the end of his Introduction that his work was completed when the first edition of Fabro's book became available to him. He did manage to incorporate various references to Fabro in the notes of his work, including points of agreement and disagreement.

82. For an overview of this controversy see Helen James John, *The Thomist Spectrum* (New York, 1966), pp. 88–97, 108–18. For a good résumé of Fabro's personal reactions to Geiger's approach see *Participation et causalité*, pp. 63–73.

83. See *La nozione metafisica*, pp. 317–18.

84. See Fabro, "The Intensive Hermeneutics of Thomistic Philosophy: The Notion of Participation," *The Review of Metaphysics* 27 (1974), pp. 471–73.

Thomas in his Commentary on the *De Hebdomadibus*—logical participation, and real participation whether of matter in form or of a substance in its accidents. By transcendental participation he rather means that the participants have in themselves only a lesser likeness or similitude of the participated perfection, which does exist in itself either as a property of a higher entity, or in the pure state as a pure and subsisting formality. In the last-mentioned case we are dealing with the participation of beings in *esse*, with the consequence that the participated perfection can be predicated only analogically of the participants, not univocally.[85]

Geiger, on the other hand, distinguishes two different systems of participation, that is, participation by composition and participation by similitude. In the first case, participation is based upon a duality of a receiving subject and an element which is received. Here the fundamental element is composition. To participate is to possess something one has received. It is also the case that if the receiving subject is less perfect than the received perfection, the subject will limit that perfection. Hence limitation is also present in almost all instances of participation. Nonetheless, philosophies which adopt this kind of participation derive limitation from composition. Composition is prior in the order of nature. Geiger proposes this as a definition of participation by composition: It is the reception and consequently the possession of an element which has the role of form by a subject which has the role of matter. If limitation also results therefrom, this is due to the imperfection of the receiving subject; but composition is essential.[86]

By participation by similitude or formal hierarchy, on the other hand, Geiger has in mind more or less perfect states of one and the

---

85. See *La nozione metafisica*, p. 318. As Fabro also writes: "La partecipazione *analoga*, in concreto, è quella della creatura dal Creatore che, essendo l'essere per essenza, in sè riassume . . . tutte le altre perfezioni, *formalmente* se sono perfezioni pure, *virtualmente* se miste." For support he cites two interesting texts: *In II Sent.*, d. 16, qu. 1, art. 1, ad 3 (Mandonnet ed., vol. 2, p. 398): ". . . convenientia potest esse dupliciter: aut duorum participantium aliquod unum, et talis convenientia non potest esse Creatoris et creaturae . . . ; aut secundum quod unum per se est simpliciter, et alterum participat de similitudine ejus quantum potest . . . et talis convenientia esse potest creaturae ad Deum, quia Deus dicitur ens hoc modo quod est ipsum suum esse; creatura vero non est ipsum suum esse, sed dicitur ens, quasi esse participans"; *De veritate*, qu. 23, art. 7, ad 10: "creatura non dicitur conformari Deo quasi participanti eandem formam quam ipsa participat, sed quia Deus est substantialiter ipsa forma cuius creatura per quandam imitationem est participativa. . . ." (Spiazzi ed., vol. 1, p. 429/Leonine ed., vol. 22.3, p. 62). In both of these texts we see Thomas rejecting a model of "many to one" in the case of creatures which are said to participate in God, and accepting only the model of "one to another."

86. Geiger, *La participation*, pp. 27–28.

same form and their hierarchical ordering; this ordering is based on their unequal degrees of perfection. In this case participation immediately expresses a diminished and particularized state of an essence each time it is not realized in the absolute fullness of its formal content. According to this approach, the many, when contrasted with the unity of the first principle, is explained first and foremost not by intrinsic composition but by formal inequality. If X and Y both imitate a common source for their perfection, this is because X does so only to its given degree, and Y does so only to its given degree. Composition may also enter in here. Hence the distinction between the two kinds of participation rests not on the presence or absence of composition, but on the relationship between composition and limitation. If composition accounts for limitation, we have participation by composition. If limitation is prior in the order of nature to composition, we have participation by similitude or formal hierarchy.[87]

According to Geiger, Thomas found himself faced with the problem of the One and the Many, and with these two different ways of accounting for multiplicity. While Geiger argues that they are indeed two complete systems of participation, he denies that Thomas simply chose one over the other.[88] Nonetheless, on Geiger's account, in developing his highly original metaphysics of participation, including that of beings in *esse*, Thomas assigns primacy to participation by similitude or formal hierarchy.[89]

Geiger acknowledges that participation by composition is implied in the second main division from Thomas's text from his Commentary on the *De Hebdomadibus*. But he notes that participation by an effect in its cause (the third main division) falls on a different level. Even so, it is in terms of the note of formal inequality (of the participated perfection in the participants) that this kind of participation bears some

87. Ibid., pp. 28–29.
88. On the two systems as Thomas was faced with them, see pp. 63–73. On Thomas's refusal simply to choose one or the other see p. 31.
89. Geiger, *La participation*, p. 47. There he concentrates on Thomas's solution for the problem faced by Boethius in his *De Hebdomadibus:* How are creatures good—substantially or by participation? Geiger finds Thomas substituting for participation by composition "la participation par similitude ou par hiérarchie formelle, où la participation n'exclut pas, bien plus où *implique identité* entre l'essence de ce qui est par participation et ce qu'on lui attribue." For continued insistence on Thomas's assigning primacy to participation by similitude see pp. 49–55. See pp. 60–61, n. 3, where Geiger maintains the same when it comes to the case of essence as participating in *esse*. He insists that if a being is this kind of being by reason of its essence, and real by reason of its existence, one must account for the diversity and inequality which arises from the side of the essence. Here one must appeal to participation by formal hierarchy. The essence "which participates in existence is itself a participation of (*de*) the First Perfection, of which it is only a limited and fragmentary aspect." Also see pp. 64–65, 67, 217, 392–98.

similarity with the first two types. The effect does not receive in all its fullness that which the cause is capable of producing.[90] This is especially true when we are dealing with *esse* as it is realized in creatures. If the *esse* of a given being is limited, this is because it imitates its unparticipated source only to that given degree. Geiger admits that in creatures *esse* is always conjoined with a distinct essence principle. But this composition of essence and *esse* does not account for the fact that *esse* is present in the creature in limited fashion. Because of this, Fabro charges that Geiger has in effect undermined the ultimate justification for defending real composition and distinction of essence and *esse* in creatures.[91]

In reacting to this, I would first recall that participation and composition are closely joined by Aquinas, and that this is also true in the case of participation of beings in *esse*. A participant is united with that in which it participates (*participatum*) as potency and act. Hence essence unites with *esse* in this way. In addition to this, though I have not yet stressed this point, Thomas insists that act as such is not self-limiting. If one finds limited instances of act, and especially of the *actus essendi*, this can only be because in every such case the act principle or *esse* is received and limited by a really distinct principle.[92]

90. Ibid., pp. 49, 78.
91. Ibid., pp. 394–96. Geiger seems to have some difficulty in dealing with Thomas's view that act is limited by a distinct potency (see p. 394, nn. 1 and 2). The text he analyzes in n. 1, p. 396 (from *De spiritualibus creaturis*, art. 1), also seems to work against his stress on the primacy of participation by similitude. He comments that composition appears as an a priori condition for the existence and possibility of a finite being! For a general presentation of Geiger's views see, in addition to Helen James John (cited above in note 82), J.-H. Nicolas, "Chronique de Philosophie," *Revue Thomiste* 48 (1948), pp. 555–64. Fabro has referred to this as the most decisive and radical critique of Geiger's conclusions. For the charge that Geiger's approach undermines the ultimate reason for defending the real distinction of essence and *esse* in creatures, see Fabro, *Participation et causalité*, p. 64, where he is quoting (with approval) from Nicolas, p. 561.
92. For discussion see Nicolas, op. cit., pp. 561–62; Wippel, *Metaphysical Themes*, pp. 157–61; J.-D. Robert, "Le principe: 'Actus non limitatur nisi per potentiam subjectivam realiter distinctam,'" *Revue philosophique de Louvain* 47 (1949), pp. 44–70. While Robert does not find Thomas reasoning explicitly from this principle to real distinction of essence and *esse* in creatures, he acknowledges that such an argument is in accord with Thomas's principles. In the context just cited I have suggested that in *In I Sent.*, d. 8, qu. 5, art. 1, such an argument is presented by Thomas, but in the *sed contra* rather than in the corpus. It seems to me that in this particular case one may safely conclude that Thomas himself accepts the argument. For some texts where Thomas accepts and uses the principle that act as such or that existence (*esse*) is not self-limiting, see *In I Sent.*, d. 43, qu. 1, art. 1 (Mandonnet ed., vol. 1, p. 1003); *In I Sent.*, d. 8, qu. 2, art. 1 (p. 202); SCG I, ch. 43; ST I, qu. 7, art. 1; *Compendium theologiae*, ch. 18 (Leonine ed., vol. 42, p. 88:7–8). For the Latin for some of these and brief discussion see Wippel, op. cit., p. 158, n. 62. See pp. 158 ff. for discussion of Thomas's reason for accepting this principle or axiom.

Hence composition is necessary if one is to account for the limitation of *esse* within a given entity. On this point Fabro is surely correct.

It is also true, of course, that according to Aquinas, the essence and the existence principle (*actus essendi*) of any creature are both created by God, since the entire being is created.[93] Hence, at least within Thomas's perspective, there is little justification for Geiger's fear that appeal to participation by composition might lead to the defense of some kind of preexisting subject or essence which would be independent from God and would wait for existence to be created and poured into it at some point in time. Any such reading of Aquinas would, of course, be a caricature, though such an understanding of essence is not far from an interpretation actually imputed to a more traditional Thomism by some such as William Carlo.[94]

Even so, one may still ask about the essence principle itself of any creature. It is only by appealing to the essence principle of any such being that one can account for the fact that the being is of this kind rather than of any other kind and participates in *esse* to its given degree. But what about the essence itself? A metaphysical explanation must also be offered for it.

Here, it seems to me, Geiger has a certain point in his favor. Both the essence and the *esse* of any finite being are created, according to Thomas. If a given being has this essence principle rather than any other, this is because its essence imitates its appropriate divine idea and depends upon it as upon its formal exemplar cause. A divine idea

---

93. See, for instance, *De potentia*, qu. 3, art. 5, ad 2: "Ad secundum dicendum, quod ex hoc ipso quod quidditati esse attribuitur, non solum esse, sed ipsa quidditas creari dicitur: quia antequam esse habeat, nihil est, nisi forte in intellectu creantis, ubi non est creatura, sed creatrix essentia" (ed. cit., p. 49). Cf. *De pot.*, qu. 3, art. 1, ad 17 (p. 41). Also see J. Owens, "The Accidental and Essential Character of Being in the Doctrine of St. Thomas Aquinas," in *St. Thomas Aquinas on the Existence of God*, J. Catan, ed. (Albany, N.Y., 1980), pp. 91–92.

94. See Geiger, *La participation*, pp. 64, 393, n. 1. For discussion and refutation of this way of viewing things see Fabro, *Participation et causalité*, pp. 69–71; Nicolas, "Chronique," pp. 561–62. For Carlo see his "The Role of Essence in Existential Metaphysics," in J. Rosenberg, *Readings in Metaphysics* (Westminster, Md., 1964), pp. 278–81, which originally appeared in *International Philosophical Quarterly* 2 (1962), pp. 584–89; and *The Ultimate Reducibility of Essence to Existence in Existential Metaphysics* (The Hague, 1966), especially pp. 103–5. This is in connection with Carlo's insistence, along with a number of other Thomists today, that essence for Aquinas, when rightly interpreted, is reducible to the given degree or mode of existence possessed by a given creature. For discussion and criticism of this reading of Aquinas see my "Thomas Aquinas on the Distinction and Derivation of the Many from the One: A Dialectic between Being and Nonbeing," *The Review of Metaphysics* 38 (1985), pp. 587–90. If one minimizes the role of essence as a receiving and limiting principle for *esse*, as Geiger tends to do, one might rather easily move on to a position somewhat like that advanced by Carlo. Geiger himself, however, never took this step, apparently because he realized that the real distinction between essence and *esse* is an integral part of Thomas's metaphysics.

is nothing but a given way in which God understands himself as capable of being imitated by a creature. Hence the essence of any creature is an expression of a particular way in which the divine idea can be imitated and in fact is imitated.[95] At this point it seems that participation by composition goes hand in hand with causal dependency, not only in the order of efficient causality, but also in the order of formal or exemplary causality. In other words, participation by composition, as it is expressed in the intrinsic structure of any created entity, receives its final explanation in the order of extrinsic causality by leading one to recognize God not only as the efficient cause but as the formal or exemplar cause of every participant. And this, it seems to me, is to bring in the element of participation by assimilation or formal hierarchy, as Geiger would have it.[96]

In sum, both composition and assimilation or imitation are involved in Thomas's explanation of the participated structure of creatures. For the philosopher, I would suggest, who must begin with finite beings and only eventually reason from what he finds in them to knowledge of God as their cause, participation in *esse commune* comes first in the order of discovery.[97] Along with this comes eventual recognition of the essence-*esse* distinction within every such being. (As I read Aquinas, demonstration of real distinction between essence and *esse* within finite beings need not presuppose prior knowledge of the existence of God.)[98]

Explicit recognition of the radically caused character of any such being comes later in the order of discovery, and with this, eventual demonstration of the existence of God. After having demonstrated God's existence, one will then be justified in speaking of participation

---

95. For a general discussion of Thomas's views concerning divine ideas and his reasons for appealing to them see Geiger, "Les idées divines dans l'oeuvre de S. Thomas," in *St. Thomas Aquinas 1274–1974. Commemorative Studies*, A. Maurer, ed. (Toronto, 1974), vol. 1, pp. 175–209. For Thomas see ST I, qu. 15, art. 1, ad 3: "Unde idea in Deo nihil est aliud quam Dei essentia" (P. Caramello ed., p. 90); ST I, qu. 15, art. 2: "Sic igitur inquantum Deus cognoscit suam essentiam ut sic imitabilem a tali creatura, cognoscit eam ut propriam rationem et ideam huius creaturae" (p. 91); *In I Sent.*, d. 36, qu. 2, art. 2: "Unde cum hoc nomen 'idea' nominet essentiam divinam secundum quod est exemplar imitatum a creatura . . ." (Mandonnet ed., vol. 1, p. 842); *De veritate*, qu. 3, art. 2: ". . . unde essentia sua est idea rerum non quidem ut est essentia, sed ut est intellecta. . . ." (Spiazzi ed., p. 66/Leonine edition, vol. 22.1, p. 104).

96. For a somewhat different way of bringing together in complementary fashion participation by composition and participation by similitude see J.-D. Robert, "Note sur le dilemme: 'Limitation par composition ou limitation par hiérarchie formelle des essences,'" *Revue des sciences philosophiques et théologiques* 49 (1965), pp. 60–66.

97. Here, of course, I am assuming that one will proceed according to the philosophical order rather than the theological order, as this is indicated by Thomas himself, for instance, in SCG II, ch. 4. See *Metaphysical Themes*, ch. 1, especially, pp. 29–32.

98. See my *Metaphysical Themes*, chs. 5 and 6.

in *esse subsistens* as distinguished from participation in *esse commune*. Appeal to God as the formal exemplar cause as well as the efficient cause of any finite being is necessary to complete the picture. Only now will one be in position to recognize the creature as a created imitation and assimilation of the divine being. Hence, if with Geiger one wishes to speak of participation by assimilation or formal hierarchy, such enters in only at this point. That is to say, it comes later in the order of discovery. But it does seem to be first in the order of nature insofar as explanation in terms of extrinsic causes is concerned. Creatures actually exist because God wills them to exist and efficiently causes them. But God can will a creature of a certain kind to exist only if it can exist. And it can exist only if it is a possible way of imitating the divine essence.[99]

The Catholic University of America

99. For discussion of this see *Metaphysical Themes*, ch. 7, especially pp. 163–71.

7   *Habitus* and *Natura* in Aquinas
BERNARD RYOSUKE INAGAKI

I

In this paper, I shall attempt to clarify Aquinas's concept of habitus through a reflection upon its relation to the nature of man, an aspect of his theory of habitus the importance of which has not been sufficiently recognized. The central thesis of my paper is that in his mature thought, Aquinas understood habitus in its essential relationship to human nature qua end. Another thesis, in support of the central one defended in this paper, is that according to Aquinas the cause of habitus is not acts or the repetition of acts, but some preexisting natural principle—in the final analysis, human nature itself. Aquinas's concept of habitus, interpreted in this way, occupies a unique place in the history of the concept of habit in that no other thinker has ever developed a theory of habit in connection with human nature in such a systematic manner.[1] The concept also plays a crucial role in our attempt to understand Aquinas's metaphysical thought. Concerning the last point, I would like to add the following observations.

The problem of experience and metaphysics in the philosophical thought of Aquinas has been the object of my research interest for many years,[2] and it was partially in search of a solution to this problem that I began to study his concept of habitus.[3] At first sight, we get the impression that these two, namely, experience (or empiricism) and metaphysics, coexist without any tension in his philosophical thought.

---

1. John Dewey, as will be seen later, developed his theory of habit in close connection with human nature in his own way. He conceived human nature, however, as totally changeable and plastic, excluding metaphysical consideration.
2. Cf. R. Inagaki, *Studies in the Philosophy of Thomas Aquinas* (Sobunsha, Tokyo, 1970).
3. Cf. R. Inagaki, *The Philosophy of Habit* (Sobunsha, Tokyo, 1981). During the initial stage of my research, I was indebted to Vernon J. Bourke, *The Perfecting of Potency by Habitus in the Philosophy of Saint Thomas Aquinas* (Toronto, 1938).

He is no less an empiricist than Ockham[4] or Locke,[5] and at the same time he is completely at ease in his metaphysical speculations. Once we begin inquiring into the problem of the possibility or ground of this coexistence of experience and metaphysics in Aquinas, however, we are struck by the immensity of the difficulty. The ultimate ground of this synthesis is to be sought in his understanding of *esse*.[6] It seemed to me, however, that the concept of habitus could mediate between these two seemingly contrary demands and exigencies, namely, those of experience and metaphysics, insofar as we can, starting with the concept of habitus, which properly belongs to the realm of experience, come to understand nature on the metaphysical level, that is, nature viewed precisely under the aspect of being. In other words, it seemed that I could make the unity of empiricism and metaphysics in Aquinas's philosophical thought highly plausible by introducing the concept of habitus.[7] And I might add in passing that I also thought that in this way I might be able to offer a third way which could mediate between the so-called transcendental Thomism and another school of Thomism which strongly insists upon the empirical approach to the apprehension of being.[8]

In advancing the thesis that Aquinas understands the concept of habitus in its essential relationship to human nature qua end, the first problem we are confronted with is the ambiguity of the term *natura*. Aquinas uses the term "nature" with such ease that we might get the impression that there is no problem as to its meaning, even though it is used in extremely diverse contexts.[9] When we discover a set of strik-

---

4. E. A. Moody, "Empiricism and Metaphysics in Medieval Philosophy," in *Studies in Medieval Philosophy, Science and Logic* (Berkeley–Los Angeles, 1975), pp. 296–97.

5. F. C. Copleston, *Aquinas* (Penguin Books, 1955), p. 25; *A History of Philosophy*, vol. 5, pt. 1 (Image Books ed., 1964), p. 84.

6. Cf. Inagaki, *Studies in the Philosophy of Thomas Aquinas*.

7. Cf. R. Inagaki, "The Degrees of Knowledge and Habitus according to Thomas Aquinas," in *Miscellanea Mediaevalia* 13/1 (Berlin–New York, 1981), pp. 270–82.

8. On transcendental Thomism, see J. Donceel, "Transcendental Thomism," *The Monist* 58 (1974), pp. 67–85. On the empirical approach to the apprehension of being, see J. Owens, "Judgement and Truth in Aquinas," *Mediaeval Studies* 32 (1970), pp. 138–58.

9. Both Schütz (*Thomas Lexikon*) and Deferrari (*A Lexicon of St. Thomas Aquinas*) list the following nine senses of the term: (1) die Geburt, (2) das innere Prinzip der Erzeugung eines Lebendigen, (3) jedes innere Prinzip einer Thätigkeit, (4) die Form und die Materie eines körperlichen Wesens, (5) die Wesenheit eines Dinges, (6) jedes Ding der Welt, (7) die Substanz, (8) das Reich der Wirklichkeit, (9) das Reich der vernunftlosen Dinge; (1) birth, (2) the inner principle of the generation of a living thing, (3) every inner principle of an activity, (4) the form and the matter of a physical being, (5) the essence of a thing precisely as it is the source of its operations and activity, (6) an entity, anything viewed in its basic aspect, (7) substance, (8) the realm of reality, (9) the realm of irrational things.

ingly agnostic statements about nature in his writings,[10] however, we begin to see the problem. The problem can be formulated in the following way: Is it possible to discover or determine the central or core meaning of *natura* in the philosophical thought of Aquinas from which all other meanings or uses can be derived? I shall argue that the metaphysical concept of nature as conceived by Aquinas is just such an attempt to determine the central or original meaning of *natura*, and that a possible way of approaching this concept is through reflection upon the concept of habitus.

Through reflection upon the concept of habitus understood in an essential relation to human nature qua end, according to my argument, we can come to the understanding of human nature itself which transcends the realm of ordinary experience, thus opening the way to the understanding of nature in the metaphysical sense. The knowledge of human nature obtained through reflection upon habitus, in other words, is the place where the metaphysical understanding of nature is to be sought. It will be argued later that nature in the metaphysical sense is precisely nature as the work of divine creation. I do not claim that I shall be able to clarify fully in this paper the metaphysical concept of nature as developed by Aquinas. I shall be satisfied if I can show that reflection upon habitus is a possible way to the metaphysical understanding of nature in the philosophical thought of Aquinas.

II

Here I must dispose of an initial objection to my thesis. Against my thesis that habitus is the way to an understanding of human nature, and further to the metaphysical understanding of nature, an objection might be raised: Is it not act, according to Aquinas, rather than habitus that reveals nature? After all, nature is defined as the principle of motion or operation by Aquinas.[11] Therefore, by reflecting upon the acts of something, we can grasp its nature (so the objection might proceed). To this objection, I would answer that it is true that we must start with acts in our attempt to understand the nature of something, but what is revealed immediately by act is only the *an sit*,[12]

---

10. ST I, q. 29, a. 1, ad 3; cf. *In I Sent.*, d. 25, q. 1, a. 1, ad 8; *Q. D. de Pot.*, q. 9, a. 2, ad 5; *In Symbolum Apostolorum Expositio*, Prol.
11. *In II Phy.*, lect. 1; *De Ente*, c. 1; ST I, q. 29, a. 1, ad 4; q. 115, a. 2; III, q. 2, a. 1.
12. On this distinction, see *De Verit.*, q. 10, a. 8; ST I, q. 2, a. 2, ad 2; *In Ana. Post.* I, 2; II, 1.

say of the human soul, and not its *quid sit,* and that it is the latter we are really seeking when we inquire into the nature of something. In this connection we might recall the distinction Aquinas makes between two kinds of the intellectual soul's self-knowledge, namely, *particulariter* (which is concerned with the *an sit*) and *in universali* (which is concerned with the *quid sit*).[13] The latter cannot be acquired through a simple reflection upon acts, but requires what he calls *inquisitio diligens et subtilis*.[14] We might also refer here to Kant's criticism of *psychologia rationalis* or *Metaphysische Seelenlehre* which fails to make a distinction between the soul's *Selbstbewusstsein* and *Selbsterkenntnis*,[15] a distinction which corresponds to that of Aquinas mentioned above. All of these considerations point to the truth that we cannot come to the knowledge of the *quid sit* of human nature by simply reflecting upon our acts.

The reflection upon habitus, however, can reveal the *quid sit* of human nature. In what way, and in what sense? A somewhat rash and simplistic answer would be to say because habit *is* human nature. Habit is identified as the "second" nature in a time-honored and common usage (*consuetudo secunda natura*);[16] William James quotes with approval the duke of Wellington's dictum that it is "ten times more nature."[17] He is joined by Pascal, who speaks as though habit and nature are simply convertible.[18] Aquinas, as we shall see, does not identify habitus with *natura*. He does see, however, a very close connection between them all through his writings. In early writings he is more occupied with the empirical indications of habitus, such as facility, promptitude, and pleasure in action, and explains these modifications of action caused by habitus in terms of *convenientia* with *natura*.[19] In later, more mature works, he takes the position that the relationship to human nature belongs to the very concept of habitus: "For it is of the notion of habit that it imply some relationship to the nature of a thing, insofar as it is in accord or not in accord [with it].... habit primarily and per se involves a relation to a thing's nature."[20] Since habi-

13. *Q. D. de Verit.,* q. 10, a. 8; ST I, q. 87, a. 1.
14. ST I, q. 87, a. 1.
15. *Kritik der reinen Vernunft,* A 341–405; B 399–432.
16. This expression goes back to Aristotle's *De Memoria et Reminiscentia* 452a27–28.
17. *The Principles of Psychology* (Dover, 1950), vol. 1, p. 120.
18. *Pensées,* Brunschvicg ed., 89, 92, 93.
19. *In III Sent.,* d. 14, q. 1, a. 2; d. 23, q. 1, a. 1; d. 33, q. 1, a. 1; *De Verit.,* q. 10, a. 9; q. 20, a. 2. It must be pointed out that this way of explaining the experiential indications of habitus in terms of the *convenientia* with nature was not abandoned in later works. Cf. *De Virt. in Com.* 1.
20. ST I-II, q. 49, a. 3. "Est [enim] de ratione habitus ut importet habitudinem

tus is the principle of our acts, just as human nature itself is, the close connection between these two is quite clear. And in the case of habitus, we ourselves are its generating cause, insofar as we can be said to cause it through our acts.[21] We can view habitus from inside, as it were, in the sense that it is we that have made it. Thus, if habitus were identified with nature itself, human nature would be completely transparent to us, which is not the case in fact.

At this stage of my argument, I can say that since habitus is the principle of acts,[22] in reflecting upon habitus, rather than upon acts themselves, we can come closer to nature itself, which is the ultimate principle of acts, and that the reflection upon habitus can reveal nature better. We might say, using a Platonic figure,[23] that human nature is written in larger letters in the case of habitus than in the case of acts. In the following, I shall try to show that in the generation or formation of habitus, something more than our acts is exercising its causality, and that this something is, in the final analysis, nature in the metaphysical sense. Hence, through reflecting upon the process of the generation or formation of habitus, we can come to grasp human nature itself as the cause or ground of habitus. This will be the main line of my argument.

III

Let us begin with human nature as it presents itself to our ordinary experience, that is, as it can be observed by the senses, measured and described in terms of some general pattern or law. According to Aquinas, this is the study of man from the side of the body (*ex parte corporis*).[24] Human nature in this sense is greatly diversified and variable, or changeable. Aquinas speaks of mutable human nature: "natura humana est mutabilis."[25] In the modern period, John Dewey understood human nature as fundamentally plastic and mutable.[26] This is human nature insofar as it becomes the subject matter of our empirical, objective knowledge.

---

quandam in ordine ad naturam rei, secundum quod convenit vel non convenit. . . . habitus primo et per se importat habitudinem ad naturam rei."
21. In what sense precisely our acts are said to cause habitus will be discussed later.
22. ST I-II, q. 49, Prol.; q. 49, a. 3.   23. *Republic* 368D–E.
24. ST I, q. 75, Prol.
25. ST II-II, q. 57, a. 2, ad 1; cf. I-II, q. 100, a. 8, obj. 1 and ad 1; *De Malo*, q. 2, a. 4, ad 13.
26. *Human Nature and Conduct* (Modern Library ed., 1957), pp. 105–6.

The term "objective" in the last sentence was used in a special sense, that is, in the sense of excluding the subject. In other words, as long as we are dealing with human nature as it presents itself to our ordinary experience, the inquiring subject itself does not enter into the range of investigation. In the empirical, objective study of human nature, the subject, the "self," the "I," is excluded methodologically. Any study of man or human nature which excludes the "I," however, cannot be called a full and radical study of man.

The decisive question to be asked at this stage of argument is: Does our inquiry into human nature terminate here, that is, with the empirical, objective study of human nature? Aquinas's answer to this question can be ascertained from the distinction he makes as to human nature, namely, between the very essence of man (*ipsa hominis ratio*) and "those things which follow upon nature, namely, dispositions, actions, and motions."[27] The former, which can be identified with human nature in the metaphysical sense, he says, is totally immutable, while human nature in the latter sense is said to be mutable in some cases,[28] which obviously refers to human nature on the empirical level. Here I might add that John Dewey reveals in his empirical account of mutable human nature that he has some metaphysical presupposition for his empirical studies. He professes to recognize only mutable human nature, rejecting every form of dualism. He speaks, however, of the "pre-sentiment" by the instinct of the integration to be achieved.[29] We are guided, according to him, by the pre-sentiment of what we ought to be in our choices and decisions through which we constantly form ourselves.[30] Such a pre-sentiment, which is a kind of self-understanding, clearly transcending the realm of ordinary experience, can be regarded as a metaphysical insight into human nature. The difference in comparison with Aquinas is that Dewey never elaborates such a pre-sentiment or insight into metaphysical theory.

Our question now may be stated as follows: How is the above-mentioned distinction between *ipsa hominis ratio* and its empirical consequences or manifestations to be interpreted? Or: How can we, starting with the latter, come to grasp the former, namely, human nature in the metaphysical sense? How can we transcend the level of the empirical study of human nature? In answering this question, the first methodological requirement is a distinction concerning the concept of nature as understood by Aquinas. According to my interpretation,

27. *In V Eth.*, lect. 12.   28. Ibid.
29. *Human Nature*, pp. 169–70.
30. Ibid., pp. 181–83; cf. *A Common Faith* (New Haven, 1966), p. 16.

human nature as the object of empirical study belongs, strictly speaking, to the category of habitus (or rather, the first species of the category of quality, as will be explained later), and not to that of substance, with which nature in the metaphysical sense is to be identified.

If my interpretation is correct, that is, if so-called human nature on the level of empirical studies in the philosophical thought of Aquinas belongs to habitus as a species of quality, a new possibility is opened for the clarification of the concept of human nature in the metaphysical sense, as the ground or cause of habitus. The inquiry into the ground or cause of habitus is possible, because as pointed out before, I myself am responsible in some way for its formation (that is, its generation and corruption, strengthening and weakening), and for this reason I am in a privileged position to know the ground or cause of habitus.[31] Here, the meaning and reality of the "I" referred to above raises a difficult problem. Dewey would object that the empirical meaning of the "I" is exhausted by the category of habit.[32] In other words, when someone says "I," there the habits speak and nothing more. To this I shall rejoin, following Aquinas,[33] that the "I," the free agent, exercising the causality of freedom, which is responsible for the formation of habitus, is not itself habitus, but is closely connected with human nature in the metaphysical sense, because that is the ultimate principle of my acts. In any case, I shall argue that one possible way to grasp human nature in the metaphysical sense is to reflect upon habitus with a view to its ground and cause.

IV

The central text in which Aquinas considers the concept of habitus in relation to the very nature of the subject (*ipsa natura subjecti*) in which a habitus is found is *Summa Theologiae* I-II, q. 49, a. 2, where he takes up the question of how the Aristotelian division of the category of quality into four species[34] is to be systematically explained. Al-

---

31. That is, we can inquire into the ground and cause of habitus by way of self-knowledge.

32. *Human Nature*, p. 25; cf. K. Dunlap, *Habits: Their Making and Unmaking* (Liveright, 1972), p. 3.

33. I have discussed elsewhere (*The Philosophy of Habit*, ch. 7, pp. 267–96) Aquinas's view of the relationship between human freedom and habitus. Here I would like to point out that he clearly maintained that habitus is formed through exercise of freedom (ST I-II, q. 49, a. 4; q. 50, a. 3; a. 5), and that the power of free will (*liberum arbitrium*) is not habitus, but something prior to habitus (*In II Sent.*, d. 24, q. 1, a. 1; *De Verit.*, q. 24, a. 4; ST I, q. 83, a. 2).

34. *Categoriae* 8b25–10a26; cf. *Metaphysica* 1020a33–b25.

though Aquinas identifies habitus as belonging to the category of quality from his earliest writings,[35] and refers to four species of quality in other writings,[36] it is only in this text that he explains the fourfold division of the category of quality in a systematic manner. And it is here also that he maintains the close connection of habitus with nature itself in the clearest, most unambiguous way.

Here Aquinas proposes his own solution in criticism of the position of Simplicius in his Commentary on Aristotle's *Categories*.[37] Simplicius' work was translated into Latin by William of Moerbeke in 1266,[38] and it is clear that his treatment of the fourfold division of the category of quality was the occasion for Aquinas to articulate his own understanding of habitus in its essential relationship to human nature. As remarked before, Aquinas's concept of habitus is unique in this regard historically. John Duns Scotus does not seem to consider the relationship to human nature itself as the essential aspect of habitus, concentrating instead upon the relationship habitus has to acts.[39] This tendency is clearly present in the treatment of habitus in William Ockham.[40] In Francesco Suarez, habitus is treated exclusively in relation to acts.[41] Among classic commentators on the *Summa Theologiae*, it was John of St. Thomas who clearly perceived the uniqueness of Aquinas's concept of habitus in this regard.[42] As for contemporary commentators, neither R. Garrigou-Lagrange[43] nor J. M. Ramirez[44] seems to recognize the uniqueness of Aquinas's concept of habitus in this regard. It is easy to overlook the philosophical significance of Aquinas's position concerning the essential relationship habitus has to nature it-

---

35. *In III Sent.*, d. 14, q. 1, a. 2; *De Verit.*, q. 12, a. 1.
36. SCG II, c. 78 (here Aquinas refers to habitus as belonging to the *second* species of quality); *De Virt. in Com.* 1; *In V Met.*, lect. 16.
37. For Simplicius' Commentary on Aristotle's *Categories* in the Latin translation by William of Moerbeke, see *Simplicius. Commentaire sur les Catégories d'Aristote. Traduction de Guillaume de Moerbeke*, Édition critique, 2 tom. (Louvain-Paris, 1971–75).
38. Ibid., tom. 1, p. xi; J. A. Weisheipl, *Friar Thomas d'Aquino: His Life, Thought, and Works* (Garden City, N.Y., 1974), p. 152.
39. *In Lib. II Sententiarum (Opus Oxoniense)*, d. 3, q. 10, n. 18; III, d. 33, n. 12; IV, d. 45, q. 1, n. 2.
40. *Quaestiones in Librum III Sententiarum (Reportatio)*, q. 12, a. 2.
41. Suarez explicitly states in his definition of habitus that "habitus est qualitas . . . per se primo ordinata ad operationem." *Disputationes Metaphysicae, Opera Omnia*, tom. XXVI, Disputatio 44, p. 664; cf. p. 673. He also maintains that "actus per se efficere habitum" (*De Habitibus in Communi*, ed. W. Ernst [St. Beno Verlag, 1964], p. 251; cf. p. 254). Cf. *Disputationes*, pp. 664, 665, 666.
42. *Cursus Theologicus*, In I–II *De Habitibus* (Quebec, 1949), pp. 41, 42; cf. *Cursus Philosophicus* (Turin-Rome, 1948), tom. 1, pp. 609–21.
43. *De Beatitudine. De Actibus Humanis et Habitibus* (Turin-Rome, 1951), pp. 416–18.
44. *De Habitibus in Communi, Opera Omnia*, tom. 6 (Instituto de Filosofia "Luis Vives," 1973), tom. 6-1, pp. 31–94.

self, because the association of habit with nature is a commonplace, almost a truism, as the expression "habit, or second nature" suggests. The uniqueness of Aquinas's position, nevertheless, can hardly be overemphasized.

Although Aquinas disagrees with Simplicius as to the consideration of various qualities,[45] the basic disagreement hinges on a matter of principle, namely, that the more natural (*naturalius*) is always the prior.[46] By applying this principle, Aquinas then reasons that, since Aristotle numbers habitus (and *dispositio*) as the first species of quality, it must be more natural than other species, that is, closest to nature itself.

Aquinas begins his explanation with the definition of quality as "a certain mode of substance." Every mode (*modus*), however, is a determination of some potentiality according to some standard (*mensura*),[47] which is an actuality of some kind. Now, in the case of quality, the potentiality in question is either the pure potentiality of matter or the unactualized potentiality of the subject. And the standards according to which the potentiality is to be determined are, respectively, substantial being (*esse substantiale*) and accidental being (*esse accidentale*). The quality which results from the determination of the potentiality of matter according to substantial being, however, is the very essence or nature of a thing (*differentia substantiae*), which properly belongs to the category of substance rather than to that of quality. The quality in the proper sense, that is, the accidental or categorical quality, is found when the potentiality of the subject is determined according to accidental being.

The mode or the determination of a subject according to accidental being, Aquinas observes, can be taken (1) in relation to the nature itself of the subject (*in ordine ad ipsam naturam subjecti*), (2) according to action and passion which follow the principles of nature, namely, the matter and form, or (3) according to quantity. What Aquinas means is this: since quality stands for the "how" (*quale*) of a thing, and nature (itself) is the first that is considered in a thing,[48] various species of quality can be ordered according to how close or remote they are from nature itself. And it is from this viewpoint that Aquinas explains the Aristotelian fourfold division of the category of quality.

The fourth species of quality, namely, *figura et forma*, results when

---

45. Such as *figura, sanitas, pulchritudo*.
46. "semper quod naturalius est, prius est." ST I-II, q. 49, a. 2.
47. Aquinas often refers to this dictum of Augustine, *Super Genesim ad Litteram* IV, 3, PL 34:299; cf. ST I, q. 5, a. 5.
48. "Natura est id quod primum consideratur in re." ST I-II, q. 49, a. 2.

the potentiality of the subject is determined according to quantity. It is the *quale* of a thing revealed by its quantitative aspects. The third (*qualitas passiva*) and the second species (*potentia activa*) are found respectively when the subject is determined according to *passio*, which follows the matter, and according to *actio*, which follows the form of the thing. Finally, the first species, namely, *habitus et dispositio*, results when the subject is determined in relation to the nature itself of a thing. Here it is clearly stated that the nature is taken in the sense of end (*finis*).[49] Precisely because the first species of quality is considered in relation to the nature qua end, that is, from the viewpoint of its *convenientia* or *non convenientia* with the nature qua end, habitus is always good or bad.[50]

It is beyond any possible dispute that Aquinas maintains that the relationship to the nature of a thing, that is, human nature itself, belongs to the very concept of habitus. In view of the general acceptance of that concept of habitus developed in later Scholasticism, notably by Suarez, it is necessary to add another clarification, however. As mentioned before, Suarez considers habitus in its essential relationship to act. He distinguishes habitus from *potentia* (active power), in this, that while the latter is the primary faculty of operation, the former contributes facility to the primary faculty.[51] Now, Aquinas does not deny that habitus can be related to acts or operations. Since habitus is related essentially to the nature itself of a thing, if the nature is further related to operation or something to be achieved through operation, then habitus will be related to operation.[52] Again, if the nature of the subject in which a habit is found consists in a relation to acts, it will follow that the habitus principally involves a relation to acts, Aquinas observes.[53] The decisive point is that the relationship to *potentia* (active power), and to acts, does not belong to the very concept of habitus; but it is rather the relationship to the nature of a thing, that is, human nature itself, that belongs to the very concept of habitus.[54]

---

49. "Et quia 'ipsa forma et natura rei est finis et cujus causa fit aliquid' ut dicitur in II Phys.; ideo in prima specie consideratur et bonum et malum" (ibid.); "Et si addatur bene vel male, quod pertinet ad rationem habitus, oportet quod attendatur ordo ad naturam, quae est finis" (ibid., ad 1).

50. ST I-II, q. 49, d. 2, ad 1; cf. *In III Sent.*, d. 23, q. 1, a. 1.

51. *Disputationes*, p. 664. According to Suarez, habitus contributes to potentia only "quaedam perfectio valde accidentaria" (*De Habitibus*, p. 251) or "quasi minimum complementum" (ibid.).

52. ST I-II, q. 49, a. 3.   53. Ibid.

54. Ibid., ad 2: "... non est de ratione habitus quod respiciat potentiam, sed respiciat naturam."

V

It has been sufficiently established that, according to Aquinas, habitus is essentially related to the very nature of a thing, that is, to human nature itself qua end. The next question to be asked is: In what way precisely is a habit related to the very nature of a thing?

In order to answer this question, it is necessary to reflect upon the process of the formation of a habitus and to elucidate its cause, for nature itself will manifest itself as the ground and cause of habitus, according to my interpretation of Aquinas's thought. Now the first thing that comes to mind as the cause of habit will be acts, or rather the repetition of similar acts. Aristotle observes that men become builders by building, and harpists by playing on the harp.[55] He also remarks that "one swallow does not bring the spring, and the spring does not come with only one balmy day."[56] It is clear that in most instances of habit formation, the repetition of similar acts with some intensity over an extended period is a necessary requirement.[57] Or, we can say that generally a fair amount of practice or performance is necessary for the acquisition of a habitus.[58] We know from experience, however, that the mere repetition of inattentive and negligent acts does not generate or strengthen habitus, but rather tends to weaken them.[59] Again, Aristotle points out that we cannot habituate a stone to move upward by throwing it up ten thousand times, or fire to go down.[60] This proves conclusively that simply to identify repeated acts as the generating cause of a habit is an oversimplification. It will be necessary to distinguish the principal and the instrumental cause of a habitus, or the true cause of a habitus from a condition which is required for its formation. The acts—and in most cases, repeated acts—may be an occasion or necessary condition for the formation of a habitus, rather than the principal cause.

Now, Aquinas does affirm that a habitus is caused by acts.[61] Upon closer reading, however, it becomes clear that he does not simply identify our acts with the efficient cause of a habitus, as Ockham and Suarez do later. For he calls our attention to the causality exercised by

---

55. *Eth. Nic.* 1103a33. 56. Ibid., 1098a18–19.
57. We must be beware of the limited validity of the common explanation of the formation of habits in terms of the plasticity of the organic matter which constitutes the subject of habits. Cf. James, op. cit., p. 105.
58. The terms "practice" or "performance" are preferable, because the so-called repetition is not strictly a repetition, but a process of repeated trial. Dunlap, op. cit., pp. 34, 35, 36, 39.
59. Cf. ST I-II, q. 52, a. 3. 60. *Eth. Nic.* 1103a21–22.
61. ST I-II, q. 51, a. 2; a. 3; q. 63, a. 2.

some active principle which preexists in the subject of the habitus. He says that a habit is generated through acts "insofar as the passive potency is moved by some active principle."[62]

What is, then, the true, principal cause of a habit? It is noteworthy in this respect that Aquinas raises the question "utrum aliquis habitus sit a natura?" at the outset of his consideration of the problem of the cause of habits.[63] He is concerned not simply with the problem of some "innate" or "inborn" habitus, according to my interpretation, but precisely with the causality exercised by nature itself in the generation of habits.[64] His question, therefore, can be formulated in the following way: Is a habitus caused by some natural principle, or is nature itself, rather than acts, the principal cause of a habitus?

In the case of the natural habit of *intellectus*, namely, the habit of principles, Aquinas maintains that it is caused, partially, by the very nature of the intellectual soul (*ipsa natura animae intellectualis*)[65] or by the agent intellect immediately.[66] For example, in the case of the first principle "every whole is greater than its part," once what is "whole" and what is "part" are known (this knowledge is to be acquired through the senses, that is, *ab exteriori principio*), to understand "every whole is greater than its part" belongs to man from the very nature of the intellectual soul, according to Aquinas. In other words, the natural habit whereby we assent to the truth of that proposition is said to be caused by the very nature of our intellectual soul. What is meant, then, by "very nature" (*ipsa natura*) here precisely, and how can we know it?

The following explanation offered by Aquinas can help us in answering that question. Since a habitus is the actualization of some potentiality, on the one hand, and is a certain perfection, it can be found only in those subjects which are *in potentia* in some way, that is, in potentiality to further perfections. On the other hand, since a habitus is not received in the subject in the mode of a *passio*, but is in the subject in the mode of a permanent quality or form, the subject of a habitus cannot be in the state of total passivity (in relation to the habitus to be received or formed), but must be active in some way. In other words,

---

62. "Habitus per actum generatur inquantum potentia passiva movetur ab aliquo principio activo." ST I-II, q. 51, a. 3; cf. q. 51, a. 2.
63. ST I-II, q. 51, a. 1.
64. Aquinas makes a reference to such causality in the following passage: "Unde si aliquis habitus sit in intellectu possibili immediate ab intellectu agente causatus, . . ." (ST I-II, q. 53, a. 1); cf. ST I-II, q. 63, a. 2, ad 3: "Virtutum acquisitarum praeexistunt in nobis quaedam semina, sive principia secundum naturam. . . . Sic igitur actus humani, inquantum procedunt ex altioribus principiis, possunt causare virtutes acquisitas humanas."
65. Ibid., q. 51, a. 1.   66. Ibid., q. 53, a. 1.

there must be some active principle (*principium activum*) in the subject as well as some passive element. Thus, it is clear that the subject of a habitus must be of a twofold structure, having both an active and a passive principle (*principium activum* and *passivum*).[67]

We may conclude in the light of the preceding explanation that Aquinas has the active principle (which is natural) in mind when he says that the natural habitus is caused by the very nature of the intellectual soul. In other words, the true, principal cause of a habitus is the active principle, which is natural, and not the repetition of similar acts or practice. Aquinas says explicitly that "all virtues [and therefore, all habits] which are acquired through our acts proceed from some natural principles which preexist in us."[68] He does not deny that habits are acquired through our acts, and to that extent our acts can be called the cause of habits. The principal cause, from which habits proceed, however, according to him, is some natural principle preexisting in us. The following metaphor used by Aquinas may be helpful in clarifying this point.

The process of habit-formation is compared to the process of the gradual drying and finally burning up of some wet object, say a piece of wood.[69] First, fire is set at one corner of the object. This initial fire must overcome the moisture, that is, the passive state of the remaining part, if the whole object is to burn up. The burning up of the whole object, that is, the complete actualization of the burning power of the object, corresponds to the formation of habits. The metaphor brings out that the true, principal cause of habit-formation is to be sought in the *principium activum*, symbolized by the initial fire. The function of acts or the repetition of acts, on the other hand, is merely to overcome the passive resistance or inertia in the subject, symbolized by moisture.

Aquinas's view of habit-formation, then, is sharply opposed to the one held by those who maintain that our acts are the efficient cause of habits. According to the latter, each act leaves or impresses some trace upon a passive and plastic material, leading to the eventual formation of a habit. Although plausible at first sight, the generation of habits cannot be explained, strictly speaking, by this theory.[70] This explana-

---

67. Ibid., q. 51, a. 1; *De Virt. in Com.* 1.
68. "Omnes virtutes . . . quae ex nostris actibus acquiruntur procedunt ex quibusdam naturalibus principiis in nobis praeexistentibus." ST I-II, q. 63, a. 3.
69. ST I-II, q. 51, a. 3.
70. Because, as Aquinas makes it clear, the acts which proceed from a habitus are definitely superior and more perfect than those acts which preceded and contributed to the formation of the habitus (*De Verit.*, q. 20, a. 3, ad 3). If acts were the only cause of habits, how could we account for the superior and more perfect quality of the acts

tion is completely mechanistic, excluding the causality exercised by nature itself, that is, nature in the metaphysical sense, both final and efficient, which alone can make the whole process of the formation of habitus intelligible.[71] In other words, this explanation does not take into account nature qua end, in relation to which habitus is formed, nor nature as the true, principal efficient cause of habitus.

The question still remains as to the precise relationship between the active principle, which is natural, and the very nature of the intellectual soul, or human nature itself. Aquinas speaks of *principium activum* in various ways. In relation to the appetitive power, the cognitive power is said to function as the *principium activum*.[72] In relation to the intellectual power as it reasons about conclusions, however, the active principle is the per se known proposition.[73] Then what is the active principle, which is natural and said to be the true, principal cause of habits? Aquinas mentions, as examples of such an active principle, *propositio per se nota* (per se known proposition) and natural desire of the good.[74] What Aquinas means by these terms are not some abstract propositions and some instinctive desires, but the natural light of reason (*lumen naturale rationis*)[75] and the will itself which is a certain nature (*ipsa voluntas [quae est] quaedam natura*),[76] as he calls them elsewhere. Hence we are justified in identifying the *principium activum*, which is natural and said to be the principal cause of habitus, with the very nature of the intellectual soul of man, in short, with human nature itself.

VI

In the preceding section, I attempted to substantiate my thesis that, according to Aquinas, the true, principal cause of habitus is human nature itself. In penetrating into nature itself as the ground and cause of habits, however, we must take the following points into consideration. First, it is important to note that there are radically different

---

which proceed from habits? Cf. Dunlap, op. cit., pp. 15, 34, 35, 36, 39, 57. G. P. Klubertanz, *Habits and Virtues* (New York, 1965), p. 131, does not emphasize this point.

71. Dunlap criticizes those theories of habits and learning which have been dominated by analogies between the results of learning processes and the results of processes of modification in nonliving objects and substances (op. cit., pp. 70–71).

72. ST I-II, q. 51, a. 2. 73. Ibid.
74. ST I-II, q. 63, a. 1; cf. q. 51, a. 2.
75. ST I, q. 1, a. 1, ad 2; q. 1, a. 5; q. 12, a. 13, and passim.
76. Cf. *De Verit.*, q. 22, a. 5; q. 24, a. 12, ad 1.

grades of perfection in habits, according to Aquinas. In the case of cognitive habits, for example, there is first the natural habit of *intellectus*, which is a natural and fundamental determination of our cognitive power (*potentia*) to its end, namely, the act of understanding *ens universale*.[77] As remarked before, this natural habit is the active principle in our cognitive power, gradually actualizing and assimilating to itself the passive-potential elements in the cognitive power. In other words, the fundamental determination of our cognitive power to its end must be perfected through the formation of other, higher cognitive habits. The acquisition of various habits of science (*scientia*), then, is the second step in the process of the perfection of our cognitive power. The many and diverse habits of *scientia* are concerned with obtaining the distinct knowledge of the various genera of being in terms of secondary, proximate causes. Third, and finally, comes the habitus of wisdom (*sapientia*), which is concerned with the knowledge of all beings in terms of their first cause.[78] The natural and fundamental determination of our cognitive power to its end, then, will be perfected only with the acquisition of the habit of wisdom, for it is with the acquisition of this habitus that the conformity of our cognitive power with *ens universale*[79] will be actually achieved. It is, therefore, as the ground and cause of the highest cognitive habitus of *sapientia* that the nature of the intellectual soul itself will be most fully manifested.

Second, we must note that since cognitive habits are, according to Aquinas, only a part of the whole complex of habits and virtues, they can manifest the nature of man only partially. In order to come to a full understanding of the nature of man as the ground and cause of habits, we must reflect upon all habits of man, infused as well as acquired,[80] which include the so-called theological virtues of faith, hope, and charity, which dispose man towards his ultimate end.[81] When we have completed such reflection, then we can obtain some insight into human nature as the ultimate end of man.[82] And it is through some insight into the ultimate end of man that we can hope to grasp human nature in the metaphysical sense, because it is only when we have grasped man's goal, the ultimate end in some way, that we can make

77. ST I, q. 5, a. 2; q. 78, a. 1; q. 79, a. 2, and passim.
78. ST I-II, q. 57, a. 2; q. 66, a. 5; II-II, q. 45, a. 1.
79. That is, this conformity belongs to the very nature of our cognitive power. *De Verit.*, q. 1, a. 1; q. 1, a. 9.
80. On the "infusion" of habits and virtues, see ST I-II, q. 51, a. 4; q. 63, a. 3.
81. ST I-II, q. 62, a. 1; a. 3.
82. Here, human nature is spoken of *participative*, that is, insofar as man is in some way *particeps divinae naturae* (I-II, q. 62, a. 1, ad 1; q. 50, a. 2; q. 110, a. 4; II-II, q. 2, a. 3).

such unqualified statements as that man *is* such and such. In the final analysis, it is only he who has actually attained the ultimate end who can see or contemplate man under the aspect of being (*sub ratione entis*), because it is he alone who knows his oneness or identity completely.[83] Compared to that, the understanding of the nature itself of man that we can obtain through reflection upon habits here, *in statu viae*, must remain very imperfect and vague indeed.

VII

Now, as a postscript, I shall venture some remarks on a problem which emerged in the course of my reflection on the relationship between habitus and *natura* in Aquinas.

The problem is this: when Aquinas says that habitus is primarily and essentially related to nature itself, nature is taken in the sense of the end, the final cause. When he maintains that habits proceed from some preexisting natural principles, however, he seems to take the natural principles or nature itself as the efficient cause. The picture which emerges here is certainly paradoxical. On the one hand, it is we ourselves, or rather "I," that form habits, which are essentially related to human nature qua end. Here habitus is formed through the causality proper to man, namely, the causality of human freedom.[84] When it is said that habitus proceeds from nature itself as the efficient cause, on the other hand, the causality involved cannot be the one proper to man. It must be the causality exercised by the Creator of nature, namely, the divine creative causality.

The formation of habitus in its essential relation to nature qua end takes place in time. The procession of habitus from nature itself, insofar as it belongs to the divine creative causality, is supratemporal. If the former process is characterized as the formation of mutable human nature, the latter may be characterized as the perfection and *re-creatio* of immutable human nature.[85] Although we are not able to explain how these two causalities are unified, we do see that the former

---

83. "unum convertitur cum ente." ST I, q. 11, a. 1; cf. *De Verit.*, q. 1, a. 1; q. 21, a. 1.

84. "Illae [ergo] actiones proprie humanae dicuntur quae ex voluntate deliberata procedunt." ST I-II, q. 1, a. 1. Aquinas clearly recognized that habitus is formed through exercise of freedom. ST I-II, q. 49, a. 4; q. 50, a. 3; a. 5.

85. ST I, q. 93, a. 4; I-II, q. 110, a. 4; III, q. 3, a. 8, ad 2. It might be objected against my interpretation that creation is presupposed, and not to be mixed with the work of nature. Cf. ST I, q. 45, a. 8. To this objection I would reply that, since the rational soul, unlike other natural forms, is created immediately by God, its perfection and *recreatio* properly belong also to the work of divine creation.

is immediately connected with the latter. In other words, the process of the self-creation of man through the exercise of his freedom is immediately connected with the work of divine creation (or rather *re-creatio*) by which human nature is perfected. In short, human activity at its highest limit, the work of self-creation, is one with the work of divine creation.

The insight into the nature itself of man which can be gained through the reflection upon habitus, then, is that it is radically open to the creative causality of God. Aquinas explicitly states that "rational nature . . . has an immediate ordering to the universal principle of being."[86] And it is this same radical openness to the divine creative causality which makes the human soul naturally capable of receiving grace (*capax gratiae*).[87] Thus, Aquinas's concept of habitus leads, through that of nature, to that of grace, the consideration of which exceeds the scope of the present paper. I would like to note merely that his concept of habitus will not be fully intelligible unless it is considered in the context suggested here.

Kyushu University
Fukuoka, Japan

86. ST II-II, q. 2, a. 3.

87. ST I-II, q. 113, a. 10.

8   Aquinas on Annihilation
JAMES F. ROSS

With the cessation of the divine operation at the same instant all things would fall into nothingness. (St. Thomas Aquinas, *De Potentia*, 5, 1)[1]

Without any doubt whatever, it must be admitted that things are preserved in existence by God and that they would instantly be reduced to nothing were God to abandon them. (Idem)

I. COSMIC CATASTROPHE?

The Doctrine of St. Thomas. Aquinas agrees with Augustine (*de Gen. ad Litt.*, IV, 12):

If the ruling power of God were withdrawn from his creatures, their form would at once cease and all nature would collapse. The world would not stand for one instant if God withdrew his support.

He also cites Gregory (*Moral.*, XVI, 37):

all things would fall into nothingness were they not upheld by the hand of the almighty.

Aquinas is unqualified:

Now the creature's whole being depends on God's simple will, since he is the cause of things by his will and not by natural necessity. Therefore, if it be his will, creatures can be annihilated. (*De Potentia*, 5, 3, sed contra, arg. 1)

    His main argument is this: God does not produce creatures out of absolute necessity (for instance, a necessity deriving from a contradiction in there not being any creatures); nor from any necessity of his nature (as he wills his goodness and happiness); nor does God's goodness depend on creatures, from which it gains nothing (*D.P.*, 5, 3). So

---

    1. Translations of passages from the *De Potentia* are taken, with some modifications, from *Saint Thomas Aquinas, On the Power of God*, trans. the English Dominican Fathers (Newman Press: Westminster, Md., 1952).

God can withdraw his causation, unless his ordained will is "that he would keep things in existence forever."

Annihilation is not an action (*D.P.*, 5, 3, ad 2). It is the withdrawal of an action; "thus the absence of the sun's action in enlightening the air causes the absence of light in the air." Although withdrawing causation *could* have an objective, cessation of willing does not *require* an objective as does an action (*D.P.*, 5, 3, ad 4), yet it *might* have one, as the cessation of a completed act may have one:

> . . . in the production of things, the end was the manifestation of God's abundant goodness. So the will's objective in the annihilation of things *can* be the *sufficiency* of his goodness, seeing that it is so self-sufficing as to need nothing from without. (*D.P.*, 5, 3, ad 4; emphasis added)

Corruption is not the same as annihilation. A corruptible thing is an unstable thing; it has a composition whose natural changes can make preserving its form physically impossible, as when wood burns, a candle melts, or meat decomposes, with the result that the thing is destroyed by a kind of "coming apart" and, thus, ceases to exist.

As Aquinas and Aristotle both insisted, for a plant to-be is to-live; for a plant to be killed is to cease to be. That kind of disintegration terminates in nonbeing but is not annihilation.

Corruption is a kind of "going out of business" toward which everything "under the sun" has an active potentiality, universal entropy. The possibility of annihilation does not, to the contrary, presuppose an active tendency toward nonbeing or even toward ceasing to be (see *D.P.*, 5, 3, ad 7). It supposes only contingency in being. Even an immortal thing, say a soul, can be annihilated. No tendency toward failure is needed, only an inability to be without God's free causation. That is enough to make annihilation possible.

Aquinas' Physical Eschatology. Still, Aquinas says firmly that *the created universe* will *never be annihilated,* and that *creatures will last forever,* as to their substance. In *D.P.*, 5, 4, corpus, he says:

> I answer that the created universe will never be annihilated. And notwithstanding that corruptible creatures have not always existed, they will last, nevertheless, forever as to their substance.

The two claims are quite different. The *first* is that God will never, even denominatively (from the creature's point of view), withdraw his sustaining causation from the cosmos. The *cosmos* will not cease to be because of the cessation of *conservation.* That is, the physical universe will not cease to be because the light that illuminates it (makes it to be) goes out, as if God's will "went off."

The *second* claim is much stronger: Not only will the divine causation not be withdrawn, the substance of the material creation *will endure forever.*

There is no tendency to *final* dissolution that will bring the cosmos to end on its own, the way an individual plant or animal eventually will cease to be. Just the opposite: form will succeed form naturally forever.

The cosmos will not be "wiped out" by withdrawal of God's conservation, annihilated the way a *dream* world of objects—say a dream world of billiard balls—would be "wiped out" by the dreamer's awakening or dreaming an unconnected sequence. The cosmos will not be "wiped out" the way a computer display is destroyed utterly when the power goes off.

Nor, even more surprisingly from Aquinas, will the cosmos blink out by cosmic entropy, by the active tendency of formal organizations, succeeding one another, to exhaust the potential energy of the components, or by the active tendency of all material things to come apart. Corruptibility is a *proprium* of all material composites. It is universal and persistent but not triumphant. Whatever can come apart, eventually does. But forms, in due course, succeed one another, forever. (See Part III, below.)

Collective decrepitude will not empty space-time and disintegrate that very framework in its wake. On the contrary, Aquinas thinks the physical universe is constructed in its substance so as to go on forever.

Until very recently scientists, had they paid any attention to Aquinas' views, would have doubted that the cosmos will naturally endure forever, except in thermodynamic death. It was also thought (*Scientific American*, April 1981) that matter is inherently unstable. However, many scientists now think the cosmos naturally endures forever, not in thermodynamic paralysis, but organized significantly above absolute zero.[2] They have remarked on the energy, the organization, required for what seems to be a *recursive* embedding of forms, of systems, in order for there to be material things *at all*. The "available" energy (information) in the material universe seems to be far greater than could have been imagined even a few decades ago, and provides for "dense energy physics," both micro- and macrostructurally, to ground "physical eschatology."[3]

2. Freeman Dyson, "Time without End: Physics and Biology in an Open Universe," 1979. *Reviews of Modern Physics* 51.3.447–60. See also Nigel Calder, *The Key to the Universe* (Penguin Books: New York, 1977), for remarks about S. Hawking's views, pp. 143–44, 154–62, 188.
3. It was Dyson (see note 2) who coined the expression "physical eschatology" and remarked on the paucity of papers on such topics.

The outcome, so far, is that the design of things inherently avoids cosmic catastrophe, just as Aquinas supposed. *Local* catastrophe, however, appears to be inevitable, from time to time, everywhere, as matter convulsively changes its forms.

II. DISPUTING ABOUT ANNIHILATION

1. *The role of the counterfactual.* I doubt that it is consistent to say, as Aquinas and most major thinkers do,[4] that God's absolute power, scientifically described, encompasses the ability to withdraw conservation from a creature.

God *could*, as far as we know, have made a cosmos that ends naturally, disintegratively, as might have happened had the number of the "entry" photons for a "big bang" been significantly smaller;[5] that is corruption, not annihilation. However, as we will see (Part III) Aquinas committed himself in *D.P.*, 5, 4, to principles that exclude God's making a self-terminating world.

An important truth, religiously and scientifically, is aptly expressed by our saying "if God withdrew his ruling hand all creation would fall instantly into nothing, just as darkness falls instantly with cessation of light" (on the object illumined). That conveys the immediacy and completeness of the creative causation. Is it to be accepted as a useful and true metaphor or as something more?

The contrary-to-fact form ("With the cessation of the divine operation, at the same instant, all things would fall into nothingness") is crucial. There is no future to God, for the simple "should-would" form.[6]

Rather, Aquinas thinks God is actively *able* to cease his supportive causation. He thought this to be more than a true metaphor, to be a scientific truth. I argue that it is a true metaphor, and somewhat more, as well, but not a scientific truth. And my basic arguments finally rest on principles of ordered goodness that Aquinas uses to explain (*D.P.*, 5, 4) why the creation endures forever.

Aquinas argues in the body of *D.P.*, 5, 3, to the effect that neither the divine nature nor the divine will needs creatures. Neither God's power nor God's goodness

---

4. A. Kenny, *Wyclif* (Oxford University Press: New York, 1985), p. 28, says Wyclif is an exception.

5. Sir John Eccles, *The Human Mystery*, the Gifford Lectures, 1977–78 (Springer-International: Switzerland, 1979). See Stephen Weinberg, *The First Three Minutes* (Basic Books: New York, 1977).

6. Aquinas acknowledged that a conditional with a necessarily false antecedent is true (*Summa theologiae*, Ia, 25, ad 2) but does not rely on that here.

depends on creatures as though it could not be without them. . . . It remains that it is not impossible for God to reduce things to nothing, since he is not under the necessity of giving them being, except on the presupposition of his decrees and foreknowledge, in that he decreed and foresaw that he would keep things in existence forever.

No reason why God cannot withdraw his creative act, the way a thinker can withdraw his imagining an object, can be found in a *need* of God's to make or keep the creature for some good to himself or out of a necessity of his nature to have creatures.

St. Thomas is also explicit, here and elsewhere, that God's *ordained* power is directed to keep things in existence "forever." So the issue concerns only what God *could* have done—whether God, not needing the creatures for anything, and even though he *will* sustain them forever, is *able* to have withdrawn *his will* from them before they were dead or disintegrated. (I do not mean that annihilation would involve a *temporal* relation, but denominatively, from the creature's vantage, it would be aptly described as "occurring" to a thing in being, not yet dead or disintegrated.)

Could God have created the very things he did, withdrawing his will before the creatures die or disintegrate? There is, of course, something peculiar about this question. Taken at face value the answer is "no," because he could not have made *all* the things he has made, withdrawing his will from *each* before it dies or disintegrates; for under that supposition the causal network of things would be so vastly different, the universe would have ceased to be long before humans came along: the cessation of the short-life particles would have changed everything. So even if God has the power to withdraw causation from each thing he makes, it does not follow that he can withdraw being from *all* things he has actually made.

To the objections in *D.P.*, 5, 3, he says (ad 1) that ceasing to cause existence in creatures would not be the same as giving them an active tendency toward nonbeing, because God does not cause nonexistence in them, but ceases to cause them to be, to "give them being." Figures in a dream may have a tendency toward breaking up into parts and combining into new patterns. For the dreamer to be able to "turn them off entirely," it is not required that on their *own* they have a tendency to "turn off entirely" as they do "to combine," but only no ability of their own to avoid it. (Of course, creating is not a kind of dreaming, as some have foolishly concluded from my examples.)[7] Nowadays,

---

7. This mistake is made by David R. Griffin, "Divine Causality, Evil and Philosophical Theology: A Critique of James Ross," *International Journal for the Philosophy of Religion*, 1973; and *God, Power and Evil* (Westminster Press: Philadelphia, 1976). "How," he

there are manmade examples of continuous dependence, like letter sequences on a computer screen that depend on a power source where nothing about the logical, semantical, or particular meaning interrelations of the images, even if they formulate all computer theory, accounts for the *being* of the sequence that is maintained by the machine's modifying an external power source.

The trouble starts with the second reply (ad 2) where Aquinas says:

Whereas, if God were to annihilate a thing, there would be no need for any action, and it would suffice if God were to withdraw the action whereby he gives things existence: thus the absence of the sun's action in enlightening [the air] causes the absence of light in the air.

The sun's ceasing to illuminate is by failure, if it occurs at all, and involves a change, as does the end of any other illumination. Aquinas is aware of that and wants only to illustrate complete and continuous dependence. Although he supposed that illumination is instantaneous (and says so in *Summa theologiae*, Ia, 67, 2c: "The diffusion of light is instantaneous"), that belief is not an element of this argument. It is the ceasing of the light *at* its *object*, not at its source, which is *instantaneous with* darkness. In fact, this is not a causal relation at all: absence of light *is* darkness and ceasing of light *is* coming of darkness. Still, even ceasing to think of a thing by "going blank" or by thinking of something else involves change. So the particular problem facing St. Thomas is to explain how creation, as act, could *end* without involving a change in God. One form I put that problem in, below, is that annihilation seems to be a contrary of creation and to presuppose it, thus requiring succession.

Aquinas argues first that there need not be a distinct *objective* to be gained to which annihilation is a means. Though creating has as its end the communication of God's love or manifestation of God's goodness, a satisfactory rationale for omitting or ceasing to create would be "the sufficiency" of God's goodness, "seeing that it is so self-sufficing as to need nothing from without."

That is enough to show that God always had a sufficient motive not to make anything and not to keep anything else in being, namely, that his "goodness was sufficient" for his perfect being. Thus he does not

---

asks, "does it express the INTENTION of orthodoxy to suggest that the world has no more reality in relation to God than an idea in the mind?" (p. 173). Robert Oakes, "Classical Theism and Pantheism: A Victory for Process Theism," *Religious Studies* 13 (1977), pp. 167–73, interprets my creation views as "esse est percipi," unhappily with no basis in the text of *Philosophical Theology* (1969 and 1980) and no defense against Phillip L. Quinn's attack, "Divine Conservation and Spinozistic Pantheism," *Religious Studies* 15 (1979), pp. 289–302.

have to undergo some change to acquire a motive for ceasing to conserve; he has such a motive all along. Moreover, that is compatible with his also having a sufficient motive for making things, too, namely, that in his abundant goodness he loves the very things he makes and that is *why* he makes them (*D.P.*, 5, 4c), something that would have been true of whatever he made. A rationale is sufficient, as I use the expression, just in case nothing beyond election is required for action, e.g., one does not need a further reason for acting from a rationale that is sufficient, even if one has sufficient rationales for opposed acts; for, of course, the rationale does not compel the action. A maximally free being will by nature have sufficient rationales for incompossible acts. In acting, such a being has in what-it-does the differentiating complete rationale for doing it. (See Part III, Aquinas' same view, below.)

So while God has a sufficient rationale for doing as he does, he also has a sufficient rationale for doing otherwise in either of two ways: (i) by making something else instead; (ii) by withdrawing conservation "at any point" within the being-in-time of a creature. Hence, no change is required for God to have a reason to cease upholding creatures, any more than a change is required for him to have one *ab initio* for making what he has made, or to have had one for making something else instead, or nothing at all. God has all his reasons by nature and unchangeably, except for the reason he has *from* the thing *done*. (One can have a reason for acting that depends on the acting, for example where the *thing* made, not the idea of it, is part of the explanation of the making [*D.P.*, 5, 4].) This is the *strength* of Aquinas' position. Having sufficient motives, and reasons, for contrary actions is necessary for perfect freedom in an immutable being, though a perfect being need not have a motive toward any imperfect action, just as a free creature, to act rightly, does not need a motive or rationale for acting wrongly.

Although one very serious obstacle seems thus surmounted, namely, the objection that there could not be an end for God to achieve by *ceasing* to conserve creatures, or that he would have to change to *acquire* that objective, it still seems that creating and withdrawing conservation from the same creature are contrary states, one of which presupposes the other. They cannot obtain nonsuccessively with respect to the same object. But succession of contrary states is not possible for God. What can Aquinas reply to this objection? I will return to that and to the question of whether Aquinas explained the issue of rationale properly. But first:

2. *Can we coherently imagine annihilation?* Would withdrawal of di-

vine will ripple across the universe, from past to future? Aquinas says, "all things would cease to be in an instant." Annihilation would negate everything instantaneously and simultaneously. Now that does not seem to be a scientific truth. The universe is enormous in ways Aquinas could not have imagined. And there can be no state that is simultaneous or instantaneous for the whole universe. The cosmos is like a symphony, going from opening chord onward (forever). It has the magnificent objective (partial) "visual" appearance of an object (stars, galaxies, etc.). But the visible heavens are more like a fireworks display or a pinwheel: our looking outward, even in close perception of ordinary objects, is looking backward, at objects that are, the further they are away, moving away faster. So what appears as a contemporaneous visible pattern of stationary objects, like a photograph of a pinwheel, is in fact a display of objects moving in various directions, at various speeds (the further away the faster), away from one another (on the whole). It is as if we made (and we could if we chose to) a visual display of a symphony performance, the first notes being the furthest away and moving fastest apart from the rest, and so on, to the end which appears in the center of the visual field, with the individual instruments describing (*forming*, when all are playing) circles around the center. That is how an essentially temporal object can appear visually, as a single unity. With the heavens, the unaided sight can see as present (as visually contemporaneous) states separated by some billion light years. There is no such thing as a *single* instant for the whole cosmos. There is no such thing as "it's all going out at *once*." That is at best a metaphor with no physical correlate because there is no such thing as "it's all going *on* at once."

Being in space is to-be-through-time. The universe is spread out temporally, like a symphony, as well as spatially, because *distance*, as transmitted natural *effect* from a given point to another, is equivalent to going pastward, and distance *to* any point from a given one, as transmitting *cause*, is equivalent to going futureward (locally).

Could annihilation, as withdrawal of being, spark across the cosmos from past to present, with the most distant galaxies "going out" (not, of course detectably by us) followed by the next most distant ones, and so forth, with the rate of "going out" just equalling the rate of gravitational and light propagation, so that the "next" exit from being does not experience the "felt" gravitational deficit of the "preceding" one? That is, could God "wipe the world out" going from farthest stars backwards? No, because there is no absolute position from which to calculate "farthest," but only *our* arbitrary vantage. Besides, annihilation might disregard the constants of nature. Just as there cannot be a *time relationship* between any point of the cosmos and the conserving creator, whose causation has to "cross" time to make spread-out things to *be*, so there can be no successive or even simultaneous (except metaphorically or denominatively vantaged) causation between God and the world, despite the efforts of Kretzmann and Stump[8] to specify such a relation.

It is confused to think everything would have to go out "all together," except metaphorically. There is no cosmic "now" at which everything would cease. That is just imaginary, like the "before the world began" that Aquinas mentions and the "now" and "then" at which the cosmos, if it was light years across in its "entry" photon mush, "began with a bang." There could *not* have been a temporally and spatially dimensionless point either physically or logically. Physical being[9] *takes time to be*. And real time requires physical being. There cannot be a real, initial point or instant, the beginning-of-time, from which physical being is *first* realized, but only an "initial" time calculated *backward*. (The same is true of a measure of music, considered internally.) There cannot be an unextended physical "now." Therefore, there cannot be a cosmic "now" to be either the instant of creation or that of annihilation.

Images of annihilation can be refined to avoid such immediate inconsistencies, but, exfoliated, their truth conditions involve inconsistencies. Why? In a word, because "conservation," unpacked, requires a kind of "creation until death." But "annihilation" requires "cessation *before* death."

Suppose the cosmos were to be annihilated. No creature in it could ever know from observation (as distinct from prophecy or revelation) that it was to happen or was happening. One could not "see" it coming. It would be not an event "within the physical world," but like the awakening from a dream or shutting off of a projector light or TV-screen power, a reality *outside it* and *indetectable*.[10] Conservation and creation are that way, too.

---

8. N. Kretzmann and E. Stump, "Eternity," *Journal of Philosophy* 78 (1981), pp. 429–57. See also Ross, "Making Time," 1982 O'Hara Lecture, Notre Dame University, in *Creation* (University of Notre Dame Press, forthcoming).

9. See "Making Time" (note 8, above).

10. Strictly speaking, all the letters in a TV display do not "go out together" because they are spatially separated and not equidistant from a power source. Imagine then an array, like a circle of covered wagons, equidistant from a constitutive light source. From the point of view of the SOURCE, the CONSTITUTIVE ILLUMINATION fails at the various objects "at the same time"; two wagons, say half a mile around the circle, go

Annihilation is like cosmic darkness hurtling unobservably across the universe. Does the prospect arouse apocalyptic terror? No. First, it is not an event in our world, it is indetectable. Second, it does not happen *to* the world because it is not a change in a subject. Third, if my arguments bear weight, it could not happen at all.

On reflection, I think Aquinas is not persuasive that God could have a rationale or motive for withdrawing conservation (*D.P.*, 5, 3, ad 4). That is because, in creating, God has a reason for the being of the creatures (*D.P.*, 5, 4). Is it, then, basically because there would have to be an alternation in God's will—a *succession* of attitudes, the latter of which presupposes the former and is its contrary? No, that is a *consequence* of the basic problem.

Suppose that God's originating will is for a cosmos that develops only so far within its natural potentiality, and ceases to be, *not* because of the inherent instability of the matter (that would be decomposition, as sketched in *Scientific American,* April 1981) but by his stopping conservation at a predetermined stage. Even if our imagining of it turns out to be incoherent, why is it not logically coherent, as Aquinas supposed? Is it not just like a pianist's choosing to play a Chopin Étude for a few lines only, when he might have gone on with it?[11] No it is not. What is it that determines the *identity* of the cosmos that *would* have been, had it not been annihilated? There must be such a determinate, in order that it be *true* that *it*, the particular, was annihilated. Except for platonists and neoplatonists, there is no such thing. It is easy to *imagine* that God has complete thoughts of what *that* free creature

---

"out" indetectably to one another because the information would have to travel far faster than light to reach the other one "before" it too "goes out." Paradoxically, each "goes out" *before* the other by an interval equal to the time light would take to travel from one to the other.

11. For this to make sense, we have to suppose that there is something that CONSTITUTES the work, over and above any performance, to determine (logically) WHAT has stopped. That is not paradoxical in the case of works of music and other abstract particulars. But that an individual or a kind of thing has its determinate reality accounted for *externally*, e.g., by participation, exemplification, or another alio-relative relation, is not only incoherent, it is explicitly inconsistent. (See discussions of Moderate Realism and "the incoherence of the philosophers" in *Creation* [note 8, above]; see also my article referred to in note 12 below.) What determines WHAT is stopped has to be internal to the being. It has to be essential. Where it must also be temporal, the being must be for that time, in order to be at all. Just as a composition has to have reality apart from the performance to be *partly* performed, so an individual would have to have some reality apart from being, in order to be annihilated. Neither natural kinds nor individual "essences" have being, even as divine ideas, as sequins on the divine robe of Light in which God chose to display himself. So, you can see that we can admit Aquinas' two premises while denying that his conclusion follows: (1) creatures *are* from God's will. (2) If God does *not* will, there is no creature. But it does not follow that (3) cessation of God's will causes loss of being *and can occur.*

would have done had he not been annihilated. But where does that knowledge come from? Not from foreseeing what will be, for there is to be no such future; not from God's effective choice because such choice is not exercised if being is suspended. An inconvenient consequence of the annihilation hypothesis is that a thing annihilated would have to be *indeterminate* with respect to some temporally later features, whereas its supposed identical thing (you or me) is *not* indeterminate in that way.

There is a difference between making a thing that by its nature ceases to be by "falling apart," by corruption (enervation, obsolescence, senescence, desiccation, erosion, exhaustion, or completion of performances, etc.), and making a thing that, whether or not corruptible, is to cease to be by failure of the cause of being before the processes of corruption (or performance) have destroyed or "finished" it. That is like making an object of thought, say a daydream, that ceases to be as attention turns elsewhere. What ceases to be, in that case, is *all* that is there, and has been, and is not *anything* that *would* have been. So that annihilated thing could not be identical with anything not annihilated. That seems to entail that God *cannot* annihilate anything he does not annihilate. Ended dreams have no real "was-going-to-be." It is also like singing, or thinking of, a phrase of a song where the will does not extend to the full thing (which is externally determined). Incomplete will, relative to the capacity of the thing, is equivalent to *cutting it off in being*, to annihilation. But that requires an extrinsic determiner of what was to be. There is no external determiner of the individuation of actual things.

Despite the broad, virtually uniform approbation of the position of St. Thomas, I think examination discloses that the notion of God's having an *incomplete will relatively to the capacity for being* of any of his creatures is explicitly inconsistent. That generates the inconsistency by which God would have to be in contrary states with respect to the same being. Moreover, it requires one to explain both the quiddity and the individuation of things *extrinsically*, a position I elsewhere argue is inconsistent on its own terms.[12] Further, it conflicts with the ordered goodness required for creation, as I will explain.

If matter is so unstable that by developing at the macroscale for long enough, the likelihood of its disintegrating to undifferentiated energy at the microscale increases to certainty (see *Scientific American*, April 1981), would that be a natural end to the universe, like a com-

---

12. See *Creation* (note 8, above) and ed. R. Audi and W. Wainwright, *Rationality, Religious Belief, and Moral Commitment*, with my "God, Creator of Kinds and Possibilities" (Cornell University Press, 1986).

position that has been played through? Yes: that is not annihilation, just disintegration, "being finished," where *what* is finished is intrinsic in the thing that is finished.

That makes clear that we have to be dealing with the withdrawal of being from a *thing that was-to-be* in some further way. Annihilation is not just wearing down, breaking up, or "being over." It involves the loss of being from a thing that is unfinished; a thing whose would-have-been states are not merely *accidentally* related to *what* it is, but necessary to what it is. Yet, unless being unfinished is incidental to *what*-is, unfinished being is impossible.

3. *Why can conservation not be withdrawn?* The way to see that withdrawing conservation from a substance involves a change of God's will is to discover the *underlying* considerations. There are three: that the thing created is God's reason for keeping it in being; that conservation throughout a thing's "being-to-its-end" is a logically necessary condition for the creature's being at all; and that annihilation is the successor, contrary to creation, requiring change.

Take a Leibnizian extreme, for a moment, where every actual attribute is essential to the thing. If my living to be eighty is essential to me, God could not have ceased to conserve me at twenty-five, as if he stopped a performance of a sonata at the end of the first movement. The potential, or conceptual, being of the sonata has to be logically independent of its performance, unlike a jazz improvisation. Otherwise, when it stops, that is *what* it was, all of it. That means that what makes it to *be* has to be distinct from the performance; otherwise, its being ends with the end of the performance. For then it would not have been *I* that God had made but some close counterpart, the same "up to age twenty-five" but different in that *I* have a "post–twenty-five" segment and the annihilated thing has none.

Besides, bivalence of all temporal properties does not apply to a thing annihilated at twenty-five, e.g., "either being or not being President at thirty-five" (I assume bivalence for clarity of argument, not as a general position). How then could *I*, for whom such properties bifurcate, have been identical with a thing for which they do not?

Analogously, for any physical thing, "being-for-its-time" is essential. That is, it is both a necessary and a *quiddative* (*per se* and *in quid*) predicate.[13] Thus there cannot be a human that does not live until death. In

---

13. A predicate is *per se* if it is necessary to a thing and applies to it on account of itself, not alio-relatively or perspectively. A predicate is quiddative if, relatively to a person's conceptual scheme for asking *what* a thing is, it says in whole or in part (e.g., by phylum, family, genus, species, or differentia) what a thing is.

fact, there is no way for a human, even atomized, to cease to be except by death.

Annihilation Is a Logical Illusion. Conservation is required, *ex parte rei*, for all beings in time, in order for them to be *at all*. And "to-be-for-its-time" is essential (and quiddative) to each temporal thing, even though a thing can be accidentally (relatively to its being-for-its-time) destroyed. Thus, there cannot be a quarter note conserved for only half its length, though one quarter note, performed, *can* be "shorter" than another accidentally. A symphony can be performed up to a point, only because there is an external (to the performance) determination for *which* thing it is; otherwise, the "part" would be the whole, a different thing. There are no external determinants of kinds and individuation of creatures.

Dying is not accidental to humans, even if it can be prevented preternaturally and supernaturally, or delayed, possibly forever, naturally. In *D.P.*, 5, 3, ad 11, Aquinas says, "that which is corruptible by nature can be made to last forever by the superaddition of glory." That may be so; but a human is still a thing-that-dies, even if it never dies. Similarly, a deciduous tree has leaves that fall, even if it is kept immobile in outer space, forever.

4. *Death essential but preventable?* We do not expect humans naturally to live forever because medical marvels cannot compete with the extinction of the sun, and the exigencies of repeatedly finding new and habitable planetary environments (every few billion years). Still, "being a thing that dies," but whose death is delayed, is not the same as having death prevented, made physically impossible. That cannot be done naturally. So it remains that a human has being-for-its-time, punctuated by death, essentially.

5. *Annihilation conflicts with conservation.* Creation of a thing-in-time requires conservation, which denominatively, from the creature's vantage, requires being through time. A material thing cannot come to be in an instant but takes time to be at all.[14] Conservation is of a *what*, of a thing with a *real* essence. Things with real essences have essential attributes. Among them are that "to-be-temporally" requires "to-be-for-its-time." Withdrawal of conservation would deny exactly that attribute: a thing of type F could not be without being-for-the-time of a thing of type F. Annihilation does not, therefore, lie within the absolute power of God.

The world God creates is not like a performance God can terminate while incomplete (from the logical vantage of the essence of anything

---

14. See "Making Time" (note 8, above).

in the created world). Such "vantage" points of incompleteness (of will) relative to "essences," whether individual or specific, require a platonism about nature and about modal logic that is indefensible.[15] To put it simply, for God to be able to terminate me, he has to be able to have made *me*, but indeterminate as to those exclusive disjuncts (President or non-President) to which I am essentially determinate.

6. *The basic argument* against Aquinas' position is twofold: that creation of material things, plants, animals, and humans is logically equivalent to conservation of their being according to their kinds, and that the things created are God's rationale for not annihilating. That is because making the things is a commitment of God's perfection to the *telos* of what is made. Thus, God cannot withdraw conservation (creation) because each actual thing is "in being to its corruption," essentially, according to its kind, and God's goodness is ordered to the *telos* of each thing. Because "annihilation" is "withdrawal of being prior to corruption of being," annihilation is inconsistent with an essential property of each created thing and with the ordered goodness of God.

Aquinas addressed the first part of that objection, though not so classifying it, in *D.P.*, 5, 3, ad 10:

If by ceasing to uphold them, God were to reduce incorruptible creatures to nothing, he would not by doing so deprive their nature of its everlastingness, so that it would remain without being everlasting: but their whole nature would cease to exist through the cause ceasing to exercise its influence over them.

No, there would not be a nature deprived of its everlastingness; a nature with everlastingness would cease to be. But what of this: if something in being, in actual being, has the ESSENTIAL property of being everlasting, then can the cause of its (essentially everlasting) being withdraw, so that it does not in fact continue to be forever? I think not, though St. Thomas says otherwise. If to-be-forever is *essential* to it, then it must actually be-forever in order to be *at all*. That's the nub.

Now, if you DEFINE "being everlasting" as that "disposition by nature to continue to be, once in being, forever, DEO CONSERVANTE," then annihilation of such a being is consistent because its *proprium* is "to be forever, once in being, provided God concurs." If that conditionalization is generalized to all properties, contradiction of the forms illustrated can be avoided. But that is because the problem is brushed

---

15. See "The Incoherence of the Philosophers," 1982 O'Hara Lecture, Notre Dame University, in *Creation* (note 8, above).

aside. WHAT kind of thing exists (e.g., a thing that exists for an oak's time, a dog's days, a star's epochs) cannot depend on *whether* God conserves it for the interval its nature requires. Just the reverse: in order for it to be at all, God MUST conserve it for that interval its nature requires. And it is not a live hypothesis that NO interval of temporal being is required by the nature of any actual being. Just the opposite: any being-in-time has a natural (relative) interval through which its being conserved is logically equivalent to its being created (caused to be) at all. Thus, withdrawal of conservation (during an interval not accidental to the thing) is the same as not having created the thing at all.

So, a thing by nature everlasting cannot be annihilated without lasting forever. For lasting forever is a necessary condition of its being at all, and its being-at-all is a necessary condition of its being annihilated.

It is objected that although immaterial things will not cease to be by corruption, by separation of form from matter, that does not assure that *esse* cannot be separated from *essentia*.[16] Immaterial things are immortal, but it is not impossible that they should cease to be. However, my argument is not directly from incorruptibility to inability to be annihilated. My argument is that for each creature, part of its essence is a particular (to each species) being-for-its-time. The being-for-its-time of rational souls and angels is "everlastingness." While we *explain* their having that particular temporality (rather, than, say, "four centuries" for some species of tree) from their incorruptibility, they are logically distinct properties, both "of the essence." I understand that Aquinas thinks they are equivalent in the creatures that have them and that the scope of "everlastingness" is limited by its explanation, "incorruptible." I think "everlasting" indicates the mode of *being* that incorruptible things have, the way they have to be to be at all.

Similarly, it is objected that although material things are corruptible, they can also be annihilated, by separation of *esse* from *essentia*, exactly as Aquinas understood the matter. I, however, am arguing that *what* exists is logically dependent on how long specifically (and in what way) it exists. In other words, for a creature that is immortal by

16. Peter Simpson stated this argument with great clarity in a letter, for which I am most grateful. He said there, "My objection is related to the *kind* of interminable existence incorruptibility bestows." That focuses the issue clearly: Are we talking of a mode of existence (roughly comparable to necessary being or infinite being) or merely (univocally) of different kinds of existents? I think the absence of matter-form composition is sufficient for analogy of "being" with, say, material things, and so we are talking of different kinds of "being" rather than just of beings of different kinds. It is a certain kind of "being" the thing must have *ab initio* and throughout its being.

nature to be at all, it must be forever. Aquinas is satisfied that it be "*such* as to be forever," should God conserve it. I am arguing that for it to be a thing of *that* sort, God must in *fact* conserve it.

Aquinas' view coheres so well with so much else that he says (except, perhaps, the *analogia entis* doctrine) that my saying "lasting forever is a condition of its being at all" will not overwhelm Aquinas' saying "being *such* as to last forever, *deo conservante*," is enough. But there is the additional factor of *God's ordered goodness* from which he has a reason not to annihilate anything he creates, despite the sufficing of his goodness for himself; for now his goodness is ordered to the *telos* of what is made. Being is a good bestowed on what is made for the good of what is made. God did not have to create, but having created, his goodness is thus ordered.

Double Talk? Double Truth? To speak of what would happen if God withdrew causation is useful to our appreciating the *scope* of God's creative power. That is like sketching out the constant power of Niagara Falls by working out what "would happen" if, *per impossibile*, the entire falls and its supply of water evaporated instantly (without other destruction). We calculate how grids of lights go out, pistons stop, switches fail, and so forth, to sketch the continuous causation of the falls. Although the resulting picture of its continuous causation is scientifically revealing, the postulated initial condition, instantaneous cessation without other destruction, is impossible. Scientific reality contains no such scenario, not even as a counterpossibility. So too with God. Yet the assertion "if God withdrew . . . ," etc., must be *made* true on account of its meaning relationship to "God is omnipotent" and not merely by the logical triviality that there is no world in which "God withdraws his ruling hand," and none in which "God withdraws his hand and some creatures continue to be." That is just truth of a counterfactual by having an impossible antecedent, a triviality. (See ST, Ia, 25, 3, ad 2.) Instead, it must be made true by SEMANTIC INHERITANCE, despite there being no "corresponding" possibility in scientific reality.

I say that God's power is properly explained in terms of annihilation, with phrases like "if God withdrew his ruling hand, all creation would fall instantly into nothingness," and yet, properly described SCIENTIFICALLY, God cannot annihilate his creatures. Is that not saying that what is religiously true may not be scientifically true? Is this "double truth" again, the very kind of doctrine Aquinas vigorously denied?

7. *Vantaged truths.* I am not attributing to Aquinas, or upholding, a

doctrine of dual truths of the kind he opposed, but of another kind that he himself acknowledged.

Several times in discussions of creation, Aquinas distinguishes truth of science from truths about the way things seem to be to common sense (for example: *D.P.*, 4, 2, ad 30; and ST, Ia, 70, 1, ad 3; 67, 4; 68, 3). He is not contrasting illusions with veridical perceptions, but contrasting *objective, stable*, public *appearances* of things to a particularly vantaged observer, that are accounted for by the scientific reality, but are not "the way things really are." In describing creation in days, before the sun was created, or in saying that "darkness was upon the face of the deep" without mentioning the air as well, "Moses was speaking to ignorant people, and out of condescension to their weakness he put before them only such things as are apparent to sense" (Ia, 68, 3c).

Secondly, differently vantaged truths may appear incompatible when they are just diverse. From afar, one might say "That house looks tiny," and up close "It is huge." Scientifically qualified statements are often too complicated for nonspecialists to understand, so statements in terms of the way things *look* (as with my astronomer example, below) are used instead. E.g., "The North Star is just overhead to your left." This is not a "double truth" doctrine as Aquinas understood the idea, one where genuinely inconsistent propositions were proposed to different audiences as true, with one set believed by initiates to be literally false and yet proposed to the unwary, who are deemed "simple," able only to take the false as the truth. Thus, some Averroists were thought to hold that the world existed forever, as scientific fact, and to teach as the revealed truth that the world was created in time.

The best way, sometimes, to convey an important truth accurately, say that God is omnipotent, is to express it as if things were only the way they APPEAR in pretheoretic understanding, despite the fact that science or superior knowledge discloses that the explanatory reality is not the apparent reality. In this case, for instance, it is efficient to explain "God is all-powerful" by what the UNREVISED ordinary meaning relations would yield as included in the meaning, "that *if* God withdrew his ruling hand, all creatures would fall into nothing." We do not, then, take into account the semantic revisions needed to describe reality scientifically, in which "God withdraws his hand" is mere metaphor, with no designated conforming reality.[17]

---

17. A designated reality is the reality picked out by a statement by way of what we *mean*; it is what we *mean*. A conforming reality is the reality a true statement conforms

In *D.P.*, 4, 2, ad 30, and ST, Ia, 70, 1, ad 3, St. Thomas says, "Moses coming down to the level of an unlettered people described things as they appear, saying that the luminaries are an adornment of the heavens." Aquinas argued that science shows that the stars are not adornments of the heavens, the way clothes are of a man, but the very stuff of the heavens, whether they are understood as Ptolemy understood them or as Aristotle did. Yet, Moses had to speak as if things were otherwise in order to be understood at all. It is as if an astronomer about to locate and discuss a comet began informally with "as you know, the sun rises in the east and sets in the west." As things appear, that is so.

So too, to explain the extent and immediacy of the power of God, as things appear to pretheoretic thought, we say that God is so powerful that if he withdrew his conservation, all the cosmos would blink out instantly and there would be nothing at all. In modern metaphor, the cosmic display would go blank, with all its data irretrievably lost. That is a true metaphor. It is also a vantaged truth.

Unbound Counterfactual Implications Can Be Blocked in a Scientific Context. When we realign descriptive categories for metaphysics and a general "world-science," some situations that are "counterpossibilities" when we talk of the world with the unrevised semantics of common sense, will not be possibilities at all. "God's having withdrawn his conserving power from a substance in being" cannot obtain. In the basically misleading parlance of possible worlds, there are no possible worlds in which God withdraws conservation from any or all creatures in being.

Nevertheless, we would not want to mislead the unwary to think God has *less* power, as if some other thing might, in principle, be able to do that. A correct description of God's power that does not provide for annihilation does not, by default, contain "If God withdrew his ruling hand, all creatures would NOT fall into nothing." That is false and contrary to the faith. Rather, a correct metaphysics of God's power involves realigned semantic relations, among "create," "conserve," "cause," etc., that make the "counterpossibility," "God's ceasing to conserve," unacceptable, inconsistent. The result is that in the scientific context, the supposition that God withdraws from his creatures is *not*

---

with. So, the designated conforming reality for "there are philosophers in Washington" is the presence of Wippel, Dougherty, Simpson, and the others there. You can have a true metaphor without a designated conforming reality: Christ will come again *at the right hand of the father.*

something about which we can have epistemic neutrality; it is something transparently impossible.

"Vantaged truth" is more easily understood when we remark: (1) vantaged truths differ from other relevant truths because their truth is *inherited*, usually by semantic relationships to other truths with designated conforming realities, EARNED TRUTHS.[18] In this case, the conditionals get their truth from "God is all-powerful," via meaning-elaboration. (2) Contrary to current fashion, the meaning of statements does not consist in their truth conditions (see Ross, *Portraying Analogy* [1982], ch. 8), and understanding statements does not consist in knowing truth conditions for them (though it can). (3) No one can provide the double decomposition (a semantic decomposition of statements, and a metaphysical decomposition of facts or realities stated) that is needed to display the CORRESPONDENCE, by isomorphism and by part-to-part matching, between a true statement and its conforming reality.[19] So, we can know something is true without knowing *how* it corresponds with reality or even *whether* it does. (4) There are truths that have a CONFORMING REALITY to which they do not stand in any correspondence relationship that could be devised on the same principles we would want to use to explain truth by isomorphic parallel decomposition, say; and there are some which, for reasons we know, do not gain their conforming reality by correspondence at all. (This is explained in my "Eschatological Pragmatism.")

Typical of the latter are truths by eschatological pragmatism: there are some revealed truths, say, about the Last Things, to whose TRUTH CONDITIONS, AT AN APPROPRIATE LEVEL OF SCIENTIFIC ARTICULATION (to form a coherent part of our world-science or scientific theology), we have NO ACCESS. Yet they are not merely *true* metaphors. Furthermore, the truth of such revelations as that Christ will come again consists not in a correspondence between what is said and a now determinate but future reality, but rather in a *cognitive consonance* of belief *in via* and experience at the Parousia; it is a fulfillment of faith by ultimate experience.

We can recognize conformity of reality to thought now, without knowing a single successful parallel decomposition into "correspon-

---

18. Do not, however, assume that when an earned truth has a designated conforming reality (e.g., "It is sunny today" has "mostly, cloudless sunshine"), the compliant (conforming reality) is what *makes* the truth-bearer true. It may not be at all. See the extensive discussion of this in my *Creation* (note 8, above).

19. This is treated in my "Eschatological Pragmatism," in *Philosophy and the Christian Faith*, ed. T. Morris (University of Notre Dame Press, 1986).

dence." So we should be unsurprised at the vast groups of truths that are *MADE* TRUE by various kinds of production (authentication, efficacious utterance, derivation from axioms) and by various inheritance relationships (e.g., logical, semantic) to other statements made true directly (in the first ways).[20] The vantaged truths INHERIT truth, and thus often depend upon alterable semantic relationships. Whether the "adornment" of the heavens can or cannot be its substance depends on whether, in context, "adornment" is the contrary of "is the substance of" or is co-applicable. That varies contextually and with theoretical framework.

Therefore, the Christian can rightly understand "and I await the resurrection of the dead" without being even remotely able to DESCRIBE what that "resurrection" consists in, e.g., whether we have the same atoms, same molecules, cells, bones, are aged thirty-three, or what an "impassible" body might be. Thus, vantaged truths are a subclass of the truths whose MEANING does not decompose into truth conditions and whose having a CONFORMING REALITY does NOT consist in a correspondence relation, and whose truth is not EARNED by a truth-making relation (like "authentication") that conforms them to a designated reality, but INHERITED by logical, semantic, and other alterable relations that DERIVE truth for them from EARNED TRUTHS but on alteration can deprive them of truth or even of a truth value. (I develop this considerably in *Creation*, the O'Hara Lectures [University of Notre Dame Press, forthcoming], and probably will do so also in *Truth Enigmatically: On Doctrinal Authority and Certitude*, forthcoming.)

So, I revise Aquinas' doctrine on annihilation, saying it is a *vantaged* truth that God can annihilate his creatures, a truth by inheritance within a prescientific semantic fabric. It is a true metaphor, but also somewhat more, as well. That is, *if* someone understood "God is the creator of all things" to *mean* that though God produced all creatures, some could continue to be without divine causation, he would *mis*understand. So, to express a proper understanding of the point, one says "if God withdrew his ruling hand, all creatures would instantly fall into nothing." Thus the latter, which is in the "scientific theology" a solecism, INHERITS truth by its meaning relation (e.g., as indispensable qualification) to a statement that DOES have a designated conforming reality, "God is creator of all things visible and invisible," and does have a coherent analogue in the "scientific theology."

20. See also my interim discussion in the Audi-Wainwright volume (note 12, above), and in an unpublished memo and two lectures at the NEH Summer Institute on Philosophy of Religion, Western Washington State University, 1986.

III. AGREEING ABOUT THE WORLD WITHOUT END

Aquinas is definite that God WILL NOT annihilate creatures and that the cosmos will go on, of its OWN (God concurring), forever. He says in *D.P.*, 5, 4, corpus:

> The created universe will never be annihilated. And notwithstanding that corruptible creatures have not always existed, they will last, nevertheless, forever as to their substance.

He does not attribute that to some gratuitous or gracious impulse of divine love but says, "it is a natural property of those immaterial things which have no contrary that they last forever, since in them there is no potentiality for nonexistence" (5, 4c). (It is clear that critics of my view should not attribute *potentiality* for nonexistence to things "composed" of *esse* and *essentia*.)

Further (and this is MOST important for explaining why God chose this world, and for explaining why the creation is not a means to any end, and furthermore it is the basis of my main argument that God has *from* creating a reason *not* to annihilate),

> He who wills a thing for its own sake, wills it to last *forever*, for the very reason that he wills it for itself. . . . *God wills the created universe for its own sake*, although he wills its existence for his own sake; for these two are not incompatible with each other. (Emphasis added)

In ST, Ia, 104, 4, Aquinas mentions that matter "is incorruptible, since it is the subject of generation and corruption." Though material things are corruptible because continuing a given form can become impossible, *matter* cannot be without form because form can be "lost" only by *replacement*, by "succession" in matter; that is one reason why formless matter cannot occur; thus, matter, as locus of succession of form, is not corruptible; matter cannot be lost from reality by change. "Matter," here, is of course not sensible matter, but the subject of structure, one manifestation of which is sensible matter.

Aquinas' discussion of the permanent endurance of the world in *De Potentia* is tense with opposition between (1) the end of the world required by faith (see 5, 5), which makes him say (in ad 11), "The last instant of all time will indeed be the end of the past, but not the beginning of the future," and (2) the scientific view that "the universe will remain forever" (5, 7–10).

He harmonizes the two by speaking of the end of the world as the end of the heavenly motions (at least what we call the solar system), with the destruction of the earth and of material earthly life, while the material world, "as to its substance," goes on forever. So he argues in a. 9 that plants and animals "will also cease then," when the past is ended and the world is renewed, and that man's animal life will "cease in that final renewal of the universe, because the body will rise not natural but spiritual . . . ; hence animals and plants will also cease to exist then." Yet, humans will (a. 10) retain their resurrected material bodies that "will contain an incorruptible principle . . . able to preserve [them] without violence."

The scriptural faith requires Aquinas to propose that there is an "end of the world" that consists, among other things, in the cessation of the heavenly motions as we know them. The "scientific" picture, consisting also of theology as well as philosophy, requires that God's "ordained will" is for the creation to continue forever, the material as well as spiritual creation. That God's ordained will requires the universe to exist forever is just an application of the principle of ordained goodness to which I appeal to say annihilation is not a scientific counterpossibility at all, only a prescientific vantaged truth.

Accord with Science. Earlier in our century, when thermodynamic death was in vogue, it seemed far less than likely that Aquinas' belief in the endurance of the universe would turn out to be true. Now speculative cosmology is more hospitable.

Although protons are no longer thought to be everlasting but individually to endure 10^{30} years (a thousand billion billion billion years), a period exceeding the interval from the "big bang" many times over, it appears also that all the components at the interatomic level, including protons, can be and are "decomposed" and also "recomposed" in cosmic gravity engines, the black holes, and spewed out from explosions and "leaked out" at the "magic circle."[21] The idea of a self-renewing cosmos has gained coherence with painstaking mathematization and conceptualization. I realize that physics, as the 1980s end, seems near chaos and bafflement because the accelerators needed to discriminate hypotheses are far beyond our powers to make and the basic supersymmetry, or string theory, and the like, elude us. We are still as uncomprehending before the wonderment of the universe as savages before a fire. Yet good science will, I think, converge with good theology: the substance of the universe endures forever.

I mentioned Freeman Dyson's papers that sketch an everlasting universe at low temperatures, yet still suitable for intelligent life. Succeeding hypotheses will include, I think, (a) that, as Hawking has suggested, despite Einstein, the laws of nature (particularly, the velocity

21. N. Calder, *The Key to the Universe* (note 2, above).

of light) will not APPEAR the same regardless of the position and acceleration of the observers (and so are harder to discover at first); (b) that matter has an infinity of strata, a recursive formal structure—the Chinese of Mao's era called quarks "stratons" to emphasize the recurrent embedding of structure—even though accessibility to "appearance" ends somewhere at or near the quark strata, unless we can somehow "recalibrate" our observing abilities; (c) that inevitably the theoretically postulated inner strata of matter will "accelerate" far beyond the experimentally detectable ones, so that a particularly virulent underdetermination of theory by observation (a kind of super-grue problem) will occur, demanding a new account of theory confirmation and discrimination; (d) that relatively more areas than were thought over the overall cool cosmos will be "hot" for intelligent things; and (e) that, as I think Hawking suggested, a universe organized locally into intelligent life endures forever, despite the obliteration of information in black holes and the apparently random introduction of matter (and information) from "leaking" and exploding black holes.

All this is, of course, speculation. Still, Aquinas' beautiful conception in *De Potentia Dei* that nature continues forever on its own (from God's ordained will) has comprehensible, though speculative, astrophysical "realizations."

With Aquinas, I think we will never discover a pit of nothingness lying at some "end" of space-time. Nor, begging his pardon, do I think, as St. Thomas did, that we will ever reach the last moment of the past, succeeded by no moment of the future, where all intelligent beings enter timeless being. We will find another way to "accommodate" the truths about the Last Things. Yet St. Thomas, I think, was right overall: God has willed that his creation, as to its substance, will endure forever.

University of Pennsylvania

9   The Tradition of Mediaeval Nominalism
CALVIN G. NORMORE

Contemporary nominalism has several faces. One of these is displayed in the first sentence of Hartry Field's book *Science without Numbers*, where Field writes that "Nominalism is the doctrine that there are no abstract objects."[1] Another is displayed in Nelson Goodman's claim that "Nominalism . . . consists of the refusal to countenance any entities other than individuals. Its opposite, platonism, recognizes at least some non-individuals."[2]

It is far from clear what these positions have to do with one another—in part because the connection between being concrete (the contrary of being abstract) and being particular or individual is itself obscure. Some philosophers write as if it were obvious that all and only concrete objects are individual, but it is hard to see what is nonindividual about either the cardinal numbers or Plato's Forms. Part of the problem here is just that we lack good theories of the abstract/concrete and individual/nonindividual distinctions, but part also seems to be that any plausible story which would make the collapse seem plausible involves strong additional assumptions which I doubt foes of either abstract objects or nonindividuals have any reason to accept.

Suppose, for example, that an object is abstract if one could imagine it emerging as the result of a process of abstraction which leaves out some features of some other object. A concrete object then would be one from which no feature was left out. Such an object would be an

---

I am heavily indebted to Christopher J. Martin for many references to texts of the *Nominales* and for much discussion of them, to Sten Ebbesen for the reference to Jacques de Vitry, and to Peter King for comments. Other versions of this material were presented at the Boston Area Medieval Philosophy Colloquium and at the University of California, Irvine. I would also like to thank the members of those audiences for their helpful discussion.

1. Hartry Field, *Science without Numbers: A Defense of Nominalism* (Princeton, 1980), p. 1.
2. Nelson Goodman, *The Structure of Appearance* (Cambridge, Mass., 1951), pp. 33–34.

individual in Leibniz's sense and an actual object (as contrasted with a mere possible) in Peirce's.[3] Against such a background the two faces of nominalism merge. But such a merger requires the identity of indiscernibles. It is because a Leibnizian individual is completely specified by a maximal collection of properties that every Leibnizian individual is, in this sense, concrete.

Nominalists are not, I think, in a position to accept the identity of indiscernibles. Why should indiscernible objects be identical? To suppose they are is to suppose that distinctness is either produced by or results in a difference of properties. But properties are neither individual nor concrete. Hence no matter which face is the true face of nominalism, nominalists will have to deny that properties exist. But then properties cannot account for the distinctness of things. This still leaves the possibility that each two things are as a matter of fact discernible, but it leaves that possibility unmotivated. So the collapse of the two claims about what nominalism is would, on this story, require an assumption which the adherents of neither need accept.

If the most plausible stories supporting the merger of the two all require assumptions which neither party need accept, we have reason to wonder whether either captures what the term "nominalism" was originally coined to express. Perhaps by investigating the history of the term we will learn something about how and why it came to be used so variously.

"Nominalist" is a mediaeval term. Perhaps the best way to find out what it means is to take that fact seriously and to try to trace the history of its mediaeval use. It is plausible to suppose that even today people use the term as they imagine their teachers did in a chain that stretches back into the Middle Ages. So perhaps the history of the use of the word "nominalist" can inform its current use.

There is considerable unease within the contemporary scholarly community about what is to be understood by "nominalism" in the Middle Ages. For example, Paul Vignaux suggests that the nominalism of the twelfth century is unrelated to that of the later Middle Ages, while William Courtenay goes so far as to suggest that there is not enough resemblance among the thinkers and views usually called "nominalist" to warrant the continued use of the term.[4] Yet even such

---

3. Because his adherence to the identity of indiscernibles is very strict, Leibniz admits possible as well as actual individuals (cf. for example his *Correspondence With Arnauld*, trans. H. T. Mason [Manchester, 1967], pp. 15–16).

4. For Vignaux's view cf. his *Philosophy in the Middle Ages* (New York, 1959), p. 52. For Courtenay's view cf. his "Nominalism and Late Medieval Religion," in C. Trinkhaus and H. Oberman, eds., *The Pursuit of Holiness* (Leiden, 1974), pp. 26ff.

sophisticated critics as these have, I suggest, queered the pitch for their investigations by assuming that we know what nominalism was, at least originally, and by assuming in particular that its roots lie somehow in the debate about universals. Thus two of the four sections into which Vignaux divides his article "Nominalisme" in the *Dictionnaire de Théologie Catholique* have "Universel" in their title, and even Courtenay is prepared to suggest that "'Nominalist' was a twelfth-century term that described a particular position on the problem of universals."[5]

It is precisely the assumption that mediaeval nominalism was, fundamentally, a position about universals which I wish to question here. I claim that mediaeval nominalism was only incidentally connected with the problem of universals and that, once that is seen, both the philosophical terrain of the Middle Ages and some of our contemporary metaphysical vocabulary look somewhat different.

When does nominalism begin? Most of our earliest sources are completely silent about this question, but there are two sentences by the twelfth-century historian Otto von Freising which just might suggest an answer. It is thought that Otto studied in Paris from about 1127 to 1133, so his testimony has some authority. In book I of his *Gesta Frederici Imperatoris*, Otto writes of Peter Abaelard that "he had for his teacher first one Roscelin, who first taught in our time the *sententia vocum*."[6] This gnomic remark could perhaps be glossed with the help of Otto's claim just a bit later in the passage that Abaelard, "holding in the faculty of natural studies the *sententia vocum seu nominum*, incautiously introduced it into theology."[7]

If the *sententia nominum* is nominalism, and if this *sententia vocum seu nominum* can be identified, as Otto suggests it can, with Roscelin's *sententia vocum*, then we have some evidence that whatever nominalism is, it was Roscelin who popularized it in the early twelfth century. But it is not easy to see how Roscelin's doctrine of *voces* could be Abaelard's doctrine of *nomina*. If the *sententia vocum* is what John of Salisbury calls in his *Metalogicon* the "opinion that *voces* themselves are species and genera," then on John's own telling, we should conclude that that opinion "has vanished readily with its author," at a time when Abaelard's views in dialectics were treated with respect. But if the *sententia vocum* to which Otto refers is not the view that genera and species are *voces*, then what is it?

5. Courtenay, op. cit., p. 52.
6. Otto von Freising, *Gesta Frederici Imperatoris*, Lib. I, in *Monumenta Germaniae Historica*, vol. 20, ed. G. H. Pertz, p. 377.
7. Ibid.

Otto suggests that Abaelard incautiously brought the *sententia vocum seu nominum* into theology. The problem of universals is not, as such, a central problem in theology, but the question of the nature of the Trinity is. The only position which we can solidly attribute to Roscelin, other than his view about universals, is the view that the distinctions among the persons of the Trinity are not distinctions among different things but distinctions among names. For this he was accused of Sabellianism.[8] As luck would have it, Abaelard was also accused of Sabellianism, and much of his effort in his *Theologia Christiana* goes to buttress his opinion against the charge. This suggests the possibility that the *sententia vocum seu nominum* includes a thesis that the various names of persons of the Trinity pick out just one thing.

Whatever we make of this suggestion about what the *sententia nominum* is, Peter Abaelard is clearly the one to whom Otto of Freising attributes it. And Walter Mappe in his *Trifles of the Courtiers* calls Abaelard the *Princeps Nominalium*.[9] Mappe's testimony is from the next generation, but still early, and it links Abaelard explicitly with the *Nominales*. If Abaelard is the author of the *sententia nominum* and the "Prince" of the *Nominales*, then we have a suspect. Does he have an alibi?

If we look at the references to the *Nominales* in twelfth-century texts, we find a curious collection of doctrines attributed to them. First, there is the view, called the *Error Nominalium*, that a syllogistic inference does not require a topical locus—this suggests that the syllogism is an inference form requiring no further justification.[10] Second, there is the view attributed to the *Nominales* in Munich CLM 2950 that a negative sentence does not follow from an affirmative nor vice versa.[11] Third, the *Compendium Logicae*—a text which recognizes Gilbert de la Poirée as master—attributes to some *Nominales* the view that a whole is nothing other than its parts.[12] Fourth, the *Obligationes Parisiensis* edited by De Rijk attributes to the *Nominales* views which imply that not everything follows from an impossibility.[13] And fifth,

---

8. Cf. Anselm of Canterbury, *Epistolae de Incarnatione Verbi*, in F. S. Schmitt, ed., *Opera Omnia* (Rome, 1938–60), vol. 1, p. 287 (*Priora Rescensio*), and 2, p. 15 (*Secunda Rescensio*).

9. Walter Mappe, *De Nuges Curalium*, d. I, c. 24, ed. and trans. M. R. James (Oxford, 1983), p. 79.

10. Cf. the treatise "Haec Est" (Paris, Arsenal 910 ff. 58ra–88vb), ed. N.-J. Green-Pederson in *Studia Mediewistyczne* 18 (1977), pp. 125–63, p. 142, n. 88.

11. Cf. the edition of Munich CLM 2950/2 by Yukio Iwakuma in *Cahiers de L'Institut du Moyen-Âge Grec et Latin* (CIMAGL) 44 (1983), p. 82.

12. *Compendium Logicae*, ed. Sten Ebbesen in CIMAGL 46 (1983), p. 39.

13. Cf. L. M. de Rijk, "Some Thirteenth Century Tracts in the Game of Obligation,"

Jacques de Vitry attributes to some *Nominales* the thesis that "nihil crescit."[14]

These theses seem quite disparate, but they have one thing in common: they are all characteristic and controversial views of Peter Abaelard. First, the view that the syllogism does not require a topical justification lies at the heart of Abaelard's theory of inference. In his *Dialectica*, Abaelard divides inferences into those which are perfect and require no rule to justify them and those which are imperfect and do require such a rule. The syllogism is his paradigm of perfect inference.[15] Second, in his discussion of the *locus ab oppositis*, Abaelard expressly denies that a negative sentence follows from an affirmative or vice versa.[16] Third, Abaelard seems to have denied that an integral whole like a house is a thing distinct from its integral parts.[17]

The fourth thesis, that not everything follows from an impossibility, is clearly Abaelard's but not so clearly a common doctrine of the *Nominales*. Abaelard not only held this view, but engaged in a bitter controversy about it with Alberic of Rheims, a controversy which seems to have been a watershed in the history of logic.[18] Abaelard resolutely denied that everything follows from an impossibility and devised two arguments which he believed decisively supported his view. In response, Alberic proved that the very arguments Abaelard used could be extended to show that the thesis Abaelard defended was inconsistent with the principles used in its defence. We do not know how Abaelard responded in turn to Alberic's proof, but in at least one text he is reported to have accepted it. This is of interest because there is confusion about the position of the *Nominales* on this point. This confusion is just what one would expect if the *Nominales* followed Abaelard into Alberic's trap and then had to find their own way out.

It is perhaps worth adding that the Alberic who bested Abaelard on this question is the same man who appears in the only mention of the *Nominales* in John of Salisbury's *Metalogicon*. John does not mention

---

Vivarium 13 (1975), pp. 22–53. Cf. also Vat. Lat. 7678, ed. in H. A. G. Braakhuis, *De 13de Eeuwse Tractaten over Syncategorematiche Termen* (Krips Repro Mappel, Holland, n.d.), vol. 1, p. 63.

14. Thus the *Dialectica Monacensis*, ed. L. M. de Rijk in *Logica Modernorum*, vol. 2, pt. 2 (Assen, 1967), p. 558, ll. 6ff., and Jacques de Vitry in his *Exempla*, Exemplum 102, in *Quellen und Untersuchungen zur Lateinischen Philologie des Mittelalters*, vol. 5, ed. P. Lehmann (Münich, 1914), p. 147.

15. *Dialectica* III, p. 256, ll. 30–35, in Petrus Abaelardus, *Dialectica*, ed. with an intro. by L. M. de Rijk, 2d rev. ed. (Assen, 1970).

16. Op. cit., III, p. 395, ll. 7ff.

17. Cf. for example op. cit., V, p. 555, ll. 10ff.

18. For Abaelard's view and the controversy surrounding it cf. Christopher J. Martin, "William's Wonderful Machine," forthcoming in the *Journal of Philosophy*, 1986.

the *Nominales* at all in his discussion of universals but in recounting his own studies tells how, after Abaelard left Paris, he, John, went to study with Alberic, "a very fierce opponent of the sect of the *Nominales*."[19]

There seems little doubt then that the *Nominales* were followers of Abaelard. But why were they called *Nominales* and what is the *sententia nominum*?

Curiously the first explicit claim about why *Nominales* are so called appears not in the twelfth century but in the thirteenth, and not among logicians but among theologians. It is found in St. Bonaventure's commentary on the *Sentences*. The problem is the unlikely one of just what the articles of faith are. A little reflection shows that the difference between heresy and orthodoxy can be marked by as little as a difference of tense—by, for example, the difference between believing that the Messiah has come and believing that the Messiah will come. Hence, it seems reasonable to say that faith requires the acceptance of particular sentences (*complexa*) at particular times. Bonaventure continues:

And if you object to them about the change of faith [that would result] on account of change in these statements [*enuntiabiles*], they respond according to the *Nominales* that the statements are not changed, because that you are going to run, that you do run, and that you have run, spoken at different times signify the same thing. There is just one statement, because there is just one thing which they signify and one time for which they are put forward. Therefore, they are one in reality and truth although they seem vocally to be diverse. (*Sent. III*, d. 24, art. 1, q. 3, c.)[20]

Bonaventure also discusses the view of these *Nominales* in *Sent. I*, d. 41, art. 2, q. 2. There he writes that

if I say now "Socrates is running today," and tomorrow I say "He ran," then since there ought not to be a different time understood with the different verb and so not a different action, the statement [*enuntiabile*] is not changed however much the consignification is changed, and because the same signification is retained, the statement is always the same. Since it is not the same except when the same signification is retained, they say that what now is true is always true. Since God forgets nothing, they say that every statement which God knew he knows. . . . And this was the opinion of the *Nominales* who are called *Nominales* because they founded their position on the unity of the name.

This very position is also ascribed by Thomas Aquinas to the "old *Nominales*."[21]

19. John of Salisbury, *Metalogicon*, bk. II, ch. 10.
20. St. Bonaventure, *Commentarius in IV Libros Sententiarum Petri Lombardi* III, d. 24, art. 1, q. 3, c.
21. Thomas Aquinas, *Summa Theologiae* I, q. 14, art. 15, ad 3.

Who held this position? M. D. Chenu, perhaps the scholar who has studied this question most deeply, thinks that the position under discussion is that of Bernard of Chartres and that it developed within the tradition of speculative grammar.[22] If his view is correct, there is a delicious irony about it, for there is no one farther from the traditional stereotype of a nominalist than Bernard. He believed firmly in Platonic Separated Forms, and the tradition of speculative grammar with which Chenu connects him was mercilessly criticized by the Buridanian "nominalists." Pierre d'Ailly even devoted a tract specifically to its refutation.[23]

But there is really no need to accept Chenu's hypothesis, for the doctrine which Bonaventure and Aquinas attribute to the *Nominales* is advanced in Peter Abaelard's *Introductio ad Theologiam* (PL 178:1102–3) where Abaelard claims that God knew before I was born that I was going to be born and does not know now that I am going to be born and yet knows now what he knew then "although then and now this knowledge of his would have to be expressed in different words." Abaelard again seems to have originated the views which the *Nominales* propounded.

But is this all? Is the secret of nominalism just that Abaelard adopted a peculiar view about the unity of names and that a band of his students followed him in this obscure and eccentric practice?

Of course not! What is at stake here, I think, is nothing less than the question of the nature of reality itself. I hypothesize that we can sum up the views that make Abaelard's theses hang together as:

(1) There are more truths than truth-makers.
(2) There are more true sentences than truths.

If this is right, then nominalism is, at bottom, a position about what makes sentences true.

Thanks especially to recent work by Martin Tweedale and Peter King, we are at last in a position to begin to appreciate Abaelard's ontology and its relation to his philosophy of language.[24] In his ontology, Abaelard seems prepared to admit two kinds of things—individual substances and individual forms. But in his philosophy of language, he is prepared to talk about statuses, dicta, and natures. Statuses, dicta, and natures are not things, and there can be changes in the status

---

22. M.-D. Chenu, *La Théologie au Douzième Siècle* (Paris, 1957), pp. 95 ff.
23. Pierre d'Ailly's tract, so far little studied, is the *Destructiones Modorum Significandi*.
24. M. Tweedale, *Abailard on Universals* (Amsterdam, North-Holland, 1976), and P. O. King, "Peter Abaelard and the Problem of Universals" (Ph.D. dissertation, Princeton, 1982).

a thing has without any change in the thing itself. For example, if you and I are similar, then I have the status of being similar to you, but

what is more ridiculous than that if someone now be born to whom I am made similar, on account of that, some new thing be born in me which necessarily leaves when he perishes?[25]

Statuses are no more real than is the relation of similarity.

When do two terms pick out different statuses? Part of Abaelard's answer is that they do so when they differ in definition. As he remarks in the *Theologia Christiana:*

we are accustomed to use "same status" or "different statuses" for what is the same in definition, and we do not call this status that status except when this thing is wholly the same as that thing in definition.[26]

Dicta are to sentences as statuses to things. Abaelard seems not to have given identity conditions for dicta in any of the works we have, but a very plausible sufficient condition for distinctness of dicta is that two dicta are distinct if terms in the sentences expressing them pick out distinct statuses. Sentences with the same copula signifying or consignifying the same time will express the *same* dictum if their terms express the *same* status. This fits the view Abaelard expresses in his *Introductio ad Theologiam* that to say today that Socrates is running and to say tomorrow that Socrates ran (yesterday) is to say the same thing, i.e., to express the same dictum. Differences in tense do not suffice to differentiate dicta. Abaelard does not indicate exactly which differences in grammatical form reveal differences in dictum or status, but what he does say suggests that differences in consignification in general would not reveal such differences. Thus, changes of gender, like changes of tense, would leave the dictum or status unaffected. Distinct sentences can express the same dictum; there are more true sentences than truths.

What of the claim that there are more truths than truth-makers? By a truth-maker, I understand an item in the ontology in virtue of which a truth obtains. The claim that there are more truths than truth-makers is then the claim that distinct dicta can correspond to the same item in the ontology. We saw earlier that it is very plausible to think that dicta are distinct if they express distinct statuses. Abaelard is very clear that (1) statuses are not themselves items in the ontology

---

25. Peter Abaelard, *Theologia Christiana*, in *Petri Abaelardi Opera Theologica*, vol. 2, ed. E. Buytaert (Corpus Christianorum, Cont. Mediaevalis), vol. 12 (Turnholt, Brepols, 1969), bk. III, par. 170.
26. *Theologia Christiana*, bk. III, par. 157.

and (2) the same thing has many statuses. Indeed his account of change depends on the possibility that the same things may come to have or cease to have different statuses.

Two of the positions we have seen attributed to the *Nominales* are views directly relevant to the theory of change. One is the view, mentioned by Jacques de Vitry, that nothing increases (*nihil crescit*). The other is the view mentioned in the *Compendium Logicae* that a whole is nothing other than its parts. How can such views be defended?

I remarked earlier that Abaelard draws a sharp distinction between things like substances and forms, and statuses. What I wish to suggest now is that it is the former and not the latter which are the subjects of predication in normal contexts. That is, when I say

(1) Socrates is a human

this can be rephrased as

(2) The thing which is Socrates is (has the status of being) human.

To see the significance of this consider the sentence

(3) Socrates is a thing-which-is-human.

Sentence 3 is true but not, I think, equivalent to sentence 1. Sentence 1 ascribes to Socrates—that very thing—a certain status—namely, that of being human. Sentence 3 on the other hand claims of Socrates that he is identical with a certain thing, which thing it picks out by the expression "a thing-which-is-human." Sentence 3 expresses, if I am right, exactly what is expressed by the claim "Socrates is that"—pointing to whatever is picked out by "a thing-which-is-human" in (3). But sentence 1 is not an identity claim at all.

Why does this matter? Abaelard is much concerned with problems of identity. The working out of an account of identity is crucial to his study of the Trinity.

Consider the following problem. Suppose a block of stone has been made into a statue by a sculptor. (What such making consists in, I suppose, is separating those bits of stone which make up the statue from other bits which do not.) Now if the block of stone is the statue—if there is just one thing there—then every feature the stone has the statue has and vice versa. After all there is just a single thing there, and for any feature it either has it or does not. But the stone was made by God and the statue was made by the sculptor and not made by God. Does this not show that the stone is a different thing from the statue?

This way of approaching the problem seems to suppose that making a statue is making a thing, and it is this which I think Abaelard would not accept. Moving bits of stone around is not making anything; it is just changing the statuses things have. Thus Abaelard's resolution of the problem is to deny that the statue, i.e., the thing which the statue is, was made by the sculptor. It was made by God (and it may be that in making it God made it with the status of being a stone because such is essential to it). The sculptor did not make anything but gave the stone the status of being a statue.

With this analysis at our disposal let us return to the two claims of the *Nominales* about change. Note first that they are connected. If a thing just is its parts, then if there are different parts there must be different things. But one way, perhaps the typical way, that a thing grows or increases is by adding new parts. So a thing which is just its parts cannot, strictly speaking, grow or increase. So growth or increase is not a change in things. Neither for that matter is alteration or local motion. Alteration is a change in status; for example, what had the status of being cold comes to have the status of being hot, and what had the status of being white comes to have the status of being black. Abaelard never explicitly says that local motion involves change of status, but what he does say strongly suggests it. Thus we can see a connection between the claims attributed to the *Nominales* and the underlying view in virtue of which they are so called. If we except generation and destruction, every change is a change of status. Just as there are more truths than truth-makers so there are more changes than things. Indeed Abaelard goes so far as to suggest that causal connections are not primarily connections among things but connections among statuses.

There seem to be no thirteenth-century figures who are called *Nominales*. Aquinas' reference to the "old *Nominales*" may suggest newer ones, but if there are such I have not yet found them. It would not be particularly surprising if the term ceased to be applied even if there continued to be people holding the characteristic positions of the *Nominales* because, so far as we can now tell, the emergence of the universities at the beginning of the thirteenth century marked the end of the twelfth-century schools as schools intellectually as well as institutionally. To find a term much like *Nominales* used again we have to turn to the late fifteenth century. There we find certain fourteenth-century figures being referred to as *Nominalistae*. The canonical list appears in a Royal Edict issued in 1473 and includes Ockham, Buridan, Pierre d'Ailly, Albert of Saxony, Marsilius of Inghen, Adam Dorp, and "other nominalists."[27] What do these folk have in common and what do they have in common with the twelfth-century *Nominales*?

The Royal Edict of 1473 provoked a reaction within the University of Paris and led to a letter addressed to the king of France defending those whom the edict mentioned. Although the authors go to some pains to tell us what nominalism is, there is, of course, no mention of universals, but there are the following terse remarks:

> Those doctors are called nominalists who do not multiply things that are principally signified by terms according to the multiplication of terms. Realists on the other hand are those who contend that things are multiplied with the multiplication of terms. For instance, nominalists say that deity and wisdom are one and the same, but realists say that divine wisdom is divided from deity.[28]

Also those are called nominalists who apply diligence and study to know all the properties of terms from which depend the truth and falsity of speech, and without which there can be no perfect judgement of the truth and falsity of propositions. These properties are *suppositio, appellatio, ampliatio, restrictio, distributio exponibilis*. In addition they know obligations and insolubles, the true foundations of argumentation and dialectic, and all their defects.

A little later the defence mentions a few concrete points of difference between nominalists and realists, claiming that

> in those matters which concern nominalism and realism the position of the nominalists is always more in conformity with the faith and frequently approved by the church, while the position of the realists is precarious and reproved in many things by the church, as is plain in the matter of universals concerning the eternity of propositions, and the multiplying of entities without cause.[29]

The theme which we saw in the twelfth-century discussions, that nominalists believe the truth-makers of sentences to be fewer than the sentences themselves, here reappears in the claim that realists posit as many things as terms while nominalists suppose fewer. But in the Royal Edict and this defence we are given not merely characteristic nominalist doctrines but a canonical list of nominalist doctors. Perhaps by looking to it we can gain some idea of how and why these figures were grouped together.

Two figures stand out among those mentioned on the list. They are

---

27. For details cf. L. Thorndyke, *University Records and Life in the Middle Ages* (New York, 1944), pp. 355 ff.
28. Ibid.
29. Ibid.

mentioned first, they are the first chronologically, and it is pretty clear that they influenced all the others. They are William Ockham and Jean Buridan. I wish to suggest that Ockham and Buridan are the common authors of an approach to the relation between language and what makes it true which is characteristic of all those on the royal list.

Like Professor M. Adams, I see Ockham as primarily an ontologist whose ultimate concern is the metaphysical furniture of the world.[30] But Ockham's method in ontology depends on a recipe which is inextricably connected with the philosophy of language. Here, very briefly, is the recipe.

First divide the expressions of your language into those which purport to pick things out (the categorematic expressions) and those which do not (the syncategorematic expressions). Then see whether some of those which purport to pick things out have nominal definitions and so can be eliminated without decreasing the expressive power of the language (these expressions Ockham calls connotative). Finally admit into your ontology whatever an undefinable (or absolute) term purports to pick out.

This is Ockham's explicit programme, and it certainly does yield the consequence that there will be many sentences containing connotative terms which express the same thing (or, in Ockham's framework are subordinated to the same mental sentence). I have argued elsewhere that although there are some differences of detail it is also Buridan's view.[31] But there is a deep difference between this approach as Ockham and Buridan employ it and the Abaelardian view that different sentences can express the same dictum. Both Ockham and Buridan believe, and Buridan repeatedly insists, that once one has said what the terms of a sentence signify, one has expressed all the signification there is. Abaelard, on the other hand, holds that the sentence as a whole signifies—though the dictum signified is in no way a thing.

This issue also divides the sides of one of the sharpest struggles among the doctors whom the Royal Edict calls *Nominalistae;* for while Ockham, Buridan, and Buridan's students all deny that sentences signify, Gregory of Rimini held what appears to be Abaelard's view, and as Gideon Gál has argued, he got it from someone deeply involved with Ockham, namely, Adam Wodeham.

We can get some perspective on the debate from the *Logica Magna*

30. Marilyn M. Adams, "Things versus 'Hows', or Ockham on Predication and Ontology," in James Bogen and James E. McGuire, eds., *How Things Are* (Dordrecht, 1985), pp. 175–88.
31. Cf. "Buridan's Ontology" in Bogen and McGuire, op. cit.

of Paul of Venice, written nearly a century later. In his *Tract on the Signification of a Sentence* Paul summarizes Gregory's position as that

the significate of a sentence is that things are somehow and *complexe significabile*.[32]

The terminology of the *complexe significabile* is apparently Gregory's, but the doctrine is clearly in Wodeham, who in the first question of bk. I, d. 1, of his commentary on the *Sentences* writes:

the total object of a sentence is its significate. Moreover its significate is to be such and such as the sentence indicates.[33]

Note the adverbial form. Both Wodeham and Gregory, like Abaelard before them, are concerned to avoid hypostasizing the total significate of sentences, and the adverbial form seems intended to do that.

Wodeham seems to have been moved to the doctrine of *complexe significabile* by the desire to find an appropriate object for verbs like "knows" and "believes." When one believes, one believes somehow. He takes Walter Chatton to task for holding that one knows or believes ordinary substances and accidents, and Ockham to task for holding that one knows or believes sentences. Thus the need for something else to know or believe and so the theory of the *complexe significabile*.

But the theory of the *complexe significabile* was, despite both Wodeham's and Gregory's claims not to be doing ontology, too rich for Buridan's taste, and he and his students attacked it mercilessly. They thought that if the theory was to do the work it was designed for, it would have to admit *complexe significabile* into the ontology, and that these entities were unacceptable. On their view only terms signify, and sentences have no signification other than that of their parts.[34]

We have come full circle. To avoid multiplying truth-makers, Abaelard introduced a layer of "non-things" between sentences and objects. But Ockham and especially Buridan find that this layer threatens to dissolve into another layer of things and so eliminate it. The doctrine which gave the *Nominales* their name divides the *Nominalistae*, and the doctrinal unity we found seems to have disappeared.

32. Paul of Venice, *De Significato Propositionis*, c. 3, in F. del Punta and M. M. Adams, eds. and trans., *Pauli Venetii Logica Magna*, pt. II, fascic. 6 (Oxford, 1978), p. 94. I have retranslated the text to focus on the adverbial form of the Latin.
33. Adam Wodeham, *In I Sent.*, d. 1, q. 1 (Gonville and Caius 281/674 f. 130rd), ed. in Gedeon Gál, "Adam of Wodeham's Question on the *Complexe Significabile* as the Immediate Object of Scientific Knowledge," *Franciscan Studies* 37 (1977), p. 87.
34. Cf. J. Buridan, *Sophismata*, ed. T. K. Scott (Stuttgart, 1977); Peter of Ailly, *Concepts and Insolubles: An Annotated Translation*, P. V. Spade (Dordrecht, 1980).

But not the underlying motivation of the twelfth-century movement, for in my discussion of Abaelard I left out something crucial; I neglected to say why he thought dicta and statuses were not things and why his followers thought that wholes were nothing other than their parts.

What I want now to suggest is that the reason Abaelard is unwilling to reify dicta and statuses and Ockham and Buridan are unwilling to countenance them at all is the same, namely, the view that if there are two things (distinct from God) then God could make or conserve one of them without the other.

That Ockham believes a restricted version of this is well known. The restriction needed for Ockham's view is that neither be God and neither be part of the other.[35] But Abaelard also accepts a similar principle. In *Theologia Christiana*, bk. III, he claims that having no overlap of parts is what characterizes numerical distinctness.[36] Because wholes cannot be created or conserved "apart" from their parts, Abaelard and his followers the *Nominales* could not consistently consider them to be distinct from their parts.

Applying the principle that numerically distinct things are wholly distinct cuts a wide swathe through metaphysics. In particular it suggests a programme for ontology—admit into your ontology as entities only truth-makers, that is, *res* which are required to account for the truth of some sentence.

What becomes of statuses, dicta, and *complexe significabile* within such a programme? They simply do not have a place. To see why, consider for a moment the status of a status—that of being human, for example. Imagine that Socrates is the only human. Suppose he is destroyed. What happens to the status of being human? One plausible answer is to say that it no longer exists either. If we take that line, then we have to deny that it is a *res* distinct from Socrates. But it is certainly not a *res* identical with Socrates, for if it were, then any other being which had it would be identical with it (by parity of reasoning) and so identical with Socrates (by the transitivity of identity). That seems absurd. So if the status "perishes" when whatever has it perishes, the status is neither identical with nor a *res* distinct from what has it. Hence it is no *res* at all. Similar reasoning will show that dicta and *complexe significabilia* are not things either. Since only *res* are in the ontology, statuses and their ilk are not. There can still be a family quarrel

---

35. Cf. *Ordinatio* I, d. 2, q. 4 (*Opera Theologiae*, 2) ed. S. Brown (St. Bonaventure, N.Y., 1970), p. 115.
36. Abaelard, *Theologia Christiana*, bk. III, pars. 148–53.

about whether one can use in semantics items which do not have a place in the ontology (and that is what Wodeham and Buridan seem to disagree about), but about the criteria of ontological commitment there is agreement.

The test for an ontological programme like this will be in its ability to provide an analysis of change. Change is expressed by differences in the truth value of the same (or of equiform) sentences at different times. It is implausible to suggest that such differences are primitive. Differences in the truth value of equiform sentences generally require differences in the world. But if the world is the collection of things, so that a world is specified by saying what there is and not also by going on to say what statuses and the like things have, by saying how it is, then all changes will have to be analyzed as changes in what there is. This suggests a slogan—all change is the creation (generation) or destruction of some real thing—which is both tempting and at least prima facie implausible.

We can see the force of the temptation in this slogan by considering how change is accounted for within supposition theory. Consider two singular categorical sentences in which all the terms occur with personal supposition—that is, are used to stand for (*supponere*) those things which they signify:

(1) Socrates is human.
(1') Socrates is pale.

At one level the truth conditions for (1) and (1') are perfectly parallel. Each is true just in case what the subject term "Socrates" stands for (namely, Socrates) is among the things for which the predicate term stands. The predicate term of (1) stands for all humans and the predicate term of (1') for all pale things. Thus (1) is true if Socrates is among the humans and (1') is true if Socrates is among the pale things—which is as one would expect.

But there is one difference which shows up when we ask what determines whether Socrates is in the extension of either predicate. "Human" is an absolute term while "pale" is connotative. One consequence of this is that "human" applies to the things it applies to essentially; they could not be what they are without "human" applying to them. "Pale" on the other hand has as its nominal definition "thing having paleness" and so applies to the pale things in virtue of their connection with paleness. One consequence of this is that "human" changes what it stands for only when some human is created or destroyed, but "pale" can change what it stands for without any substances being created or destroyed—they need only alter their connections with palenesses. The question arises whether for a substance to gain or lose a connection with a quality involves the creation or destruction of anything. The conventional wisdom about supposition (in which I partake) has it that the supposition of a phrase like "thing having paleness" is completely determined by the suppositions of its categorematic parts, "thing" and "paleness," and the meaning or consignification of its syncategorematic expressions—in this case "having." But if this is so then "pale thing" can change its supposition only if "thing" or "paleness" does. These are absolute terms and change their supposition only if something is created or destroyed. But both Ockham and Buridan think that a thing can be separated from its accidents by the power of God without either the thing or the accidents being destroyed.[37] Thus nominalism taken together with the standard interpretation of supposition theory can lead one to search for new entities to be what is created or destroyed when more ordinary things are just altered or moved in space. I believe that at least part of the history of the *Nominalistae* is the history of the working out of this programme, but this, the saga of the nominalist search for an adequate theory of change and its connections with the rise of the New Physics, is another story.[38]

What, then, is mediaeval nominalism and with which of the two faces of twentieth-century nominalism does it connect? My argument here has been that mediaeval nominalism began in a series of worries about the relation of sentences and clauses to the world, worries made central by Abaelard, and that it is as much a problem in semantic theory as in metaphysics. I have argued that it has nothing to do with the problem of universals and that seeing it as focused on the problem of universals simply distorts our picture of what went on. I think it less distorting but still inaccurate to see it as a position about the ontological status of abstract entities. The impulse toward eliminating a layer of semantic entities for sentences to signify would support a parsimony about abstract entities but does not absolutely require it. Nominalists resist multiplying things when they multiply terms, but there remains ample room for disagreement about how this economy is to be obtained. This disagreement about the methods by which language can describe the world without being in any way isomorphic with it is what underlies the debate between supporters of the *complexe*

---

37. Cf. Normore, op. cit., for discussion.
38. It is also a large one. Some of the beginnings can be found in Normore, op. cit.

significabile and their opponents. It is a family quarrel and I suspect just one of the many which a thorough investigation of the tradition of mediaeval nominalism and the efforts to do physics and theology from a nominalist perspective will reveal.

Erindale College
University of Toronto

10 William Ockham: Voluntarist or Naturalist?

MARILYN McCORD ADAMS

1. INTRODUCTION

It is almost a cliché in treatments of medieval philosophy to say that the Franciscans are voluntarists, and Ockham is the most radical among them. Like most stereotypical judgments, this one contains elements of truth along with considerable distortion. Before we can arrive at a more accurate focus, however, we must get clearer about the meaning of the term and the issues at stake.

(1.1) Preliminary Distinctions.

Usually, in the secondary literature, voluntarism is set against naturalism. Both the voluntarist and the naturalist among medieval philosophers will believe in will and nature. But the former will tend to locate his baseline explanations of things in the will and its choices, whereas the latter will ground them in the natures of things. Unlike Aristotelian substances, voluntarism and naturalism admit of more and less: between these poles stretches a spectrum of opinion, and philosophers will be identified as one or the other relative to each other.

In answering whether, for a given philosopher, will dominates over nature or the reverse, we must also ask *whose* nature—the agent's own or those of other things? Some philosophers contend that the created agent's own appetitive natural inclinations combine with his sensory awareness and intellectual beliefs to necessitate his volition, e.g., for the end of happiness. Here some naturalists may be said to give prominence to intellect over will in explaining human choice and action. It is another matter whether the created natures have such an integrity of their own that not even the omnipotent divine will is free so to tamper with them as, e.g., to make fire a coolant.

(1.2) "Aristotelian" Naturalism.

Nor is it in relation to just any naturalism that Ockham has been dubbed a voluntarist, but a kind of "Aristotelian" naturalism. (i) Aristotle the scientist had begun with observed regularities and assumed things (substances) to which they belonged. (ii) He posited natural tendencies or potencies in the things to explain the regularities. (iii) Further, he concluded that individuals are grouped into genera, species, and subgroups on the basis of shared natural potencies, and (iv) posited natures or natural kinds defined in terms of them. (v) Metaphysically, he contended against Plato that the essences of things exist in reality only within the individuals whose essences they are, but (vi) posited substantial and accidental forms as primitive explanatory entities that either are essentially or essentially give rise to the power to produce effects of the relevant sort. (vii) Where human beings are concerned, Aristotle recognized a unique human function in rational self-government whose end was happy contemplation. Endowed with generally reliable sensory and intellectual faculties, each individual is to make his own value judgments and then conform his choices to them. Virtues are the acquired habits that incline (but do not necessitate) a person to exercise this function well.

(1.3) Ockham's Alleged Voluntarism.

That Ockham was a radical voluntarist is allegedly proved in many connections. (i) First, it is widely claimed that Ockham's nominalism makes the classification of individuals into genera and species a function of *human free choice*. For it is supposed to turn "things into words" which have their meaning by human convention.[1] (ii) Further, Ockham's accounts of *divine omnipotence and freedom* assign God the power to arrange the created causal order however He likes, and so make the causal potencies of a given nature a function of God's free and contingent choices.[2] (iii) The same divine omnipotence and freedom are supposed to undermine the natural reliability of created cognitive faculties. For Ockham's explicit concessions—that God is free and able to

---

1. For example, James Weisheipl exemplifies this sort of interpretation in "The Place of John Dumbleton in the Merton School," *Isis* 50 (1959), pp. 439–54, in connection with the category of quantity.
2. Étienne Gilson, "The Road to Scepticism," *The Unity of Philosophical Experience* (New York, 1937), ch. 3, pp. 82–87. Cf. Harry R. Klocker, "Ockham and Efficient Causality," *Thomist* 23 (1960), pp. 106–23.

produce the created mental act while removing its intentional object, and that He is free to deceive creatures—seem to open the Pandora's box of Cartesian skepticism so that Ockham is unable to close it again.[3] (iv) Again, Ockham's understanding of freedom, created and divine, appears to cut the connections between the agent's will and natural appetitive inclinations when he grants that either God or man could will evil under the aspect of evil, or choose something precisely because right reason is against it! (v) In the sphere of morals, Ockham's putative advocacy of an unmodified divine command theory, in which God's free and contingent commands are the overriding norm, is thought to explode Aristotle's ideal of rational *self*-government, by destroying the regulative function of the agent's own intellect in choice-making.[4] (vi) In soteriology, Ockham is thought to overemphasize the divine will at the expense of divine wisdom, when he insists that the categories of merit and demerit are entirely dependent on free and contingent divine legislation. At the same time, his claim that God looks to foreseen created free choices in predestination and reprobation won him the charge of Pelagianism in his own day.

My present purpose is not a minute refutation of the errors in this characterization of Ockham, which in any event I have undertaken in other places.[5] Instead I wish to sketch an alternative portrait of Ockham, the Aristotelian naturalist, who gives unique consideration to the will. Often, underlying (i)–(vi) is the tendentious assumption that free will and nature may be so opposed that the former dissolves the latter. I hope to show how, for Ockham, nothing could be further from the case.

---

3. E.g., Étienne Gilson, "The Road to Scepticism," *The Unity of Philosophical Experience*, pp. 77–82. Cf. Anton Pegis, "Concerning William of Ockham," *Traditio* 2 (1944), pp. 465–80.

4. Paul Helm reflects this consensus when he presents Ockham's moral theory as paradigmatic of "unmodified" divine command theory: ". . . What can be labelled an Ockhamist Divine Command Theory holds that morality is founded upon a free divine choice. If God commands fornication, then fornication is obligatory, and it is within God's power to do so. He could establish another moral order than the one he has in fact established and he could at any time order what he has actually forbidden. From this position Ockham could consistently only regard ethics as a matter of special divine revelation in Scripture or elsewhere, and not a matter of natural law discerned through reason or conscience." (Introduction, *Divine Commands and Morality*, ed. Paul Helm [Oxford, 1981], p. 3.)

5. Principally in my book *William Ockham*, forthcoming from Notre Dame University Press in the spring of 1987.

2. OCKHAM AS A MODIFIED ARISTOTELIAN NATURALIST IN METAPHYSICS

(2.1) Hylomorphism.

To begin with, in physics and metaphysics, Ockham is an Aristotelian hylomorphist. (i) Rejecting atomism, he repeats the arguments of Aristotle's *Physics* to conclude that matter and form are the metaphysical constituents of changing things. Matter is that which persists through a change and is the subject of inherence of successive forms.[6] Forms are primitive explanatory entities which account for a thing's having the literal shapes, potencies, and tendencies to function that it has. Further, Ockham follows Aristotle in accepting a partition between the properties that belong to a thing essentially, and those that pertain to it accidentally. Accordingly, he distinguishes between substantial form and accidental forms.[7] Further, he believes that in living things, there is a plurality of substantial forms (e.g., in a cow, prime matter, corporeity, and sensory soul; in a human, prime matter, corporeity, sensory soul, and intellectual soul) which are in and of themselves apt to unite with prime matter and with each other to make a being that is one per se.[8] Ockham thus thinks that an individual or primary substance is a metaphysical composite of really distinct constituents—prime matter, and one or more substantial forms—and that this composite which makes one per se is its individual essence or substance nature.

(ii) In addition, Ockham recognized that there were accidental forms. While some moderns posited a distinct kind of accidental form for each of the nine Aristotelian categories of accident, Ockham spills a lot of ink to argue that forms really distinct from substance are to be found only in the category of quality, and takes himself thereby merely to be expounding the position of the Philosopher.[9] But Ockham does not draw the conclusion that because there are not quantitative or

---

6. *Philosophia Naturalis* I, cc. 15–16 (Roma, 1637; repr. by The Gregg Press Establishment, Vaduz-Liechtenstein, Holland, pp. 18–21).

7. Ockham defends the real distinction of qualitative forms from substance in *Quodlibeta* VII, q. 2, *Opera Theologica* (St. Bonaventure, N.Y.) (= OTh) IX 706–8, where his arguments are dominated by the intuitions of Aristotelian physics, and not by the doctrine of transubstantiation. And Ockham attributes the same view to Aristotle in *Summa Logicae* I, c. 55; *Opera Philosophica* (St. Bonaventure, N.Y.) (= OPh) I 179–82.

8. *Quodlibeta* II, qq. 10–11; OTh IX 157–59, 162–64; *Reportatio* II, q. 20; OTh V 429–30, 444; *Reportatio* III, q. 4; OTh VI 135–39; *Reportatio* IV, q. 9; OTh VII 160–66.

9. *Ordinatio* I, d. 30, q. 1; OTh IV 306; *Ordinatio* I, d. 30, q. 3; OTh IV 340; *Summa Logicae* I, cc. 49–50; OPh I 158–62.

relative forms really distinct from substantial and qualitative forms it is an arbitrary and subjective matter whether things are quantified or related. On the contrary, one of his central contentions is that a complete description of reality, of things as they are prior to and independently of any human intellectual activity, will not consist merely of a list of which things there are, but will also include a consideration of how they are. Prior to and independently of any intellectual activity, things really exist somehow and not otherwise.

(2.2) The Problem of Universals.

(i) In his commentary on Porphyry, Boethius expounds Alexander of Aphrodisias' "Aristotelian" solution to the problem of universals, which assigns genera and species a double mode of existence: in reality as numerically multiplied in numerically distinct particulars, and in the mind as an abstract general concept naturally apt to be predicated of many.[10] Thirteenth- and early fourteenth-century philosophers developed many variations on this theme. Aquinas held that while human nature of itself exists neither in the mind nor in reality, it could have a double mode of existence: in reality in particulars and as such fully particularized and numerically multiplied in numerically distinct particulars; in the intellect, as universal.[11] By contrast, Scotus maintained that even existing in reality, numerically multiplied in numerically distinct particulars, the nature is common, in that although this humanity exists in Socrates as really the same as and formally distinct from his haecceity, it is not incompatible with the humanity of itself to exist in Plato instead.

(ii) Ockham argued at length that all such "moderate realist" positions were contradictory,[12] and instead took his own position to be truly representative of Aristotle.[13] As Ockham reads the Philosopher, the latter's main point was to deny that the essences of things existed in some Platonic heaven, separated from the particulars whose essences they are.[14] It was not Aristotle's intention to affirm, strictly

---

10. Anicius Manlius Torquatus Severinus Boethius, *The Second Edition of the Commentaries on the Isagoge of Porphyry*, book I, sec. 11, in *Selections from Medieval Philosophers*, ed. Richard McKeon (New York, 1929), pp. 95–98.
11. *De Ente et Essentia*, c. 3; ed. Roland-Gosselin (Paris, 1948), pp. 25–29.
12. *Ordinatio* I, d. 2, qq. 4–7; OTh II 99–266.
13. E.g., *Summa Logicae* I, c. 15; OPh I 51–52.
14. Ockham gives Platonism short shrift, simply rehearsing Aristotle's arguments against it, and concurring in the Philosopher's conclusion that "no one in his right mind" would hold that the natures of particulars exist in separation from them the way Platonic ideas were supposed to do (*Ordinatio* I, d. 2, q. 4; OTh II 117).

speaking, that human nature is *in* Socrates, as if a human being were a composite of common human nature and individuating principles.[15] After repeatedly reducing to contradiction the central "moderate realist" idea—that the nature of itself is indifferent to universality and particularity, but has a double mode of existence, so that it can be universal in one and particular in another—Ockham concludes that everything real is individual and particular, whereas universality is a property that pertains only to names and that by virtue of their signification relation. Because he identifies the primary names with naturally significant concepts, which pick out their significata by suitable resemblance relations,[16] Ockham would better be counted a conceptualist than a nominalist. Whereas a realist about universals such as Burleigh held that natural-kind terms such as 'animal' or 'man' named the really existing genus- or species-thing, respectively, Ockham maintains that such common concepts are universal in that they actually or potentially signify a plurality of individuals, in such a way that one is signified no more than another.[17]

(iii) Ockham would deny that the nominalism/conceptualism which he thinks he shares with Aristotle renders the genus- and species-classification of individuals arbitrary and subjective. Just as what makes individuals fall under a given genus- or species-concept is the requisite degree of similarity, so what makes individuals co-generic or co-specific is the fact that they bear to one another a primitive relation of generic similarity or species-wise similarity, respectively. To be sure, Ockham does deny that similarity is a thing really distinct from particular substances and qualities.[18] But here, too, he believes himself a follower of Aristotle.[19] Indeed, Ockham contends, in this matter Aristotle would go further to deny that there are any relative things really distinct from substance and quality, whereas the Saints and the Church require him to affirm real relations of Paternity, Filiation, and Spiration in the Godhead and a real relation of assumption between the human nature of Christ and the Divine Word, as well as real relations of inherence between accident and substance and substantial form and prime matter, and real relations of union among parts of a con-

---

15. *Ordinatio* I, d. 2, q. 6; OTh II 224.
16. *Ordinatio* I, d. 2, q. 8; OTh II 270, 272.
17. Cf. Walter Burleigh, *De Puritate Artis Logicae*, cc. 1 and 3, ed. Philotheus Boehner (St. Bonaventure, N.Y., 1955), pp. 1–3, 6–9. Ockham, *Expositio in librum Perihermenias Aristotelis*, Proemium, sec. 6-7; OPh II 355, 356–57; cf. *Ordinatio* I, d. 2, q. 8; OTh II 270, 272.
18. *Ordinatio* I, d. 30, q. 1; OTh IV 292–93.
19. *Ordinatio* I, d. 30, q. 1; OTh IV 306; *Ordinatio* I, d. 30, q. 3; OTh IV 340, lin. 13–17; cf. *Summa Logicae* I, cc. 49–50; OPh I 158–62 (esp. 160–61).

tinuum.[20] And in any case, he thinks that similarity is a real relation in the intelligible and important sense that it obtains or not between/among individuals prior to and apart from any intellectual activity comparing and contrasting them;[21] hence its holding or not is not "subjective." Further, similarity is an intrinsic relation, which cannot but obtain, given the existence of the relata, and hence hold or not independently of not only the human will but the divine as well.[22] Ockham's view is that individuals whose prime matter and substantial forms are maximally similar are co-specific; in certain other lesser degrees, co-generic.[23]

(2.3) Theological Modifications.

Where Ockham does self-consciously depart from Aristotle's doctrine of substance and accident is with regard to the Philosopher's claims that

(A) Individual substance natures subsist per se (are essentially their own supposita) and cannot exist in or be sustained by anything else,

whereas

(B) Accidents can exist in substances as in a subject and cannot exist in reality otherwise than in a subject.

So far as (A) is concerned, Ockham understands Aristotle to assume that the individual human nature belonging to Socrates *is* Socrates and cannot exist without being Socrates. And given his nominalist/conceptualist readings of Aristotle and Averroes, he attributes to both the view that abstract and concrete nouns in the category of substance are altogether synonymous.[24] From these, Aristotle would derive the corollary

(C) Particular substances are numerically multiplied as substance natures are (numerically or specifically) diversified

as a necessary truth.

Given the doctrine of the Incarnation, according to which the sup-

---

20. *Ordinatio* I, d. 30, q. 4; OTh IV 366–72.
21. *Ordinatio* I, d. 30, q. 5; OTh IV 385.
22. Thus, for example, Ockham says that God cannot make two white things and bring it about that they are not similar (*Reportatio* II, q. 2; OTh V 39).
23. *Reportatio* III, q. 9 Q.
24. *Summa Logicae* I, c. 7; OPh I 23–24; *Quodlibeta* V, q. 11; OTh IX 524.

positum which is the Divine Word assumes an individual human nature, however, there is at least one individual substance nature that is not its own suppositum, and hence neither (A) nor (C) can be necessary truths.[25]

Likewise, the doctrine of transubstantiation, the then-favored interpretation of the real presence of Christ in the Eucharist, seemed to disqualify (B) from being a necessary truth as well. For according to it, when the priest says the eucharistic words of institution, the substance of the bread and wine cease to exist while the accidents remain, and the substance of the Body and Blood of Christ come to be present in the same place as the accidents.[26] It seems to follow that every time the priest says mass, accidents are miraculously preserved in existence apart from inhering in any substance as in a subject.

In both cases, Ockham follows Scotus in insisting that Aristotle's account of substance natures and accident natures stands in need of correction. Scotus maintained that substances have a natural aptitude to be their own supposita and hence independent,[27] while accidents have a natural aptitude to depend on a subject of inherence.[28] Yet, the Subtle Doctor observes, every creature is in obediential potency to the divine will, to be used as God wishes,[29] so that He can obstruct any natural aptitude in any creature. And this is what God did when the Divine Word assumed the individual human nature of Christ, and what He regularly does whenever transubstantiation occurs in the Eucharist. Although basically inspired by Scotus' tactic, Ockham denies that substance natures have a natural aptitude in either direction—whether to be their own supposita or to be sustained by another; rather they are in "neutral potency" to each.[30] Although "the nature is actively inclined no more to one than to another" (by contrast with heat, which is actively inclined to heat production), still, if left to itself, the substance nature will be its own suppositum.[31] But if God causes it to be sustained by another, He will thereby contradict no inherent active tendency in created natures.[32]

---

25. *Reportatio* III, q. 1; OTh VI 28.   26. *Reportatio* IV, q. 8; OTh VII 148–50.
27. *Op. Ox.* III, d. 1, q. 1, n. 9; Wadding-Vives (= WV) 14, 26.
28. *Op. Ox.* III, d. 1, q. 1, n. 9; WV 14, 26.   29. *Op. Ox.* III, d. 1, q. 4, n. 2; WV 14, 84.
30. *Quodlibeta* IV, q. 7; OTh IX 336.   31. Ibid.
32. Marilyn McCord Adams, "Relations, Inherence, and Subsistence: or, Was Ockham a Nestorian in Christology?" *Noûs* 16 (1982), pp. 62–75. Cf. "The Metaphysics of the Incarnation in Some Fourteenth Century Franciscans," in *Essays Honoring Allan B. Wolter*, ed. William A. Frank and Girard J. Etzkorn (St. Bonaventure, N.Y., 1985), pp. 21–57.

(2.4) Efficient Causality.

In his views about causality, Ockham follows a Christianized Aristotelian naturalism. Confronted by regular correlations in nature, Aristotle posited substance- and accident-things as primitive explanatory entities which are essentially or essentially give rise to the powers (*virtus*) that lie behind the regularities. Thus, for example, donkey-nature is essentially or essentially gives rise to the powers (*virtus*) for nutrition, growth, reproduction, locomotion, etc.; heat is essentially the power (*virtus*) to produce heat in nearby combustible materials.

(i) So, too, Ockham distinguishes *sine qua non* causality from efficient causality properly speaking, on the ground that where the latter is involved it is by *A*'s own power (*virtute propria*) or nature[33] that the correlation between *A*s and *B*s obtains; by contrast *A*s are *sine qua non* causes of *B*s when it is by the will of another that the correlation obtains. And he denies that there are any *sine qua non* causes in nature.[34]

(ii) Again, Ockham follows Scotus in believing that created natures are as they are and are possible of themselves, and are such independently of their relationship to anything extrinsic, such as the divine thought or will.[35] Since on Ockham's view created substance- and quality-things are essentially the power (*virtus*) to produce a given range of effects, it follows that not even omnipotent divine freedom can change the natural causal powers of creatures, say by bringing it about that heat is the power to cool or to produce whiteness or that acorns naturally produce frogs. Rather Ockham's remarks about actual or possible divine interference in the natural order should be understood in the light of the fact that, although essential, "Aristotelian" productive powers are in principle obstructible, often by other creatures here below and a fortiori by omnipotent divine freedom. Thus, the regular correlation between fire and heat-production notwithstanding, God has the power to obstruct the natural order of fire (or, more precisely, of the heat in fire)[36] on a regular basis with the result that the combustible material is heated by the natural activity of the sun, a universal cause, instead.[37] Likewise, God could obstruct the natural productive power of any created cause and act to produce its usual effect all by Himself.

33. *Reportatio* IV, q. 1 L–M.
34. *Philosophia Naturalis* II, c. 3, p. 35; cf. *Reportatio* IV, q. 2 N.
35. *Ordinatio* I, d. 43, q. 2; OTh IV 649–50.
36. *Expositio in Octo Libros Physicorum*, book II, t. 34, vol. 21 VA.
37. *Reportatio* II, qq. 3–4; OTh V 72–73.

(iii) Since Ockham believes the substance natures of individuals within a given species to be maximally similar, he joins his predecessors in taking for granted the a priori principle of *the uniformity of nature*—viz., that all individuals of the same species have the same kind of effect on an equally disposed patient.[38]

(iv) Further, Ockham assumes that essential causal potencies are determinate not only with respect to kind of effect produced but with respect to the *individual* effect of that kind. Thus, if a particular instance of heat (call it heat-1) is in fact produced by another (call it heat-2), it is logically or metaphysically impossible for heat-1 to be produced by any created cause other than heat-2, even another instance of heat.[39] Nevertheless, God could obstruct such determinate causal potencies and replace the action of heat-2 with His own.

Thus, it is clear that for Ockham—as for any other Aristotelian naturalist—the natural potencies of things are independent of any will, created or divine. And Ockham only agrees with his predecessors and contemporaries when he allows that whether or not natural causes act to the limit of their powers depends on the divine will.

(2.5) Summary.

Our survey so far has shown that, according to Ockham, created natures are not defined by the will, whether created or divine. Rather they are as they are prior to and independently of any one's thought or contingent free choice. Just as created natures in and of themselves are defined by natural potencies (*virtus*) many of which can be obstructed by natural causes, so any and all can be blocked by divine omnipotence. But not even God can make a creature an *active* cause of anything contrary to its natural inclinations.

3. SKEPTICISM VERSUS COGNITIVE RELIABILITY

In epistemology as elsewhere, Ockham sees Aristotle as his philosophical mentor.[40] And if Ockham's psychology with its rejection of sensible and intelligible species and focus on intuitive and abstractive cognition departs markedly from traditional developments of Aris-

---

38. *Ordinatio* Prologue (= Prologue), q. 2; OTh I 86–87, 92–93.
39. *Reportatio* II, qq. 12–13; OTh V 287–91.
40. This is especially clear in his discussion of sensation, which is littered with references to Aristotle's *De anima* and the *Parva naturalia*. See *Reportatio* III, qq. 2–3; OTh VI 43–129.

totle's thought, (i) the More than Subtle Doctor joins the Philosopher in taking the general reliability of our cognitive faculties for granted. Ockham begins with the assumption that we have certain knowledge of mind-independent material things,[41] as well as of our own present mental acts.[42] He then proceeds to trace such evident judgments to a distinctive species of acts of awareness—intuitive cognitions[43]—which are the power to produce evident judgments regarding their objects. Likewise, where our sensory faculties are concerned, Ockham cites without further defense the Aristotelian maxim that where the sensory faculty is well disposed and close enough to its object, and where conditions in the medium are suitable, the sense does not err with respect to its proper object.[44]

(ii) Like any Aristotelian naturalist, Ockham recognizes that natural potencies can be obstructed. (a) Sensory illusion is a fact of nature, and Ockham discusses the causal and metaphysical analyses of it at considerable length.[45] Again, Ockham matter-of-factly observes that while we have evident knowledge of sensible things—e.g., that Socrates is white—through intuitive cognitions, sometimes the flow of information can be blocked "because of an imperfection in the intuitive cognition, say because it is somehow imperfect and unclear, or because of some impediments in the objects, or because of any other obstacles."[46] (b) In addition, Ockham joins his medieval colleagues in taking a step beyond Aristotle, when he envisions the possibility of supernatural obstruction of our cognitive functions. (bi) For example, he opines that sensory illusion is sometimes caused by the clever placement of mirrors by demons[47] and that the angels can even interfere with our internal perceptions by manipulating our humors.[48] (bii) Where creatures can obstruct, a fortiori God can intervene. Thus, Ockham maintains, the God who miraculously brought Shadrak, Meschak, and Abednego through the fiery furnace unsinged by blocking the natural tendency of heat to burn flesh, can also interfere with the natural tendency of intuitive cognitions to cause evident

---

41. *Quodlibeta* I, q. 15; OTh IX 83; Prologue, q. 1; OTh I 23.
42. Prologue, q. 1, corollary 2; OTh I 40, 43; *Quodlibeta* I, q. 14; OTh IX 79.
43. Prologue, q. 1, a. 1; OTh I 31–32; *Reportatio* II, q. 13; OTh V 256–58.
44. *Reportatio* III, q. 2; OTh VI 57.
45. In *Ordinatio* I, d. 27, q. 3, OTh IV 230–58, where Ockham's concern is refuting Peter Aureol's argument from sensory illusion that the intentional objects of sensation have a nonreal mode of existence. Likewise in *Reportatio* III, qq. 2–3, OTh VI 43–129, where he is rejecting the notion that sensation involves the production of species in the medium or in the sensory faculty—to both of which he gives a negative answer.
46. Prologue, q. 1; OTh I 32–33.
47. *Ordinatio* I, d. 27, q. 3; OTh IV 250; *Reportatio* II, q. 16; OTh V 370.
48. *Reportatio* II, q. 16; OTh V 370.

judgments, by preventing them from causing any judgments whatever.[49] Further, by the "substitution" principle, God can obstruct any secondary efficient cause and supply its action Himself. Accordingly, whereas intuitive cognitions are naturally caused and conserved by the action of the intellect together with the existent and present object, God can produce and/or conserve an intuitive cognition of a nonexistent object[50] or an extant but absent object,[51] in which case one would be caused to judge that the object was nonexistent or absent. But, Ockham insists, God could no more bring it about that an intuitive cognition was an efficient partial cause of a false judgment (and so *acted* contrary to its natural inclination) than He could make fire or the heat in fire *act* to cool anything; for the supposition that He did would entail "an obvious contradiction."[52] (biii) Finally, Ockham believes that God could deceive us by acting together with an abstractive cognition to produce a false belief in us,[53] or by acting alone to produce a habit that would incline us to form false beliefs about the past.[54] Contrary to the impression given by the secondary literature, Ockham is no innovator here. In *Quodlibeta* V, q. 5, Walter Chatton objects to Ockham's account of intuitive cognition, on the ground that it excludes the possibility that God should deceive us, contrary to the theological consensus gelled in the wake of the Condemnation of 1277.[55] Ockham's response is simply to explain how his theory allows for this possibility and thereby conforms to standard teaching.

(iii) It is a measure of Ockham's Aristotelian posture that he nowhere hints that such naturally and/or metaphysically and/or logically possible obstructions to the human knowing process in any way undermine the certainty of their usual deliverances. If Henry of Ghent gives Academic skepticism careful and ponderous consideration,[56] and Scotus rejects Henry's apparent concessions to the Academics by refuting their position in detail,[57] Ockham mentions them by name once only and then merely to reiterate Augustine's observation that

---

49. Prologue, q. 1; OTh I 70; *Quodlibeta* V, q. 5; OTh IX 499.
50. Prologue, q. 1, a. 1; OTh I 38–39; *Quodlibeta* VI, q. 6; OTh IX 605.
51. *Reportatio* II, qq. 12–13; OTh V 258.   52. *Quodlibeta* V, q. 5; OTh IX 498.
53. *Quodlibeta* V, q. 5; OTh IX 498.   54. *Reportatio* IV, q. 14; OTh VII 311.
55. See Jeremiah O'Callaghan, "The Second Question of the Prologue to Walter Chatton's Commentary on the Sentences: On Intuitive and Abstractive Knowledge," in *Nine Medieval Thinkers*, ed. J. Reginald O'Donnell (Toronto, 1955), pp. 233–69 (esp. 246–47).
56. *Summa Quaestionum Ordinarium* (Paris, 1520; repr. St. Bonaventure, N.Y., 1953), a. 1, q. 1; a. 2, q. 1.
57. *Ordinatio* I, d. 3, p. 1, q. 4; Vaticana III 123–72.

however much the Academics have cavilled about sensory knowledge, "they have never been able to cast doubt on" the mind's knowledge of propositions such as 'I know that I am alive'.[58] Like Aristotle and Scotus, Ockham understands certainty to involve not freedom from the *natural or metaphysical or logical possibility* of error, but absence of *actual* doubt and error, and so does not anticipate Cartesian worries either.

4. THE FREEDOM OF THE WILL

Strictly, to speak of an Aristotelian doctrine of will is an anachronism, as the notion of will entered philosophy via the Stoics and was passed on by Augustine and others to medieval philosophy and theology. Nevertheless, Aristotle does have a view about choice and its relation to nature, and medieval commentators mapped talk of the will onto that.

Here it must be admitted that Ockham moves, more than his predecessors, to sever connections between the will and the agent's own nature. (i) For example, *Aquinas* had contended that human nature evidences a natural inclination to the good in general, and towards happiness, and concluded that humans necessarily will these as the end of their actions,[59] while the will is free to deliberate and choose among means to those ends.[60] And he concludes that the will is thus unable to will evil under the aspect and/or for the sake of evil,[61] but can will only the real or apparent good for the sake of happiness. Aquinas also held that given a volition for the end, and a certain intellectual judgment regarding the means to the end, the will is necessitated to will the prescribed means.

(ii) *Duns Scotus*[62] rejected this characterization, advancing a high doctrine of the freedom of the will as a self-determining power for opposites, the only genuine "Aristotelian" rational power.[63] Following out various quotations from Augustine, the Subtle Doctor maintains

---

58. Prologue, q. 1; OTh I 43.   59. *Summa Theologiae* I, q. 82, a. 1c.
60. *Summa Theologiae* I, q. 82, a. 2c, ad 2.
61. *Summa Theologiae* I, q. 82, a. 2, ad 1; q. 83, a. 4c.
62. For detailed treatments of Scotus' position, see Allan B. Wolter, "Native Freedom of the Will as a Key to the Ethics of Scotus," in *Deus et Homo ad Mentem I. Duns Scoti* (Rome: Societas Internationalis Scotistica, 1972), pp. 360–70. Cf. Wolter, Introduction to *Duns Scotus on the Will and Morality*, ed. and trans. Allan B. Wolter, O.F.M. (Washington, D.C., 1986) (= AW).
63. *Quaest. Metaph.* IX, q. 15; WV VII 611; AW 157.

that the will is not the kind of thing that can be necessitated by anything else, whether without or within the agent, created or divine.[64] Indeed, in his early works, Scotus is even uncomfortable about assigning the intellect's awareness of the object a role as partial efficient cause of the volition.[65] Nevertheless, Scotus does not endow the will with freedom by cutting it off from the innate tendencies of the agent; on the contrary, he appears to see the former as emerging from peculiar features of the latter. Taking a page from Anselm, Scotus attributes to the created will two innate "affections" (*affectiones*)—the affection for what is advantageous (*affectio commodi*) and the affection for justice (*affectio iustitiae*)—which are metaphysically nothing really distinct from the will, but the will itself innately inclined one way and the other.[66] Insofar as the natural inclination of a thing is its inclination or tendency to seek its own proper perfection, Scotus maintains that the affection for the advantageous corresponds in humans and angels to the natural inclinations of other things, so that if it were the will's only affection, humans and angels would necessarily choose out of self-interest what appeared to be their own advantage.[67] The will's inclination to justice is a tendency to love things because of their own intrinsic worth.[68] Since its presence in the will frees it to choose against its own advantage, Scotus styles this affection "the innate liberty of the will."[69] He holds that it is always within the power of any will *to act or not to act*. Yet, to the extent that the will's freedom is the resultant of two inclinations for good, its scope is not unlimited. With regard to real or apparent goods—whether means or the ends (the good in general, happiness, or God)—it has the option to will (*velle*) in their favor or not to act at all;[70] with respect to evils, it has the option to will-against (*nolle*) them or not to act.[71] But no one can will-against happiness or in favor of misery.

(iii) *Ockham's* position takes something from each and ventures be-

64. Summarized by Ockham in *Ordinatio* I, d. 1, q. 6; OTh I 487–90. See also Scotus, *Ordinatio* IV, d. 29; WV XIX 218; AW 175, 177.
65. See Bernardine M. Bonansea, "Duns Scotus' Voluntarism," in *John Duns Scotus, 1265–1965*, ed. John K. Ryan and Bernardine M. Bonansea (Washington, D.C., 1965), pp. 83–121.
66. *Ordinatio* III, d. 17; WV XIX 654–55; AW 183. Scotus seems to hold that both affections are inseparable from the will, while Anselm implies that the affection for justice is lost at the Fall and restored only little by little by grace through participation in the sacraments.
67. *Ordinatio* III, d. 17; WV XIV 654–55; AW 183; *Ordinatio* IV, suppl. d. 49, qq. 9–10; WV XXI 382; AW 191. For the case of an angel, *Ordinatio* II, d. 6, q. 2; AW 469.
68. *Ordinatio* III, suppl. d. 26, q. u.; WV XV 340–41; AW 179, 181.
69. *Ordinatio* II, d. 6, q. 2; AW 469; *Ordinatio* III, d. 17; WV XIV 654–55; AW 183.
70. *Ordinatio* IV, suppl. d. 49; WV XXI, 332–33; AW 193.
71. *Ordinatio* IV, suppl. d. 49; WV XXI 332–33; AW 193.

yond both. Like Scotus, he maintains that the will is a self-determining power for opposites and thus an "Aristotelian" rational power. But he finds causal models as appropriate to action theory as to epistemology, and in any event does not see how to exclude the *possibility* and even the occasional *actuality* of the will's being necessitated. For in the Godhead, the divine will necessarily wills the procession of the Holy Spirit,[72] while among creatures, acts of will are created qualities and hence—by the "substitution" principle, according to which God can cause all by Himself whatever He causes in conjunction with secondary causes—can be produced by God acting alone.[73] Similarly, Ockham maintains that some mental acts are incompossible with others, so that a general efficacious volition (say an efficacious volition to do whatever right reason dictates) together with a particular belief (say that right reason dictates that one ought to give alms to this beggar) necessitates a particular volition—namely, to give alms to this beggar.[74] And he explains the sure happiness of the Blessed and the unavoidable misery of the damned in terms of God's acting as the total efficient cause to produce a wholehearted love of God in the former[75] and a hatred of punishment and the will for happiness in the latter.[76] Even when the will determines itself and so acts freely, intellectual and sensory acts may be *partial* efficient causes of acts of will.[77]

Unlike his distinguished predecessors, however, Ockham does not see the scope of the will as limited in any way either by the agent's innate appetitive inclinations or by the dictates of right reason.[78] (a) Although he does recognize in the will innate inclinations—to pursue sensory pleasure (*delectatio*) and avoid sensory distress (*dolor*),[79] to will (*velle*) the advantageous (*commodum*) and to will-against (*nolle*) the disadvantageous (*incommodum*), as well as to will (*velle*) the just and to will-against (*nolle*) the unjust—he insists that, strictly speaking, they are not *natural* inclinations, because they do not necessitate the will, and its movement contrary to them does not count as violent.[80] (b) He does not try to construct the will's power for opposites as a kind of vector resultant of their interaction, but sees the will's freedom as primitive. In characterizing it as the liberty of indifference or contingency,[81]

72. *Ordinatio* I, d. 1, q. 6; OTh I 491–96.
73. *Reportatio* II, q. 15; OTh V 350.
74. *De Connexione Virtutum* (= *DCD*), q. 7, a. 3; OTh VIII 353. Cf. *Ordinatio* I, d. 1, q. 6; OTh I 491–96; *Quaestiones Variae* (= *QV*), q. 6, a. 10; OTh VIII 277.
75. *Ordinatio* I, d. 1, q. 2; OTh I 397, 399; *Reportatio* II, q. 15; OTh V 341.
76. *Ordinatio* I, d. 1, q. 1; OTh I 399; *Reportatio* II, q. 15; OTh V 341.
77. *DCD*, q. 7, a. 3; OTh VIII 363; *DCD*, q. 2, a. 2; OTh VIII 447.
78. *Ordinatio* I, d. 1, q. 6; OTh I 502.   79. *QV*, q. 8; OTh VIII 447.
80. *Reportatio* II, q. 15; OTh V 351, 355.
81. *Ordinatio* I, d. 1, q. 2; OTh I 399; *Ordinatio* I, d. 1, q. 6; OTh I 502.

Ockham understands the will's options with respect to any given object to be not merely action versus inaction, but also willing (*velle*) versus nilling (*nolle*). (c) The only limitation is that an agent cannot wittingly choose a contradictory object. (d) Thus, Ockham concludes that the will can will-against (*nolle*) the good. The created will can do this by willing to hate God;[82] by willing-against enjoyment of the clearly viewed divine essence;[83] by willing-against its own happiness;[84] by willing-against its ultimate end, whether ignorantly[85] or perversely[86]; or by willing-against the good in general.[87] (e) Likewise, Ockham maintains, the will can will (*velle*) evils—in particular, will to do the opposite of what right reason dictates;[88] will unjust deeds precisely because they are unjust, dishonest, and contrary to right reason;[89] and will evil under the aspect of evil.[90]

Ockham's account of freedom of the will makes for a bigger contrast between rational and nonrational natures than many of his "Aristotelian" contemporaries would allow. For the natural tendencies of nonrational natures not only incline, but—barring obstructions—necessitate their action towards the perfection of their built-in ends. But Ockham assigns the will of rational natures a measure of independence from the agent's intellect and innate motivational inclinations, in that the latter neither necessitate the will nor define its scope. Nevertheless, so far from not divorcing the will from the agent's nature altogether, he is saying that such free will is an aspect of the best (human, angelic, and divine) natures. And while neither right reason nor appetitive inclinations necessitate the will, they do have an important regulative function in choice and deliberation (see section 5 below).

5. MORALS

Ockham scarcely charts new territory either when he defines 'moral science' one way as "precisely about mores [*moribus*] that are within our power,"[91] or when he divides the field into two parts—nonpositive and positive morality, respectively. (i) According to Ockham, the for-

---

82. *Reportatio* IV, q. 16; OTh VII 352.   83. *Ordinatio* I, d. 1, q. 6; OTh I 505.
84. *Reportatio* IV, q. 16; OTh VII 351–52.
85. *Ordinatio* I, d. 1, q. 6; OTh I 503; *Reportatio* IV, q. 16; OTh VII 350.
86. *Reportatio* IV, q. 16; OTh VII 350.   87. *Reportatio* IV, q. 16; OTh VII 351.
88. *DCD*, q. 7, a. 3; OTh VIII 367; *QV*, q. 6, a. 10; OTh VIII 285.
89. *Reportatio* IV, q. 16; OTh VII 357–58.
90. *QV*, q. 8; OTh VIII 444–45.   91. Prologue, q. 12; OTh I 360.

mer constitutes the subject matter cultivated by Aristotle's *Ethics*[92] and is that which "directs human acts apart from any precept of a superior" or authority,[93] and includes propositions known per se (e.g., 'Every intrinsic good should be sought', 'Every intrinsic evil should be avoided', 'The will should conform to right reason', etc.)[94] or from experience (e.g., 'An angry person is to be calmed with soft words')[95] and their entailments. (ii) On the other hand,

positive moral science is that which contains divine and human laws which oblige one to pursue or avoid those things which are neither good nor evil except because they are prohibited or commanded by a superior to whom it belongs to make [*statuere*] laws.[96]

It includes both the science of jurisprudence (which studies contingent human laws) and sacramental theology (which covers certain extant divine precepts).[97]

(5.1) Intrinsic Imputability.

Ockham brings the will into the spotlight of moral theory (both broad-sense and narrow) when he argues that its acts (omissions) are the intrinsic and essential locus of imputability.

Focusing on the properties of (narrow-sense) moral virtue and vice, Ockham argues as follows that no moral theory can be adequate which does not identify some act that is necessarily and intrinsically virtuous:

> 1. Suppose a is contingently virtuous in such a way that it is possible for a to be virtuous and it is possible for a to be vicious, depending on its relation to a second act b.
>
> 2. Either (i) b is contingently virtuous in such a way that it is possible for b to be virtuous and possible for b to be vicious depending on its relation to a third act c; or (ii) b is necessarily and intrinsically virtuous.
>
> 3. If (not-2ii) b is not necessarily and intrinsically virtuous, then (i) either there will be an infinite process, or (ii) there will be a stop at some necessarily and intrinsically virtuous act.
>
> 4. An infinite process is impossible.
>
> 5. Therefore, (not-3i).

92. *Quodlibeta* II, q. 14; OTh IX 177.   93. *Quodlibeta* II, q. 14; OTh IX 177.
94. *Quodlibeta* II, q. 14; OTh IX 177; cf. *QV*, q. 6, a. 10; OTh VIII 281–82.
95. *QV*, q. 6, a. 10; OTh VIII 281–82.   96. *Quodlibeta* II, q. 14; OTh IX 177.
97. Ibid.

6. Therefore, (3ii): some act is necessarily and intrinsically virtuous.[98]

(4) reflects the Anselmian intuition that value scales must have a top, and is used by Ockham to prove the existence of a nature than which there is none nobler and better.[99] Behind premiss (2) is an implicit assumption that

    1.1. Any virtuous (vicious) act is virtuous (vicious) either (i) necessarily and intrinsically, or (ii) by relation to another virtuous (vicious) act,

which instantiates the general principle

    1.2. If something is contingently F, there is something else that is necessarily and intrinsically F/F-*ness* through which the former is F contingently.

All three claims—(2), (1.1), and (1.2)—were rejected by Scotus, who had argued that moral virtue is a matter of an act's "fit" with the circumstances. Going to church is a generically good kind of thing to do, but whether or not a given act of going to church is in fact morally virtuous depends upon its being done at the right time and place, in the right manner, and for the right end. Thus, according to the Subtle Doctor, a given act of going to church may be contingently virtuous, and indeed first be virtuous and then vicious because first done in the right circumstances and then not (or vice versa).[100] Nevertheless, those things in relation to which the act is deemed one or the other are not themselves virtuous or vicious either. Moral virtuosity and viciousness are properties that supervene on combinations dictated by right reason.

Ockham grants the instantiation of (2) for sensible qualities such as whiteness and sweetness, but he rejects those for the other eight categories of accident (see section 2.1 above). Nor does he reason that because Socrates is contingently similar to Plato there must be something that is similarity intrinsically and necessarily. Rather, he insists that similarity is nothing really distinct from Socrates' and Plato's existing similarly. Again, according to Ockham, the fact that Socrates

---

98. *DCD*, q. 7, a. 1; OTh VIII 327–28; *DCD*, q. 7, a. 4; OTh VIII 381.

99. *Quodlibeta* I, q. 1; OTh IX 3; *Quodlibeta* VII, q. 15; OTh IX 761. Ockham does not think it possible to demonstrate that there is only one top-grade nature, and so denies demonstrative force to the further inference that some nature is nobler than all others.

100. John Duns Scotus, *God and Creatures: The Quodlibetal Questions*, trans. Felix Alluntis and Allan B. Wolter (Princeton, 1975), secs. 18.8, p. 400; 18.15–23, pp. 403–6.

is first spatially proximate to Plato and then not does not imply that there must be something that is spatial proximity intrinsically and necessarily. Why, then, does Ockham treat virtue and vice like whiteness rather than like similarity and proximity?[101] Indeed, given Ockham's views about the role of free and contingent divine commands in determining the content of morality, broad sense and narrow (see sections 5.2 and 5.3 below), it is difficult to see how he can consistently regard any created action as intrinsically and necessarily virtuous.[102]

In my judgment, Ockham's real concern is with imputability. And the thesis to which his theory is most deeply committed is not (1.1) but the instantiation of (2) for imputability:

> 7. If an act is imputable to an agent, there must be some act that is intrinsically and necessarily imputable to the agent,

from which he reasons further as follows:

> 8. No act is imputable to an agent unless it is within his power.
> 9. Only acts of will are within an agent's power intrinsically and necessarily.
> 10. Therefore, only acts of will are intrinsically and necessarily imputable.[103]

Once again, (9) seems to be jeopardized by Ockham's adherence to the "substitution" principle, according to which God could be the total efficient cause of any created volition. Thus, by his own admission, if created volitions were caused apart from any activity of the created will or dictate of its reason, they would not be imputable.[104]

In the face of this, Ockham could admit that the "substitution" principle drives a wedge between what is intrinsically true of an agent and what is necessarily true. He could have maintained that a creature is intrinsically *F*, provided there is no possibility in the created order of its not being *F*; but it may not be necessarily *F*, where God could intervene to prevent it from so being. Given his above-mentioned views about causality (see section 2.3 above), Ockham might reply that where a given volition (call it *v*-1) is in fact imputable, it did in fact have the agent's will and practical dictates among its efficient causes.

---

101. *Reportatio* III, q. 11; OTh VI 388–89.
102. For a survey of the problems that arise for Ockham, see Rega Wood and Marilyn McCord Adams, "Is to Will It as Bad as to Do It? The Fourteenth Century Debate," *Franciscan Studies* 41 (XIX), pp. 5–60, esp. 18–30. I now think our discussion there did not sufficiently attend to Ockham's distinction between the two value categories of nonpositive and positive morality.
103. *DCD*, q. 7, a. 4; OTh VIII 381; *Reportatio* III, q. 11; OTh VI 390.
104. *DCD*, q. 7, a. 3; OTh VIII 347–50; *Reportatio* II, q. 15; OTh V 340–45.

Hence, the only possible created causes v-1 could have had must include the agent's own will and reasoning. It would follow that since that volition could not have been produced in the created order without being imputable, it is intrinsically imputable.

(5.2) Nonpositive Morality.

Ockham begins his account of nonpositive morality with the ideal of rational self-government shared by Aristotle and other pagan philosophers, according to which morally virtuous action involves the free coordination of choice with right reason. Thus, Ockham maintains that "no one acts virtuously unless he acts with *knowledge* and *freedom*."[105] (i) Each agent is obliged to make his own value judgments: neither acts done mindlessly nor acts done in slavish obedience to authority are candidates for virtue; rather a dictate of the agent's own intellect must be an efficient partial cause of any virtuous act.[106] Invincible ignorance excuses,[107] but culpable ignorance doubles the offense. For if the individual follows the dictates of his own intellect and performs an act contrary to *right* reason, he is guilty of mistaken judgment and wrongheaded choice alike. But if he follows someone else's correct dictate instead of his own erroneous one, he adds a sin against conscience[108] to his crime of careless calculation. (ii) In addition, as discussed above, an act is morally virtuous only if it lies within the power and is produced by the efficient causality of the will itself.[109]

Moreover, Ockham recognizes that virtue comes in degrees. *First-degree moral virtue* is a matter of willing

> to do just deeds (a) in conformity with right reason dictating that such deeds should be done, (b) according to the required circumstances for precisely this deed, and (c) for the sake of the end of the intrinsic value of the deed itself[110]

or for some other intrinsically good end. For example, suppose a king follows his own right reason which dictates that he withdraw his troops from occupied territory, at a specific time and place and in a certain manner, and do so in the interests of peace. *Second-degree moral virtue* exceeds the first in perseverance, willing such acts

> with the intention of in no way abandoning such deeds for the sake of anything contrary to right reason—not even because of death, if right reason

---

105. DCD, q. 7, a. 3; OTh VIII 362.
106. DCD, q. 7, a. 3; OTh VIII 358; QV, q. 8; OTh VIII 414–16.
107. QV, q. 8; OTh VIII 429.   108. QV, q. 8; OTh VIII 429–30.
109. DCD, q. 7, a. 3; OTh VIII 363; cf. QV, q. 8; OTh VIII 411.
110. DCD, q. 7, a. 2; OTh VIII 335.

were to dictate that such a deed should not be abandoned even to avoid death.¹¹¹

Third-degree virtue differs from the first two in its end, and is a matter of willing first-degree contents precisely because right reason has commanded them;¹¹² its *heroic version* involves extraordinary persistence contrary to the will's innate inclination to seek sensory pleasure and avoid suffering.¹¹³

So far, Ockham thinks, Christians and pagans can travel together.¹¹⁴ And this common ground identifies the norm of nonpositive morality with the deliverances of right reason, as prior to and independent of the agent's choices and/or the free and contingent legislation of any external authorities. Indeed, on the scheme presented, conformity to an external authority could be virtuous only if it were free and dictated by right reason. But what if right reason were informed of the existence of an infinite being, who acts by intellect and will? What would it dictate about relations between it and human or angelic persons?

Scotus thought unaided natural reason could demonstrate a priori the existence of God under just such a description.¹¹⁵ Since 'good' (in its transcendental sense) converts with 'being' and signifies being under the aspect of amiability or desirability, it follows that the infinite being is the infinite good and infinitely desirable or lovable; finite beings are merely finite goods and finitely desirable or lovable. Accordingly, since the infinite good is both compatible and incommensurate with any finite good, right reason would afford no reason for not loving it and would dictate universally, to all agents, that God should be loved above all and for His own sake.¹¹⁶ Following as it does from the intrinsic worth of the divine essence, this practical principle has its normative status prior to and independently of any precept of the divine will.¹¹⁷ Although the affirmative version of this maxim may not belong to the natural law, taking that term in its strictest sense, be-

---

111. *DCD*, q. 7, a. 2; OTh VIII 335.   112. *DCD*, q. 7, a. 2; OTh VIII 335.
113. *DCD*, q. 7, a. 2; OTh VIII 336–37.
114. *DCD*, q. 7, a. 2; OTh VIII 336–37; cf. 354–55, 357.
115. Scotus offers this argument in many places, including *Ordinatio* I, d. 2, and *De Primo Principio*.
116. *Ordinatio* III, suppl. d. 27, a. 1; AW 425–27; cf. *Lectura*, Prologue, pars 4, qq. 1–2; AW 127–43.
117. *Ordinatio* IV, d. 46; AW 241. Note that Scotus grounds the obligation of rational free creatures to love God primarily not on the causal relation between them, but on the natural goodness of God considered in His own right, contrary to the suggestion of much contemporary literature about divine-command ethics. Cf. *Divine Commands and Morality*, p. 3.

cause someone might—through no fault of his own—be unable to engage in the relevant philosophical reasoning, the negative or conditional versions—'No irreverence must be shown to God' or 'If God exists, He alone must be loved as God'—do.[118]

Similarly, Ockham recognizes that the dictates of reason are influenced by the agent's information. Less optimistic than Scotus about the prospects of natural theology, Ockham grants unaided natural reason the demonstration of a nature than which there is none nobler and better, but denies the further proofs of unicity[119] and personality. Thus, a person guided by natural reason alone would calculate that God ought to be loved in the highest degree,[120] and negatively that no one should be led to do anything contrary to the precept of his God.[121] And he could further infer that if there were only one God, and if He were personal, then wholehearted love of Him would be expressed in trying to please Him in every way: by loving Him and what He wills to be loved, not-willing what He wills not to be willed, and willing-against what He wants to be willed against.[122] Enlightened by revelation as to the unicity and personality of God and contents of the divine precepts, created right reason would issue the positive and unconditional dictates—that "whatever is pleasing to God ought to be done,"[123] that His will regarding creatures should be fulfilled,[124] that the created agent should love God and what He wills to be loved and hate what He wills to be hated,[125] and that these things should be done for God's sake.[126] Thus, Ockham can remark that Eleazar's refusal to eat pork in violation of positive divine legislation under the old covenant manifests heroic determination not to do anything "contrary to right reason" and a willingness to "sustain death according to the dictate of right reason."[127]

Therefore, for Ockham as for Scotus, suitably informed right reason, the primary and internal regulator of action, discovers another rule in God's commands, and the authority of the latter is derivative from that of the former. And there is, accordingly, yet another species, a *fourth-degree virtue*, which the pagans do not share: the habit to

---

118. *Ordinatio* III, suppl. d. 37; AW 277.
119. *Quodlibeta* I, q. 1; OTh IX 3; cf. *Quodlibeta* VII, q. 15; OTh IX 761; *Ordinatio* I, d. 1, q. 5; OTh I 464.
120. *Ordinatio* I, d. 1, q. 4; OTh I 447; *DCD*, q. 7, a. 2; OTh VIII 335–36; *DCD*, q. 7, a. 3; OTh VIII 358.
121. Ockham says this negative precept is known per se; *DCD*, q. 7, a. 3; OTh VIII 366.
122. *QV*, q. 6, a. 11; OTh VIII 314.   123. *DCD*, q. 7, a. 3; OTh VIII 365.
124. *Ordinatio* I, d. 41, q. u.; OTh IV 610.
125. *DCD*, q. 7, a. 3; OTh VIII 359.   126. *DCD*, q. 7, a. 4; OTh VIII 399.
127. *QV*, q. 6, a. 10; OTh VIII 280.

will deeds whose object and circumstances conform completely to right reason, and to will them for twin ends—viz., because they conform to right reason and for the love of God.[128] Only such acts are *perfectly* virtuous, according to Ockham,[129] who repeatedly exemplifies virtue in terms of acts which have such a double end.[130]

It is at this point that Ockham's distinctive doctrine, which equates freedom of the will with the liberty of indifference or contingency, makes a difference. For if a theory lays down a double criterion of something, it is important that those norms agree. According to Scotus, God in His freedom can either command what right reason would dictate or refrain from commanding at all; but He cannot issue commands contrary to right reason or the natural law, any more than He can will evil under the aspect of evil.[131] But for Ockham, the scope of God's options matches the range of His omnipotent power (whose boundaries are defined only by the principle of noncontradiction). And the More than Subtle Doctor has the courage of his convictions as he concludes that God could command us to act contrary to other dictates of right reason—e.g., He could enjoin acts of the species now labeled "hatred of God,"[132] "fornication,"[133] "adultery," and "theft."[134] And in this logically and metaphysically possible eventuality, right reason would lead to contradictory dictates.[135] Even if some first- and second-degree virtuous acts would still be possible, third- and fourth-degree actions would be rendered impossible for the morally witting. For, according to Ockham, the volition to do A for the sake of right reason and/or for the wholehearted love of God has correct partial descriptions as "a volition to do whatever right reason dictates" and/or

---

128. *DCD*, q. 7, a. 2; OTh VIII 335; *DCD*, q. 7, a. 3; OTh VIII 348; cf. *DCD*, q. 7, a. 4; OTh VIII 399.
129. *Reportatio* III, q. 11; OTh VI 386.
130. *DCD*, q. 7, a. 2; OTh VIII 338; *DCD*, q. 7, a. 4; OTh VIII 386; *Reportatio* III, q. 11; OTh VI 387.
131. *Ordinatio* IV, d. 14, q. 2, n. 5; WV XVIII 52; cf. AW 24–25.
132. *Reportatio* IV, q. 16; OTh VII 352.   133. *DCD*, q. 7, a. 4; OTh VIII 391.
134. *Quodlibeta* II, q. 15; OTh V 352.
135. Armand Maurer apparently hopes to avoid this consequence with the suggestion that just as God acts freely and contingently in commanding, so He acts freely and contingently in shaping human reason, and He always does so so that the dictates of conscience or right reason always line up with what He has actually commanded. Thus, he writes: "The consciences of men prompt them to perform some acts as good and to avoid others as bad, and they are obliged to follow the dictates of their conscience or right reason. These dictates, however, are not rooted in human nature, nor are they necessary consequences of that nature. They are simply expressions in men of God's free decision that they should act according to given norms." (*A History of Philosophy: Medieval Philosophy* [New York, 1962], p. 287.) This thought stems from Maurer's mistaken impression that for Ockham the active causal potencies of created natures are fully malleable in the Creator's hands (see section 2.3 above).

"a volition to do whatever God commands."[136] But he also maintains that such general volitions combine with beliefs about what right reason dictates and/or what God commands, to necessitate the corresponding particular volitions—which in the case hypothesized would be contradictory and thus incompossible. It follows that where God issued commands contrary to other dictates of right reason, no well-informed agent could will something because right reason commands it and/or for the wholehearted love of God. Given such divine legislation, the moral ideals of a life of third- or fourth-degree moral virtue would break down.

Thus, it is fair to say that Ockham's recognition of divine commands as a norm in nonpositive morality gives the will a prominence unprecedented in medieval Aristotelianism; for the notion that God is free to issue commands contrary to other dictates of right reason, opens the possibility that nonpositive morality might break down.[137] Nevertheless, commentators are wrong to characterize Ockham's ethics as a "divine-command theory," as if God's precepts were the only norm,[138] with a resultant collapse of nonpositive morality into positive morality. Nor is it right to say that Ockham begins with divine commands but allows right reason a role as a derivative norm, or at least prima facie approximation thereto.[139] A closer fit is found with so-called modified divine-command theories which are said to break down if God's commands run contrary to what would be good for human beings. But the label "modified right-reason theory" might better bring out the primacy of right reason as a norm in this value sphere.

---

136. *Ordinatio* I, d. 1, q. 1; OTh I 385; *QV*, q. 7, a. 4; OTh VIII 381.

137. D. E. Luscombe surely underestimates the seriousness with which Ockham regards God's freedom when he suggests, "Perhaps he [Ockham] meant to exaggerate when he supported his view that God could have sanctioned anything that falls short of logical contradiction by saying that he could have commanded even hatred of himself" ("Natural Morality and Natural Law," in *The Cambridge History of Medieval Philosophy* [Cambridge, 1982], 714).

138. Paul Helm, Introduction, *Divine Commands and Morality*, p. 3.

139. Copleston recognizes that Ockham mentions both divine commands and right reason and struggles to characterize their relation. At times he suggests that Aristotelian morality is the "substructure" and divine commands the "superstructure" (*A History of Philosophy*, vol. 3: *Late Medieval and Renaissance Philosophy*, part I: "Ockham to the Speculative Mystics" [New York, 1968], p. 119). But in the end, he understands Ockham's morality to be "markedly authoritarian in character" (ibid., 114–16, 121), while "[r]ight reason is depicted as ... at least the proximate norm of morality" (ibid., 117–18) which provides "a provisional code of morality, based on non-theological considerations" (ibid., 122).

(5.3) Merit.

With the sphere of positive morality, we arrive at a category in which Ockham's theory is fundamentally voluntaristic rather than naturalistic, and that by definition. For he says that it deals with things that are good or bad, not in themselves, but only in relation to the legislation of some authority.[140]

Ockham follows Scotus and opposes "naturalists" such as Aureol and Lutterell when he locates the category of merit and demerit as a subdivision of positive morality, created by free and contingent divine statutes[141] the way the commercial value of metal or paper money is fixed by the governmental decree. Following theological conventions, Ockham understands that an action is *accepted by God* if and only if He regards its agent as thereby prima facie worthy of eternal life; a *meritorious action* is one that is freely performed and accepted by God,[142] whereas a *mortal sin* renders its doer prima facie worthy of eternal punishment.[143] Against his naturalist opponents, Ockham defends the theses that

(D) No creature is necessarily and intrinsically acceptable (unacceptable), none necessarily or intrinsically worthy of eternal life (eternal punishment);

instead

(E) If anything is acceptable (unacceptable), worthy of eternal life (punishment), it is so through a relation to an extrinsic cause—viz., the divine will issuing certain legislation.[144]

He argues that nothing in creatures is either a logically necessary[145] or a logically sufficient[146] condition of either eternal blessedness or eternal punishment. (a) His metaphysical proof rests on the observation

---

140. *Quodlibeta* II, q. 14; OTh IX 177.   141. *Quodlibeta* II, q. 14; OTh IX 177.

142. *Ordinatio* I, d. 17, q. 2; OTh III 473–74. That a meritorious act must be done freely is emphasized in numerous places, e.g., *Ordinatio* I, d. 1, q. 2; OTh I 402; *Quodlibeta* III, q. 19; OTh IX 275; cf. *Quodlibeta* VI, q. 1; OTh IX 588. That the possibility of merit or demerit depends on the agent's ability to use reason is asserted in *QV*, q. 8; OTh VIII 437–41.

143. *Reportatio* IV, qq. 10–11; OTh VII 195, 223.

144. So far as acceptance or worthiness of eternal life is concerned, see *Ordinatio* I, d. 17, q. 1; OTh III 446, 449, 452, 454–55; d. 17, q. 2; OTh III 471–72; *Reportatio* IV, qq. 3–5; OTh VII 55. Regarding God's hatred of creatures, *Ordinatio* I, d. 17, q. 1; OTh III 447, 449. Regarding a deed or person worthy of eternal punishment, *Reportatio* IV, qq. 3–5; OTh VII 43–46.

145. *Ordinatio* I, d. 17, q. 1; OTh III 445.

146. *Ordinatio* I, d. 17, q. 1; OTh III 452, 455; *QV*, q. 1; OTh VIII 17, 21.

that the existence of creatures at one time is logically independent of the existence of that and/or other creatures at another time. It follows that no matter what created acts or habits (acquired or infused) exist in a created agent during this mortal life, it is within God's power and freedom to annihilate him immediately upon death, so that he enters into no eternal destiny whatever.[147] (b) Arguing from the sphere of morality, Ockham contends that God is a debtor to no one,[148] and so cannot sin by failing in His obligations, no matter what He does. In particular, He is under no requirement (i) to assign eternal destinies to any creatures, (ii) to distribute eternal happiness and eternal damnation on the basis of created free choices (and hence on the basis of merit and demerit) instead, say, of race, gender, or national origin,[149] or (iii) to accept morally virtuous acts and reject morally vicious ones; nor was He bound in His distribution scheme either (iv) to link merit and demerit to the present sacramental system of the Church, (v) to conform His distribution scheme to "Ockham's Razor,"[150] or (vi) to connect either with the infusion of theological virtues.[151] Ockham regards this recognition—that the whole system of eternal rewards and punishments is entirely a product of God's free and contingent volitions—as the strongest possible antidote to Pelagianism. By contrast, the naturalists—who say that there is some configuration of created agents, acts, and habits which God is metaphysically and morally bound to accept and eternally reward (or punish)—come too close for Ockham's comfort to the spirit of that famous heresy.[152]

Free from any obligation to legislate the category of merit and demerit into existence, or to give it one shape rather than another, God is in fact pleased with created free agents who exercise their unique function of rational self-government to the full. Accordingly, God in fact wills that humans and angels follow the dictates of nonculpable reason[153] and so, apart from invincible ignorance, conform their acts

---

147. *Ordinatio* I, d. 17, q. 1; OTh III 453–54; *QV*, q. 1; OTh VIII 19; *Reportatio* IV, qq. 10–11; OTh VII 209; *Reportatio* IV, qq. 3–5; OTh VII 55; *DCD*, q. 7, a. 4; OTh VIII 389; *QV*, q. 8; OTh VIII 435; *Reportatio* II, q. 15; OTh V 353.

148. *QV*, q. 1; OTh VIII 23–26; *Reportatio* IV, qq. 10–11; OTh VII 209; *Reportatio* IV, qq. 3–5; OTh VII 55; *DCD*, q. 7, a. 4; OTh VIII 389; *QV*, q. 8; OTh VIII 435; *Reportatio* II, q. 15; OTh V 353.

149. And therefore apart from merit and demerit; cf. *Reportatio* IV, qq. 3–5; OTh VII 45; *Reportatio* III, q. 9; OTh VI 281. Ockham toys with the idea that the Blessed Virgin Mary was predestined to eternal life apart from any merit on her part; cf. *Ordinatio* I, d. 41, q. u.; OTh IV 606–7; *Reportatio* III, q. 5; OTh VI 154–56.

150. *Ordinatio* I, d. 14, q. 2; OTh III 432.

151. *Reportatio* III, q. 9; OTh VI 279.

152. *Ordinatio* I, d. 17, q. 1; OTh III 455–56; *QV*, q. 1; OTh VIII 21; *QV*, q. 6; OTh VIII 318–20.

153. *QV*, q. 8; OTh VIII 436.

to right reason.[154] If sin is fundamentally a matter of displeasing God, flouting right reason is one way to sin under existing divine statutes.[155] Another way, of course, is to fail to conform in some way to the sacramental regulations of the Church.

As things now stand, then, divine commands and right reason are twin criteria in the category of merit and demerit as well as that of nonpositive morality. But this time God's commands are fundamental and right reason's role derivative, whereas before it was the other way around. What if, however, God were to issue commands contrary to other dictates of right reason, as (we have seen) He is free to do? Would the whole value category of merit and demerit break down as well? Not according to Ockham. For God cannot efficaciously will or command contradictories.[156] Therefore, He could not simultaneously enjoin free creatures to follow right reason in everything, and command them to act contrary to some of its dictates. To issue the latter command, He would have to retract the former. Hence, Ockham's notorious remark that if God commanded the acts now labeled "adultery," "fornication," and "theft," and even "hatred of God," these acts—which could never be morally virtuous, because they are contrary to right reason—could be done without demerit and even meritoriously.[157]

(5.4) Summary.

In the sphere of morals, Ockham exceeds his predecessors in giving prominence to the will, both created and divine. For, in effect, he makes the valuation of acts of will the exclusive subject matter of broad-sense morality, given his view that only such are appropriately within our power. Even more dramatic is Ockham's move to bring the divine will to center stage—both in narrow-sense morality and in the category of merit—not only by recognizing it as a norm for each, but also by emphasizing divine freedom not simply to "rubber stamp" the dictates of right reason.

Nevertheless, Ockham would not have seen his focus on will as a denigration of nature. His identification of acts of will as the locus of imputability seemed to him a step towards a partial characterization of the *nature* of free agents, whereas the divine will functions in morality to perfect and complete it. That divine commands are a deriva-

---

154. *QV*, q. 8; OTh VIII 411.
155. *QV*, q. 8; OTh VIII 428–29, 435; *DCD*, q. 7, a. 4; OTh VIII 387, 390.
156. *Reportatio* II, q. 15; OTh V 352.
157. *Reportatio* II, q. 15; OTh V 352; cf. *Ordinatio* I, d. 42, q. u.; OTh IV 621; *Reportatio* IV, q. 16; OTh VII 352, 355.

tive norm in ethics is a necessary truth. When Ockham singles out fourth-degree virtue—according to which acts are willed, not only because they are commanded by right reason, but also for the love of God—as the only really perfect virtue, his thought is that the natural perfection of rational self-government comes to its summit when it reaches out beyond itself into a love relation with the infinite being. This move of the creature towards the creator has, for Ockham, the flavor not of fearful and slavish obedience of an underling to an authority, but of a self-governing adult freely and with deliberation choosing to make the fullest self-development an offering of love to the Supreme Good.

That right reason is a derivative norm in the category of merit is a contingent fact, entirely dependent on divine free choice. In the category of merit, God expresses His free and contingent love for creatures, by being so well pleased by the person who perfects the unique function of rational free creatures, and does so within the framework of the sacraments of the Church, as to reward it with eternal life. When Ockham draws out the implications of how He didn't *have* to do it, he is not trying to scare people, but trying to offer a measure of His generosity. In reply to the naturalists, he says, "it is not necessary for God to love from any motive; rather He liberally and freely loves whom He loves."[158] "[B]y His sheer grace, He will give with liberality to whom He will give. . . ."[159] "Whatever He does for us, He does by grace alone."[160]

6. CONCLUSION

In my opinion, Ockham is best understood as a Franciscan Aristotelian. In metaphysics, he practices Franciscan poverty: so far as the basic structure of the world is concerned, Ockham does not see God doing with more what He could do with fewer. But Ockham was far too Aristotelian to anticipate Berkeley or Hume by deleting a material substratum and/or natures with their primitive causal potencies; he is content to argue that, from a philosophical point of view, the only things in the created world are particular substances and qualities. Ockham's failure to embrace Academic or to anticipate Cartesian skepticism reflects both an Aristotelian optimism that natures "work"

---

158. *Ordinatio* I, d. 17, q. 1; OTh III 463–64.
159. *Ordinatio* I, d. 17, q. 1; OTh III 455.
160. *Reportatio* IV, qq. 3–5; OTh VII 55.

always or for the most part, and a Franciscan confidence that God made created natures because He liked them, and not with a view to frustrating them. In the sphere of morality, Ockham's watchword is not parsimony but liberality. It naturally befits those rational free creatures made in God's image to command themselves to make wholehearted love of Him their end. It is with a Franciscan sense of proportion that Ockham insists that God does not *have* to be impressed by this. Equally Franciscan is his assurance that divine courtesy and generosity will bless the best that Aristotelian nature has to offer with the incommensurate reward of the beatific vision. In one case, God has gone further still, by determining the neutral potency of an individual human nature so that it is sustained forever by the Divine Word itself.

University of California, Los Angeles

11   Ockham and Final Causality
STEPHEN F. BROWN

I. ANNELIESE MAIER ON FINAL CAUSALITY

In her article "Das Problem der Finalkausalität um 1320," Anneliese Maier attempted to show the historical roots of William of Ockham's view of final causality.[1] The remote source, assuredly, was Aristotle, who provided his most explicit treatment of final causality in book II of the *Physics*.[2] Ockham's more immediate scholastic predecessors based themselves on this *Physics* treatment of final causes when they both agreed and disagreed over final causality. Thomas Wylton, whom Maier believed to be one of Ockham's immediate sources, noted this as he introduced the *problèmatique* of his era in *Quodlibet III* (ca. 1314):[3]

The question: whether an end [*finis quo*] is a cause? In regard to this question all agree in concluding that it is, for the Philosopher, II *Physics*, shows by demonstration that every agent, whether acting naturally or through understanding and will, acts in every action for the sake of an end. If it is a natural agent, then it acts for the sake of an end prearranged by a superior agent, that is, the author of nature. If it is an agent acting through knowledge, then it acts for an end that is intended, known, weighed, or at least imagined. Yet, even though this conclusion is one that all are sure about, still it is very difficult to assign the manner in which an end causes, if we are speaking about the causality of the end in bold contrast to the causality of an efficient cause and as distinct from the other types of causes.[4]

---

1. A. Maier, "Das Problem der Finalkausalität um 1320," in *Metaphysische Hintergründe der Spätscholastischen Naturphilosophie* (Rome, 1955), pp. 273–99.
2. *Physics* II, cc. 8–9 (198b10–200b8). Cf. Guillelmus de Ockham, *Expositio in libros Physicorum Aristotelis* II, tt. 75–92, ed. G. Leibold (*Opera Philosophica* IV; St. Bonaventure, N.Y., 1985), pp. 366–408.
3. Maier, ibid., pp. 296–97 and n. 36.
4. Cod. Burgh. 36, f. 83rb: "Quaestio est an finis quo sit causa. In hac quaestione omnes conveniunt in una conclusione, quod sic, nam Philosophus, II *Physicorum*, ostendit demonstrative quod omne agens per naturam et per intellectum et voluntatem in omni actione agit propter finem. Si sit agens naturale, agit propter finem ab agente superiori, scilicet ab auctore naturae, praestitutum. Si sit agens per cognitionem agit

It is this last—most difficult—question, i.e., how a final cause causes, that served as the focus of that portion of Maier's article which centers on Ockham. In the treatment of this specific problem in the texts attributed to Ockham, Maier judged that the then unedited *Expositio in libros Physicorum Aristotelis* (for her, Ockham's earliest treatment of finality) deserved slight attention, since it offered little that was noteworthy and provided nothing of importance for the historical development of the question treating how a final cause causes.[5] The works which drew her attention were principally the *Quaestio disputata 'De fine'*[6] and to a lesser extent the *Summula Philosophiae Naturalis*, which she considered "doubtlessly" Ockham's final treatment of the issue, and one where he already manifested a certain distance from the problem.[7]

In her reading of these three works attributed to Ockham, Maier saw no inconsistency in the position they represented. The author of these three texts was, for her, Ockham himself, and when he faced the issue directly, as he did in the *Quaestio disputata* and *Summula*, his consistent answer was: "A final cause moves metaphorically."[8] Nor was Ockham, she believed, being an innovator in his position: Thomas Wylton and others, no matter how they might explain their position in detail, also held that "a final cause moves metaphorically."[9]

II. GERHARD LEIBOLD AND OCKHAM'S WORKS

By 1982, when Gerhard Leibold published his article "Zum Problem der Finalität bei Wilhelm von Ockham,"[10] he had completed the

---

propter finem intentum, cognitum, deliberatum vel saltem imaginatum. Tamen licet ista conclusio sit certa omnibus, attamen difficilimum est assignare modum secundum quem finis causat, loquendo de fine ut distinguitur omnino a causalitate efficientis et a ceteris generibus causarum." Cf. Maier, ibid., p. 290.

5. Maier, ibid., p. 296: "Die Expositio zur Physik bringt, wie gesagt, wenig Eigenes und jedenfalls nichts was für die problemgeschichtliche Linie, die wir verfolgen, von Bedeutung wäre."

6. Guillelmus de Ockham, *Quaestiones variae*, q. 4, ed. G. Etzkorn, F. Kelley, and J. C. Wey (*Opera Theologica* VIII, St. Bonaventure, N.Y., 1984), p. 154. Cf. Maier, ibid., pp. 296–98.

7. Guillelmus de Ockham, *Summula Philosophiae Naturalis* I, cc. 4–13, ed. S. Brown (*Opera Philosophica* VI, St. Bonaventure, N.Y., 1984), pp. 220–47. Cf. Maier, ibid., pp. 295 and 298–99.

8. Maier, ibid., pp. 295–97.

9. Maier, ibid., pp. 273–99.

10. G. Leibold, "Zum Problem der Finalität bei Wilhelm von Ockham," *Philosophisches Jahrbuch* 89 (1982), pp. 347–83.

critical edition of book II of Ockham's *Expositio in libros Physicorum Aristotelis*, as part of the *Habilitationsschrift* he wrote under the direction of Father Vladimir Richter, S.J.[11] Leibold judged that the *Expositio* treatment of finality deserved more attention than Anneliese Maier had given it. It deserved further study for a number of reasons. First of all, Maier's study of the *Expositio* presentation was founded on a limited manuscript check. Surely a critical edition allows a more careful examination. Furthermore, his detailed perusal of book II of the *Expositio* supplied him with results that brought important corrections to the reigning portrait of Ockham's finality theory. Going beyond the context of Ockham himself, a careful look at the certainly authentic text of the *Expositio* raised serious objections to Maier's implicitly asserted uniformity in the historical development of the finality *problèmatique*. The Ockham of the *Expositio*, according to Leibold, broke with the late scholastic approach to the question, where the type of finality characteristic of the field of art (*technē*) is dominant. Ockham in the *Expositio*, Leibold argued, was a truer Aristotelian. The Venerable Inceptor made his own the fundamental intuition of the Philosopher's teaching about finality. Aristotle distinguished two different territories of finality—finality in art and finality in nature. The late scholastics, as portrayed by Maier, tended to bring the two arenas together, speaking of the finality of nature according to the model of finality found in the field of art. Ockham, in Leibold's careful reading of the *Expositio*, kept the two fields of finality distinct. He recaptured Aristotle's basic metaphysical intuition regarding the finality of nature in itself—where the final cause is tied to the form.[12]

Ockham, as the certain author of the *Expositio*, not only differed from the late scholastics with whom Anneliese Maier acquainted us. Leibold found that the *Expositio* Ockham was also in conflict with the "Ockham" of many other works attributed to him. So, not only did the *Expositio* deserve further attention; all the other treatments of finality attributed to Ockham also deserved attention. Leibold lined them up and patiently measured them, using the indubitably genuine *Expositio* as his yardstick of evaluation.[13]

Following the lead of his teacher, Father Vladimir Richter, S.J., who noted contradictions between the *Expositio* and *Summula* treatments of

---

11. Leibold, ibid., p. 347, n. 1; cf. Guillelmus de Ockham, *Expositio in libros Physicorum Aristotelis*, ed. S. Brown (*Opera Philosophica* VI, St. Bonaventure, N.Y., 1984), pp. 213–408.
12. Leibold, ibid., pp. 348–50, 378–80.
13. Leibold, ibid., pp. 350–51.

final causality a decade earlier,[14] Leibold studied the *Summula*. In this work he found the final cause connected to efficient causality ("... Quamvis finis non sit in re extra, est tamen in intentione agentis"), whereas in the *Expositio* it is linked up with the form.[15] He found such a clear contradiction between the two presentations that he judged it impossible to explain the difference in terms of a development in Ockham's thought concerning final causality.[16] Since the *Expositio* is undeniably authentic, and no reconciliation between the two presentations is possible, it was not difficult for Leibold to conclude that the *Summula* is not authentic, especially since Weisheipl and Brampton had already indicated some doubts concerning Ockham's authorship of that work.[17]

Leibold next examined the *Quaestio disputata 'De fine'*, which in the Lyons edition of 1494–96 was presented as the third *quaestio* of book II of Ockham's *Sentence* commentary.[18] Leibold informed us that we

14. V. Richter, "Zu Ockhams naturphilosophischen Schriften," in *Proceedings of the XVth World Congress of Philosophy* (17–22 September 1973; Varna, Bulgaria), p. 817: "Ausserdem ist mir bei der Durchsicht des Textes des 2. Buches der Expositio aufgefallen, dass auch die in den *Summulae* vertretene Auffassung über die Finalursache in den unbeseelten Körpern verschieden ist von derjenigen der Expositio." Cf. Leibold, ibid., p. 373, n. 135.

15. Leibold, ibid., p. 370: "Aus diesen ersten terminologischen Erklärungen können wir bereits ersehen, wie weit sich die hier verwendete Begrifflichkeit von der in der *Expositio* entfalteten Finalitätslehre entfernt hat. Wir haben hier einen deutlichen Beleg für die von A. Maier gemachte Beobachtung, dass als Folge des Zusammenfalls der beiden Arten von Finalität in Natur und Kunst die ganze Problemstellung am planenden Handeln ausgerichtet ist und die Rolle des finis und seiner Kausalität im Naturgeschehen demgegenüber vernachlässigt wird.

"Desgleichen tritt die grundlegende Veränderung des Ursachenbegriffs bezüglich des finis zutage. Der causa finalis wird im Entstehensprozess eine Rolle nach Art der causa efficiens zugeschrieben, in der sie im Zusammenwirken mit anderen, auf der gleichen begrifflichen Ebene stehenden Ursachen einen Effekt hervorbringen soll.

"Damit haben sich die *Summulae* eine Auffassung von Finalität zu eigen gemacht, die mit der in der *Expositio* dargestellen Lehre des Aristoteles kaum noch Ähnlichkeit aufweist. Dort war das Problem der Finalität grundgelegt worden in dem Gedanken, dass die Natur auch in der Weise des finis Ursache ist, wobei dieser finis als forma angesprochen wurde."

16. Leibold, ibid., p. 372: "Ich halte es für unmöglich, dass ein so eklatanter Widerspruch zur *Expositio* durch die Vermutung einer Entwicklung Ockhams in der Frage der Finalität beseitigt werden könnte. Ausserdem bleibe auch dann immer noch die Berufung auf Aristoteles für diese Auffassung ein unwiderlegliches Zeugnis für das vollkommene Unverständnis des Autors der *Summulae*."

17. Leibold, ibid., p. 373 and p. 350, n. 7. Cf. C. K. Brampton, "Ockham and His Authorship of the *Summulae in libros Physicorum*," *Isis* 55 (1964), pp. 418–26, and J. A. Weisheipl, "Ockham and Some Mertonians," *Mediaeval Studies* 30 (1968), pp. 163–74. We have attempted to defend the authenticity of the *Summula Philosophiae Naturalis* in Guillelmus de Ockham, *Summula Philosophiae Naturalis* (OPh VI, pp. 25*–27*).

18. Leibold, ibid., pp. 375–77. Cf. Guillelmus de Ockham, *Quaestiones variae*, q. 4 (OTh VIII, pp. 98–154).

would not be too far off the track if we considered this *quaestio* as the source for the *Summula* treatment. Certainly there is, in his judgment, an affinity between the two works.[19] The *Quaestio disputata*, like the *Summula*, linked the final cause to the efficient cause, not to the form, and it likewise spoke of the motion of the final cause as metaphorical ("Causa finalis non dicitur causa finalis amoris quo agens amat ipsum, sed dicitur causa finalis effectus causandi ab agente propter amorem finis in quantum amatus movet agens ad efficiendum. Et eius motio non est nisi metaphorica.").[20]

Since Boehner had already noted a confusion regarding the location of this *Quaestio disputata* within Ockham's corpus[21]—and its content, like that of the *Summula*, conflicts with the definitely authentic *Expositio*—Leibold also called the authenticity of this work into question.[22]

Leibold then moved beyond the sources examined by Maier and next studied the conception of finality in the *Quodlibeta* attributed to Ockham. The questions from *Quodlibeta II* and *IV* which deal with final causality were, in Leibold's estimation, even more radical and decisive in their denial of a final cause having an autonomous mode of causality than were the *Summula* and the *Quaestio disputata 'De fine'*. The *Quodlibeta* admitted only a distinction of reason between the final

19. Leibold, ibid., p. 377: "Aus dem Vergleich dieser terminologischen Bestimmungen wird meines Erachtens die Verwandtschaft dieser Quaestio zu den *Summulae* deutlich. Da *Sent.* II, q. 3 wohl früher als die *Summulae* anzusetzen ist, scheint mir die Vermutung, diese Quaestio könne zu den Quellen gehören, die in irgendeiner Form bei der Komposition der *Summulae* herangezogen wurden, nicht abwegig."

20. Cf. Leibold, ibid., p. 376, n. 161. For a slightly altered reading see the new edition (OTh VIII, p. 109).

21. Cf. P. Boehner, "The *Notitia intuitiva* of Non-existents according to William of Ockham," *Traditio* 1 (1943), esp. pp. 240–43 (reprinted in E. M. Buytaert, ed., *Collected Articles on Ockham* [St. Bonaventure, N.Y., 1985], pp. 293–98). Cf. Leibold, ibid., p. 350, n. 7, and 377, n. 168.

22. Leibold, ibid., p. 377: "Es ist nun höchst aufschlussreich, dass Boehner in seiner textkritischen Studie zur *Reportatio*, in der er als erster versuchte, Ordnung in die Konfusion der Quaestionen zu bringen, *Sent.* II, q. 3, die, abgesehen von der einzigen Edition (Lyon, 1494–1496), nur in zwei Handschriften überliefert ist, als fremdes, nicht zum ursprünglichen Textbestand der *Reportatio* gehöriges Element erwiesen hat. Vielmehr, so hat er vermutet, bilde diese Quaestio zusammen mit anderen Quaestionen augenscheinlich den 'nucleus' eines anderen Werkes von Ockham, dem er den fiktiven Titel 'Quaestiones disputatae Ockham' gegeben hat.

"A. Maier hat diese Vermutung Boehners für 'sehr plausibel' gehalten und seine Meinung geteilt, dass *Sent.* II, q. 3 als quaestio disputata nachträglich zur *Reportatio* hinzugekommen ist.

"Trotz dieser Versicherungen muss man die textgeschichtliche Überlieferung von *Sent.* II, q. 3 als unklar bezeichnen. Diese Unklarheiten machen sie in Verbindung mit der inhaltlichen Verwandtschaft mit den aus guten Gründen in ihrer Authentizität bezweifelten *Summulae* zu einer 'quaestio dubia'."

The authenticity of this *quaestio disputata* is treated in Guillelmus de Ockham, *Quaestiones variae* (OTh VIII, pp. 12*–13*).

cause and the efficient cause of a natural event. This completely un-Aristotelian conception was so in conflict with the truer Aristotelian view Leibold found in Ockham's authentic *Expositio* that a closer look at the authorship of the *Quodlibeta* was necessary.[23]

Now Joseph C. Wey, C.S.B., in the introduction to his 1980 edition of the *Quodlibeta* found their authenticity hardly questionable and argued that at least *Quodlibeta I–V* were probably based on disputes carried on at the Franciscan convent in London during the years 1322–24. In his care not to push beyond his evidence, and because certain questions of *Quodlibeta VI* and *VII* refer to the Avignon Commission that examined Ockham's writings in 1325, Wey thought it reasonable to say that Ockham did the final redaction of all his *Quodlibeta* in Avignon, after his arrival there in the middle of 1324.[24]

Leibold still remained unconvinced by Wey's arguments for the authenticity of the *Quodlibeta*. The conflict between the conception of final causality in the *Expositio*, certainly the direct product of Ockham, and the conception of finality in *Quodlibeta II* and *IV* was too strong to say the same person directly authored the two works which have come down to us as Ockham's.[25]

In brief, the certainly authentic *Expositio*, directly authored by Ockham, conflicts essentially in the conception of finality with the treat-

---

23. Leibold, ibid., p. 350: "Ockham erweist sich nämlich in der *Expositio* als treuer Aristoteliker. Das bedeutet, dass er die grundlegenden Anschauungen der aristotelischen Finalitätslehre übernommen hat. So macht sich Ockham in der *Expositio* die aristotelische Unterscheidung der Finalität für den Bereich des planenden Herstellens und des natürlichen Geschehens zu eigen und lässt sich somit nicht denen zurechnen, für die diese beiden Arten von Finalität zusammenfallen. Die planende, intelligente Instanz, die für den Bereich der Kunst charakteristisch ist, lehnt Ockham für den Bereich der Natur gerade entschieden ab." Cf. also p. 378.

24. Cf. Guillelmus de Ockham, *Quodlibeta Septem*, ed. J. C. Wey, C.S.B. (*Opera Theologica* IX, St. Bonaventure, N.Y., 1980), pp. 32*–41*.

25. Leibold, ibid., p. 381, n. 190: "In seiner Einleitung (7*–41*) zur kritischen Ausgabe der Quodlibeta septem hat der Herausgeber P. Joseph C. Wey, C.S.B., die Authentizität der Quodlibeta für kaum bezweifelbar gehalten (32*–34*). Im einzelnen nimmt er an, dass die Quodlibeta das literarische Zeugnis von Disputationen seien (30*–32*), die wahrscheinlich 1322–1324 im Londoner Franziskanerkonvent stattgefunden hätten (36*–38*), verlegt aber ihre Redaktion nach Avignon in das Jahr 1325 (40*–41*). Die vorgelegte Begründung der Authentizität vermag mich nicht zu überzeugen. Abgesehen davon, dass man bisher aus guten Gründen gezögert hat, Ockham in der Avignoner (und Münchner) Periode eine philosophische oder theologische Schrift oder Tätigkeit zuzuschreiben (vgl. noch zuletzt V. Richter, Zu Ockhams Entwicklung, a. a. o. 184), stellt die Inkonsistenz in wichtigen Lehrpunkten, z. B. in der Frage der Finalität, ein schweres Hindernis dar, Ockham persönlich als den Autor dieses Werkes anzusehen. Die zahlreichen Anmerkungen, mit denen in der Edition etwa bei den von mir behandelten Quaestionen des II. und IV. Quodlibet auf das 2. Buch der Expositio in libros Physicorum zum Vergleich verwiesen wird, können diese Unterschiede nicht aus der Welt schaffen."

ments of finality in the strangely compatible *Summula*, the *Quaestio disputata 'De fine'*, and the *Quodlibeta* also attributed to Ockham. The latter three works tie final causes to efficient causality, and speak of the motion of the efficient cause as real, while describing the motion of the final cause as metaphorical. The *Expositio*, in Leibold's evaluation, links the final cause of natural events to the form, and never speaks of the metaphorical motion of the final cause.

If I present an afterthought to Leibold's thesis, it is because Leibold also presented the same afterthought. It is this: even though the *Quaestiones in libros Physicorum Aristotelis* attributed to Ockham do not discuss final causality, still Leibold indicated in a note that these *Quaestiones* also cannot survive an authenticity challenge. They cannot be the work of Ockham himself, but are a collection of texts taken from Ockham's "other" works.[26] I do not know why the *Quaestiones in libros Physicorum Aristotelis* entered into a discussion of final causality, except perhaps because they are so closely tied to the authenticity of the *Quodlibeta*. If you deny the authenticity of the *Quodlibeta*, you must also deny the authenticity of the *Quaestiones in libros Physicorum Aristotelis*, and vice versa. The two works are so intertwined that their authenticity seems to be a single question: there cannot be an authenticity "yes" for one and an authenticity "no" for the other. To apply this to the present case, if one could prove the authenticity of the *Quaestiones*, then the *Quodlibeta* (with their conception of final causality) would have to be considered the authentic teaching of Ockham himself.

III. EVALUATION OF LEIBOLD'S THESIS

I will thus begin my evaluation of Leibold's thesis by attempting to show why the *Quaestiones*, and therefore the *Quodlibeta*, must be accepted as authentic works of Ockham.

Not only are the *Quaestiones* and the *Quodlibeta* linked by location (all three copies of the *Quaestiones*[27] are found in manuscripts which

---

26. Leibold, ibid.: "Wird man die Frage der Authentizität der Quodlibeta noch weiter diskutieren müssen, steht es für mich fest, dass die Quaestiones in libros Physicorum, die Ockham neben der Expositio und den Summulae als drittes naturphilosophisches Werk zugeschrieben werden, kein Werk von Ockham selbst sind. Meine Zweifel in dieser Richtung habe ich schon früher (s. Anm. 7) begründet. Die Quaestiones in libros Physicorum sind eine Kompilation aus anderen Werken Ockhams." Cf. also G. Leibold, "Zur Authentizität der Quaestiones in libros Physicorum Wilhelms von Ockham," *Philosophisches Jahrbuch* 80 (1973), pp. 368–78.

27. Guillelmus de Ockham, *Quaestiones in libros Physicorum Aristotelis*, ed. S. Brown (*Opera Philosophica* VI, St. Bonaventure, N.Y., 1984), pp. 31*–32*.

contain the *Quodlibeta*), but they are also connected interiorly. The *Quodlibeta* frequently promise a future treatment of certain issues, and these promises are fulfilled in the *Quaestiones*. E.g., *Quodlibet II*, q. 18 (OTh IX, p. 192, lin. 96–98), says: ". . . sicut sunt distincti actus temperantiae specifice, ita sunt distincti habitus, sicut alias patebit." This is fulfilled in Q. 84 (OPh VI, p. 628, lin. 47–48), where the author reworks materials from the earlier *Quaest. in III Sent.*, q. 9 (OTh VI, p. 303, lin. 5–13). The reference of *Quodlibet IV*, q. 33: ". . . sicut post [note well] patebit" (OTh IX, p. 460, lin. 129–33), is fulfilled in Q. 61 (OPh VI, p. 563, lin. 38–49). The "sicut alias patebit" of *Quodlibet V*, q. 24 (OTh IX, p. 576, lin. 46–48), finds its referent in Q. 59 (OPh VI, pp. 557, lin. 14–558, lin. 57).

Similarly the *Quaestiones* refer back to the *Quodlibeta*. The varying character of these references also commands attention. Some just indicate the *Quodlibet* (e.g., OPh VI, p. 429, lin. 121: "sicut patet in primo Quodlibet"). Others provide the number of the *Quodlibet* and the question (e.g., ibid., p. 398, lin. 19: "Istas rationes quaere ultima quaestione quarti Quodlibet"). There are some references which tie the *Quaestiones* to the *Quodlibeta* even more closely (e.g., ibid., p. 476, lin. 83: ". . . responsum est prius, nona quaestione secundi Quodlibet," and p. 607, lin. 79–80: "Ad secundum dico sicut prius dictum est quaestione quarta primi Quodlibet"). In these latter two examples we not only have the numbers of the *Quodlibet* and the *quaestio*, but also the notation *prius*, as though the author (*dico*) considers the *Quodlibeta* a closely connected work.[28] Perhaps this helps solve the riddle in Q. 2 (ibid., p. 399, lin. 18: "sicut prius probatum est")—this surely does not refer to Q. 1 or an earlier place in the *Quaestiones*, but it does have its fulfillment in *Quodlibet III*, q. 12 (OTh IX, pp. 247, lin. 19–250, lin. 98).

Another connection between the *Quodlibeta* and the *Quaestiones* is found in their common, and seemingly unique-to-them, use of the new formulation of the razor (cf. OPh VI, p. 413, lin. 7–8: "Quando propositio verificatur pro rebus, si res permanentes sufficiunt ad verificandum, frustra ponitur alia res"). This phrase will be treated as so familiar that it is later truncated to the form "quando propositio verificatur pro rebus etc." (e.g., ibid., p. 423, lin. 13). The old form of the razor also continues to be used here (as in the *Quodlibeta*), but the new form suggests a connection of both the *Quaestiones* and the *Quodlibeta*

---

28. As in *Quodlibet IV*, q. 33 (OTh IX, p. 460, lin. 129–33), the author simply says "sicut *post* patebit" (pointing to *Quaestio* 61), so in *Quaestio* 2 he says simply "sicut prius probatum est" to refer to *Quodlibet III*, q. 12. The author, speaking always in his own name (*dico*), in these unobtrusive ways acts as if these two works belong together.

with Walter Chatton, who so strongly defended, in his *Lectura*, the anti-*rasorium* principle captured in the *Quod sic* of Q. 13 (ibid., p. 425, lin. 4–6: "Quando propositio est vera pro rebus, si res permanentes non sufficiunt ad eius veritatem oportet addere aliquid ultra"). Chatton, in his *Reportatio*, tells us that Ockham has attacked his anti-razor, and these two works (the *Quodlibeta* and the *Quaestiones*) are the only works attributed to Ockham where such an attack is found.[29]

The various connections, through reference, of the *Quaestiones* with other authentic works of Ockham also seems well established. In the one direction, we find in Q. 112, as L. Baudry[30] observed, a reference back to *Scriptum in I Sent.*, d. 24, q. 1 (ibid., p. 697, lin. 79–80): "Ista dicta de unitate et numero possunt [inveniri] dist. 24 libri primi Sententiarum."[31]

In the other time direction the *Expositio Physicorum*, that certainly authentic work of Ockham, points to future treatments of issues of natural philosophy. All the references to future treatments do not necessarily point to the *Quaestiones*, but in our judgment the following samples from *Expositio Physicorum* II, which Leibold edited, do find their fulfillment in the *Quaestiones*:

---

29. Cf. Gualterus Chatton, *Reportatio in I Sent.*, d. 8, q. 3 (Cod. Paris. Bibl. Nat. lat. 15, 887, f. 39va): "Ego autem utebar et utor non alia propositione, sed aliter explicata, videlicet quod omnis propositio simpliciter affirmativa verificata pro rebus, si potest non esse vera istis rebus exsistentibus, alia res requiritur ad eius veritatem; et ista non sufficiunt, quia non plus requiritur ad veritatem propositionis nisi quod ipsa propositio sit et quod sic sit in re sicut propositio significat. Et licet istam viam meam negent aliqui, scilicet Ockham et sui sequaces, in hoc tamen quia non videtur eis quod propositio talis fiat vera plus quam falsa vel e converso nisi aliqua res se habeat aliter, ideo dicunt quod numquam fit hoc nisi per productionem alicuius rei vel per motum localem vel per transitum temporis, igitur saltem in illis casibus ubi transitus temporis vel motus non sufficit, oportet quod concedant propositionem meam. Nam in casu eorum, quare oportet ponere motum localem vel successionem temporis ad successivam verificationem propositionis verificabilis solum pro re? Quia ad hoc necessario oportet quod res aliter se habeat. Ergo, ex quo per illa duo in aliis casibus non potest salvari verificatio post falsitatem huius propositionis, oportet dicere quod plus requiritur. Ex quo propositio verificatur pro re, mens statim assentit. Cogitavi multas instantias, sed non possum omnes solvere una vice." I would like to thank Fr. Joseph C. Wey, C.S.B., for bringing this text to my attention. Cf. Guillelmus de Ockham, *Quodlibeta Septem* (OTh IX, pp. 35*–36*) and *Quaestiones in libros Physicorum Aristotelis* (OPh VI, p. 38*).

30. L. Baudry, "Sur trois manuscrits occamistes," *Archives d'Histoire Doctrinale et Littéraire du Moyen Âge* II (1935–36), p. 142. In *Quaestio* 3 (OPh VI, p. 476, lin. 95–96) we have another reference, a problematic one: "Pro ista materia quaere [responsionem] ultima quaestione II." We believe it refers to Ockham, *Quaest. in IV Sent.*, q. 12 (OTh VII, pp. 255–56). However, the numbers given here might suggest that it was once located at the end of *Quaest. in II Sent.*

31. Cf. Guillelmus de Ockham, *Scriptum in I Sent.*, d. 24, qq. 1–2 (OTh IV, pp. 72–121).

1. (*Expositio Physicorum* II, t. 3; OPh IV, p. 235, lin. 610–13)

Secondly, we must see how the nature is the principle in an increase. And we have to say that in this case it is some substantial form which is the active principle of such an increase; and this is likewise the active principle for any decrease. We will say *elsewhere* how this is so.

(*Quaestiones in libros Physicorum Aristot.*, OPh VI, Q. 125, lin. 22–34)

A third conclusion is that frequently the nature is the active principle in any kind of increase. This is clear in the case of an increase which takes place in rarefaction. For, if water is rarefied by heat and afterwards surrenders to its nature, it is clear that once again it will be condensed by being cooled. Since this form of cold will be from the substantial form of water, and this cold causes this cooling, as was stated before, it follows that the substantial form of water is the efficient principle, at least in the sense of the mediate efficient principle, of this condensation. And we would have to say the same thing in regard to the rarefaction of fire when fire is later condensed. The same is also clearly the case in an increase which takes place by the arrival of some elementary substance, because certainly in this case one substantial form is immediately the principle of that increase, as will be clear at another time [cf. Q. 143, lin. 35–47].

2. (*Expositio Physicorum* II, t. 70; OPh IV, pp. 353, lin. 61–354, lin. 65)

In the sixth place you should note that although sometimes an efficient cause, that is, the form through which the efficient cause acts, may belong to the same species as the form which is produced, still it is not the case that they always belong to the same species. For, frequently the agent and the form through which he acts are of a different species than the form of that which is generated. And *on another occasion* it will be made clear how one should respond to the authority of Aristotle, taken from VII *Meta-*

(*Quaestiones in libros Physicorum Aristot.*, OPh VI, Q. 143, lin. 35–40)

A second conclusion is that the intention of the Philosopher and his Commentator is that the elements are produced partially by the substantial forms of the elements. And this is proved first because the Philosopher says in book VII of the *Metaphysics* that whatever is generated is generated by something which is like it; and this is especially true in the case of the simple generation which takes place in the generation of a substance.

physics, which seems to say the opposite.

3. (*Expositio Physicorum* II, t. 3; OPh IV, pp. 236, lin. 657–237, lin. 664)

From what we have said it can be made clear by induction that every nature which is simple—such as a heavenly body and even every prime matter and substantial form—is a principle of some change, taking change in a broad sense of the term. Now not only is this the case, but it could also be proved—if we assume what Aristotle suggests in the *Categories* and in other places, namely, that every accident is received immediately in some substance,—that the nature is the principle, at least the passive principle, of every change. But we will speak of this *on another occasion*.

(*Quaestiones in libros Physicorum Aristot.*, OPh VI, Q. 125, lin. 8–36)

In this question I state four conclusions. The first is that according to the Philosopher's intention the nature is the immediate passive and receptive principle of any sudden change whatsoever, and this is the case because he does not assert that a quantity differs from a substance and a quality; and consequently he claims that every accident is immediately received into some substance.... The second conclusion is that the nature is the active immediate principle of an alteration to some sensible quality.... The third conclusion is that often the nature is the active principle of every type of increase. The fourth conclusion is that in generation and corruption the nature is only the immediate passive principle of that sudden change.

The third example seems most compelling, since it sets up two items which the future treatment should provide: *that every accident is received immediately into some substance* and *that the nature is the principle, at least the passive principle, of every change*. Both these points promised in the *Expositio Physicorum* are fulfilled in Q. 125 (OPh VI, pp. 733 ff.).

It seems reasonable to conclude that what Ockham promised us in book II of the *Expositio Physicorum* is fulfilled in the *Quaestiones*, and that he is the author not only of the *Expositio Physicorum*, but also of the *Quaestiones*—and, because of their interconnection, of the *Quodlibeta*.

We have, furthermore, witness to Ockham's authorship of the *Quaestiones* in the *Lectura* of Walter Chatton, Ockham's confrere at the Franciscan convent in London. For there is no doubt that the texts of Walter Chatton's *Lectura in I Sent.*, d. 2, q. 1, a. 1, and *Quaestiones* 131–36 of Ockham's *Quaestiones in libros Physicorum Aristot.* are intertwined. In a large number of places they are verbally the same.[32]

32. Cf. Guillelmus de Ockham, *Quaestiones in libros Physicorum Aristotelis* (OPh VI, pp. 40*–41*), and S. F. Brown, "Walter Chatton's *Lectura* and William of Ockham's

If, for example, we compare the text of the *Lectura* with *Quaestio* 132, we see that Chatton is quoting Ockham verbatim. The marginal note of the *Lectura* text of cod. Paris., Bibl. Nat. lat. 15, 886, written in the same scribal hand as the text itself, also indicates that it is Ockham who is Chatton's opponent here:

(Chatton, *Lectura*, n. 16)[33]

(Ockham, *Quaestio* 132; OPh VI, pp. 754, lin. 26–755, lin. 44)

In regard to the second doubt, where the question is whether in the case of essentially ordered causes a second cause depends on a first, the opinion of some authors is that a second cause does not any more depend on a first cause than vice versa, because I ask: what is it for a second cause to depend on a first cause? Either it means the same thing as this—that a second cause cannot produce an effect without the first cause. And this is not convincing, because the first cause similarly depends on the second, because neither can a first cause produce an effect without the second. Or it means that the second cause depends on the first in being. And this is not convincing, first because in accidentally ordered causes a second cause can also depend on a first cause in being. But it is not convincing secondly, because then a cause of a cause would always be a cause of what the other cause caused. Yet this is false, because sometimes a cause depends on something on which even if it did not depend, still it would cause the same effect. Or the meaning could be, as a third alternative, that for a second cause to depend on a first means that it receives some influence from that through which it acts. But this is not necessary, be-

But against this I ask: what is it for a second cause to depend on a first cause? Either it means the same thing as this—that a second cause cannot produce an effect without the first cause. And this is not convincing, because the first cause similarly depends on the second, because neither can a first cause produce an effect without the second. . . . Or it means that the second cause depends on the first in being. And this is not convincing, first because in accidentally ordered causes a second cause can also depend on a first cause in being. But it is not convincing secondly, because then a cause of a cause would always be a cause of what the other cause caused. Yet this is false, because sometimes a cause depends on something on which even if it did not depend, still it would cause the same effect. Or the meaning could be, as a third alternative, that for a second cause to depend on a first means that it receives some influence from that through which it acts. But this cannot be admitted,

---

Quaestiones in libros Physicorum Aristotelis," in *Essays Honoring Allan B. Wolter*, ed. W. A. Frank and Girard J. Etzkorn (St. Bonaventure, N.Y., 1985), pp. 90–93.

33. S. F. Brown, "Walter Chatton's *Lectura* . . . ," p. 97.

| cause this influence could only be local motion or some absolute form. Yet often a second cause causes without receiving this type of influence. | because this influence could only be local motion or some absolute form. Yet often a second cause causes without receiving this type of influence. |

But Chatton's quoting of Ockham is not the only information we get when we compare the *Lectura* and *Quaestiones*. In *Quaestio* 135, after giving a number of reasons by Duns Scotus, the author of the *Quaestiones* says: "Et fortificantur prima et secunda rationes ab alio sic . . . ," and then he gives us verbatim an argument from the *Lectura* of Chatton, I, d. 2, q. 1, a. 1:

(Chatton, *Lectura*, n. 48)[34]	(Ockham, *Quaestio* 135; OPh VI, p. 764, lin. 39–49)
I only present the aforesaid argument, which is that of Aristotle. I argue in this way: I point out the totality of things each of which is caused. Now whether this totality is finite or infinite, it has a cause— and here I am speaking indifferently concerning both efficient and final causes. Now that cause does not itself have another cause, therefore it is the first uncaused cause. The first assumption is clear, for every part of that totality is caused in so far as nothing is pointed out except a totality of caused things. Therefore, the totality is caused, since for a totality to be caused only means that all its parts are caused. The second assumption is clear, because a cause preceding this totality by a priority of causality itself is not part of this totality, otherwise it would not be a cause preceding the totality. Thus, such a cause itself is not caused, because our starting point was to consider that everything which is caused is pointed out and included in this totality. Consequently, a cause preceding this totality of caused things is an uncaused cause.	And the first and second reasons are strengthened by another author in this way: I point out the totality of things each of which is caused. If such a totality is finite, then I argue: this totality has an efficient cause, and the latter efficient cause does not itself have another efficient cause. Thus it is the first uncaused cause. The first assumption is clear: since each part of this totality is caused, then the totality itself is caused, because for a totality to be caused only means that all its parts are caused. The second assumption, according to Scotus, is clear, because a cause which precedes this totality is not part of the totality, otherwise it would not be a cause preceding the totality. Consequently, it would not be an uncaused cause.

34. Brown, ibid., p. 106.

Even further, the text of Q. 135 provides us with three *instantiae* or objections to Chatton's position which Chatton himself then quotes verbatim and to which he responds in the very same article of the *Lectura*.[35] In short, at this juncture of their lives they know one another's positions in some written form that is identical with the texts at these places in the *Quaestiones* and *Lectura*.

This is the case not only for the *Quaestiones*, but also for the *Quodlibeta* and Chatton's Prologue to the *Lectura*. Wey has shown that in a number of places Chatton's Prologue cites Ockham, and that the closeness of the texts shows that when Chatton provides Ockham's arguments he does so in a form that is found nowhere else in the works attributed to Ockham except in the *Quodlibeta*.[36] Yet, on the other hand, Ockham in the *Quodlibeta* also quotes Chatton's Prologue, and the texts are verbally very close:

(Ockham, *Quodlibet V*, q. 5)[37]

But against this position I argue: if this is granted, then it follows that God could not cause in us one act of knowing through which a thing which is absent appears as present to us. And this is false, since God's doing so does not include a contradiction. What we assume is proved because such knowledge is not intuitive according to you, because through intuitive cognition a thing appears to be when it is and appears not to be when it is not. Neither is it abstractive cognition, because by abstractive cognition a thing does not appear to be present.

Furthermore, what belongs to an

(Chatton's Prologue, q. 2, a. 3)[38]

Against this opinion I prove that perfect intuitive cognition in creatures, if it is conserved by God, does not represent that a thing does not exist. First, because in such a case God could not cause in us one act of knowing some thing through which it would appear to us to be present when it would be absent. And this is false, because nothing should be denied as within God's power unless its positing would imply a contradiction. I prove the consequence: either that cognition of the thing would be intuitive, and such is false according to you, because you assert that intuitive cognition is that cognition by which a thing appears not to be when it is not. Or else it would be abstractive; and this is not the case either, because according to you and in fact by abstractive cognition a thing does not appear to be present.

Thirdly, just as above, what be-

---

35. Brown, ibid., pp. 91–92.
36. Cf. Guillelmus de Ockham, *Quodlibeta Septem* (OTh IX, p. 27*).
37. Guillelmus de Ockham, *Quodlibetum V*, q. 5 (OTh IX, pp. 496–99).
38. J. O'Callaghan, "The Second Question of the Prologue of Walter Chatton's Commentary on the Sentences: On Intuitive and Abstractive Cognition," in *Nine Mediaeval*

act according to its substance, if the substance stays the same, no matter what else might be posited, still it can continue to belong to that act. Now, by divine power the substance of sight remains the same, even if the thing seen does not exist any more. Therefore, it is not repugnant to this vision to cause at least partially the kind of assent it caused before when the thing existed; and consequently this causal power can belong to it.	longs to an act through the act's substance, if its substance stays the same, no matter what else might be posited, still it can continue to belong to that act, granted that the substance of the act remains.... If, therefore, when the thing no longer exists, the sight remains just as it did before in the substance of the act, then it is not repugnant to that substance in its type of causing partially that it causes an assent just like the one before; at least it is not repugnant to it that in its type of causing it cause a similar assent.
Furthermore, if you grant your position, it follows that there could be sight and yet by means of it a thing would neither appear to be or not to be. This consequent is against what you hold. The assumption is proved by this common principle: when each of some alternatives belongs to something contingently, if there is no contradiction, then God can make something belong to it without all the other alternatives existing at the same time. For it is in this way especially one proves that matter can exist without every form. Now, by the power of sight someone can sometimes know that a thing exists and sometimes that a thing does not exist. Therefore, it is not a contradiction that neither of these alternatives belongs to sight.	Fourthly, according to that position you would have to hold that this act of seeing could exist, and yet that by means of it a thing would not appear to be nor would it appear not to be.... I prove the consequence: when each of some alternatives belongs to something contingently, if they are not contradictories, then God can make something to belong without all the other alternatives existing at the same time. For it is in this way that one proves that matter can exist without every form, according to you.... If therefore this act of sight is of such a nature that by virtue of it sometimes a thing is known to be and sometimes it is known not to be, then it is not a contradiction that neither of these alternatives belongs to it.

In other words, just as Ockham's arguments have been communicated to his respondent, so the objections of his respondent have been communicated to Ockham. This is the case with *Quodlibet V*, q. 4, as well, where the "Si dicis..." corresponds, as Wey indicated, to Chatton's Prologue, q. 2, a. 6.[39]

From the information we already have in the introductions to vari-

---

Thinkers, ed. R. O'Donnell (Pontifical Institute of Mediaeval Studies, Studies and Texts I, Toronto, 1955), pp. 246–47.

39. Guillelmus de Ockham, *Quodlibetum V*, q. 4 (OTh IX, p. 493).

ous volumes of Ockham's *Opera theologica et philosophica* concerning Chatton and Ockham, and from a study of the interrelationship of the *Lectura* of Walter and the *Quodlibeta* and *Quaestiones* of William, we can arrive at a number of conclusions. First, Chatton's *Lectura* guarantees that Ockham is the author of the *Quodlibeta* and *Quaestiones*. Second, these works of Chatton and Ockham were produced in London, where Ockham and Chatton were in the same convent. Third, at least in some cases Ockham and Chatton each had available to them a written formulation of some of one another's arguments and objections before working on or overseeing the final redaction of these works.[40]

So far, against Leibold's denial of the authenticity of Ockham's *Quodlibeta*, we have tried to establish that the *Quodlibeta* and the *Quaestiones* are so closely tied to one another that their authenticity is intertwined. We have also argued that they are Ockham's works. Our chief argument is that Walter Chatton guarantees the authenticity of these two texts. The account of final causality contained in the *Quodlibeta*, therefore, should not be set aside without making every effort to see if the difficulties raised by Leibold cannot be resolved in another way than by denying the authenticity of the *Quodlibeta* guaranteed by Chatton.

Wey already argued for the guarantee Chatton brought to the authenticity of the *Quodlibeta* in the introduction he wrote to his edition of that work. I have tried to strengthen Wey's argument by showing that in some places Chatton quotes both these works, the *Quodlibeta* and the *Quaestiones*, word for word. Since Leibold was not swayed to alter his opinion by Wey's evidence, I imagine that the elements I have added so far will not be any more successful in convincing him. It seems that he holds as a basic principle that his reading of the *Expositio*, which is certainly an authentic work, conflicts with the teaching on finality in all the other works attributed to Ockham, and that the authenticity of these works at least can be questioned. The *Expositio* itself is unchallengeable as regards its authenticity; the *Quodlibeta*, *Quaestio disputata 'De fine'*, and *Summula* lack for him this same unchallengeable character.

Although, then, Chatton vouches for the authenticity of the *Quodlibeta*, such a guarantee was not strong enough to shake Leibold from his position. So, let us leave this warranty out of our consideration for the present and see if we can find another approach in examining Leibold's basic assumptions regarding the conflict between final

---

40. Cf. Brown, "Walter Chatton's *Lectura* . . . ," pp. 92–93.

causality in the certainly authentic *Expositio* and the position on final causality represented in the other works he judged to be wrongly attributed to Ockham. Our approach follows this form: is there any other indubitably authentic work of Ockham besides the *Expositio* that treats of final causality and that Leibold has not examined? We believe that there is—the *Scriptum in I Sententiarum*. In the Prologue of Ockham's *Scriptum in I Sententiarum*, q. 5, where Ockham fights against Richard of Conington, he answers Richard as follows:

> Furthermore, what he says, that "an end causes the efficient cause and form causes matter"—these words are either metaphorical and improper or simply false, because it would follow that something would cause God, since He is an efficient cause. Likewise, it would follow that whenever the sun would cause some effect due to pursuing its end, the sun would be caused. Also, the intellective soul doing something for the sake of an evil end would then be caused by that evil end. The way in which these metaphorical words are to be understood will be clear on another occasion.[41]

In this certainly authentic work, and in a passage which has no authenticity problem about it, Ockham tells us Richard of Conington's words "finis causat efficientem et forma materiam" are to be taken metaphorically and improperly, or that, if taken properly, they are false. Furthermore, he tells us that he will make it clear elsewhere how these metaphorical words are to be understood. Here then is a certainly authentic Ockham work promising us the kind of treatment we find in the *Summula*, the *Quaestio disputata 'De fine'*, and the *Quodlibeta*.

Leibold, then, has to push his examination a little further and tell us how the certainly authentic *Scriptum* presentation of "finis causat metaphorice" is reconcilable with his reading of the certainly authentic *Expositio* presentation. Surely, his answer cannot be that the *Scriptum* is inauthentic.

IV. AN ALTERNATIVE TO LEIBOLD'S POSITION

I would like to suggest a possible way by which the *Expositio* presentation of final causality might be reconciled with the *Scriptum* (as well as the *Summula*, *Quaestio disputata 'De fine'*, and *Quodlibeta*) treatments.

---

41. Guillelmus de Ockham, *Scriptum in I Sent.*, prol., q. 5, ed. G. Gál and S. F. Brown (*Opera Theologica* I, St. Bonaventure, N.Y., 1965), p. 164: "Praeterea, quod dicit quod 'finis causat efficientem et forma materiam': ista sunt verba vel metaphorica et impropria vel simpliciter falsa, quia sequeretur quod aliquid causaret Deum, cum sit causa efficiens. Sequeretur etiam quod sol quandocumque causaret aliquem effectum propter finem quod tunc causaretur. Et tunc anima intellectiva faciens aliquid propter malum

In book II, chapter 13, section 5, of the *Expositio in libros Physicorum Aristotelis* (OPh IV, p. 404, lin. 20–29) Leibold's edition of the text reads:

Et ideo notandum est quod non est intentio Philosophi quod necessitas non est in naturalibus aliquo modo ex materia, sed intendit quod non est sufficienter nec mediate nec immediate ex materia, nec contingit ultimate respondere ad quaestionem per 'quare' per materiam. Sed isto modo necessitas in naturalibus est ex fine. Quia mediate vel immediate est sufficienter ex fine et per finem contingit ultimate respondere ad quaestionem per 'quare' de re naturali; et hoc quia finis est quodammodo causa causarum, quia aliquo modo MEDIATE movet efficientem ad agendum et efficiens producit formam in materia quae est propter formam.

I have capitalized the last use of the word *mediate* in this paragraph to draw the reader's attention. It is not capitalized, of course, in Leibold's edition. *Mediate* is a very plausible reading, given the frequent use of the same word in the paragraph. Very likely the scribes of manuscripts EFGH even read the abbreviation (*me*^{ce} or *me*^{te}) as *mediate*, since they added the abbreviations for *vel immediate* right after it.[42] The abbreviation for Leibold's reading, *mediate*, is *me*^{ce} or *me*^{te} in manuscripts ABDI. Only manuscript C (Naples, Bibl. Nat., cod. VIII.E.26, f. 33rb) offers an alternative abbreviation. C has *me*^{ice} or *me*^{ite} in my capitalized instance, whereas the same scribe wrote *me*^{ce} or *me*^{te} for the other instances of *mediate* found in Leibold's text. The alternative to Leibold's reading of *MEDIATE* which could reconcile, at least to some degree, the certainly authentic *Scriptum* and the certainly authentic *Expositio* is the reading *METAPHORICE*. The fuller abbreviation for *metaphorice*, of course, is usually *meta*^{ce}; but manuscripts often do not give the clearer abbreviation: they give *me*^{ce} or *me*^{te} often in this time period when the context might demand *mediate, mediante, metaphysicae, metaphorice*, etc.

In any case, even though the *Expositio* is an authentic work of Ockham, Leibold's reading of the *Expositio* text is not as unproblematic as he has assumed. I do not think that the issue of *MEDIATE* or *METAPHORICE* can be settled on paleographical grounds alone. Given, however, the claim of Ockham's certainly authentic *Scriptum* that Conington's "finis causat efficientem" must be understood metaphorically, and its pointing to a fuller treatment later of how this *causare metaphorice* is to be understood, I think *metaphorice* is a worthy

---

finem causaretur ab illo malo fine. Qualiter autem ista verba metaphorica sint intelligenda alias patebit."

42. Cf. Guillelmus de Ockham, *Expositio in libros Physicorum Aristotelis* II, t. 90 (OPh IV, p. 404, lectiones variantes: lin. 27).

possible reading. Nor is the reading *metaphorice* in connection with the movement of the final cause totally alien to Aristotle. In the *De generatione et corruptione* the Philosopher himself declared: "The active principle is a cause, as being the source of movement, but the end is not active—thus health is not active except metaphorically [εἰ μὴ κατὰ μεταφόραν]."[43]

Furthermore, when Chatton considered the Venerable Inceptor's view of the causality of a final cause in another passage of Ockham's prologue, he argued:

To the argument it should be said that if he is speaking about the final cause and dependency metaphorically,[44] the major is true, because an end has to move metaphorically[45] in either of two ways, namely, either a love of it moves the agent or the effective causation by the agent is ordered to the end according to the natural order of things prearranged by the author of nature. . . . If you were to speak of dependency and motion properly, then the major is false. . . .[46]

Here Chatton tells us that the only reasonable way to interpret Ockham's major premiss is to understand the motion of a final cause as metaphorical, since the *finis* has to move *metaphorically* in either of two ways: *either* the love of the end moves the agent, *or* the agent is ordained to that end according to the natural order of things established by the author of nature. In interpreting the major premiss of Ockham's *Scriptum* argument[47] in this way, Walter Chatton provides, I believe, a clue to understanding the reading I am suggesting for the *Expositio* text we are considering: ". . . quia ALIQUO MODO METAPHORICE movet efficientem ad agendum. . . ." I would take this reading of Ockham to mean that when an agent acts with knowledge and deliberation, it is the end as loved which moves metaphorically, but that when we are dealing with a natural agent, acting without knowledge and deliberation, it is the end established in the natural order of things by the author of nature which moves the agent meta-

---

43. Aristotle, *De gener. et corrupt.* I, c. 7 (324b14–16).
44. metaphorice: me^{ce} A (Paris, B.N. lat. 15, 886), metha^{ce} B (Paris, B.N. lat. 15, 887), me^{ce} F (Flor. B.N., Conv. soppr. C. 5. 357).
45. metaphorice: me^{ca} (!) A, me^{ce} B, me^{ce} F.
46. Gualterus Chatton, *Lectura in I Sent.*, prol., q. 7, a. 3 (cod. A, f. 55vb): "Ad argumentum igitur dicendum quod si loquatur de causa finali et dependentia metaphorice loquendo, sic maior est vera, quia finis habet movere metaphorice altero duorum modorum: scilicet vel quod eius amor moveat, vel quod causatio effectiva agentis ordinetur ad ipsum secundum naturalem ordinem rerum praestitutum a conditore naturae. . . . Si loqueres de dependentia et motione proprie, tunc maior est falsa. . . ."
47. Cf. Guillelmus de Ockham, *Scriptum in I Sent.*, prol., q. 11 (OTh I, p. 305, lin. 17–24).

phorically. Now this end, and this natural order of things, have been chosen by a higher being, as is noted in the *Summula*[48] and in the *Quaestio disputata 'De fine'*.[49] Yet the natural order itself of things functions as an order, and this is stressed in the *Expositio*.[50] That the natural order is a *chosen* order does not undercut the fact that it is a chosen *order*, functioning according to its own principles.

Perhaps Leibold's reading *mediate* could be justified, even though I wonder what meaning can be given to the phrase *aliquo modo mediate* in our problematic passage. That manuscripts EFGH added *vel immediate* suggests not only that they read *mediate* but that the *aliquo modo mediate* reading represented a problem for them or their source(s). Yet, even if his reading of *mediate* in this *Expositio* text could be justified, still the point we must face and resolve remains. The authentic *Scriptum* prologue, with its claim that "finis causat efficientem" is a metaphorical statement, and its promise that an explanation of its meaning will be provided elsewhere, must be reconcilable with the authentic *Expositio* presentation of final causality. If the *Scriptum* is reconcilable with the *Expositio*, then so must be the works consistent with the *Scriptum*, such as the *Summula* and the *Quaestio disputata 'De fine'*. The *Quodlibeta* provide a similar presentation of final causality, although perhaps more particularized, since they frequently relate to Chatton's *Reportatio* II, d. 1, q. 1, art. 1–4.[51] Given the guarantee by Chatton of their authenticity, and their consistency with Ockham's *Scriptum* on final causality, the *Quodlibeta* also cannot be declared as "not a direct work of Ockham" simply on the grounds that it differs from the *Expositio* account of final causality.

V. OCKHAM ON FINAL CAUSALITY

All these four works—*Scriptum, Summula, Quaestio disputata 'De fine',* and *Quodlibeta*—give essentially the same position regarding final

---

48. Guillelmus de Ockham, *Summula Philosophiae Naturalis* II, c. 6 (OPh VI, p. 230, lin. 61–63): "Et sic loquitur Philosophus de causa finali, II *Physicorum* versus finem. Et ideo ponit in natura finem, quia eodem modo fit sicut si fieret ab arte."

49. Guillelmus de Ockham, *Quaestiones variae*, q. 4 (OTh VIII, p. 120): ". . . Dico quod—loquendo de causa finali praestituta a voluntate quae proprie est causa finalis, et non de fine intento ab agente superiori dirigente. . . ."

50. Guillelmus de Ockham, *Expositio in libros Physicorum Aristotelis* II, t. 80 (OPh IV, p. 376, lin. 42–44): "Notandum est quod eodem modo fierent naturalia si fierent ab arte quantum ad ordinem fiendorum. Non tamen oporteret quod agens esset intrinsecum vel naturaliter operans sicut nunc."

51. Cf. Guillelmus de Ockham, *Quodlibetum IV*, qq. 1–2 (OTh IX, pp. 293–309).

causality ("finis movet metaphorice"). The *Quaestio disputata 'De fine'* provides the greatest detail concerning this issue and best fulfills the promise enunciated by Ockham in the Prologue of the *Scriptum:*[52] "Qualiter autem ista verba metaphorica [i.e., 'finis causat efficientem'] sunt intelligenda alias patebit." We will follow its lines in presenting the explanation Ockham promised us in the *Scriptum*.

Two of the central issues regarding the causality of a final cause in the *Quaestio disputata 'De fine'* are (1) the nature of the causation or motion of the final cause, and (2) whether for something to move as an end it has to have some real being outside the mind. In brief, the two main issues concern the *causation* of the final cause, and the *entity* of the final cause.[53]

In regard to the causation or motion of the end Ockham notes that each of the four causes has its own type of causality. The causation of an efficient cause, he says, is well enough known: it is to produce something or to act. However, the causation of every type of cause is not a certain kind of doing or acting, for not every type of cause is an efficient cause.[54]

Yet, the way we commonly speak of a final cause and its causation is to say "it *moves* the efficient cause to act." But what is the meaning of this word "moves"? A strong tendency, since we can be swayed by a greater familiarity with the way an efficient cause acts, is to imagine that a final cause, because it causes or moves, moves in the same way as an efficient cause causes or moves. But when we say "a final cause *moves* an efficient cause to act," we mean by "move" that the *finis* (or end) is loved by the agent. And this, Ockham continues, is really nothing more than to say that the agent loves the *finis* or end. From the fact that the end is loved in this way, or that the agent loves it, no new *res* or reality is acquired by the *finis* or end; nor does it as final cause have anything come from it ("nihil realiter adquiritur ei vel etiam est ab eo").[55]

If, in speaking of the *movement* of the final cause, we mean that something is acquired by it or from it, we have to deny that any such thing happens. If we take the word "moves" *in its efficient cause sense*, then in speaking of the final cause as *moving* the agent to act, we are only speaking metaphorically. The final cause does not move the way an efficient cause does. It "moves" as "that which the agent loves."[56]

52. Guillelmus de Ockham, *Scriptum in I Sent.*, prol., q. 5 (OTh I, p. 164).
53. Guillelmus de Ockham, *Quaestiones variae*, q. 4 (OTh VIII, pp. 98–154, esp. 107–17).
54. Ibid., p. 107.   55. Ibid., pp. 107–8.
56. Ibid., p. 108.

Ockham thought that this confusion was the mistake one of his contemporaries made when he spoke of final causality in the following way: an efficient cause could be considered in two ways: according to its entity and according to its causality. In the first sense, the final cause, according to this opinion, does not have any causation in regard to the agent. But in regard to the *causality* of the efficient cause, the final cause does have causation.[57]

Ockham balks at this explanation. It is not precise or subtle enough. You might argue, Ockham tells us, that the final cause moves the agent in the sense that the love the agent has for the end is caused by the end (*finis*) as an object. This may well be, Ockham admits, but the end as an object causing love does not have the character of a final cause. If the end were to cause the love of itself in the agent, it would move the agent not as a final cause but as an efficient cause. It is *its being loved*, and thus being the reason for the agent's action, that makes it a final cause as such.[58]

Another way of putting it is this: a final cause as a final cause is not in any way an efficient cause producing love of itself in the agent. To be exact, the final cause as final cause is not the final cause of the agent; it is the final cause of the effect being produced. The efficient and final cause produce the same effect; one does it *effective* (as an efficient cause), the other *finaliter* (as a final cause).[59]

Ockham's main point in discussing the causation of the final cause appears to be that we can too easily be led by the descriptions of final cause which say that it "causes" or "moves" to imagine wrongly that the final cause as such is involved in some kind of activity in its causation which is like the causation of an efficient cause. The causation of the final cause, for Ockham, is real. So is that of the material and formal cause. But the causations of these causes are not efficient causations, since these causes are not, as such, efficient causes. We do not normally speak of material or formal causes as moving or causing something. We do, most rightly, speak of an efficient cause as causing or moving something; and that is a correct or proper expression. We also say that a final cause moves or causes; and according to Ockham this is an improper expression. It is an improper or metaphorical expression not because a final cause is not a real cause; it is a real *final* cause. It is an improper or metaphorical expression because nothing really is acquired from it ("nihil realiter est ab eo") as a final cause, whereas in the case of the efficient cause something really is acquired

57. Ibid.   58. Ibid., pp. 108–9.
59. Ibid., p. 109.

from it. It is in this sense, I believe, that "finis movet efficientem" is to be understood as a metaphorical statement, both when we are referring to agents who act with knowledge and deliberation and when we are referring to natural agents which act without knowledge and deliberation.

If we turn to our second question, regarding the *entity* of the final cause, the question is this: in order that the end (*finis*) "move" the agent, does it have to have being outside the mind?

Ockham's discussion of this issue is represented simply as a debate between Avicenna and Averroes.[60] Avicenna's position is represented by a brief citation from book VI of his *Metaphysics:* "Causa finalis in suo esse in anima prior est ceteris causis, et isto modo est causa finalis et causa aliarum causarum."[61] A final cause in its being in the mind is prior to the other causes, and in this way (i.e., in the being it has in the mind) it is the cause of the other causes. Ockham's own position on the previous question might pull him to this Avicennian side of the debate. He argued that the final cause "moves" as being *loved,* and *its being loved* takes place in the soul.[62]

Averroes saw the need, in book XII of the *Metaphysics,* for a distinction not made by Avicenna.[63] It is by the form of something desired as it exists in the mind that the agent is "moved"; but it is according to the being as it exists outside the mind that it is an end. If what an agent loves is a bath, then it is, according to Averroes, a real bath that he loves, not just a bath as it exists in the mind.

Ockham, in an attempt to reconcile Avicenna and Averroes—and also to resolve their problem—wants a further distinction: there is a difference between the kind of being that a final cause must have to "move" an agent to act and its real extramental being. Certainly when we choose to go for a walk to become healthy, we do not have as our end or goal to be healthy in our mind. We want to be healthy in our bodies. In this Averroes was correct. But, in order for an agent to be "moved" by the real entity of something, it is not necessary that this *finis* have that entity *in act* outside the mind. In fact, the real entity of the end *must be loved,* and therefore, be in the mind in order to be a final cause. I am able to love something, and even to love the real existence of something, although it does not yet exist according to that real entity, just as I am able to understand something in its reality, al-

60. Ibid., pp. 111–14.
61. See Avicenna, *Metaph.* VI, c. 5 (ed. Venetiis 1508, f. 94va); *Liber de philosophia prima V–X,* ed. S. Van Riet (Louvain-Paris), p. 338.
62. Guillelmus de Ockham, *Quaestiones variae,* q. 4 (OTh VIII, pp. 111–14).
63. Averroes, *In XII Metaph.,* t. 36 (ed. Iuntina [Venice, 1550–53], vol. 8, f. 149v).

though it does not now exist according to that reality. For Ockham, this was the point Avicenna was, or should have been, making.[64] In brief, Avicenna and Averroes can be harmonized. For the one accentuated the fact that a final cause is that which is loved, while the other stressed that what is loved is the real being of that which is loved.

We have attempted in this study to examine the contention of Gerhard Leibold that Ockham's *Expositio* treatment of final causality is so in conflict with the presentation of final causality in the *Summula*, *Quaestio disputata 'De fine'*, and *Quodlibeta* attributed to Ockham that all of the latter works must for this reason be considered inauthentic. For our part we have tried to show that Walter Chatton vouches for the authenticity of the *Quodlibeta*. Then we indicated that the prologue of the certainly authentic *Scriptum in I Sent.* holds one of the elements which Leibold found incompatible with the *Expositio* treatment: "finis movet metaphorice." Furthermore, the Prologue of the *Scriptum* promises a further explanation of "finis movet metaphorice," and such a treatment is exactly what we find in the *Summula* and the *Quaestio disputata 'De fine'*. Our conclusion is that the works set aside by Leibold as not being Ockham's cannot be so easily discounted. They must be reconcilable with the *Expositio*. That Ockham would change his mind back and forth (e.g., from the *Scriptum* to the *Expositio* to the *Quodlibeta*) seems unlikely. We have tried to suggest some directions for a reconciliation of the various treatments, but realize that our efforts are only a beginning.

Boston College

64. Guillelmus de Ockham, *Quaestiones variae*, q. 4 (OTh VIII, pp. 114–17).

12   Themes and Problems in the Psychology of John of Jandun

EDWARD P. MAHONEY

Despite Siger of Brabant's eventual abandonment of the Averroist psychology and the severe blow of the Condemnation of 1277, Averroism did not disappear from the University of Paris.[1] The philosopher of Averroist inclination who most influenced late medieval and Renaissance thought was an early fourteenth-century master of arts, John of Jandun (d. 1328).[2] He makes a radical distinction between faith and reason, arguing that since Aristotle and Averroes took sense knowledge as their starting point they could not demonstrate the rational soul to be the true substantial form of the body, united to it in existence, and created by God.[3] Such a view involves a miracle and can

---

1. On Averroism in the late thirteenth and early fourteenth centuries, see Maurice De Wulf, *Histoire de la philosophie médiévale*, 6th ed., III (Louvain and Paris, 1937), pp. 125 and 128; R. A. Gauthier, "Trois commentaires 'averroistes' sur l'ethique à Nicomaque," *Archives d'histoire doctrinale et littéraire du moyen âge* 16 (1947–48), esp. pp. 187–89 and 331–36; Zdzislaw Kuksewicz, *De Siger de Brabant à Jacques de Plaisance: La théorie de l'intellect chez les averroïstes latins des XIII et XIV siècles* (Wroclaw, 1968), pp. 97–99 and 118–20. On the evolution of Siger's psychology, see Antonio Marlasca, "La antropología sigeriana en las 'Quaestiones super librum de. causis,'" *Estudios filosóficos* (Santander) 20 (1971), pp. 3–27; Edward P. Mahoney, "Saint Thomas and Siger of Brabant Revisited," *The Review of Metaphysics* 27 (1974), pp. 531–53. For some references to the Condemnation of 1277, see note 48 below.

2. On Jandun's life and works, see Noel Valois, "Jean de Jandun et Marsile de Padoue, auteurs du *Defensor Pacis*," *Histoire littéraire de la France* 33 (1906), pp. 528–602; Stuart MacClintock, *Perversity and Error: Studies on the "Averroist" John of Jandun*, Indiana University Publications Humanities Series, No. 37 (Bloomington, Ind., 1956); Jose Terraro, "Juan de Janduno y el Gandavense," *Salmanticensis commentarius de sacris disciplinis* 7 (1960), pp. 331–43; Ludwig Schmugge, *Johannes von Jandun (1285/89–1328): Untersuchungen zur Biographie und Sozialtheorie eines lateinischen Averroisten*, Pariser Historische Studien, V (Stuttgart, 1966), pp. 1–26 and 121–32. For discussion regarding his relations with Marsilius of Padua, see Valois, "Jean de Jandun et Marsile de Padoue," pp. 560–602; Alan Gewirth, "John of Jandun and the *Defensor Pacis*," *Speculum* 23 (1948), pp. 267–72; Schmugge, *Johannes von Jandun*, pp. 26–28 and 95–119.

3. John of Jandun, *Super libros Aristotelis de anima subtilissimae quaestiones* (Venice,

be known only by faith.⁴ It is instructive to note that when Jandun explains that Aristotle and Averroes could not know that God was of infinite power, since their demonstrations are based on what can be sensed, he appeals to Albert the Great to distinguish the natural from the supernatural.⁵

Jandun explains that in the philosophy of Aristotle there are two meanings of "form of the body" (*forma corporalis*), namely, a perfection which is united in existence to the body and an agent only appropriated to and operating within the body (*operans intrinsecum appropriatum corpori*)—he credits Siger as his source for the latter concept. The intellective soul (*anima intellectiva*), which is one for all men, is thus man's form in the same way that the sailor is the form of his ship,

---

1552), III, q. 5, f. 6orab; q. 12, f. 71rb; q. 29, f. 92rb. See also I, q. 1, f. 51ra. On Jandun's conception of the relation of faith and reason, see Étienne Gilson, "La doctrine de la double vérité," in *Études de philosophie médiévale* (Strasbourg, 1921), pp. 64–75, and *History of Christian Philosophy in the Middle Ages* (New York, 1955), pp. 522–24; Pierre Duhem, *Le système du monde*, VI (Paris, 1954), pp. 560–64 and 572–75; Armand Maurer, "John of Jandun and the Divine Causality," *Mediaeval Studies* 17 (1955), pp. 185 and 189; Stuart MacClintock, *Perversity and Error*, pp. 69–101; Arrigo Pacchi, "Note sul commento al 'De anima' di Giovanni di Jandun; IV: La questione della 'doppia verità,'" *Rivista critica di storia della filosofia* 15 (1960), pp. 354–75. Étienne Gilson, *La philosophie au moyen âge* (Paris, 1952), p. 691, remarks: "Il est donc très probable que l'averroïsme de Jean de Jandun est une forme savante de l'incredulité religieuse et qu'on peut le considérer comme un ancêtre des libertins." However, he softened his judgment when he later (1955, p. 524) wrote: "It is therefore possible that John of Jandun's Averroism was a learned form of religious incredulity. Yet, strictly speaking, there is no way to prove this. Was he sneering at Christian faith itself? Or was he sneering at the simplicity of the theologians who pretended to demonstrate what they can only believe? We do not know." An echo of Gilson's earlier, harsher judgment appears in Armand Maurer, *Medieval Philosophy* (New York, 1962), p. 345. For a more nuanced view, see now Maurer's "Siger of Brabant on Fables and Falsehoods in Religion," *Mediaeval Studies* 43 (1981), pp. 515–30.

4. Ibid., III, q. 6, ff. 64ra–66ra; q. 29, f. 94rb. Jandun is also careful to point out that creation *ex nihilo* cannot be demonstrated but must be held on the basis of religious faith. See *Super octo libros Aristotelis de physico auditu subtilissimae quaestiones* (Venice, 1551), I, q. 22, f. 20rab; III, q. 11, ff. 48rb–49ra; VIII, q. 3, ff. 107rb–108rb; VIII, q. 22, f. 129rab; *In libros Aristotelis de coelo et mundo quaestiones subtilissimae* (Venice, 1552), I, q. 29, f. 19vab.

5. "Et dicit Albertus primo de generatione 'Quid mihi de miraculis dicitur cum de naturalibus disseramus'...." John of Jandun, *Quaestiones in duodecim libros metaphysicae iuxta Aristotelis et magni Commentatoris intentionem* (Venice, 1553), I, q. 4, f. 25vb. See Albert the Great, *De Generatione et corruptione*, *Opera omnia*, IV, ed. A. Borgnet (Paris, 1890), I, tr. 1, c. 22, p. 363: "... dico quod nihil ad me de Dei miraculis cum ego de naturalibus disseram." On Siger's use of the same text from Albert, see my "Sense, Intellect, and Imagination in Albert, Thomas, and Siger," in *The Cambridge History of Later Medieval Philosophy*, ed. Norman Kretzmann, Anthony Kenny, Jan Pinborg, and Eleonore Stump (Cambridge, 1982), pp. 602, 618–19; Bruno Nardi, *Studi di filosofia medievale* (Rome, 1960), pp. 119–20; Fernand Van Steenberghen, *Maître Siger de Brabant*, Philosophes médiévaux, XXI (Louvain and Paris, 1977), p. 236.

whereas the vegetative and sensitive souls are united in existence to the body.[6] Jandun has also taken over from Siger the view that the intellective soul is not distant in place or in subject from the human bodies of which it serves as form.[7]

6. "Ad evidentiam quaestionis considerandum est diligenter quod in philosophia Aristotelis forma corporis accipitur dupliciter quantum spectat ad propositum. Uno modo forma corporis dicitur quaecunque perfectio dans esse corpori et unita corpori secundum esse sic quod esse ipsius corporis sit actuale sicut esse illius perfectionis. Et hoc modo communiter et famose sumitur forma, unde quod sic accipiatur forma declaratione non indiget. Alio modo sumitur forma corporis pro operante intrinseco appropriato corpori. Dico autem quod operans intrinsecum appropriatum corpori est illud operans quod non est distinctum a corpore loco et subiecto et cuius actus proprius proprie et praecise dependet ab illo corpore vel ab aliquo existente in illo corpore, ita quod operans intrinsecum et illud corpus, licet non sint unum in esse, ita quod esse unius sit esse alterius, sunt tamen unum in uno opere proprio, quod ab utroque dependet immediate. Et hoc modo intelligentia movens coelum dicitur esse forma eius, non quod det esse formaliter, ut demonstratum est in 8 physicorum, quia ipsa est movens intrinsecum appropriatum tali corpori. Non enim est divisa ab ipso loco et subiecto eo quod incorporalis existens nec locum occupat nec subiectum. Et actus proprius ipsius intelligentiae, scilicet motus proprie et praecise, dependet a caelo. Quaelibet enim intelligentia movet, aliquod corpus coeleste proprie et immediate, et aliquod non movet, ut habet videri in 2 coeli et mundi. Et sic actus eius dependet a corpore huiusmodi, saltem a subiecto in quo recipitur. Quod autem isto modo sumatur forma sive actus corporis, ut patet in libris Aristotelis et Commentatoris." John of Jandun, *Super libros de anima*, III, q. 5, f. 58vb. Jandun has clearly adopted Siger's conception of the *operans intrinsecum corpori*. Indeed he goes on to mention Siger by name and indicate the source of his remarks: "Et debes scire quod istam solutionem huius rationis, qualiter homo intelligit quantum ad aliquid, posuit reverendus doctor philosophiae Remigius de Brabantia in quodam suo tractatu de intellectu, qui sic incipit: 'Cum anima sit aliorum cognoscitiva.'" Ibid., f. 60ra. Jandun is referring not to the *De intellectu* but rather to the *De anima intellectiva*, since the quoted words are indeed the incipit of the latter work. For Siger's espousal of the *operans intrinsecum* concept, see my "Sense, Intellect, and Imagination," pp. 617–18. For other passages in which Jandun puts forth this view of how the intellective soul serves as the form of the human body see his *Super libros de anima*, I, q. 11, f. 14vab and f. 15rb; II, q. 5, f. 23vab; III, q. 5, f. 59ra; q. 7, f. 64rb–va; *Super libros de physico auditu*, VIII, q. 6, f. 111vb; *In libros metaphysicae*, V, q. 7, f. 61ra; VIII, q. 2, f. 107vb; XII, q. 4, f. 129va; q. 12, f. 134ra. For discussion see Karl Werner, "Der Averroismus in der christlich-peripatetischen Psychologie des späteren Mittelalters," in *Sitzungsberichte der Philosophisch-Historischen Classe der Kaiserlichen Akademie der Wissenschaften*, Bd. 98 (Vienna, 1881), pp. 266–68; Marcel Chossat, "Saint Thomas d'Aquin et Siger de Brabant," *Revue de philosophie* 24 (1914), pp. 553–75; Bruno Nardi, *Sigieri di Brabante nel pensiero del Rinascimento italiano* (Rome, 1945), pp. 100–102; Stuart MacClintock, "Heresy and Epithet: An Approach to the Problem of Latin Averroism," *The Review of Metaphysics* 8 (1954–55), pp. 188–91, 198, and 536–42; *Perversity and Error*, pp. 55–58; Pacchi, "Note sul commento al 'De anima' di Giovanni di Jandun; II: L'unicità dell'intelletto e l'unità della scienza," *Rivista critica di storia della filosofia* 14 (1959), pp. 437–40; Kuksewicz, *De Siger de Brabant*, pp. 205–9.

7. Charles Ermatinger, "The Coalescent Soul in Post-Thomistic Debate" (Ph.D. dissertation, Saint Louis University, 1963), has argued that this conception of the soul is more basic than Siger's theory of the soul as a *forma operans intrinsecum* and that such a conception of the soul is central to Giles of Rome's explication of Averroes (pp. 6–15, 31–40, and 72–74) as found in his *De plurificatione intellectus possibilis* (pp. 41–58). Ermatinger attempts to show that Jandun tacitly admits that Siger and Giles of Rome hold the same view regarding Averroes' doctrine of the soul (p. 74). On the other hand

There are thus two substantial forms in the human being: man is put in the species of human both by the cogitative soul, the highest of the material forms, which Aristotle calls the "passive intellect" (*intellectus passivus*), and by the separate intellective soul, whose thinking man comes to share.[8] The intellective soul is itself composed of two diverse essential parts, namely, the agent intellect and the possible intellect.[9] Although they are one in substance, they have different essences and respective functions, namely, to render that which is potentially intelligible actually intelligible and to receive the intelligible.[10] The possible intellect is a passive power which is in potency not only to all universal and abstract intelligible species but also to the act of thinking.[11]

One of Jandun's contemporaries, Thomas Wilton, claimed that according to Averroes the possible intellect is a potency only in regard to the universal intentions which it receives, whereas it is something actual when taken in itself. He argued that what was a pure possibility could not immediately receive such intentions, since the latter are accidents. Presumably what Wilton meant was that as existing accidents the intentions required an actual or existent thing as a subject in which to inhere.[12] He also maintained that for Averroes the agent in-

---

Kuksewicz, *De Siger de Brabant*, pp. 100–101, 110–11, and 215, attributes the conception of the soul as not distant in place or in subject to Giles of Orleans and never mentions Giles of Rome. He is following the tentative reconstruction of the psychology of Giles of Orleans presented by Wladyslaw Senko, "A la recherche d'un commentaire sur le 'De anima' de Gilles d'Orleans," in *La filosofia della natura nel medioevo, Atti del Terzo Congresso Internazionale di Filosofia Medioevale* (Milan, 1966), pp. 691–98. Senko bases himself on marginal references to an "Egidius" in manuscripts of Harvey Nédellec and Durand of Saint Pourçain. For a restatement of his own position on Giles of Rome, Harvey, and Durand, along with a critique of Senko and Kuksewicz, see Charles J. Ermatinger, "Giles of Rome and Anthony of Parma in an Anonymous Question on the Intellect," *Manuscripta* 17 (1973), pp. 91–98.

8. John of Jandun, *Super libros de anima*, I, q. 10, f. 13va; III, q. 5, ff. 59vb–60rb. See also his *In libros metaphysicae*, I, q. 4, f. 5rab; q. 5, f. 5va; VII, q. 17, f. 100ra. For discussion see Pierre Duhem, *Le système du monde*, VI, pp. 549–58; MacClintock, "Heresy and Epithet," pp. 539–40; *Perversity and Error*, pp. 58–62; Nardi, *Studi di filosofia medievale*, p. 175, n. 2, and pp. 187–88; Kuksewicz, *De Siger de Brabant*, pp. 206–9. MacClintock's puzzling claim that Jandun's psychology reveals Augustinian tendencies has been effectively answered by Zdzislaw Kuksewicz, "Jan z Janduno a Augustynizm Sredniowieczny: Polemika z oceną poglądów awerroisty paryskiego dokonaną przez MacClintocka," *Studia Filozoficzne* 5 (14) (1959), pp. 98–99 (English summary), and by Arrigo Pacchi, "Note sul commento al 'De anima' di Giovanni di Jandun; I: La teoria del senso agente," agente," *Rivista critica di storia della filosofia* 13 (1958), p. 373; see also pp. 442 and 456–57.

9. John of Jandun, *Super libros de anima*, I, q. 3, f. 4rb; II, q. 5, f. 23va; III, q. 26, f. 90ra and f. 90vb.

10. Ibid., I, q. 8, f. 10ra; q. 10, f. 13vb; III, q. 5, f. 57rb.

11. Ibid., I, q. 10, f. 13va; III, q. 2, f. 54vb.

12. See Thomas Wilton, *Quaestio disputata de anima intellectiva*, ed. Wladyslaw Senko, in *Studia Mediewistyczne* 5 (Warsaw, 1964), p. 78, ll. 30–34.

tellect and the possible intellect are two distinct substances, each of which subsists in itself.[13]

Jandun examines Wilton's views on the possible and agent intellects at length but rejects them as opposed to Aristotle and Averroes.[14] In opposition to Wilton and others in the Averroist tradition, Jandun rejects the position that the agent intellect is for Aristotle and Averroes a substance distinct from the possible intellect, and he explicitly denies that it is God.[15]

Unlike Siger, Jandun does not believe that sensation can be wholly accounted for by the sensible thing outside the body, by the sensible species which that thing produces, or by the sense which passively receives the sensible species. Neither singly nor taken together do they provide the causal agency required to explain the act of sensing itself. Jandun argues that the same power cannot of itself be both an active and a receptive principle, thereby excluding the passive sense as the required causal agent. The sensible species is eliminated on the grounds that the act of sensing cannot result from something of less dignity than itself. Since the sensible thing is at a distance from the sensing organism, and sensation requires an active principle immediately present to sense, the sensible thing is also rejected as a causal agent explaining sensation. Jandun derides as ridiculous the notion

13. Ibid., pp. 81–82. On these doctrines of Thomas, see Senko, "La Quaestio disputata De anima intellectiva de Thomas Wilton dans le ms 53/102 de la Bibliothèque du Grand Séminaire de Pelplin," *Miscellanea Mediaevalia* 2 (Berlin, 1963), pp. 466–67, and "Les opinions de Thomas Wilton sur la nature de l'âme humaine face à la conception de l'âme d'Averroes," *Rivista di filosofia neo-scolastica* 56 (1964), pp. 594–98 and 601–2; Kuksewicz, *De Siger de Brabant*, pp. 185–88.

14. Jandun, *Super libros de anima*, III, q. 6, ff. 60va–63ra; q. 26, ff. 88vb–90vb. Senko, "Jean de Jandun et Thomas Wilton. Contribution à l'établissement des sources de 'Quaestiones super I–III De anima' de Jean de Jandun," *Bulletin de Philosophie Médiévale (S.I.E.P.M.)* 5 (1963), pp. 139–43, presents textual comparisons which demonstrate that Jandun is attacking Wilton's *De anima intellectiva* in his own questions on the *De anima*. Kuksewicz, *De Siger de Brabant*, pp. 209–14, also makes evident how seriously Jandun took Wilton. The most comprehensive study on Wilton is the introductory essay published by Senko in his edition of Wilton's *Quaestio disputata de anima intellectiva*, pp. 5–73. He compares Wilton's position with those of three of his contemporaries, namely, Jandun (who followed a similar path), William Alnwick (who fought him bitterly), and John Baconthorpe (who respected and quoted him), showing by a selection of textual comparisons that Jandun borrowed both ideas and formulations from Wilton and that Baconthorpe gave a reliable presentation of his views (pp. 40–46). Of particular note is Senko's analysis of the material intellect as actual of itself (pp. 59–65). I am indebted to my colleague at Duke Professor Kazimierz Grzybowski for translating from the Polish original relevant passages of this essay. Charles Ermatinger, "John of Jandun in His Relations with Arts Masters and Theologians," in *Arts libéraux et philosophie au moyen âge* (Montreal and Paris, 1969), pp. 1181–84, has noted that Jandun is also dependent on Wilton in a discussion regarding divine infinity.

15. John of Jandun, *Super libros de anima*, III, q. 2, f. 55ra; q. 26, f. 88vb; *Super libros de physico auditu*, I, q. 1, f. 2rb; *In libros metaphysicae*, XII, q. 4, f. 130ra.

that some had of an agent sense whose action went forth outside the soul to external objects and thereby enabled them to generate sensible species in the media and also in the sense organs. The agent sense (*sensus agens*) which he proposes is a natural power of the sensitive soul, namely, the passive sense, but only as the latter has already been disposed and prepared for sensation by the reception of the sensible species. Inasmuch as a particular sensible species serves as the necessary condition for the passive sense having sensation of a particular sensible object, it is not surprising that Jandun refers to it as the immediate receptive principle (*immediatum per se principium receptivum*) of the act of sensing.[16]

The causal analysis that Jandun presents of sensation and the terminology that he adopts regarding the agent sense and the sensible species closely resemble his analysis of the causal factors involved in intellectual cognition and his terminology for the agent intellect and the intelligible species.[17] The problem of the agent sense remained a topic debated vigorously by various philosophers from the fourteenth through the sixteenth century.[18]

16. John of Jandun, *Super libros de anima*, II, q. 16, ff. 32ra–37va. Jandun is quite explicit that the passive sense and the agent sense exist together in the same subject as two different powers (f. 34va). He also points out that the agent sense acts not on the sensible according to the real, corporeal existence (*esse reale et corporeum*) which it has in the world about us, but on the spiritual or intentional existence (*esse spirituale seu intentionale*) which it has in the passive sense by means of the sensible species representing it (f. 34va). Although such a notion of sensation is clearly at odds with Aristotle's own doctrine, Jandun argues that they are identical, and he interprets all texts from Aristotle so as to favor his own position (ff. 32va, 34ra–va, 35ra–vb, and 36vb). For further analysis see Arrigo Pacchi, "Note sul commento al 'De anima' di Giovanni di Jandun; I: La teoria del senso agente," pp. 372–83, and Edward P. Mahoney, "Agostino Nifo's *De Sensu Agente*," *Archiv für Geschichte der Philosophie* 53 (1971), pp. 124–25, n. 23. We have summarized Jandun's treatment of the agent sense in the question found in his questions on the *De anima*. For discussion regarding the different treatises he wrote on the topic and for information about Bartholomew of Bruges, with whom he was in controversy on the same topic, see MacClintock, *Perversity and Error*, pp. 104–10; Charles Ermatinger, "Some Unstudied Sources for the History of Philosophy in the Fourteenth Century," *Manuscripta* 14, pp. 3–11; Adriaan Pattin, "Pour l'histoire du sens agent au moyen âge," *Bulletin de Philosophie Médiévale (S.I.E.P.M.)* 16–17 (1974–75), pp. 104–7.

17. Jandun himself alludes on occasion to the parallel. See *Super libros de anima*, II, q. 16, f. 34vab; III, q. 23, ff. 83vb–84ra. Jandun argues that there is a twofold agent or active principle, one that disposes and prepares a subject for receiving its final or complete act, and another that perfects and completes the prepared subject by inducing its final act or complement. He applies this distinction when analyzing both sensation and intellection. See II, q. 16, f. 35ra; III, q. 23, f. 83vb.

18. For studies on later philosophers who interested themselves in the topic, see Ermenegildo Bertola, "La questione del 'Senso Agente' in Gaetano di Thiene," in his *Saggi e studi di filosofia medioevale* (Padua, 1951), pp. 53–69; Leonard A. Kennedy, "Sylvester of Ferrara and the Agent Sense," *The New Scholasticism* 40 (1966), pp. 464–77; Mahoney, "Agostino Nifo's *De Sensu Agente*," pp. 119–42; Pattin, "Pour l'histoire," pp. 100–113.

While Jandun interrelates the possible intellect, the agent intellect, and the internal senses in his various writings and indicates their connections to the phantasm, the intelligible species, abstraction, and the act of thinking, it is not clear that he consistently maintains the same doctrine in all these works. Because these variations appear to have been overlooked by his historians, who have tended to concentrate almost exclusively on his *De anima*, we shall attempt to set out these variations in at least a cursory fashion.[19]

In his questions on the *Metaphysics*, whose date of composition is not certain, Jandun indicates that all human intellectual knowledge takes its start from sense knowledge, and he attributes differences in intellectual ability to the fact that some people have superior internal senses—in particular they have better cogitative powers and memories.[20]

Following a lead in Albert the Great, he distinguishes in our "experience" (*experimentum*) both a material element, namely, the sensible species retained in memory, and a formal element, namely, the act of comparing (*collatio*) these preserved species in regard to something in which they agree. This ability to compare individuals previously sensed in order to find some likeness (*similitudo*) in which they agree belongs only to the cogitative power in humans and not to the estimative power in animals, because the cogitative works in conjunction with the intellect and the estimative does not. Presumably Jandun means that the cogitative power is joined to the agent intellect, since he remarks that when the lower power is joined to the higher power, it is more illuminated and operates in a more excellent fashion.[21] A few questions earlier, he had indicated that the agent intellect abstracts and illuminates the phantasms and also acts to prepare the possible intellect for the act of thinking.[22]

If we collect some of Jandun's scattered remarks about the agent intellect in his questions on the *Metaphysics*, we learn that it is a cause of

---

19. Kuksewicz, *De Siger de Brabant*, pp. 202–43, analyzes only Jandun's questions on the *De anima*. Even in regard to that work Kuksewicz does not completely confront the seemingly conflicting things which Jandun says concerning the agent intellect and the production of the intelligible species.

20. John of Jandun, *In libros metaphysicae*, I, q. 4, f. 5vb; II, q. 2, f. 21vb; q. 3, f. 22va; XII, q. 12, f. 133ra. See also IV, q. 13, ff. 53vb and 54rb. Schmugge, *Johannes von Jandun*, p. 130, lists this work among those whose date is not known. See also note 26 below.

21. Ibid., I, q. 9, f. 7va; q. 11, f. 8rb; q. 12, f. 8vab. See Albert the Great, *Metaphysica: libros quinque priores*, ed. Bernhard Geyer, *Opera omnia*, XVI, part I (Aschendorff, 1960), I, tr. 1, c. 6, p. 10a. Jandun may also be influenced here by Aquinas, *In libros metaphysicorum*, I, lect. 1, who specifically attributes to the cogitative power the ability to make such comparisons.

22. Ibid., II, q. 1, f. 20vb.

the intelligible species in the possible intellect; that it sees the likeness existing among individuals and forms one intention of them; that it abstracts and illuminates the phantasms; that we grasp self-evident principles in its light and without any need for reasoning; that it must illuminate the possible intellect if the latter is to have knowledge, that is, receive the intelligible; and that phantasms are the instrument of the agent intellect.[23] Moreover, Jandun makes it clear that after the agent intellect has abstracted all sensible substances and produced intelligible species of them in the possible intellect, the latter knows directly the agent intellect itself and even rises to knowledge of higher separate substances including God.[24] The possible intellect, which Jandun also calls "our intellect" (*noster intellectus*), thus knows primarily by means of intelligible species to which it stands in potency.[25]

Jandun also makes some interesting remarks regarding cognitive psychology in his questions on the *Physics*, which recent scholarship dates as having been completed around 1318.[26] Although sense knowledge and intellectual knowledge have in common that they are caused by species from the thing known, they differ insofar as sense knowledge is brought about by a species representing one individual thing and no other, while intellectual knowledge is brought about by a species representing the essence of the thing and not absolutely (*praecise*) one individual thing.[27]

Both phantasms and intelligible species are likenesses (*similitudines*) of things, but the intellect needs the former in order to have the latter.[28] Jandun explains that the phantasm acts in a spiritual fashion

---

23. Ibid., I, q. 1, f. 1va; q. 12, f. 9rb; II, q. 1, f. 20vb; q. 2, ff. 21vb–22ra; q. 4, ff. 24vb–26ra; XII, q. 13, f. 135va. See also I, q. 16, f. 11vb. In XII, q. 1, f. 128rb, Jandun attributes to Averroes the position that the possible intellect considers the likeness among individuals. Also of interest are his remarks on the three degrees of abstraction which distinguish natural philosophy, mathematics, and metaphysics. See I, q. 2, f. 3ra; q. 21, f. 17ra; VI, q. 3, ff. 79vb–80ra.

24. Ibid., I, q. 1, f. 1va; q. 23, f. 19vb; VII, q. 7, f. 91ra; IX, q. 15, f. 119rb.

25. Ibid., VI, q. 8, f. 82vb; IX, q. 14, f. 118va; XII, q. 4, f. 129vb; q. 21, f. 143ra. Jandun occasionally refers to "concepts" (*conceptus*), but he appears to take them to be intelligible species. See V, q. 12, f. 62vb; q. 33, f. 74rb; XII, q. 21, f. 143ra.

26. On the dating see MacClintock, *Perversity and Error*, p. 111, and Schmugge, *Johannes von Jandun*, pp. 126–27 and 129. The latter author suggests (p. 130) that Jandun's *Metaphysics* is later than his *Physics*. Whatever be their respective chronology we shall assume that the *De anima* is the last of the three works, since it contains the most nuanced examination of key problems regarding psychology and even admits uncertainty about the functions of the agent intellect. But see note 38 below.

27. John of Jandun, *Super libros de physico auditu*, I, q. 5, f. 6ra.

28. Ibid., I, q. 1, f. 1va; q. 4, f. 5ra–va. Jandun is careful to stress that we know neither the sensible species nor the intelligible species prior to knowing the things of which they are species or likenesses. See I, q. 5, f. 6ra.

(*spiritualiter*) by impressing on the intellect a species which the intellect receives. From the perspective of this causal relationship, the phantasm is of greater dignity than the intellect, since the former is active and the latter is passive. However, the intellect itself has an operation that is of greater dignity than the activity of the phantasm, namely, the act of thinking (*intelligere*), which occurs only after the possible intellect has been informed by the intelligible species and which it perhaps (*forte*) owes to the agent intellect.[29]

In this work Jandun distinguishes two different kinds of intellectual abstraction (*abstractio intellectualis*) which he attributes to the agent and possible intellects respectively. The abstraction pertaining to the agent intellect is simply to make that which is potentially intelligible actually intelligible. However, Jandun refuses to settle here whether the agent intellect does this by causing the intelligible species in conjunction with the phantasm or whether it does this by causing the act of thinking directly. On the other hand, the possible intellect abstracts by knowing something which is prior without that which usually accompanies it as the posterior, as when it knows the species without the individual or the genus without the species. Jandun indicates that such an abstraction of the prior from the posterior is the abstraction of the universal from its particular, an abstraction common to every science, since in every science the superior can be considered apart from its inferior.[30]

What is remarkable is that Jandun has here assigned to the possible intellect, and not to the agent intellect, the task of abstracting the universal from the particular. Since Jandun also holds in this work that the possible intellect must first be informed by intelligible species to know and that the possible intellect enjoys universal knowledge through intelligible species which it does not cause, it is difficult to see how it could be the source of such an abstraction.[31]

In his questions on the *De anima*, which were probably composed

---

29. Ibid., I, q. 1, f. 2va. See also IV, q. 27, f. 74ra. The possible intellect has the receptive power to receive intelligible species. See I, q. 12, f. 12va.

30. Ibid., II, q. 4, f. 30va. Jandun remarks (f. 30va) that all concede the effect of the agent intellect to be either the intelligible species or the act of thinking or both.

31. See ibid., I, q. 5, f. 6ra, and IV, q. 27, f. 74ra. In his *Quaestio de notioritate universalium* (ed. Zdzislaw Kuksewicz, "La 'Quaestio de notioritate universalium' de Jean de Jandun," *Mediaevalia philosophica polonorum* 14 [1970], pp. 87–97), which was completed in 1314, Jandun argues that knowledge of the genus, which is more universal, must precede knowledge of the species, which is less universal. The example given is the knowledge or the concept of animal which must precede the knowledge or the concept of man. For a briefer version of this question, see Jandun, *Super libros de physico auditu*, I, q. 6, f. 7rb–vb. It is not clear how these remarks are to be reconciled with the possible intellect abstracting the genus from the species.

between 1315 and 1318, Jandun shows particular interest in Albert's fivefold division of the internal senses, but he considers phantasy (*phantasia*) to be reducible to what Averroes calls the cogitative power.[32] Moreover, he notes that by phantasy Aristotle sometimes means the imagination and at other times the cogitative power. Jandun's own list of the internal senses is identical with that of Averroes, namely, the common sense, imagination, the cogitative or estimative power, and memory. While the role of imagination is simply to retain the sensible species received by the common sense, both the common sense and the cogitative power have judgmental tasks.[33] However, Jandun takes it as probable that the cogitative power cannot know itself, since it is an organic power—Albert is cited as an authority that an organic power cannot have self-knowledge.[34]

Jandun attributes to the internal senses and to the cogitative power in particular the ability to cause a preparation (*praeparatio*) in the possible intellect, namely, an intelligible species, which serves as the receptive and disposing principle (*principium receptivum et dispositivum*) but not as the active principle of the act of thinking (*per se principium effectivum intellectionis*).[35] Although he refers to the phantasm as the immediate active principle causing the intelligible species (*principium immediatum activum speciei intelligibilis*), when he speaks more precisely he states that it is in fact the activity of the cogitative, the highest of the sense powers, together with its phantasm which induces the most immediate disposition required for the act of thinking. Imagination and memory, on the other hand, evoke only a certain disposition or as it were preparation.[36] Jandun is careful to stress not only that the

---

32. On the dating see MacClintock, *Perversity and Error*, pp. 105–10; Schmugge, *Johannes von Jandun*, pp. 123–25.

33. John of Jandun, *Super libros de anima*, II, q. 17, f. 38ra; q. 37, ff. 52va–54ra; III, q. 15, f. 73va. Elsewhere Jandun also notes the differences in Aristotle's treatment of the internal senses in his various works. See Jandun, *Super parvis naturalibus Aristotelis questiones perutiles ac eleganter discussae* (Venice, 1505), q. 5 in the *De memoria*, f. 26vb. For Albert's views on the internal senses see my "Sense, Intellect, and Imagination," pp. 602–4; Nicholas H. Steneck, "Albert the Great on the Classification and Localization of the Internal Senses," *Isis* 65 (1974), pp. 193–211.

34. Ibid., III, q. 4, ff. 56va–57ra. See also II, q. 33, f. 50vab. The relevant passage in Albert is his *De anima* (ed. C. Stroick, *Opera omnia*, VII, part 1 [Aschendorff, 1968]), III, tr. 2, c. 14, p. 196, l. 92, to p. 197, l. 8. Jandun emphasizes in III, q. 8, f. 66vb, that the intellect can know in a universal fashion, since it is not an organic power. While the cogitative power can distinguish individual things from one another, it cannot distinguish them in a universal and abstract fashion. It thus knows this animal and this relationship, but it cannot grasp their essences by a universal knowledge.

35. Ibid., III, q. 11, f. 70rab; q. 16, f. 73va and f. 74ra; q. 17, ff. 75vb–76ra; q. 35, f. 98rb.

36. Ibid., III, q. 14, f. 72vb; q. 15, f. 73rab; q. 16, f. 74vab; q. 30, f. 94va. In III, q. 35, f. 98rb, Jandun speaks more loosely of the phantasm as the species which exists in

cogitative power is not to be found in animals, who have merely an estimative power, but also that imagination and memory in humans differ from the same faculties in the brutes.[37]

There is some evidence that while composing his questions on the *De anima*, Jandun shifted somewhat his position on the respective roles of the agent intellect and the possible intellect in the production of the intelligible species and universal knowledge.[38] At various points in the work he indicates that the phantasm produces the intelligible species in the possible intellect only because it operates in conjunction with the agent intellect.[39]

He describes the intelligible species as an abstract and spiritual form that is produced by the intellect and that represents the abstracted material thing in a universal fashion. On the other hand, the act of thinking (*intellectio*), which is distinct from the intelligible species, is the knowledge that the intellect has of the thing presented to it through the intelligible species. Jandun maintains that while the phantasm cannot be the immediate active principle of the act of thinking, it alone can serve as the immediate active principle of the intelligible species. The possible intellect cannot play that role, since it stands in the state of a receptive potency to the intelligible species. Nor can the agent intellect be the immediate and proper principle of any particular intelligible species, since it is the universal cause of all of them.[40] Jandun overcomes the objection that the phantasm, being ma-

---

imagination, in memory, or in the cogitative power and which disposes the human intellect, that is, the possible intellect, for the act of knowing.

37. Ibid., III, q. 30, f. 94va; q. 35, f. 98rb–va.

38. Both MacClintock, *Perversity and Error*, pp. 107–8, and Schmugge, *Johannes von Jandun*, p. 125, propose the possibility that book III was originally a separate treatise. This may account for some of the tensions in the work.

39. John of Jandun, *Super libros de anima*, I, q. 10, f. 13va; II, q. 16, f. 34va; q. 19, f. 41ra; III, q. 7, f. 64vb.

40. Ibid., III, q. 14, f. 72vab. Jandun rejects (f. 72ra) the position of those who take the intelligible species to be identical with the act of thinking. One of their arguments is that if the intelligible species and the act of thinking are distinct then the intellect would have to know the intelligible species before it knew the essence of the thing. They also point out that we can know the likeness (*similitudo*) of something only after we have come to know the thing itself. Jandun replies (ff. 72vb–73ra) that in fact the intelligible species and the act of thinking occur in the same instant. Moreover, what causes cognition is not known first, as is clear in the case of the sensible species of color and our knowledge of color. Jandun had earlier composed a treatise *De specie intelligibili* which attacked someone who had used fourteen arguments to show that the intelligible species is really distinct from the act of thinking. Charles Ermatinger, "Notes on Some Early Fourteenth Century Scholastic Philosophers," *Manuscripta* 4 (1960), pp. 34–38, showed that Jandun is attacking Bartholomew of Bruges's *Sophisma de specie intelligibili*. For a close and valuable comparison of Bartholomew's *Sophisma* with Jandun's treatise and also with his discussion on intelligible species in his *De anima*, III, q. 14, see Edward

terial, cannot be the cause of the intelligible species, which is immaterial, by explaining that the phantasm can do this only by virtue of the agent intellect. However, he then admits that the nature of the agent intellect's contribution remains hidden and requires further inquiry.[41]

Several questions later, Jandun remarks that it is commonly held that the agent intellect abstracts the essence of the thing known and that such an abstracting is simply to produce an intelligible species which represents the essence in a universal fashion. But he adds that the way in which the agent intellect does this in conjunction with the phantasm will be examined later.[42]

In the question devoted to whether there must be an agent intellect, Jandun argues that since the intelligible species is the immediate receptive principle of the act of thinking (*immediatum per se principium receptivum intellectionis*) and the possible intellect is the receptive potency which receives the thinking, something else must serve as the immediate active and perfective principle of the act of thinking (*immediatum per se principium activum perfectivum ipsius intelligere seu intellectionis*). Having previously ruled out the phantasm, Jandun concludes that the agent intellect alone can play this role, and he takes both Aristotle and Averroes to have held such a position. To render that which is potentially intelligible actually intelligible the agent intellect does nothing to the stone outside the soul, nor does it do anything to our phantasm of the stone. But the agent intellect does do something to the intelligible species which the stone and its phantasm have caused in the possible intellect. One objection that Jandun brings against this account is that the agent intellect would then serve both as the remote active principle causing the intelligible species in the possible intellect and as the immediate active principle causing the act of thinking in

---

G. Smith, "John of Jandun's Dispute with Bartholomew of Bruges on the Intelligible Species" (M.A. thesis, Saint Louis University, Saint Louis, Missouri), esp. pp. 14–66. It should be emphasized that Jandun is careful to present Averroes himself as upholding the distinction between intellection and the intelligible species. See *Super libros de anima*, III, q. 15, f. 73va. This explication of Averroes by Jandun would become the focus of a vehement philosophical dispute at Padua in the late fifteenth century and helped trigger off a continuing debate on intelligible species in the sixteenth century. On these late discussions see Antonino Poppi, *Saggi sul pensiero inedito di Pietro Pomponazzi* (Padua, 1970), pp. 139–94; idem, *La dottrina della scienza in Giacomo Zabarella* (Padua, 1972), pp. 97–108; Edward P. Mahoney, "Antonio Trombetta and Agostino Nifo on Averroes and Intelligible Species: A Philosophical Dispute at the University of Padua," in *Storia e cultura al Santo di Padova fra il XII e il XX secolo*, ed. Antonino Poppi (Vicenza, 1976), pp. 289–301.

41. Ibid., III, q. 15, f. 74ra.
42. Ibid., III, q. 20, f. 79va. See also f. 80ra.

the possible intellect. The only apparent escape would be to say that the phantasm alone causes the intelligible species, which seems absurd. Another objection is that all previous Latin expositors of Aristotle have held that the agent intellect abstracts intelligible species from phantasms, not that it causes the act of thinking. Jandun escapes the latter difficulty by unabashedly taking the "abstracting" proper to the agent intellect to be its producing not the intelligible species but rather the act of thinking in the possible intellect. The first objection seems to cause him more concern. While he gives here the facile solution that the same thing can be both a remote and an immediate cause but in different ways, he obviously remains puzzled as to the agent intellect's role in the producing of the intelligible species.[43]

When he turns directly to the problem in the following question, he confesses that he finds the thesis that the agent intellect causes the intelligible species by the means of the phantasm to lack necessity, and he adds that he does not understand what sort of causality the agent intellect could share with the phantasm. Jandun takes as the more defensible position that the agent intellect does not cause the intelligible species either directly or by means of the phantasm.[44] Having established this conclusion, he reasserts that when the agent intellect "abstracts" it simply causes the act of knowing; it does not remove or separate an intelligible species from a phantasm.[45]

What remains puzzling in Jandun's account is the source of the immateriality and universality of the intelligible species. Apparently Jandun would now admit that the cogitative power, although it is not immaterial, can generate universal intelligible species and that it can do so without the help of the agent intellect.[46]

Indeed, Jandun does not allow that the intellect could have an intelligible species proper to a particular individual, since such a species would be material. Since the intellect is an abstract or separate power (*virtus abstracta*), that is, not bound to the here and now, it is fit by nature to receive only an abstract or universal species, that is, one which represents in a universal way. While he maintains that the intellect knows the universal essence first and directly, he denies that the intel-

43. Ibid., III, q. 23, ff. 83ra–86rb. He suggests (f. 86rab) that the Latin expositors (*expositores latini*) failed to set forth the correct view of the agent intellect not because they did not know it but because they gave themselves more to theology than to philosophy and were too busy to write it down. Elsewhere he mentions Albert and Aquinas among the *expositores latini*. See II, q. 6, f. 23vb; III, q. 37, f. 101rb.
44. Ibid., III, q. 24, f. 88ra and 88va.
45. Ibid., III, q. 25, f. 89vb. See also III, q. 21, f. 82rb–va.
46. This stand puts Jandun in conflict with Averroes' own views in his long commentary on the *De anima*.

lect knows the sensible particular through a reflection back on the phantasm, expressing puzzlement as to what such a reflection could be. His own solution is that the intellect knows the sensible particular through the intelligible species taken as it is in conformity to some particular phantasm and not as it is representative of the essence. Since the phantasm is itself the product of an individual cognition by the senses, we may say that the intellect of itself grasps the universal essence, while it grasps the sensible particular only by means of the senses.[47]

Despite his emphasis on phantasms as the necessary starting points for intellectual knowledge, Jandun attacks certain of the Latin expositors, especially Thomas and his followers, for arguing that since the human intellect can know nothing without phantasms, it cannot in this life know the essence of God and of the Intelligences. He argues that if knowledge of the essences of separate substances and of God is the proper and highest operation of the human soul—as Thomas would admit in regard to the soul's beatific vision of God in Paradise—then it should be attainable in this life.[48]

Developing remarks of Averroes, Jandun defends the thesis that the more intelligible species the possible intellect receives the more it is disposed to take the agent intellect as its own object of cognition and, through the agent intellect, the other separate substances.[49] After a man has so developed his speculative intellect that he is united to all the intelligible species in the possible intellect he becomes, as Themistius says, Godlike, since he is then united to the agent intellect, knows directly and intuitively through the agent intellect and in an ascending order all the separate substances, including God, and thereby achieves

---

47. John of Jandun, *Super libros de anima*, III, q. 22, ff. 80vb–81va. Jandun's own stand seems as vulnerable to attack as the notion of a reflection by the intellect back on the phantasm.

48. Ibid., III, q. 37, ff. 100ra–101va. See also III, q. 26, f. 89vb; *In libros metaphysicae*, II, q. 4, esp. f. 23vb. For relevant references in Thomas see *Summa theologiae*, I, q. 12, aa. 2–5, 9, and 11; I-II, q. 3, a. 8. Jandun's thesis that the human intellect can know the essence of God during this life was among the propositions condemned by Etienne Tempier in 1277. See Pierre Mandonnet, *Siger de Brabant et l'averroisme latin au XIII siècle, IIme partie: Textes inédits*, 2d ed. (Louvain, 1908), p. 177, nos. 8–9; H. Denifle and A. Chatelain, *Chartularium Universitatis Parisiensis*, I (Paris, 1889), p. 545, no. 36, and p. 555, no. 211. For discussion see John F. Wippel, "The Condemnations of 1270 and 1277 at Paris," *The Journal of Medieval and Renaissance Studies* 7 (1977), pp. 187–88; Roland Hissette, *Enquête sur les 219 articles condamnées à Paris le 7 Mars 1277*, Philosophes médiévaux, XXII (Louvain and Paris, 1977), pp. 27–32.

49. John of Jandun, *In libros metaphysicae*, VII, q. 7, f. 91ra. See also II, q. 4, ff. 25vb and 26rb; XII, q. 4, f. 130ra. Kuksewicz, *De Siger de Brabant*, pp. 232–34, presents only a brief summary of Jandun's doctrine on human felicity as a consequence of our union with separate substances. He does not cite Jandun's questions on the *Metaphysics*.

the highest felicity possible to a human being.[50] This doctrine became a favorite topic of discussion in Renaissance Italy, especially after the publication of Averroes' *De beatitudine animae*.[51]

This study has attempted not only to bring together key themes of Jandun's psychology but also to underscore in particular various topics and problems that are overlooked or played down in general summaries of his psychological thought. Some effort was made to pay attention to Jandun's different writings and not to rely solely on his questions on the *De anima*. As a result, it was noted that Jandun does not always hold the same position on a particular topic in his different writings. Indeed it became apparent that even within the questions on the *De anima* there appear to be certain tensions if not discrepancies.

All this should perhaps discredit characterizing Jandun as a rigid Averroist and lead us to view him as trying out various solutions to certain philosophical problems. Of particular interest is the parallel that was seen to exist between Jandun's analysis of sensation and his analysis of intellectual cognition. This led him to certain views regarding the functions of the agent intellect and the potential intellect, and yet he seemed not to have been locked into those views but to have shifted on their respective functions. The very nature of "abstraction" was evidently a serious problem for him and one with which he wrestled.

Other topics that caused him concern were the level of cognition achieved by the internal senses, the cogitative sense in particular, the

50. John of Jandun, *Super libros de anima*, III, q. 37, ff. 102rb–103rb. In his *In libros metaphysicae*, I, q. 1, f. 1va, and II, q. 4, f. 25rb, Jandun calls this condition *status supremus*. In II, q. 3, f. 25rb, he combines the language of *status* with that of *adeptio* and *adeptus intellectus*. In I, q. 1, f. 1vb, he appears to indicate that Boethius, *Consolatio Philosophiae*, III, 2, is the source of the *status* terminology. However, we might do well to observe that Albert the Great had also used the *status* terminology in the context of discussing man's union with the agent intellect: "Mirabilis autem et optimus est iste status intellectus sic adepti; per eum enim homo fit similis quodammodo deo, eo quod potest sic operari divina et largiri sibi et aliis intellectus divinos et accipere omnia intellecta quodammodo." *De anima*, III, tr. 3, c. 11, p. 222b, ll. 80–84. For further discussion see my forthcoming article, "John of Jandun and Agostino Nifo on Human Felicity (Status)," in *L'homme et son univers au moyen âge* (Actes du septième congrés international de philosophie médiévale [30 août–4 septembre 1982]), ed. C. Wenin (Louvain-la-Neuve, 1986), vol. 1, pp. 465–77.

51. On Jandun's influence on Italian Renaissance philosophers, see Martin Grabmann, "Die Aristoteleskommentar des Heinrich von Brüssel und der Einfluss Albert des Grossen auf die mittelalterliche Aristoteleserklärung," *Sitzungsberichte der Bayerischen Akademie der Wissenschaften, Philosophisch-Historische Abteilung Jahrgang 1943*, Heft 10 (Munich, 1944), pp. 55–56; Nardi, *Sigieri di Brabante*, pp. 166–67; Pierre Duhem, *Le système du monde*, VI, pp. 542–43; Maurer, "John of Jandun and the Divine Causality," pp. 185–207; MacClintock, *Perversity and Error*, pp. 2 and 132; Mahoney, "Agostino Nifo's *De Sensu Agente*," pp. 122–23.

nature and role of intelligible species, and whether and how the human intellect achieved union with the separate intellects and finally with God during this life. Several of these topics deserve further investigation by historians of fourteenth-century philosophy, but such investigations should be carried out with a sensitivity to the questioning and probing manner in which Jandun himself approached many of these problems.[52]

Duke University

52. An earlier version of this essay was written during the tenure of a fellowship from the John Simon Guggenheim Foundation.

Index of Authors

Adam Dorp, 211
Adam Wodeham, 212, 213, 215
Adams, M., viii, 212, 221n, 226n, 237n
Alcibiades, 92, 93
Al-Farabi, vii, 35, 61n
al-Ghazali, 23, 50n, 55, 56
Alan of Lille, 65
Alberic of Rheims, 205, 206
Albert of Saxony, 211
Albert the Great, 81, 101, 106, 274, 279n, 282, 285n, 287n
Alexander of Aphrodisias, 23n, 29n, 32n, 223
Alexander of Hales, 71n, 72
Allen, R. E., 119n
Altmann, A., 61n
Alvarez-Gomez, M., 107n
Ambrose, 66
Amin, U., 37
Andrea Alpago, 25n
Anselm of Canterbury, 72, 204n, 232, 236
Anthony of Parma, 276n
Aristotle, 1, 2, 6, 23, 24, 25, 26, 27, 28, 29, 30, 31, 33, 34, 35, 36, 37, 38, 39, 40n, 43, 45, 47, 48, 49n, 50, 51, 52, 53, 54, 56, 57, 58, 59, 66, 94, 95, 107, 108, 111, 113, 115, 118, 125, 128, 142n, 143, 149n, 151n, 162n, 165, 166, 169, 194, 220, 221, 222, 223, 224, 225, 226, 228, 229, 230, 231, 235, 238, 246, 247, 249, 251, 254, 267, 273, 274, 277, 282, 284, 285
Augustine, 64, 81, 82, 85n, 96n, 97n, 99, 100, 101, 102, 103, 104, 105, 106, 113, 115, 177, 230, 231
Averroes, 23, 50n, 56n, 76, 81, 95, 133n, 225, 271, 272, 273, 274, 275n, 276, 277, 280n, 282, 284n, 285n, 286, 287

Avicebron, 136
Avicenna, 23, 25n, 27n, 54, 59, 61n, 76, 79, 149n, 271, 272

Bartholomew of Bruges, 278n, 283n
Baudry, L., 257
Becker, J., 47n
Beierwaltes, W., 96n, 97n, 101n
Berkeley, G., 246
Berman, L., 47n
Bernard of Chartres, 207
Bernard of Clairvaux, 65, 67, 68, 69, 83, 113n
Bertola, E., 278n
Blaise, A., 100n
Boehner, P., 253
Boethius, vii, 64, 65, 68, 72n, 99, 121, 122, 124, 223, 287n
Boisacq, E., 101n
Bonansea, B. M., 232n
Bonaventure, 69, 82, 102, 206, 207
Bourke, V. J., 159n
Bouyges, M., 32n
Brampton, C. K., 252n
Brown, S. F., viii, 255n, 259n, 260n
Brugmann, 101n
Busa, R., 108n

Calder, N., 179n, 198n
Carlo, W., 156
Cassiodorus, 10, 106
Chalcidius, 66
Chatelain, A., 286n
Chenu, M.-D., 63n, 64n, 70n, 71n, 207
Chossat, M., 275n
Chrysippus, 7, 8, 9, 12, 96n
Cicero, 1, 2, 4, 5, 8, 9, 10, 11, 13, 17, 18, 19, 20, 21, 66, 95, 96n
Clarembaldus of Arras, 65, 70n, 72n

Clarke, W. N., 118n, 132n, 133n, 149n
Claudianus Mamertus, 106
Clement of Alexandria, 86, 87n
Congar, M. Y., 73n
Copleston, F. C., 160n, 242n
Courtenay, W., 202, 203
Cruz Hernandez, M., 25n

Daly, J., 85n
Davidson, H. A., 32n, 41n, 43n, 47n
De Couesnongle, V., 112n
de Rijk, L. M., 1n
de Saussure, F., 101n
De Wulf, M., 273n
Deferrari, R., 160n
Del Prado, N., 117n
Delphic oracle, 94
Democritus, 96n
Denifle, H., 286n
Descartes, R., 221
Dewey, J., 159n, 163, 164, 165
Dietrich of Freiberg, 82
Diodorus Cronus, 7
Dümpelmann, L., 134n
Dod, B. G., 73n
Doig, J. C., 76n
Donceel, J., 160n
Druart, T.-A., vii, 25n, 32n
Du Roy, O., 101n
Duhem, P., 274n, 276n, 287n
Dunlap, K., 165n, 172n
Dunlop, D. M., 27n, 30n,
Durand of Saint Pourçain, 276n
Dyson, F., 179n, 198

Ebbesen, S., 201n
Eccles, J., 180n
Eckhart, Meister, 63, 79, 101n, 106
Einstein, A., 198
Empedocles, 91
Epicurus, 96n
Ermatinger, C. J., 275n, 276n, 277n, 278n, 283n
Etienne Tempier, 286n
Eudemus, 2

Fabro, C., 117, 120n, 121n, 122n, 130n, 135n, 136n, 144n, 152, 153, 155, 156
Fackenheim, E., 61n
Faes de Mottoni, B., 114n
Fakhry, M., 26n
Field, H., 201
Finnegan, J., 32n
Flasch, K., 82n
Forcellini, A., 100n

Frede, M., 6, 9, 10, 11, 12, 13, 20, 21
Friedlaender, P., 89n

Gaetano di Thiene, 278n
Gaius, 5
Gál, G., 212, 213n
Galston, M., 24, 25n, 26n
Garrigou-Lagrange, R., 166
Gauthier, R. A., 273n
Geiger, L., 117, 118, 122n, 128n, 152, 153, 154, 155, 156, 157n, 158
Genequand, C., 23n, 29n
Gewirth, A., 273n
Gilbert de la Poirée, 204
Giles of Orleans, 276n
Giles of Rome, 101, 114, 275n, 276n
Gilson, E., 64n, 117n, 220n, 221n, 274n
Glücker, J., 47n
Godfrey of Fontaines, 83, 114
Goodman, N., 201
Gorgias, 90, 92
Grabmann, M., 63n, 287n
Green-Pederson, N. J., 1n
Gregory, 177
Gregory of Rimini, 212, 213
Gregory, T., 70n
Griffin, D. R., 181n
Grzybowski, K., 277n
Guttmann, J., 47n, 61n

Hadot, P., 5n, 122n
Häring, N., 65n, 72n
Harvey Nédellec, 276n
Harvey, W. Z., 47n
Hawking, S., 179n, 198
Hegel, G., 116
Helm, P., 221n, 242n
Henle, R., 117–18
Henry of Ghent, 65, 82, 114, 230
Heraclitus, 86, 91
Hissette, R., 286n
Hödl, L., 71n
Hubbell, H. M., 2n
Hugh of St. Victor, 67
Hume, D., 246
Husik, I., 47n
Huxley, G. L., 85n
Hyamson, M., 49n
Hyman, A., vii, 54n

Ibn Sina, *See* Avicenna 27n
Ibn Tibbon, 38
Inagaki, R., viii, 159n, 160n, 165n
Isaac of Stella, 64
Isaye, G., 107n

Isidore of Seville, 10, 106
Ivry, A., 61n

Jacques de Vitry, 201n, 205, 209
James of Plaisance, 273n
James, W., 162
Jansen, W., 72n
Jean Buridan, 211, 212, 214, 215, 216
Jerome, 100
Jesus Christ, 64, 195, 224, 226
John Baconthorpe, 277n
John Damascene, 101n
John Dumbleton, 220n
John Duns Scotus, 63, 166, 223, 226, 230, 231, 232, 233, 236, 239, 240, 241, 243, 261
John, H. J., 152n, 155n
John of Jandun, viii
John of St. Thomas, 130n, 166
John of Salisbury, 64, 66, 68, 203, 205, 206
John Peckham, 81
John Philoponus, 10
John, Saint, 64
John Scotus Eriugena, 63, 64, 79
Jolowicz, H. F., 5n
Julius Paulus, 5

Kant, I., 162
Kaplan, L., 47n
Kennedy, L. A., 278n
Kenny, A., 180n
King, P., 201, 207
Kirk, G. S., 86n
Klein-Braslavy, S., 47n
Klibansky, R., 80n, 83n
Klocker, H. R., 220n
Klubertanz, G. P., 172n
Kluxen, W., 70n, 81n
Kneale, W. and M., 7n, 8n, 9n, 10, 11, 12n, 17, 20, 21
Kogan, B. S., 23
Köpf, U., 73n
Kramer, J., 54n
Kremer, K., 80n, 136, 138n
Kretzmann, N., 22n, 185n
Krings, H., 101n
Kuksewicz, Z., 273n, 275n, 276n, 277n, 279n, 286n
Kullmann, W., 96n

Lang, A., 73n
Leibniz, 188, 202
Leibold, G., 250, 251, 252, 253, 254, 255, 257, 264, 265, 266, 268, 272

Lerner, R., 26n
Little, A., 117
Locke, J., 160
Lohr, C. H., 73n
Lucchetta, F., 25n, 32n
Luscombe, D. E., 242n
Lutterell, 243

MacClintock, S., 273n, 274n, 275n, 276n, 278n, 280n, 282n, 283n, 287n
MacDonald, S., 135n
Madkour, I., 25n
Mahdi, M., 24
Mahoney, E. P., viii, 107n, 114n, 273n, 274n, 275n, 278n, 282n, 284n, 287n
Maier, A., 249, 250, 251, 253
Mandonnet, P., 286n
Manser, G. M., 117n
Mao Tse-tung, 199
Marius Victorinus, 5, 6
Marlasca, A., 273n
Marrou, H.-I., 91, 92n
Marsiglio Ficino, 79
Marsilius of Inghen, 211
Marsilius of Padau, 273n
Martianus Capella, 9, 10, 17–18
Martin, C. J., 201n, 205n
Mates, B., 7n, 12n
Maurer, A., 241n, 274n, 287n
McEvoy, J., vii, 85n, 87n, 106n
McInerny, R., 122n
McMichael, A., 22n
McTighe, T. P., 23n
Merobaudes, 5
Michot, J., 25n
Monica, 104
Montagnes, B., 117n, 132n, 144n
Moody, E. A., 160n
Moses, 194
Moses Maimonides, vii, 38, 45, 47
Munk, S., 38n
Mutakallimuūn, 45, 55

Najjar, F. M., 42n
Nardi, B., 274n, 275n, 276n, 287n
Nicholas, B., 5n
Nicholas of Cusa, 63, 64, 79, 83, 95, 106, 107, 115
Nicolas, J.-H., 155n
Nietzsche, F., 116
Nifo, Agostino, 278n, 284
Normore, C. G., vii, viii, 212n, 216n
Nuriel, A., 47n

Oakes, R., 182n
O'Callaghan, J., 230n, 262n

Orpheus, 88
Otto von Freising, 203, 204
Owens, J., 117n, 156n, 160n

Pacchi, A., 274n, 275n, 276n, 278n
Pascal, B., 162
Pattin, A., 278n
Paul of Venice, 213
Pegis, A., 221n
Peirce, C. S., 202
Penido, M. T., 117n
Peri, I., 101n, 106n
Peter Abelard, 4, 64, 75, 83, 203, 204, 205, 207, 208n, 209, 210, 212, 213, 214, 216, 243
Peter Aureoli, 243
Peter of Ailly, 207, 211, 213n
Petrarch, 83
Pines, S., 23, 24n, 47n
Plato, 24, 25, 28, 35, 48, 50, 51, 52, 85, 87, 88, 89n, 91, 92, 93, 94, 97, 99, 105, 108, 113, 114, 115, 118, 119, 125, 128, 140n, 142n, 143, 163, 201, 220
Plotinus, 96, 97
Plutarch, 86n
Pomponazzi, Pietro, 284n
Poppi, A., 284n
Porphyry, 223
Proclus, 78, 82, 96, 97, 98, 99, 107n
Protagoras, 87, 88, 91, 92, 93, 95, 96n, 107n, 108, 113
Protarchus, 90
Pseudo-Dionysius, 64, 76n, 99n, 100, 107, 131n, 136n, 140, 141
Ptolemy, 40n

Quinn, P. L., 182n

Rabinowitz, N., 61n
Rachid, A., 27n
Rahman, F., 25n
Ramirez, J. M., 166
Ramón Guerrero, R., 24, 25n, 27n
Raven, J. E., 86n
Ravitzky, I., 47n
Rhabanus Maurus, 106
Richard of Conington, 265, 266
Richter, V., 251, 252n
Rief, J., 101n, 102, 103
Robert Grosseteste, 80n, 85, 106
Robert, J.-D., 155n, 157n
Roche, W. J., 101n
Roscelin, 203, 204
Rosenthal, F., 25n
Ross, D., 49n, 50n

Ross, J. F., viii, 181n, 185n, 186n, 187n, 189n, 190n, 195

Schmugge, L., 273n, 279n, 280n, 282n, 283n
Schneider, A., 64n, 66n
Schrimpf, G., 64n, 122n
Seidl, H., 107n
Senko, W., 276n, 277n
Sextus Empiricus, 7
Sharif, M. M., 25n
Shiel, J., 5n
Siger of Brabant, 82, 114, 273, 274, 275, 277, 287n
Silverman, D. W., 47n
Simplicius, 166, 167
Simpson, P., 191n
Smith, E. G., 284n
Smyth, S., 85n
Socrates, 88, 90, 91, 92, 93, 94
Solon, 86, 114
Stadler, M., 107n
Steinschneider, M., 38n
Steneck, N. H., 282n
Strato, 2
Strauss, L., 47
Stump, E., vii, 1n, 2n, 5n, 185n
Saurez, Francis, 166, 168, 169
Sylvester of Ferrara, 278n
Syrianus, 95

Taylor, R., 139n
Terraro, J., 273n
Theaetetus, 93
Themistius, 23n, 286
Theophrastus, 2
Thierry of Chartres, 65, 67, 68, 73, 79
Thierry of Freiberg, 106
Thomas Aquinas, viii, 46n, 49n, 50n, 63, 72, 76, 77, 78, 80, 81, 82, 95, 96, 100, 101, 106, 107, 108, 109, 110, 111, 112, 113, 114, 115, 206, 207, 223, 231, 273n, 274n, 275n, 279n, 285n, 286
Thomas Wilton, 249, 276, 277
Thorndyke, L., 211n
Trebatius, 1
Trombetta, Antonio, 284n
Tweedale, M., 207
Twersky, I., 47n

Ulpian, 2, 5, 6

Valois, N., 273n
Van Steenberghen, F., 63n, 114n, 274n
Vignaux, P., 202, 203

Virgil, 5
Virgilius Maro Grammaticus, 101n
Voegelin, E., 87n, 93n, 94
von Brüssel, H., 287n

Walter Burleigh, 224n
Walter Chatton, 213, 230, 257, 259, 260, 261, 262, 263, 264, 267, 268
Walter Mappe, 204
Walzer, R., 26n, 27, 40n, 42n
Wéber, E. H., 101n, 106n, 113n
Weinberg, S., 180n
Weisheipl, J. A., 106n, 124n, 166n, 220n, 252n
Werner, K., 275n
Wey, J. C., 254, 257n, 262, 263, 264
Wieland, G., vii, 63n, 72n
William Alnwick, 277n

William of Auxerre, 73
William of Conches, 65
William of Moerbeke, 166n
William of Ockham, viii, 63, 75, 106n, 160, 166, 169, 210, 212, 213, 214, 216
William of St. Thierry, 206
Williams, G. H., 47n
Wippel, J. F., vii, 114n, 126n, 135n, 151n, 155n, 156n, 157n, 158, 286n
Wolfson, H. A., 47n, 49
Wolter, A. B., 226n, 231n
Wood, R., 237n
Wyclif, J., 180n

Zabarella, G., 284n
Zeno, 96n
Zimmermann, A., 106n
Zimmermann, F. W., 36n

Index of Subjects

Absolute, 116
absolute term, 215, 216
abstract, 123
abstract entities, 216
abstract objects, 201
abstraction, 136, 279, 281, 284, 285, 287
Academics, 230, 231
accident, 120, 121, 124, 127, 128, 129, 130, 134, 140, 224, 225, 226, 227. *See also* being, accidental
accidental form, 120, 149
accidents, 126, 132
accuracy, 90
act, 128, 131, 132, 133, 134, 146, 151, 155, 236, 237; immanent, 109; infinite, 131; not self-limiting, 155; of existing, 117, 150; of will, 233
act-potency composition, 145
actio, 168
action, 114, 162, 164, 183, 219; reason for, 270
actions, classified, 57
active principle, 171, 172
acts, 159, 161, 166, 168, 170, 171, 235, 238, 241, 244, 246; arbitrary, 56, 57, 59; incompossible, 183; principle, 163; repetition, 169; volitional, 57, 58, 59
actual, 202
actuality, 53
actus essendi, 117, 124, 128, 145, 148, 151, 152, 155, 156
advantageous, 233
aesthetics, 116
aevum, 141
affectio commodi, 232
affectio iustitiae, 232
affection, 232
agent, 219, 231, 232, 237, 238, 239, 242, 244, 269, 270; free, 245; natural, 249, 271
Agent Intellect, 29, 30, 31, 32, 33, 39, 40, 42, 60
allegorical interpretations, 70
alteration, 210
ampliatio, 211
an sit, 161, 162
analogia, 99
analogy, 117, 130, 134, 144, 153
anapodeiktos, 8
angel, 127, 191, 244
animals, 283
appearance, 199
appellatio, 211
appetite, 219, 221, 233
aptitude, natural, 226
Arabic philosophy, vii, 23
argument forms, 8
argumentation, 211
Aristotelian corpus, 34
Aristotelianism, vii, 66, 234, 242
arithmetic, 106
art, 251
artistic creation, 109
artistic quality, 115
Arts Faculty at Paris, 78
ascent, 28, 35, 37, 38
assimilation, 144, 145, 157, 158
assumption, 224
astronomy, 74
atomism, 222
attribute, 188; divine, 54
authority, 63, 72, 73, 238, 239, 243, 246
Averroism, 273, 274n, 287
Averroists, 193

beatific vision, 247, 286
beauty, 91, 99, 103, 104, 114

Index   295

becoming, 91, 92
being, 81, 115, 118, 121, 122, 123, 126, 129, 130, 133, 135, 151, 156, 160, 188, 239; absolute, 110; accidental, 112, 167; actual, 190; divine, 112, 114, 148, 158; everlasting, 190; finite, 111, 112, 115, 131, 152; grades, 112, 114; heirarchy, 111; immaterial, 191; immutable, 183; infinite, 110, 111, 115, 239, 246; nature, 135; self-subsisting, 136, 143; simple, 112; substantial, 167; withdrawal, 184, 188, 190
being as being, 149
being in general, 137, 149
being qua universal, 26
being-for-its-time, 188, 189, 191
beings, 128, 131, 134, 149; created, 118, 134, 140; spiritual, 104
beings qua beings, 26
believers, ordinary, 46
biblical religion, 45
big bang, 180
bodies, 61, 140
bodies, kinds, 39
body, 66, 163, 273, 274, 275

canon law, 74
catastrophe, 177, 180
categorematic: expressions, 212; part, 216
categories, 30, 31n, 75, 222, 236
causal: connections, 210; potencies, 246
causality, 96, 97, 115, 141, 174, 227, 267, 270; divine, 49, 110, 274n (*See also* God, cause); *sine qua non*, 227
causation, 185, 269; creative, 180; divine, 196; theories of, 6
cause, 56, 98, 99, 103, 134, 140, 143, 144, 155; of being, 96; efficient, 53; infinite, 111; metaphorical, 253
causes, 249; four, 34; volitional, 53
celestial: bodies, 31, 32, 33, 35, 39, 40, 42 (*See also* heavenly bodies); motion, 59; sphere, 60; spheres, 40, 53, 59; world, 56
certainty, 230, 231
chance, 48
change, 28, 49, 52, 86, 90, 105, 106, 209, 210, 214, 215, 216
charity, 102, 104
Chartres, School of, 67, 68, 70, 72
choice, 219, 220, 234, 238, 239
Christian doctrine, 63, 64, 65, 68, 69, 70, 71, 72, 74, 78, 82
Christian wisdom, 67, 68, 69, 70, 74, 80
Christianity, 65, 66, 116

Church, 244, 245, 246
circumstances, 236
citizens, 87
cogitative power, 279, 282, 283, 285, 287
cognition, 77, 109, 228; abstractive, 230, intellectual, 278, 287; intuitive, 229, 230; structures, 75
cognitive: faculties, 220, 229; power, 173
collatio, 279
commands, divine, 237, 241, 242, 245
commodum, 233
common, 139; sense, 193, 194, 282
complexe significabile, 213, 214, 217
composite, 60, 127, 128, 222; entities, 124, 125; material, 179
composition, 118, 121, 125, 126, 127, 131, 134, 152, 153, 154, 155, 156
concept: abstract, 233; common, 224
conceptualism, 224, 225
concrete, 123, 202; objects, 201
Condemnation of 1277, 273
conditionals, 7, 12, 15, 18; negation, 17
conjunction, 12, 14, 18
connotative term, 212, 215
conservation, 180, 185, 189, 190, 192, 214; withdrawal of, 180, 183, 186, 188, 191, 192, 194
consignification, 208
consonance, 100
constants, 185
contemplation, 90, 95, 220
contingency, 178, 233, 241; human, 79
contradictions, 46
copula, 208
correspondence, 195, 196
corruption, 103, 178, 180, 187, 190
cosmogony, 73
cosmology, 85, 198
cosmos, 86, 95, 97, 179, 180, 194, 197, 199; identity, 186; self-renewing, 198
creation, 52, 65, 78, 101, 103, 104, 106, 107, 108, 110, 111, 113, 115, 161, 175, 185, 189, 191, 193, 197, 215, 216; and emanation, vii; atemporal, 50; by the divine will, 47; cessation, 182
creative causality, 174
creator, 246
creature, 112, 129, 156, 157, 180, 181, 183, 188, 227, 243, 246
creatures, 99, 118, 130, 146, 150, 155, 177, 178, 194, 196, 197; existence, 244; free, 247

death, 244
decomposition, semantic, 195
deficiency, 104

degrees: of beings, 140; of perfection, 154
delectatio, 233
deliberation, 234, 271
delight, 105
delusion, 87
demonstrated truth, 46
dependence, continuous, 182
descent, 28, 35, 37, 38, 43
desirability, 239
desire, 104
destruction, 215, 216
dialectic, 105, 114, 116, 211; Stoic, 6
dialectics, 70, 71
dicta, 207, 208, 214
dictum, 212
difference, 128, 135
dimensions, 89
disintegration, 178, 188
disjunction, 11, 12, 19
disorder of the polis, 87
dispositions, 164
dissolution, 179
distance, 88, 100, 184
distinctness, 214
distress, 233
distributio exponibilis, 211
diversity, 71, 121
divine beings, 24
divine command theory, 221, 242
divine science, 25, 30, 36, 37, 39, 40, 41, 43
Divine Word, 64, 247
divinity, 34
division, 89
dolor, 233
double truth, 192, 193
doubt, 231
doxa, 87
dualism, 164; Manichaean, 103
duration, 105

earth, 86
education, 91, 92
effect, 97, 98, 134, 228
effective causation, 267
efficient: causality, 61, 157, 227, 238, 252, 255; cause, 142, 158, 171, 172, 174, 233, 237, 253, 254, 265, 269, 270; secondary, 230
elements, 29
emanation, vii, 78, 115
emanationism, 34
emanationist texts, 38
empirical studies, 165
empiricism, 79, 92, 159, 160

end, 57, 99, 160, 161, 168, 231, 234, 249, 265, 267, 268, 270, 271; as loved, 267, 269, 271, 272; of man, 173; of the world, 197, 198
Enlightenment, 116
ens, 122, 123, 129, 130, 135, 144, 150, 151
ens commune, 137, 138, 149, 150, 151
ens inquantum ens, 149
entia rationis, 140
entropy, 178, 179
enuntiabiles, 206
Epicureans, 48
episteme, 89, 114
epistemology, 107, 109, 228
equivocation, 54, 55
equivocity, 144
error, 231
esoteric method, 46
esse, 102, 104, 118, 121, 122, 123, 124, 125, 126, 127, 128, 129, 130, 131, 132, 133, 134, 135, 139, 141, 144, 145, 146, 147, 148, 149, 150, 152, 153, 155, 156, 160, 197; *accidentale*, 167; *commune*, 118, 125, 135, 136, 137, 138, 140, 141, 142, 143, 147, 148, 149, 150, 151, 158; *subsistens*, 135, 136n, 140, 143, 146, 148, 158; *substantiale*, 167; *tantum*, 138; divine, 137, 138, 139, 144; formal, 136; not composed, 124; pure, 138; self-subsisting, 134, 138, 140, 148, 149, 151; signified abstractly, 123
essence, 117, 125, 127, 128, 129, 132, 134, 144, 146, 147, 150, 152, 154, 155, 156, 157, 189, 191, 280, 284, 285, 286; divine, 137, 146, 147, 158, 239; of man, 164
essences, 220, 223
essentia, 197
estimative power, 279, 282, 283
eternal: beings, 26; time, 50
eternity, 50, 86, 94, 97, 98, 99, 105; of the world, 45, 46, 47, 48, 50, 53, 57, 66
ethics, 66, 77, 79, 104, 246
Eucharist, 226
evil, 103, 221, 231, 232, 241, 265
excellence, human, 87
excess, 104; or deficiency, 89
exemplar cause, 142, 157, 158
existence, 28, 49, 92, 97, 111, 117, 124, 125, 131, 150, 156, 273; cause, 30, 33; in general, 125; of God, 96; rank, 31
existing, act, 117
experience, 159, 160, 161, 164, 235, 279
extension, 215

Index

faith, 65, 71, 73, 74, 75, 206, 273, 274
false belief, 230
Fate, Stoic views, 6
faydh, 41, 42
felicity, 287
fifth element, 59
final cause, viii, 29, 43, 142, 174
finality, 115; in art, 251; in nature, 251
finis, 168
finiteness, 76, 77, 78
fire, 86
First, 43, 133
First Act, 144, 145, 147
first being, 36, 95, 143, 144, 145, 146, 147; cause, 27n, 36, 37, 39, 40, 41, 138, 145, 151, 173; principles, 33, 34, 35, 73, 96, 154; soul, 98; sphere, 95
form, 29, 39, 68, 96, 97, 111, 115, 120, 125, 127, 128, 132, 134, 137, 145, 146, 153, 168, 179, 209, 222, 251, 252, 253, 255, 265, 274; and matter, 30; accidental, 220, 222; divine, 68, 72; qualitative, 223; spiritual, 283; substantial, 220, 222, 223, 224, 225, 273, 276
formal cause, 157
forms, 89, 106, 118, 201; individual, 207; Platonic, 207; subsisting, 125
Franciscans, 219, 246, 247
free choice, 228, 244
freedom, 165n, 174, 175, 183, 232, 233, 234, 238, 241, 244; created, 221; divine, 220, 221, 227, 242, 243, 244, 245, 246; human, 220; Stoic views, 6

genera, 203, 220, 223
generation, 215; and corruption, 197; and destruction, 210
genus, 3, 112, 128, 129, 135, 137, 224
God, 25, 28, 36, 37, 48, 49, 54, 55, 57, 58, 59, 60, 65, 76, 85, 86, 87n, 102, 103, 104, 105, 107n, 111, 112, 113, 114, 115, 118, 129, 130, 132, 134, 136, 137, 140, 141, 142, 143, 144, 145, 146, 147, 148, 149, 150, 151, 156, 157, 175, 177, 181, 182, 185, 186, 187, 189, 190, 193, 196, 197, 210, 214, 220, 221, 226, 227, 230, 233, 237, 240, 243, 244, 245, 246, 247, 265, 273, 274, 280, 288; apart from time, 53; cause, 48, 157, 178, 192 (*See also* causality, divine); choice, 187; commands, 242; essence, 286; existence, 48, 76, 158, 239, 240; freedom, 183, 241; goodness, 180, 182, 183, 190, 192; omnipotent, 193; perfection, 190; personality, 240; power, 180, 181, 192; unicity, 240

god, 92, 93, 98
gods, 86, 87, 94
good: the, 87, 90, 91, 95, 96, 99, 102, 232, 234, 239; and evil, 88, 89, 105; in general, 231
good life, 90
Good, Supreme, 246
goodness, 87, 104, 180; divine, 139
grace, 69, 175, 246
grammar, speculative, 207
grammatical form, 208

habits, 220, 244; of principles, 170, 173; of science, 173
habitus, viii; cause, 163, 165, 169, 170, 171, 172; grades, 173
haecceity, 223
happiness, 79, 219, 231, 232, 233, 234; eternal, 244
harmony, 100
heaven, first, 33, 42
heavenly bodies, 29, 30, 32n. *See also* celestial bodies
heavens, 184
hedonism, 90
heresy, 206
heterodoxy, 79
hierarchy, in knowledge, 90
historical reality, 69
human, 283; beings, 220, 242, 244, 276; destiny, 68; existence, finite, 77; nature, 223, 247
humors, 229
hylomorphic: bodies, 41; composition, 39, 139n; substances, 42
hylomorphism, 42, 43, 81, 222

Idea, 96
idea, divine, 156, 157
idealism, 106; Romantic, 116
Ideas, 118, 125, 128
identity, 202, 209, 214; conditions, 208
ignorance, 238
illumination, 64, 81, 99, 100
imagination, 50, 282, 283
imitation, 118, 145, 146, 147
immanence, divine, 113
immaterial: beings, 26, 30, 34, 36, 37, 38, 39; movers, 29, 31; non-mover, 31
immateriality, 285
immortality, personal, 78
immutability, 90; divine, 55
impediments to cognition, 229
impossibility, 204, 205
impossible, 51, 56
imputability, 235, 237, 238

Incarnation, 64, 69, 71, 225
inclinations, natural, 233
incorruptibility, 191
increase, 205, 209, 210
indifference, 233, 241
indiscernibles, 202
individual, 118, 120, 128, 134, 139, 145, 201, 202, 220, 222, 224, 225, 228, 280, 285
individuation, 139, 187
inference, 204, 205
infinity: bad, 116; divine, 107n
inherence, 224, 226
insolubles, 211
instant, 184, 185
intellect, 28, 29, 31, 33, 35, 40, 60, 77, 97, 100, 108, 136, 151, 219, 221, 223, 230, 232, 234, 238, 239, 281, 286, 288; agent, 170, 276, 277, 278, 279, 280, 281, 283, 284, 285, 286, 287; divine, 107, 108, 110; first, 36, 59, 60; human, 32, 110, 111; passive, 276; possible, 276, 277, 279, 280, 281, 282, 283, 284, 285, 286; potential, 31, 287; separate, 61
intellectual power, 172
intelligences, 40, 61
intelligible content, 97, 119, 120
intelligibles, 31, 32, 40
intension, 106
intention, 280
intentions, order of, 124
interpretation: allegorical, 67; moral, 67
Islam, 69, 70
Islamic Theology, 28

Jewish philosophy, vii
judgment, 88, 94, 230, 231, 238
jurisprudence, 74, 235
just, 233
justice, 86n, 232

Kalam, 28
knowledge, 76, 87, 90, 91, 95, 97, 107, 108, 109, 111, 114, 238; certain, 229; empirical, 163; human, 109, 111; intellectual, 279, 280; objective, 163, 164; sense, 279, 280; universal, 283

language, 90, 216; philosophy of, 207, 212
Last Things, 199
law, 2, 3, 87, 235
Law of Moses, 45, 48, 51
legislation, 239, 243; divine, 240
liberal arts, 72

life, 97, 98; eternal, 243, 246; human, 93, 95; intelligent, 198, 199
light, 100; of reason, 172
likeness, 141, 144, 146, 147, 148, 279, 280, 283n
limit, 90, 96, 97
limitation, 104, 118, 152, 153, 154, 156
local motion, 210
logic, 1, 27, 64, 66; Aristotelian, 8; Stoic, 8, 9
logica nova, 73, 75
logos, 86
love, 104, 105, 113, 270, 271, 272; of God, 240, 242, 246, 247; divine, 197

making, 209, 210, 214
man, 92, 115, 163, 164, 172, 173, 174, 175, 276; nature, 114
mankind, 65
many, 154
material, 85
material things, 229
mathematics, 35, 87, 90
matter, 29, 32, 39, 49, 50, 51, 52, 85, 96, 120, 121, 123, 125, 126, 127, 128, 132, 134, 145, 146, 153, 167, 168, 179, 197, 199, 265; prime, 224, 225
matter-form union, 128
mean, 89, 95
meaning, 195
means, 231
measure, vii, 104; divine, 105, 110, 113; of qualities, 114; of quantity, 114
medicine, 74
memory, 279, 282, 283
mental acts, 229, 233
merit, 243, 244, 245, 246
Mertonians, 106n
metaphor, 250, 265, 266, 267
metaphysical: beings, 34; insight, 164
metaphysics, viii, 24, 25, 26, 27, 28, 30, 34, 35, 43, 66, 76, 77, 78, 81, 104, 107, 108, 113, 115, 116, 117, 118, 124, 159, 160, 194, 216; and logic, 6; subject, 149, 150
mind, 50, 85, 87, 105, 107, 111; divine, 110; human, 72, 106, 110
miracle, 57, 273
mirrors, 229
misery, 233
mixture, 90
mode, 102
moderation, 87, 91, 104, 114
modus, 103, 104
moment, 199
moral science, 234, 235

morality, 237, 244, 245, 247; nonpositive, 238, 239, 242, 245; positive, 243
mores, 234
mortal sin, 243
motion, 50, 52, 59, 61, 85, 95, 98, 100, 161, 164, 269, 271; metaphorical, 250, 255, 267, 269, 270, 272
movers, 40
mutability, 103
Mutakallimūn, 50
mysticism, 67

names, 224; unity of, 207
natural, 274; beings, 34, 41; bodies, 29, 30; forms, 32; law, 241; order, 267, 268; philosophy, 29; science, 30, 35, 39, 67, 74; theory, 30
nature, 57, 70, 71, 134, 135, 145, 185, 190, 191, 199, 207, 219, 224, 225, 226, 227, 228, 231, 236, 240, 245, 246, 247, 249, 267; created, 148; divine, 103, 180; human, viii, 159, 161, 162, 164, 165, 166, 168, 169, 172, 173, 174, 175; nonrational, 234; qua end, 168, 172, 174; rational, 234; senses, 160
natures, 220; created, 118
necessary: causes, 54, 56, 58; creation, 51; laws, 59
necessity, 50, 52, 53, 60, 177, 181, 243
negation, 54
Neo-Scholasticism, 116
Neoplatonism, 24n, 33, 39, 64, 76n, 78, 79, 80, 82, 96, 97, 99, 100, 107, 111, 112, 114, 115, 186
nilling, 234
nolle, 233, 234
nominal definitions, 212
nominalism, vii, viii, 225
non-individuals, 201
nonbeing, 178, 181
noncontradiction, 241
nonexistence, 49, 51, 197
nominalism, 216, 224
nothing, 49, 50, 51
nothingness, 199
nouns, 225
nous, 91
number, 88, 89, 95, 96, 97, 101, 102, 103, 104, 105, 106, 112, 113, 115
number speculation, 68
numbering, 90

obedience, 238, 246
object, 110, 232; absent, 230; nonexistent, 230; of knowledge, 108, 109, 111, 113

objects, 213
obligations, 211
One and the Many, 119, 142n, 154
One, the, 71, 96, 98, 104, 112, 115
ontology, 207, 212, 213, 214, 215
operation, 161, 168
opinions, true, 46
optimism, 246
order, 57, 58, 94, 97, 99, 101, 102, 103, 104, 105, 113, 114, 220, 268; ascending, 286; material, 105, 106; natural, 227; of being, 152; of discovery, 28, 148, 157, 158; of exposition, 28; of extrinsic causality, 157; of investigation, 28; of nature, 148, 153, 158; of thought, 136
ordo, 103
orthodoxy, 206

pantheism, 116, 147
participation, viii, 81, 97, 98, 99, 100, 104, 112, 114; by assimilation, 157; 158; by composition, 152, 153, 156, 157; by formal hierarchy, 152, 154, 157, 158; by similitude, 152, 153, 154; degrees, 143; intentional, 120; logical, 120, 126, 134, 153; ontological, 121; predicamental, 121n, 152; real, 121, 126, 131, 132, 134, 153; transcendental, 152, 153
particular, 119, 223, 281, 286
particularity, 224
particularization, 55
parts, 86, 127, 210
parts and wholes, 214
passio, 168, 170
passive principle, 171
passivity, 109, 170
Pelagianism, 221, 244
perception, 108
perceptions, internal, 229
perfect being, 36
perfection, 91, 119, 121, 126, 130, 134, 143, 151, 153, 170, 173, 232; divine, 112
persons, 146
phantasm, 279, 280, 281, 282, 283, 284, 285, 286
phantasy, 282
philosopher, 90, 91
philosophy, 63, 64, 66, 70, 76, 77, 78, 79, 80, 81
phronesis, 91
physical: being, 85; eschatology, 179
physics, 30, 66, 70, 76, 198, 216, 217; Stoic, 6

Platonism, 65, 66, 68, 186, 190, 201, 223n
Platonists, 118, 119
pleasure, 88, 90, 91, 114, 233, 239; and pain, 87, 88, 89
plenitude, divine, 111
point, 185
political works, 26
politics, 28, 86
pondus, 102, 103, 104, 106
possibility, 56, 194
possible, 202; beings, 42; worlds, 194
potency, 128, 131, 132, 133, 134, 146, 151, 155, 220; causal, 228; neutral, 226; obediential, 226
potentia, 168
potentiality, 53, 167, 168, 170, 178; and actuality, 55
power, 99, 227, 228, 245; active, 168; divine, 141, 142, 194, 244; infinite, 274; productive, 227; rational, 231; self-determining, 233
praeparatio, 282
precept, 239, 242; divine, 240
predicables, 2
predication, 130
preparation, 282
prime matter, 41, 42
prime mover, 28, 29, 36, 37, 53
principle: of being, 30, 38; of change, 29; of discovery, 37; of existence, 28, 29, 34, 43; receiving, 121
principles: discovery, 28; of demonstration, 36; of instruction, 30, 34
priority, 53; and posteriority, 130
privation, 49, 54
procession, 97; of creatures, 146, 147; of the Holy Spirit, 233
production, 109; and truth, 196
properties, 202, 211, 222, 224
proportion, 90
propositions, 211; known per se, 235
psychology, viii, 107
punishment, eternal, 243
pupil, 88
Pythagoreans, 89n, 118

quality, 96, 165, 166, 167, 170, 222, 224, 227, 236, 246; species, 166, 167, 168
quantity, 96, 111, 168
quid sit, 162
quiddity, 151, 187
quod est, 121, 122n
quod quid est, 151

rank, 41, 42, 51
ratio, 164

rational: animals, 41; part, 94
rationalism, 75, 77
rationality, 69, 70, 71, 73, 74, 75, 80, 81, 82, 83, 105
rationalization, 76
razor, 256, 257
real: composition, 123; distinction, 117, 123, 124, 125, 126, 129, 155, 157
realism, 109, 113, 211, 224; moderate, 224
reality, 112, 124, 223
reason, 67, 71, 72, 73, 83, 90, 97, 105, 115, 238, 240, 273; human, 75
receptivity, 109
Redemption, 69, 71
regularities, 220
relation, real, 224, 225
relativism, 92, 95, 97
relativity, 88, 89
remission, 106
res, 127, 214
rest, 104
restrictio, 211
revealed truth, 71
revelation, 72, 195, 240
reversion, 97, 115
rhetoric, 90; and Roman philosophy, 5
rhetorical terms, Greek, 6
right judgement, 114
right reason, 236, 238, 239, 240, 241, 242, 245, 246
Royal Edict of 1473, 211, 212

Sabellianism, 204
sacramental: regulations, 245; system, 244
sacraments, 246
salvation, 71
Scholasticism, 75, 106, 168
scholastics, 4
science, 30, 67, 71, 72, 75, 76, 78, 80, 89, 91, 193, 194, 281
sciences: plurality, 74, 77; self-sufficiency, 74, 77
second causes, 39, 40, 41, 233
second intellect, 60
self, 164; -creation, 175; -government, 220, 221, 244, 246; -knowledge, 162, 282; -understanding, 164
semantics, 215, 216
sensation, 272, 277, 278, 287
sense, 219; agent, 278; passive, 278
senses, 108, 286; internal, 282, 287
sensible, 286; beings, 31n
sensing organism, 277
sensory: faculties, 229; illusion, 229

Index   301

sentence, 204, 205, 207, 208, 211, 212, 213, 214, 215
sententia nominum, 203, 204, 206
sententia vocum, 203, 204
separate: intellects, 288; substances, 133, 139, 143, 280, 286; substances, knowledge of, 23
sight, 88
signification, 206, 212, 224
similarity, 224, 225
similitude, 153
similitudo, 279, 283n
simple, 60; being, 126; entities, 124, 125
simplicity, divine, 54, 114n
simultaneity, 97, 184
sin, 245
skepticism, 221, 228, 230; Academic, 246; Cartesian, 246
Sophists, 88
soteriology, 221
soul, 28, 29, 39, 60, 66, 85, 88, 92, 94, 95, 98, 100, 104, 105, 106, 109, 110, 162, 265, 278; cogitative, 276; human, 99, 286; intellective, 274, 276; intellectual, 170, 171, 172, 173; rational, 191, 273; sensitive, 275; vegetative, 275
souls, 32, 41, 140; celestial, 41
sound, 85, 88
space, 184
space-time, 179
species, 102, 103, 118, 120, 128, 129, 135, 137, 203, 220, 223, 224, 228
species, intelligible, 276, 278, 279, 280, 281, 282, 283, 284, 285, 286, 288; preserved, 279; sensible, 277, 278, 279, 283n
spirituality, 85
stability, 86
state, 93
statements, 206
status, 207, 208, 209, 210, 214, 215
statutes, divine, 243, 245
Stoic logic, vii
Stoicism, 96
Stoics, 11, 12, 231
strife, 86
subdisjunction, 12, 20
subject, 109, 110, 120, 121, 124, 126, 127, 134, 153, 168; determination, 167; of being, 122; substantial, 123
subjectivism, 92
subjectivity, 116
subjects of predication, 209
sublunar world, 50, 53, 58, 59
subsistence, 225
substance, 112, 113, 121, 123, 127, 128, 130, 132, 133, 141, 165, 167, 209, 222, 224, 225, 226, 227, 228; finite, 150; primary, 222; separate, 127
substances, 220, 224, 246; corporeal, 140; individual, 207; separate, 125
substantia, 129, 132
substantial form, 120, 121, 126, 128; subsisting, 149
"substitution" principle, 227, 230, 237
supernatural, 274
supposition, 211, 215, 216
suppositum, 225, 226
syllogism, 204, 205
symbolical interpretations, 70
syncategorematic expression, 212, 216

telos, 190, 192
temperateness, 93
tense, 206, 208
terms, 211, 212, 213, 216
tertium quid, 127, 134
that which is, 121, 122, 123, 125
theology, 39, 71, 73, 74, 75, 78, 79, 81, 82, 83, 217; Christian, 72; natural, 240; sacramental, 235
theoretical sciences, 36, 37
thermodynamic death, 179
thing, 112, 127, 209, 210, 214
thinking, 276, 279, 281, 282, 283, 284, 285
thought, divine, 227
time, 48, 49, 50, 52, 53, 85, 95, 98, 100, 174, 184, 185
topical justification, 205; locus, 204
topics, 1, 2, 4
tradition, 80, 81, 83
transcendence, 79, 85; divine, 113
transcendental Thomism, 160
translation, 66
translations, 77
translunar world, 58, 59
transubstantiation, 226
Trinity, 65, 67, 146, 204; distinction of persons, 204
truth, 87, 88, 89, 90, 91, 100, 196; earned, 195n, 196; inherited, 196; vantaged, 195, 196
truth conditions, 195, 215
truth-maker, 207, 208, 210, 211, 213, 214

ultimate principle, 35
uncaused being, 35; cause, 27n
undefinable, 212
undemonstrated modes, 7
underworld, 88

unenlightened, 24
union, 224
unity, 86, 95, 97, 98, 102, 104, 112, 113, 115, 134, 154; of God, 45
universal, 119, 123, 126, 150, 224, 281
universality, 70, 72, 119, 120, 224, 285
universals, 6, 203, 204, 206, 216, 223
universe, 53, 102, 106, 179, 184, 198
University of Paris, 211, 273
university, medieval, 75
univocity, 130, 134, 144, 153
unmoved mover, 33
utility, 90

value judgments, 220, 238
velle, 233, 234
vice, 95, 235, 236, 237
Victorines, 67
violence, 233
virtue, 88, 113, 220, 235, 236, 237, 238; degrees, 238, 239, 240; moral, 95; perfect, 246; theoretical, 34, 173, 244
virtus, 227

volition, 242; general, 233
voluntarist, viii

weight, 101, 102, 103, 104, 105, 106, 113, 115
whole and parts, 103, 204, 205, 209
will, 104, 172, 219, 221, 227, 228, 232, 233, 234, 235, 237, 238, 239, 241, 242, 245; created, 234, 245; divine, 48, 49, 50, 51, 52, 53, 54, 55, 56, 57, 58, 60, 180, 181, 186, 187, 198, 199, 219, 221, 225, 226, 227, 233, 239, 243, 245; human, 54, 55, 57, 225; undetermined, 56
willing, 234
willing-against, 234
wisdom, 63, 64, 90, 102, 173; divine, 48, 49, 50, 57, 58, 59, 68, 221
world, 56, 64, 65, 185, 186, 197, 198, 215, 246; cause, 68; destiny, 79; order, 86; origin, 79

yliatim, 139

www.ingramcontent.com/pod-product-compliance
Lightning Source LLC
Chambersburg PA
CBHW031408290426
44110CB00011B/306